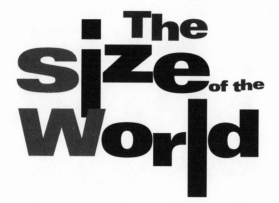

The Size of the World

By

Jeff Greenwald

The Globe Pequot Press

Old Saybrook, Connecticut

Library of Congress Cataloging-in-Publication Data is available.
ISBN 1-56440-623-7

Portions of this book have appeared in WIRED, Condé Nast Traveler, EcoTraveler, the San Francisco Examiner, Travelers' Tales Mexico, and in Big World on the Global Network Navigator's Travelers' Center.

Manufactured in the United States of America
First Edition / First Printing

For Debra Sue,
who never goes anywhere

If you want to make God laugh, tell Him
what your plans are.

—Yiddish proverb

And I learned there are troubles
of more than one kind—
Some come from ahead
and some come from behind.

—Dr. Seuss

Acknowledgments

If I asked all the people who assisted me on my journey to join hands, the human chain would probably stretch across every inch of my 29,127-mile route. I've tried to thank most of those people here. Friends, fellow travelers, angels and knaves who appear in the narrative itself are not mentioned, although I've taken the opportunity to note a few individuals whose specific roles in my story, disguised by canny pseudonyms, are best left vague.

In the United States I wish to acknowledge the help, love and/or inspiration given by Richard Bangs, Barbara Banks, John Battelle, Monique Brechet, Rob Breszny, Jay Brown, Mimi & Peter Buckley, Gia Capadona, Sue Cliff, Dan Clurman, Neil Diamant, Matt Fassberg, Pat Fish, Donald W. George, Roslyn Greenwald-Miller, Jane Heaven, Albert O. Hirschman, Pamela Holm, Pico Iyer, Lisa Jarahian, Louis B. Jones, Kathi Kennedy, Richard Kohn, Dave Levy, Patricia Loftus Lee, Valerie MacLean, Laurie Marks-Wagner, Lisa Menna, Harold Miller, John Miller, Cara Moore, Ray Rodney, Amy Schwartz, Diane Seigel, Devorah Symansky, Ben Shapiro, Joan Walsh and Nina Wise. Health care, Lomotil and pre-trip inoculations were ably dispensed by Dr. Bernard Sklar and the staff of the Alameda Travel Vaccination Clinic.

Among the other-worldly organizations and individuals who smoothed my path I am especially beholden to the Mexico Tourism office in Oaxaca, Blue Bubble Divers in Cozumel, Salif Badiane of Top Tours Senegal, Sylvia Kamara of the Senegal Tourism Board, the Hotel Sofitel Teranga in Dakar and the American Peace Corps in both Senegal and Mali. Consul Roger John Daley went out of his way to assist me at the American Embassy in Istanbul, while Moira Sherwood and Ferhat Dikicil unfolded a very welcome couch (complete with a somewhat less welcome cat) in Ankara.

For friendship and support during my travels in Asia I warmly thank Chrissy Gregory, Frances Howland, Yasmine Rana, Patricia Roberts, Sanjib Raj Bhandari and Kiran Gautam of Mercantile Office Systems, Médecine Sans Frontières, Steve Marshall, Fabiola, and David Firestein of the Guangzhou (Canton) USIS office. The Mandarin Oriental extended lavish hospitality during my stay in Hong Kong — as did my good friends Jill Kluge and Shaun Kelly, who gave me the run of their lovely flats whilst I "blundered through the wilderness in search of inner peace."

o   o   o

Outfitting the trip was a mammoth project in itself, made infinitely more managable (and affordable) by the generosity of a half-dozen big-hearted corporations. My sincere thanks to Eagle Creek, which supplied our sturdy backpacks, padlocks and money belts, to Sierra Designs for providing lightweight rain gear, and to Cascade Designs in Seattle for what might have been the most indispensible items of all: Therm-a-Rest mattresses, cushions and pillows. A Pür water filter bravely battled micro-organisms in Mexico, Guatemala and West Africa.

I am indebted to the Hewlett-Packard Corporation for the "loan" of an OmniBook 300 computer, as well as to Pacific Rim Systems for lending me a compact, battery-powered P35 external floppy drive. A tip of the water bottle goes to Ms. Ümit Çelebioglu of Hewlett-Packard's Ankara office, who made sure my OmniBook got a thorough ear-cleaning after its trial-by-sand.

Thanks also to Larry Habegger, James O'Reilly and Linda Sirola of O'Reilly & Associates in Sebastopol, as well as to Marguerita Castanera and William and Elaine Petrocelli of Book Passage in Corte Madera. Less metaphorical passages were furnished by Carnival Cruise Lines, Delmas AAEL, Fleet Trans International, Jebsen & Company and the Hapag-Lloyd Corporation. Lastly, I am deeply grateful for the spiritual retreat offered by the Vedanta Society in Marin County — where I was able, at long last, to catch my breath.

o   o   o

Mike Urban, maverick editor at Globe Pequot, had the guts, imagination and foolishness to rope this project in; if I've satisfied his trust I ask no more. Laboring behind the scenes were a handful of friends and interns who helped me corral a thousand pages of notes, eight hundred pages of manuscript, twenty-eight maps and many hours of taped interviews into slightly more user-friendly form. These intrepid souls included Shelley Buck, Christopher Crossen, Sheila Davies, and Carolyn Miller. Big thanks also to Michael Coffino, the Elvis of Researchers, who drummed up the skinny on everything from fortune cookies to Islamic law. Copyeditor Debbie Jacobs applied a final, meticulous rouge and shine; she also eliminated about six thousand semicolons.

Finally, with a deep bow and a sly wink, I bequeath three oxen, two fatted calves and one road-weary laptop to Maia Hansen, my private and incontrovertible proof that the Universe sometimes gives you exactly what (or who) you need the most. Tireless intern, brilliant editor and on-call therapist rolled into one, Maia performed the astounding feat of *making the entire journey without uttering a single word of complaint.* Such perpitatetic heroism would have amazed even Moses.

o   o   o

• 1 •

Let's Call the Whole Thing Off

It was on the eleventh of November, 1993—exactly six weeks before my estimated date of departure—that I started to get scared.

Scared enough to race around my Oakland flat with a Kool-Aid pitcher, watering the hell out of my houseplants; scared enough to attack with my hammer and rusted sculpting chisel the hardy extragalactic fungus growing between the cracks of my living room picture-window frame. Scared enough to run out to PayLess and buy, for $14.95, one of those Dr. Seuss–inspired, *Carnaval*-on-acid feather dusters especially designed for cleaning venetian blinds. Scared enough, in short, to pretend to a throne of unthreatened domesticity; as if the warm and comfortable one-bedroom flat I was waking up to every morning was not about to vanish like a snapped-away magician's handkerchief.

Scared enough, easily, to call the whole thing off.

What I did instead was call my friend Blake, a psychotherapist specializing in decision management. This seemed a consummately marketable skill; everyone from stymied shoppers ("Starkist or Chicken of the Sea?") to world leaders ("Economic embargo or carpet bombings?") could avail themselves of his services. Blake was a good enough pal not to charge me for his time. All he asked in return for an hour's counseling was the guarantee that I'd vouchsafe my entire Bill Evans CD collection to him when I left—a condition that, in my distracted state, I failed to recognize as a conflict of interest.

Half an hour later we sat at my dining table over strong coffee. I had to shovel six newspapers, a month's worth of accumulated mail and a monstrous tapeworm of fading fax paper off to the side before, my notebook splayed, I initiated our "dialogue."

"What it amounts to," I said, "is that I have no idea how I got myself into this state. A year ago this seemed like a perfect thing to do, the perfect next step in my evolution as a writer. But now that I have a book contract—now that I'm *obligated* to do it—I'm completely terrified."

"What is it, exactly, that you're afraid of?"

I launched into my list. First of all there was the trip itself. There were too many unknowns; my imagination couldn't cope with them all. Next in line came the issue of separation anxiety. The older I got, the more difficult it was to forsake the familiar. Not just Coriola, not just my friends and my flat, but the whole sketchy continuity of my life. I'd been working on a novel, *Snake Lake,* for six months, and it seemed fatal to set it aside. Finally—worst of all—I'd developed a violent aversion to *rushing.* The idea of trying to circle the world overland in six short months seemed utterly insane.

"All I can envision," I said, "is running like a madman from one country to the next, unable to ever stop or relax if I hope to get the book in on time."

Blake shrugged. "Seems like plenty of time to me. Phineas Fogg did it in. . . ."

"That was a novel. Fiction. Fantasy."

"What about Michael Palin? That BBC guy?"

I rolled my eyes. "That guy had an advance team the size of the Desert Storm strike force, and a bankroll to match. Their sunscreen bill was more than my entire budget."

"Okay. So what if the book's late?"

"It can't be." I shook my head peremptorily. "Globe Pequot's a relatively small house, and my editor's reputation is on the line. I can't let him down."

"Good. That's unambiguous. So what are you going to do about it?" No matter how old Blake gets, he'll always look like a kid I used to dissect dead birds with in fourth grade.

"What I want to discuss is the feasibility of backing out. And whether or not my career—not to mention my self-esteem—could survive it." I started doodling little cages in my notebook. "The problem is I know that, whatever I do, I'll wish I'd done the opposite. If I go, I'll wish I'd stayed and finished my novel. If I stay, I'll always regret that I didn't face up to a great challenge."

Blake settled back into his chair, hands behind his head. He might have been on the beach in Malibu. *"Mit eyn hint'n,"* he intoned soulfully, *"ken men nisht zayn oyf tsvey yaridem."*

"Meaning what?"

"With one rear end, you can't be at two circuses. Listen. Do you have a copy of the proposal here? The one you used to sell this book to your publisher?"

"Of course."

"Pull it out. I want you to remind me—and remind yourself—why you wanted to do this thing in the first place."

Why I Wanted to Do This Thing in the First Place

Nine years earlier, on a solo trek up the Arun Valley in remote northeastern Nepal, I'd wandered into a tiny village called Num. It was early afternoon; frost still clung to the moss in the shadows of large stones. Women with dark hair and darker eyes squatted in the clearings outside homes of packed and painted clay, hand-feeding grain into the center of spinning millstones.

I had a long and difficult day ahead of me and planned to keep walking. But as I approached the grassy field at the edge of Num— marked by a simple cement schoolhouse, beyond which a steep and ancient trail of worn stone steps descended a thousand feet to the Arun River—I was stopped by a surreal sight. School was in recess, and ten boys in shorts and tattered shirts were playing a highly spirited game of volleyball—*without a ball.* They leapt into the air on either side of a threadbare net, pantomiming serves, passes, and deadly spikes. So acutely was their attention focused on this imaginary ball that, when a wild serve sailed in my direction, they shouted in unison: *"Look out, mister!"*

As so often happens in Nepal, my initial amusement gave way to admiration. The schoolyard was situated on a small plateau at the end of Num's high ridge; a bad serve or foul would send a real ball bouncing into oblivion. The river valley a quarter mile below was probably littered, I imagined, with lost balls. Then again, maybe not— in Nepal, where the per capita income is about $150 a year, a regulation volleyball would cost a month's salary. Losing one wasn't a mistake the school district could afford to make twice.

I sat down to record the scene in my journal. After a few minutes I was joined by a grinning, neatly dressed man who appeared to be in his late twenties. He introduced himself as one of the school's two teachers and, encouraged by my rudimentary Nepali, took the liberty of making a small request. Recent rains, he said, had delayed a shipment of educational materials; was there any chance I had a world map that he could look at?

In fact, I did. It always came in handy. One of the first things that people in remote villages asked me was where I came from. My reply— "Oakland, California, U.S.A."—was marvelously exotic but virtually meaningless; few rural Nepali shepherds or subsistence farmers had ever heard of nearby Okuldunga, let alone Oakland. Over the years I'd learned to carry some helpful props: snapshots of my family, post-cards of San Francisco Bay, and an up-to-date map of the world.

I dug the map out of my backpack. The teacher unfolded it care-fully and spread it across his lap. We were soon joined by his com-rade—another clean-shaven young man in a spotless white shirt and knockoff Levi's. It became clear that, strange as it may seem, neither of these men had ever closely examined a world map before.

First, of course, we found Nepal. The two men blanched at the sight of their own country, sandwiched between the geopolitical mon-sters of India and China. They nodded respectfully at the elegant landmass of North America and bit their lips sizing up the Soviet Union.

The teachers were well aware of current events and, like tourists at the Russian Tea Room, tried to spot the "celebrity" countries they'd heard about on Radio Nepal. First they hunted out the most volatile areas of the world—at that time Korea, Iran and Iraq—then broke off to search for more inviting hot spots, like Hong Kong and Bangkok. Returning to the Middle East, they peered around for a moment in bewilderment, gasping audibly when they finally located the tiny sliver of Israel. *"Kasto sano!"* they cried. "It's even smaller than Nepal!"

The volleyball game ended, and we were soon surrounded by kids. Their eyes and fingers centered on Nepal, then fanned out to find India, Tibet, Africa, Australia. As they mouthed the names of dis-tant cities—New Delhi and Sydney, London and New York—it seemed as if they were actually tasting these places; creating whole worlds in their imaginations, as convincingly as they'd created their foolproof volleyball.

Observing their faces observing the map, I sensed what they might be feeling. To these penniless kids, growing up in a tiny Himalayan village a week's walk from the nearest lightbulb, the planet Earth was as impossibly large as the galaxy.

I remember feeling just a little bit envious. It had been a while since I had basked in sheer wonder at the size of the world or felt so gleefully helpless in the face of the seemingly insurmountable obsta-cles that lay in the way of exploring it. I well knew where such think-ing could lead; it was the kind of thinking that had built my travel-writing career and had led in a rather direct line to the very trip I was on.

Why, then, did I envy a bunch of impoverished Nepali grade-school students who gawked at Boston as if it were Betelgeuse? Maybe because, for an instant, I remember what it had felt like when this planet seemed utterly vast, mysterious and inaccessible. When I wandered onto that volleyball field in Num I was only thirty years old—but the world was shrinking beneath by feet.

o   o   o

The central cause of my disillusionment, I finally realized, was a fact of life that every one of us, young and old, now takes completely for granted. The fact is, simply, *flight*.

I had begun my life of travel as an explorer: an individual who wanted to plumb, in some small way, the secrets of the planet. My mission was to get joyfully lost—to become a sort of global Theseus, deciphering this spherical labyrinth of infinite passageways and possibilities. "Strange travel suggestions," Kurt Vonnegut, Jr., counseled my generation, "are dancing lessons from God." I believed old Kurt entirely, and embraced travel as the spiritual chisel that could reveal the hidden shape of my soul.

But the culture of air transportation, so sanitized and monotonous, dulled my edge. The anxious rush to the airport, the in-flight movies and rubbery chicken, the ceaseless jet roar that the body finally mutes (along with everything else), the hypnotic ballet of battered luggage followed by days of jet lag—it took a while, but I finally wised up. These journeys weren't explorations; they were long commutes.

The moment one climbs onto an airplane, I realized, one enters into a Faustian bargain. Comfort, convenience and the ability to buy duty-free perfume in any nation on Earth are ours. In return we need only utter, in our heads and our hearts, the mantra of the modern age: *"The world is getting smaller."*

I had sold myself short. Pretending to get to know the world, I had succeeded only in redefining my worldview. The Earth was no longer an enormous, mysterious and infinitely varied globe. It had become a vast plain, whipped by the jet stream, marked by bare-walled departure lounges and the honey glow of runway lights.

An essential quality of travel had been lost. If I had to define it, I'd use the word *continuity:* the sense that the sidewalk in front of one's house is connected, physically, with every other spot on Earth. I wanted to reclaim that feeling. I wanted to remind myself that the longest journey begins not at an international airport, but at the threshold of one's own front door.

By the time I reached my late thirties I had covered more ground than Magellan, Marco Polo and Columbus combined, but I realized I had cheated. Arriving at ever more exotic destinations, I slouched through customs with a guilty mien. I knew that important rituals and rites of passage had been overlooked, and that I didn't truly deserve to be in the places I was landing. And I also knew, beyond a shadow of a doubt, what was required of me if I was ever to recapture my fascination for the allure, the mystery and the size of the world.

In March of 1994, I would turn forty. As a birthday present to myself—and as the ultimate challenge of my career—I wanted to rediscover that the Earth is round. I wanted to embrace its mass, feel its gravity, ambulate its circumference. I wanted to travel forward, without a return ticket, and let the topology of the planet's sphere carry me back to the place I had started from.

There was only one way to do this. I would have to travel around the world—from Oakland, California, to Oakland Calfornia—without ever leaving the ground.

Choice and Choicelessness

"So what's changed?" Blake had wandered over toward the stereo to appraise my John Coltrane collection, but returned as I refilled our coffee cups and dumped a bag of tortilla chips on the table between us. "It still sounds like a good idea to me. You don't think it's important anymore?"

"I don't know if it's important enough to give up everything else for."

"Okay. So tell me this: What, exactly, are you giving up?"

"Sn—"

"Your novel isn't going anywhere, so let's forget about that. What are you *actually giving up* to make this trip?"

"B—"

"Bagels? Lox schmeer? Maureen Dowd? Are you so attached to your morning ritual with coffee and the *New York Times* that you'll throw away a chance to go around the world for it? *Think*, man, *think*. Imagine, for a moment, that you stay. Imagine that you call your publisher, that you call your agent tomorrow and tell her it's no-go. What are the consequences?"

"I'll never eat lunch in New York City again."

"That's beside the point. What will your life really be like if you cancel this trip and spend the next six months here? Where will you be half a year from now? Think about it. Will you be better off?" He leaned forward and selected a perfectly triangular chip, nipping off one 60-degree corner with a twiggish snap. "You tell me."

He was right. Freelancing, more than ever, seemed a dead-end street. I'd encountered enough once-celebrated word wranglers on dark corners, mooning about their Precambrian cover stories for *Esquire* while they sucked Night Train from brown paper bags. My novel was stuck in mid-molt, and hours of pecking at my Word 5.1 toolbar wasn't prying anything loose. To ice the cake, my next-door neighbor—the infamous Winchester Woman—had broken ground on an elaborate sundeck that promised months of shrieking carpentry.

"The main problem," I said, "is that I've got the whole thing so tied up with my birthday. I can conceivably put off the trip, but I can't put off turning forty. I know in my heart of hearts that, if I chicken out, I'll always remember this as 'The Year I Turned My Back on Destiny.'"

"So what we're talking about here," Blake postulated, "is *choice* versus *choicelessness*. It seems to me that what we're looking at is a situation that's already irreversible. Bailing out is not an option. I think you know that. The only choice you have, really, is to identify your anxieties, acknowledge them, and forge ahead. The consequences of *not* doing this trip, in other words, are more dire than the consequences of doing it. Agreed?" I said nothing. "Anything else?"

I bit the bullet. "Coriola," I confessed.

"Did you ask her if she wanted to go with you?"

"She can't. Impossible. She has no money. She's been temping for ages, and every cent she earns goes to pay off her student loans and parking tickets. What she needs in her life right now is a real job, not another huge loan. Besides." I blew air through my lips. "Our relationship is dead in the water. We're still seeing each other, but more out of habit than anything else. She's already involved with some other guy. Part of it is that she never really forgave me for the affair I had while she was in India two years ago."

"That was with. . . .?"

"Sally. Sal and I haven't been lovers for over a year—she's like a sister to me now—but Cori doesn't believe it. There's nothing I can do. And maybe I don't want to do anything." A sudden image of Coriola in my bed, her kelp-green eyes reflecting the candlelight, made me wince. "It's totally irrational. I know it's over, but I can't let go. The thought of leaving her drives me nuts. Go figure."

"There's nothing to figure. The relationship is over, you know it and she knows it, but you still want to hang on to her. Either you take her with you—and pay her way—or you go without her, and realize that it's gonna hurt for a while. Of course you can also stay here, declare your love, and ask her to move in with you. But I don't get the impression you're considering that option."

I nodded slowly and rhythmically, like one of those thirsty glass ducks that operate on the sublimation of alcohol vapor.

"Everything you've said is true," I sighed, resigned. Blake stood up, stretched and moseyed back toward my jazz shelf. "But at the end of the day, there's still one thing I can't reconcile. It's this idea of a time limit. When I first dreamed up the idea I meant the trip to be a *pilgrimage*—a spiritual circuit of the Earth. It seems to defeat the entire purpose if I have to race around the world in six months."

"Not at all." My therapist peered up. He was leaning over a scrap of blue note paper and compiling a lengthy list of titles, ostensibly for my records. "In fact, it's perfect. A spiritual pilgrimage with a time limit and deadline! Very nineties." He tacked the list to the wall above my CD player. "How soon can you leave?"

• 2 •

Unnatural Selection

Whenever an 0 passes in my life, I get an irresistible urge to jump through it. The round-the-world overland journey I envisioned was my gut response to a long-anticipated need—as March 6, 1994, crept ever closer—to perform a worthy and appropriate ritual. What better way to celebrate the circle, as cycle, shape and circus hoop?

But there was something else, even more compelling. In Indo-Tibetan Asia, performing a *kora*—a clockwise circumambulation around revered shrines, holy cities or sacred mountains—is considered a supreme act of pilgrimage. This, then, was my goal: to perform a kora around the Earth itself.

о   о   о

The idea had looked great on paper. As I plotted my route, though, and fathomed the lonely logistics of such a voyage (weeks at sea, days on trains, hours on oxcarts), my heart sank. Six months was a long time. It was a very long time. It was more time, I realized, than I could bear to spend with myself.

Finding a less familiar companion proved difficult. Friends who had money had no time, friends who had time had no money, and everyone else had children. Also, I felt that my ideal partner should be a woman. It seemed self-evident that a man and a woman traveling together would have access to a greater variety of people and socal situations than two men. A single man cannot always approach single or married women in Africa, India or the Middle East, but "couples" are acceptable currency wherever humans tread.

The frustrating thing was that I already knew who I wanted to travel with. My consort of choice was Sally Knight, a beautiful Australian who'd entered my life two years earlier, when Coriola was off in Dharamsala. I'd been hired to edit a book about the political turmoil in Burma, and Sally was assigned as my research assistant. If intelligence is the ultimate aphrodisiac, a day working with Sally was like an oyster banquet at a lingerie party. As the project progressed we'd moved our chairs closer and closer together until, one afternoon, she was close enough to bite me. This appetizer was followed by a six-course meal; and though we stopped sleeping together before Coriola's return, our appetite for each other's company remained insatiable. We still got together at least once a week to study Tibetan, collaborate on magazine articles and compose, among other dreams, the proposal for this very book.

I was sure she'd be perfect. For one thing, we had traveled together before. The previous January we had met briefly in India, spending a few days exploring the sights of New Delhi before journeying off to meet her guru—affectionately known as "Papaji"—in Lucknow. Though young by conventional standards (she was twenty-two), Sally had been deeply immersed in meditation and eastern philosophy since her teens. Her centered and stable approach would be the ideal complement to my manic-depressive psychosis. To ice the cake, Sal was supernaturally lucky: If the IRS ever decided to audit her, Stephen Hawking would show up to balance her books.

Unfortunately, like Coriola, she was dead broke. Sally's budget for a big night out permitted *Star Trek*, take-out Szechwan and a scratch-off lottery ticket.

As the weeks ticked by and a solo voyage seemed ever more likely, I launched a desperate ploy. Ignoring the advice of my friends ("You'll be swamped by crackpots!"), I ran an ad in the Personals section of the local weekly:

Writer with book contract seeks female companion for round-the-world overland trip. I'm 39, and a seasoned traveler. My partner must be fit, adventurous, adaptable and engaging. I'm looking for someone who's always dreamed of making such a journey, and has her own vision and motive for the trip. Some expenses will be covered, but self-sufficiency is required. Note: this is *not* a relationships ad! Sexual orientation or marital status is no bar.

I braced myself, expecting to be buried beneath an avalanche of responses. There were eight.

During the next two weeks I met each of my potential companions for lunch at King Yen—a bow to the old Jewish proverb that you can learn everything you need to know about someone by ordering Chinese food with them.

The first candidate, a professional storyteller at the Oakland Public Library, was eager to collect local folktales from around the world. I was intrigued until, to my horror, she ordered pork-flavored gluten in oyster sauce. The second woman was the recently widowed wife of a famous yacht racer and a renowned carnivorous plant breeder in her own right. We were having a great time until, allergic to prawns, she accidentally blew her nose into our last *mu shu* pancake. I actually did hear from one married woman: a feisty, green-eyed pet-liability lawyer whose husband had eagerly welcomed the suggestion of a six-month hiatus. The comic potential of such a tryst grew on me, but her fortune cookie—"You will soon survive a great natural disaster"—compelled me to reconsider.

After six more episodes of trial by sizzling iron platter, I had narrowed the field to two. The finalists had absolutely nothing in common, except that (*a*) they had exactly the same birthday, and (*b*) both had been crazy enough to answer my ad.

Lucy showed up for lunch in a ten-gallon hat and frilled leather vest with a vintage sixties button pinned above her breast: *Feed Your Head.* Blond and petite, she made a good living providing manicures and conversation to bedridden elderly women. One of them—a San Francisco art collector—had recently passed away, leaving Lucy a small Degas sketch. The drawing had fetched a bundle at auction, and Lucy had earmarked part of the money for travel.

And Lucy needed a change of scene. Her condo was stale with portraits of Elvis, dog-eared Shirley MacLaine books and the pet-shop smell of hamster droppings. She'd come home from work the previous evening to find her ex-boyfriend changing the lightbulb in her bedroom. He was standing on her pillow—in his boots.

"I knew then and there," she said, "that your ad was destiny speaking." Her fortune cookie seemed to concur. "This marks the beginning," it declared, "of an unforgettable vacation."

Lucy had no qualms about circling the globe with a total stranger; her main concern was finding her precise shade of lipstick in Senegal or Tibet. This thorny obstacle was removed when, at our third meeting, she located a San Francisco body-piercing salon that would tattoo her makeup on for her.

"It lasts five years," she gleefully declared. "The savings practically pay for the entire trip."

Zelda, on the other hand, was a professional magician. She'd been performing since the age of twelve, entertaining audiences from Tokyo to Madrid. Any doubts I had about her talent were dispelled at our second encounter, during a heated argument about the "psychic surgeons" of the Philippines (I believed, she didn't). To make her point, she "extracted" a roll of breath mints from my spleen.

The Great Zelda had other impressive attributes as well. She was a martial arts expert, with a street-tested ability to defend me from irate rickshaw wallahs, drunken sailors and rabid temple monkeys.

There was just one problem: We bickered. Warning lights flashed at our very first encounter, when we nearly came to blows trying to decide between pan-fried string beans and Mongolian chicken.

"I'm not a team player," she warned me, narrowing her eyes and twirling her chopsticks like kung fu weapons. "I'm used to having my way."

This gave me pause. Though the thought of roaming the globe with a magician was nearly irresistible, I could imagine any number of situations in which she might decide to make me disappear.

o   o   o

I told Lucy and Zelda that I'd make my decision by 10:00 P.M. the following Friday. As the hour drew closer, however, my doubts grew. Both women had their attributes and idiosyncrasies. Both had charisma and charm. Either would be a colorful character in my book. And either one, Sally sagely pointed out, could just as easily turn out to be a total nightmare. . . .

Several minutes before ten I picked up my world globe, placed it on the dining table and gave it a dizzying spin. I closed my eyes and pointed. If my finger touched land, Lucy would be my companion; if it touched sea, Zelda.

La!

I looked down. My finger rested squarely on the Panama Canal.

Five minutes later the telephone rang. I hesitated, still debating what I'd say to either of the hopeful candidates.

To my great surprise, it was neither. Sally was calling from a restaurant in Marin; and I could tell by her tone of voice that someone's wish, for better or worse, had come true.

"Pack your bags," she commanded. "I've just won the lottery."

Pennies from Heaven

"Winning the lottery," as it turned out, was Sally's shorthand for a rather different sort of luck.

She had spent the evening having dinner with friends of a friend. The well-to-do couple had recently returned from three weeks in India, where they'd attended the morning *satsangs,* or teachings, of one Hari Lal Poonja, a gigantic eighty-five-year-old guru capable of triggering one's nascent enlightenment instantly, sometimes with a mere finger snap. The fact that Sally had previously spent six months in the home of this luminous being was not wasted on them, and when she demurely added that her most passionate earthly desire was to visit Papaji again, reaching him this time via an emotionally and physically demanding around-the-world overland route, the couple began to share sly glances of conspiratorial generosity.

But the chain of spiritual coincidence did not end there. This very same couple, it seemed, then insisted on sharing with Sally their favorite brain food: an hour-long videotape, made in India about nine months earlier, of their esteemed mutual guru being interviewed by a skeptical, aggressive but basically good-natured and certainly good-looking foreign journalist. When the tape ended, Sally grinned radiantly and revealed that it was that very journalist with whom she had been invited to make her odyssey.

Over dessert the glances became whispers. Presently the man of the house asked Sally, "How much do you think you'll need?"

Assuming a six-month trip, at somewhere between $25 and $30 a day, Sally picked the closest millennial figure. "Five thousand dollars?"

"If you'll permit us," these superb individuals proposed, refilling her wineglass, "we'd like to make it possible for you to go."

And so Sally had come up with the money. Neither she nor I realized quite yet that the agreed-upon sum contained a fatal miscalculation. By the time the otherwise penniless Sally had finished paying for the requisite bedding, shoes, visas, toiletries, inoculations, clothes, books and so forth, her total budget would have shriveled down to a pathetic $18 a day. But for the time being we were very happy campers—dancing in Safeway parking lots, whirling through wilderness supply outlets and feeding each other *kung pao* chicken in front of the television as Captain Jean-Luc Picard unraveled the cosmos: *"Engage!"*

Clockwise

The traditional direction in which to perform a kora is clockwise. The object of veneration, in other words, is kept on one's right.

It is generally accepted, in social as well as astronomical circles, that the world turns counterclockwise. From the point of view of an observer above the North Pole, in other words, the globe appears to spin right to left. To travel clockwise around it required that Sally and I begin our trip by crossing the Pacific Ocean. Sally was eager to start out this way as well; it would bring us directly to Asia, where her deepest interests lay.

The problem was, we couldn't find a ship willing to carry us that way. After dozens of phone calls and yards of faxes we pretty much knew the score: Late autumn to midwinter was the high season for passenger ships traveling from the West Coast to balmy Australia and New Zealand, and none of the companies offering this service had room for two complimentary passengers. (Paying was out of the question; the fare for both of us would have run to nearly $10,000.)

The few shipping lines that plied that route were unwilling to help us, for union or liability reasons. While it might be possible to find a cargo ship heading for Taiwan or Japan, the thought of arriving in extortionate Tokyo in dead winter—forgoing Australia and Indonesia entirely—left us flat.

We would clearly have to rethink our spiritual strategy.

"Who says," I challenged Sally, "that the Earth spins counterclockwise, anyway?"

"I have no idea. It just does. Doesn't it?"

"Only if you assume—as we've all been brought up to assume—that north is 'up.'"

"Well, isn't it?"

"Not at all. It's a completely Eurocentric concept. The earliest explorers—I mean the ones who published their maps first—naturally put themselves on top, and started the idea that the axis of our hemisphere, the North Pole, was up. In reality, the world is a tiny blue sphere, spinning through infinite space. And there's no up or down in space. To a person in the Southern Hemisphere, the world spins clockwise; and anyone from a Southern Hemisphere country—you, for example—would perform a kora by heading east, not west."

"But this is *your* fortieth-birthday kora—and you're from the Northern Hemisphere."

"Geopolitically that's true. But if I look at myself as a citizen of the Earth—rather than as an 'American'—I can elect to circle the world either way. I don't have to buy into this whole cartographic missionary position thing."

"Well, if you're going to put it that way . . ."

o   o   o

We began investigating transatlantic routes. I maintained a healthy dread of the prospect, having read John McPhee's *Looking for a Ship:* "To make the North Europe run in winter is something that many American sailors do everything they can to avoid and others just refuse to do. No matter how straitened they may be and hungry for work, they will pass up the winter North Atlantic."

McPhee's intelligence, however, applied mainly to routes between the East Coast and German or Scandinavian ports. If we could find a ship heading toward North or West Africa—Alexandria, for instance, or Casablanca—we would remain well south of those tempestuous seas.

Africa is not one of the world's great international trading centers. There are very few lines that provide direct service between the United States and, say, Guinea-Bissau. Lykes Lines, out of New Orleans, fit the bill, but my attempts to secure passage on one of the containerships came to naught. Farrell Lines also passes through the Strait of Gibraltar and discharges cargo in Alexandria, but I had no better luck with their bureaucracy.

"The Panama Canal!" another friend cried. "Go to Panama! There are millions of ships going that way!" No doubt; but on investigation, a bizarre international shipping regulation seemed to forbid the picking up or discharging of passengers on Panamanian soil.

It was early December. We had to leave soon, very soon, if I hoped to complete the trip and write my book by the contracted deadline. Thanksgiving week had been worthless, and with twenty-one days left until Christmas I found myself on the phone from dawn to dusk.

I was sitting at my desk, applying for an extension on my 1993 income taxes, when the telephone rang. The caller was Dwayne Newton, a friend I'd met about a dozen years before in Santa Barbara. Fine-art photographer, San Francisco firefighter, *capoeira* dancer and Civil War rifle collector, Dwayne was the ultimate nineties Renaissance man. Some friends thought he looked like Eddie Murphy on a good day, but I didn't think Murphy had ever had a day that good.

"You ought to let me make some calls," he offered. "My uncle was practically a legend in the Merchant Marine. Sometimes just mentioning his name is enough to thin out the red tape."

I sighed heavily. "You're welcome to try. But I've already made a million calls."

"Never mind. Just tell me, exactly, where you want to go."

I told him. He hung up. I finished my IRS form, walked it to the post office, bought a third of a pound of turkey roll at the grocery store and returned home forty-five mintues later to find the message light blinking on my answering machine.

"Yo, dude. Newton here. I found you a ship."

o   o   o

"It leaves from *where?*"

"Brooklyn. January twenty-fifth. Ten days from Red Hook to Dakar."

"That's incredible." Sally shook her head. "Dwayne is amazing."

Sally knew Newton well; I had first pointed him out to her during the free-for-all Gulf War protest marches that filled the streets of San Francisco in late 1990. Walking tall, a proud and solitary figure positioned between the morose Adult Children of Distant Fathers United for Globel Reconciliation and the tribally percussive Gay and Lesbian Drummers Say NO! War for Oil, Dwayne wore a hand-lettered sandwich sign announcing himself as the lone political herald of African Americans for the Metric System.

"So the new question is: What do you want to do between now and the end of January?"

"I vote we get out of here as quickly as possible," Sally said, teething on a purple pen. "We're just spinning our wheels—and I'm spending money I don't have. I may as well be spending it on the road."

Her comment, I knew, concealed bravely suppressed misgivings. The more we'd stared at maps, the more Sally had realized that the initial appeal of the trip—for her, at least—had been the prospect of visiting Asia. Indonesia, Thailand, India, Nepal; those were the cultures that excited her, that would slake her spiritual thirst. If we began by traveling eastward, it would be months before we reached them.

Her curiosity about the intervening geography was, at best, scant. In her darker moments she viewed Africa and even Europe as total waste of her resources and time. At one point she broached the possibility of flying ahead to Bombay, and waiting for me there. I spent two days convincing her—in some distress—that the pilgrimage was an organic whole, based on the idea that every part of the world was interconnected. This argument (combined with her sense of loyalty and a certain component of guilt) finally won the game, but putting off the inevitable any longer would drive both of us insane.

A decision was reached. Rather than traverse the frozen heartland of the U.S.A., we would head south to sunny Mexico, dip into Guatemala and backtrack up through Belize and the Yucatan. Finding passage from Mexico to Florida would be relatively straightforward. Once we arrived in Miami we would play it by ear.

"And I thought you'd like to know," Sally said liltingly, "that I've been doing some research of my own. There's a school of Tibetan Buddhism—it's called Bon—whose pilgrims go around shrines *backward*. Counterclockwise. One of their saint-practitioners, I forget his name, has a great line about it . . . hang on, I'll find it . . ." She leafed through the oversize legal pad that served as her notebook. "Here. Are you ready?"

I nodded that I was.

"'While the other orders seem content to follow the Buddha,'" she read triumphantly, "'we prefer to come around and meet Him.'"

Dancing Lessons

During the final days before our departure, two oblique but irresistible travel suggestions fell from the cosmos into my lap.

The first was an invitation, from Wilderness Travel in Berkeley, to join their three-week Mount Kailas expedition in early May. Led by Gary McCue—whose *Trekking in Tibet* was already a minor classic—the trip would begin in Simikot, northwestern Nepal. A weeklong trek would bring us to the Nepal-Tibet border, where waiting Land Cruisers would carry us to Lake Manasarovar.

This was my dream trip. Kailas is far more than a mountain: It is the center of Hindu and Buddhist cosmology, the abode of Lord Shiva, the Center of the Universe. Sally and I would have to circle the Earth about a billion times to obtain the spiritual merit of one Kailas kora; and the ritual bathing in holy Manasarovar, at the mountain's base, would cleanse us of all imaginable impurities.

The Chinese, who have occupied Tibet since the 1950s, enjoy making money, and permits for such expeditions can be outrageously expensive. Sally and I met with Bill Abbott, the Wilderness Travel director, to discuss this.

"We'd like to invite you to come as our guest," he offered magnanimously, "at no charge. But as far as Sally goes, we'll have to ask you to cover her permits and so forth. We'll be glad to comp her on the Wilderness Travel end of things—she won't have to pay for meals or gear or transportation or leaders' fees—but whenever we're asked to lay out money ourselves we'll pass that expense on to her. Fair enough?"

"More than fair," I agreed.

"Do you have any idea how much money we're talking about?" That was Sally.

"Not at this point." Abbott leaned so far back in his chair I thought the stem would snap. "We estimate a thousand or so—but that's a ballpark figure. You know the Chinese; it all depends on what the officials had for breakfast that morning."

It was worrisome, but workable. If worse came to worst, Sally could always ask her Marin patrons for an extra few thousand dollars. Surely they wouldn't deny her the opportunity to circle the holiest mountain in the world . . . ? And I would be more than happy to split her expenses with them, since the free ride essentially kicked three weeks back into my budget.

"Count us in," I announced. "The way I see it, this trek could be the centerpiece of my whole book."

o   o   o

The second proposition I received was almost frightening, for it threatened to compromise, albeit in a strictly cerebral fashion, the motivating thesis behind my trip.

Ten days before Christmas—less than two weeks before our ETD—I received a phone call from an editor at O'Reilly & Associates in Sebastopol, California. O'Reilly was a well-established publisher of software and computer manuals; they'd recently made forays into the equally congested universe of travel literature as well. Snippets of my work had appeared in a few of their *Travelers' Tales* anthologies, and I anticipated, greeting the editor, a generalized plea to keep my eyes open.

What he had in mind was far more specific. O'Reilly & Associates, it seemed, had recently launched an enterprise on the Internet: the mushrooming, electromagnetic labyrinth of on-line singles clubs, Grateful Dead databases and other hyperspecific peer interest groups (African Americans for the Metric System?) that was beginning to define, for better or worse, the polis of the future. The name of this new enterprise was the Travelers' Center, and it was the hottest thing in travel since Lomotil.

"What we'd like you to do," the editor said, "is write a column for us, from the road. Your dispatches can be as short or as long as you like, and you can write them whenever you feel like it. No pressure, no deadlines and—sorry—no money. But we promise you'll get great exposure, and it might open up a whole new audience for your book."

Nerds! The great untapped market in travel literature! I contemplated the prospect of hundreds, thousands of cowlicked, whitesocked, penny-loafered Internet hackers tearing themselves away from their *Star Trek* forums to find out how long my Tenochtitlan tapeworm was.

The long and short of it was, he sold me on the idea. There was just enough mystery to the Net, just enough evidence that maybe it really was only the tip of some dazzling iceberg, to get me (who'd been, after all, president of the Space Science Club in high school) interested. Nonetheless, I had to acknowledge there was something subversive about the enterprise. There I was, about to set off to rediscover, in the most physical way possible, the immensity of the world by traveling its girth without airplanes. But it's not just the airplane that has made the world seem small; forces like the telephone, the fax/modem and the Internet were doing their part as well. This, then, would be the odd paradox of my odyssey. While my body would be compelled to creep across the Earth's surface like an inchworm, my brain would shuttle hither and yon at the speed of light.

The only hurdle was hardware. If I was going to be uploading stories from various global backwaters, I needed a notebook computer small enough and light enough to carry in my daypack. It had to have a long battery life, contain very few moving parts and be tough as nails. It also had to be easy to service. Nothing is more frustrating than lugging a useless piece of sophisticated electronic equipment—impossible to fix but too expensive to throw away—around the world.

After considerable frantic research I found such a machine. Produced by Hewlett-Packard, it was called an OmniBook. Aside from its garden-variety virtues, which included near-weightlessness, it had one particular feature that knocked my socks off: If the battery died like a dog in the middle of a trans-Saharan balloon ride, the Omnibook would run for about five hours on four AA batteries.

In the near future, that selling point will probably sound as ingenious as vulcanized rubber wheels on a horse-drawn buggy. But in 1993 it was a technological masterstroke that made my jaw drop.

I called up Hewlett-Packard, told them what a big shot I was and asked them to send me a "demonstration" unit on the double.

"No," they replied.

Forces were marshaled. O'Reilly representatives wrote letters, my publisher made a personal plea, and *Wired* magazine, in a decorous ceremony that included computer-generated heralds, wind-up sushi and an elephant in a VR body suit, promoted me to contributing editor. This did the trick. Three days later a UPS courier arrived at my door, accepted my illegible scrawl on a liquid crystal pad and handed me an enormous box containing, hidden among politically correct non-Styrofoam peanuts, my very own OmniBook on six-month "editorial loan." That same afternoon an HP product reviews coordinator phoned me, confirming my receipt of the unit and offering a few words of professional advice.

"Don't lose it," she said.

o   o   o

At this point my relationship with O'Reilly & Associates was honed to a single point man: Allen Noren, editor of the Traveler's Center.

A mild-mannered Scandinavian who could have easily modeled for nautically named colognes in *GQ*, Noren was no couch potato. Working nights in a converted garage, he was putting together a book of his own: an account of a grueling three-and-a-half-month trip around the Baltic Sea that he and his girlfriend had made on a BMW K100 motorcycle. Sensing my eleventh-hour panic, he cruised down from Sonoma County to familiarize me with the maddening series of commands needed to link up with his office in Sebastopol.

There is' no need to re-create my education, an approximation of which anyone can see by renting *The Miracle Worker*. Noren's patience would have made a bonsai gardener look like a Formula One pit-stop mechanic, and after two lengthy sessions I was able to perform a simple fax transfer without biting my own teeth.

The day before Christmas we said farewell, shaking hands at the top of my stairwell and, unexpectedly, hugging.

"I know you and Sally will have a great trip," he said with real emotion. "If you ever run into trouble, or even if you just need to talk with someone, call me." He handed me a slip of paper with his calling-card number on the back. "I mean it. I know what it's like to be out there."

I saw him out the door. There is a certain weightless abdominal feeling one gets when, in the final days before a long trip, one sees familiar faces for the last time. I stood in my driveway, weak-kneed with the realization that, in three days, Sally and I would be gone.

Allen was halfway to the sidewalk when he turned around. "Hey, I almost forgot to ask," he called. "Have you got a name for this column of yours yet?"

Indeed I did: "Big World."

• 3 •

The Paradise of Fortune Cookies

The inventor of the fortune cookie appears to have been a Chinese immigrant named David Jung, who managed a small bakery in Los Angeles in 1918. After the Great War, Jung used to see people standing around in the streets looking hungry and lonely; he wanted to give them something to eat and a bit of encouragement. He began by wrapping messages in sweet egg rolls, finally developing a crispier recipe and the signature pinch 'n' fold.

Literary aspects of production were assigned to a Presbyterian reverend who favored biblical maxims. Around 1922, though, authorship shifted to more contemporary minds—and the messages acquired the uncanny prescience we rely upon in the fortune cookies of today.

o   o   o

It seemed to Sally and me that the entire practice reached its height, its literary apex, during the month before our departure.

"Do you think this is true?" Sally dropped the fortune in front of her lips and blew it over to me. It settled, face-up, in my tea:

> Your ability to read minds sometimes
> frightens the people around you

I narrowed my eyes. "If you don't know the answer, you don't need to ask. What do you make of this one?"

> You will play an historic role in Earth's first visit
> by extra-terrestrial beings

She was silent for a while. "I wasn't planning to reveal myself until the appropriate moment, but you might as well know the truth right now . . ."

> Never mistake motion
> for action

"Uh-oh. You think we should make that the motto of our trip?"
"I like this one better."

> You are in the right place,
> at the right time

"Even now?"
"It's always Now," she replied.
"Ahh. This one's a keeper." I grasped the spearmint-green slip by its wings and displayed it to Sally like a butterfly specimen.

What you are looking for
is who is looking

"Saint Francis." She nodded. "And the Buddha. And Papaji. We should both have that tattooed on the backs of our eyelids." She cracked open her cookie. I watched her eyes widen until, silently, she passed the benediction over to me:

You will successfully
navigate the Bardo

"Well, Jesus," I said.

"You can't imagine what a load off my mind this is."

The *bardo,* of course, is the territory, the spooky twilight zone, mapped out in that great metaphysical classic known in the vulgate as *The Tibetan Book of the Dead.* In that ancient treatise—one of the first great travel books—*bardo* is the name given to the usually horrifying interregnum that lies between death and rebirth. While migrating through this zone, the human soul faces all manner of self-created demons and obstacles, and attempts, using every tool at its terrified disposal, to influence the conditions and circumstances under which it will be reborn.

But the word *bardo* has a broader meaning as well. It can indicate any interim journey, from a long commute to a wait in the dentist's chair.

"Has it occurred to you," I asked Sally, "that this whole pilgrimage we're about to embark on is a kind of bardo?"

She scrunched up her face. "Well, hopefully, not just a bardo. There are other realms in Tibetan mythology, too. Right? There are paradise realms; there's a bunch of hell-realms; and there are loads of bardos."

"So then maybe it's fair to say that we'll pass through a few paradises, a bunch of hells, and a hell of a lot of bardos."

"Probably. But you also have to remember that it's all relative. All of these hells, bardos, paradises are *self-generated* realms. They're projections of your own inner nature."

"You're a clever one, Ms. Knight." I lapsed into our *Avengers* mode.

"Thank you, Mr. Greenwald. You know what I think? We should get one more fortune. Just for the trip. Agreed?"

I shrugged, suspicious of putting so much weight on a cracker.

"Of course," she added, "we reserve the right to reject anything it says if we don't like it."

"All right, then."

She ran over to the King Yen cash register, grabbed another fortune cookie from the bowl and set it between us with a flourish. We held the cookie like a wishbone—"Here goes nothing"—and snapped it open, nearly bumping heads as we leaned forward to read the brief but unsettling message:

> Nothing is written

On Our Backs

What do you bring along on a six-month overland voyage that will take you from the Arizona desert to the Himalaya?

Nothing? Or everything? There was, I discovered, no middle ground.

Our luggage of choice, selected after innumerable reconnaissance missions to camping supply stores, was the Eagle Creek "Endless Journey" backpack. Though the name threatened to reawaken all the separation anxiety I had experienced in my earlier knee-to-knee conversations with Blake, two practical considerations prevailed.

The first was that the packs, large enough to accommodate a Toyota Tercel, featured zip-off daypacks just the right size for my computer. The second was that Eagle Creek offered to send us the gear for free. All they asked in return was a sheet of color slides showing their equipment at work in assorted exotic locales. Easy enough . . . for though I had no illusions about my own credibility as a real-life model, Sally was a decidedly different story.

I reserved December 26, the day before our departure, for packing. Two hours into the process I was ready to order an industrial trash compactor. It is astounding how socks, shirts, and bathing trunks, so light and airy when taken individually, quickly condense into a mass with the approximate weight and density of a neutron star. Add to these AA batteries, binoculars, Celestial Seasonings tea bags, a down vest, echinacea tablets, floppy diskettes, guidebooks, a hairbrush, an inflatable camping mattress, jazz tapes, Kodak film, Lomotil, mittens, nasal spray, Off! insect repellent, polypropylene socks, rubber thongs, sunscreen, Travel Scrabble, underwear, vitamin C, water purification tablets, Xeroxes of my passport, a Yashica camera and my black dress shoes (you never know), and you're grappling with the only earthly object capable of pinning Konishiki, the beloved Samoan sumo wrestler, to the mat.

Friends, neighbors and the local chiropractor dropped by to watch me put it on. This accomplished, I moved about my flat gingerly, cautious as a moon man. But the pack was superbly designed, and the weight well balanced. It was no worse than having an adult hippopotamus strapped to my back.

But by the time the sun had set, and the backpack and I faced each other across the now-ravaged wasteland of my bedroom, I realized that one of my worst traveler's nightmares was about to come true.

I was about to carry something heavy around the world.

Video Night in Oakland

The evening before my departure found me glued to my television, blearily digesting the four videotapes I'd rented as part of a crash course in spiritual pilgrimage. The movies had been suggested by Geoffrey Hill, a Jungian therapist famous for his unique method of treating clients. Eschewing conventional antidepressants like Prozac and Zolaft, Hill prescribed films.

I'd telephoned Hill at his cabin in the San Bernadino Mountains, some miles southeast of LA. A storm had closed the roads, trapping him indoors. Recognizing a captive audience, I launched into a long soliloquy about our pilgrimage—describing its long evolution and the various apprehensions I'd experienced in connection with it.

"I would guess," Hill responded, "that what you're feeling is a combination of trip anxiety as well as some midlife issues. Let me ask you this: Do you feel like (*a*) you've already gone through a midlife transition; (*b*) that you're going through one now; or (*c*) that most of it is still to come?"

"All of the above."

"Well then, it's likely the trip itself is part of the 'working out' of the crisis. It's a common thing for a man going through such a transition to embark on a journey of some type. A trip of this scale—even the *idea* of doing this—could be something that you're creating, consciously or unconsciously, in order to resolve that natural process."

"It's unclear to me," I said, "how a pilgrimage like this could resolve my midlife crisis."

"Oh, it could." There was a pause; Hill sneezed violently. "The problem is, you never get the redemptive value until *after* you've redeemed yourself. You never know the end result until after the journey is over. And I'm glad you use the world 'pilgrimage,' because that's what they were in the old days; nowadays most travel is a form of entertainment.

"The reason you called me, though, is for examples of films that would be good for you to see. I have a few in mind; all of them describe what we might call the Odyssean Journey. I'm talking here about a mythical wandering: a trip which is a homecoming, ultimately, to one's own self."

Hill proceeded to recommend a dozen films. These included Volker Schlondorff's *Voyager,* Wim Wender's *Until the End of the World,* Ingmar Bergman's *Seventh Seal,* John Ford's *Long Voyage Home* and Stanley Kubrick's *2001: A Space Odyssey.* I was alarmed by how many of them ended with the protagonist's death.

"Aren't there any movies," I inquired, "in which the traveler returns victorious and collects the rich rewards that he deserves?"

"No." Hill laughed. "One does have to die. I wouldn't take it too literally, though. The transition from youth to adulthood—the very midlife swing you're experiencing—often feels like a kind of death. A seed has to be buried in the ground; it has to die before new fruit can come up. The journey merely fertilizes the process."

"I'm not sure I understand."

"All right, then. Consider Odysseus. It seemed he would never get home. Once he did, Ithaca was full of rivals who were getting drunk and going after Penelope. At the end of the book he chases off the rivals and reconciles with his wife—but we know it's not over. Some of the suitors might come back to take revenge on him, a month or two after Homer's story ends. There's trouble ahead. But the lessons that he's learned on his journey have prepared him well. They prepared him to win back Penelope, and they've prepared him to deal with whatever new obstacles he might face in the future. Odysseus might not have lived 'happily ever after'; but he was wise enough, strong enough and crafty enough to win a certain amount of peace in the end.

"And that," Hill concluded, "is why myth is so useful. It's not about a single story, or episode; it's about a worldview. The rewards you spoke of don't come until *after* the narrative—when the original personality that set off has died, and we complete the story in our own minds."

Zero Hour: A Baptism

The twenty-seventh of December dawned cold and clear. I had spent the night pretending to sleep, lying inert and cross-eyed beside Coriola, and reached over to turn off the alarm clock before it woke her up. But she had been faking it as well.

"Omygod. Today's the day. Eeeeeeee! Are you excited?" Her own voice sounded strangely neutral.

"No," I answered honestly. "Just terrified."

She had long ago lost patience with this kind of talk and bounded out of bed into a bathrobe, the bathroom, the kitchen. I heard the door of the refrigerator—a vintage General Electric Combination with rotating half-moon shelves and art deco cubicles for Meats, Cheese and Ice Cream—slam shut, followed by the throaty glug of apple juice on the move. She returned with two glasses and sat near my hip.

"Poor Duck-duck." This is what she called me. "Don't be scared. You'll have a wonderful time. You've got a great assignment, and you're going with one of your best friends." Did she believe this at last? "Just try to relax. Six months from now, when it's all over, you won't believe how fast it went by. Just concentrate on your writing, and have a great time." She leaned over to kiss me, slipping a cool hand under the sheet. "I know you will."

I knew she was seeing someone else, and it irked me that I could not put her out of my mind once and for all before setting off on my enormous trip. The proverbial clean break. But how many couples have struggled in vain against the hot undertow of Good Chemistry? I was happy, for the moment, to let go.

o   o   o

Coriola left for work at eight-thirty, promising to take the early afternoon off. I spent the next two and a half hours cleaning the house, and writing a note to my subtenants. Sally turned up at eleven, laden, antlike, with a load many times her body weight. Her first move—after dumping the pack in a corner—was to prance over to the stereo and slip *Our Time in Eden,* programmed to the second cut, onto the CD player.

> *These are days you'll remember*
> *Never before and never since, I promise*
> *will the whole world be warm as this*
> *And as you feel it, you'll know it's true*
> *that you*
> *are Blessed and Lucky*

She grabbed my hands and danced me around the living room, a brat *dakini,* careless, loaded, free.

o   o   o

Dwayne arrived an hour later, parking his Stealth-black Pathfinder in the driveway and loading Sally's gear into the back. The plan was as follows: He'd take Sally to San Francisco, where she'd pick up her American reentry visa. This should take about thirty minutes. The two of them would continue on to the Civic Center BART station. I would emerge from the exit nearest Burger King and, after bidding farewell to the theoretically waiting Coriola, the three of us would leave the Bay Area and drive about 450 miles south, to Santa Barbara. Dwayne would have the option of leaving us there or, if so moved, spiriting us even farther south.

Sally and I were drinking champagne in my living room when a loud knock startled us back into a semblance of workaday consciousness. I hopped down the stairs to find a deliverywoman holding out a cereal-box-size Fedex Pak and confirmation padlet. I carried the box upstairs.

"What is it?" Sally wanted to know.

"I've got no idea. Nothing too surprising, I hope. . . ."

Within was a bulging manila envelope and, inside that, a knotted plastic bag containing a small beveled jar sealed with a wide, tight cork. There was also a greeting card, silk-screened with an image of the Green Tara, goddess of compassion and protectress of the Kathmandu Valley.

"Om Shalom, Jeffji and Sallyji," the card read. "Blessings, pilgrims, on your journey. Enclosed please find the Elixir of Eternal Life, bottled at the Source; Lake Manasarovar, June 1993. Much love, Carroll."

I sat on my ass, unable to speak. I knew that Carroll Dunham, one of my closest friends in Nepal, had made a summer pilgrimage to Mount Kailas; I even knew she was back in the United States promoting her new book about Tibet. But this gift, and its timing, were beyond belief.

Sally, who had a deep and abiding love for rituals, took over. "You guys sit down," she instructed me and Dwayne. We did. She then proceeded to walk around us—clockwise—three times, uttering as much as she could remember of the Green Tara invocation before uncorking the crystal flask and spritzing us with Manasarovar nectar.

"There." She touched her finger, the spritzing instrument, to her own forehead. "If we're not ready now, we never will be."

Surprisingly, we did feel ready. There was nothing more to say. Dwayne and Sally threw their arms around me, picked up their bags and left the flat.

This was it, then. I stood in the center of my living room, pulse racing. I looked at my dragon tree; at the rice-paper lanterns hanging from the ceiling; at the painting of Ganesha on the wall. I walked into the kitchen and touched the coffee grinder, the hot-water faucet, a knife. Soon, sooner than I dared to believe, all these objects would seem impossibly distant; for the instant I stepped out of my apartment, the circumference of the world would lie between this moment and being here again.

It's always now, Sally had told me over a fortune cookie. Is it?

I slipped my arms through the Endless Journey and hiked it onto my shoulders.

"Farewell, beautiful home. Don't go away."

Southern Exposure

An elderly black man sat on a folding stool on the sheltered patio outside the MacArthur BART station, running a glorified pipe cleaner through the throat of a battered clarinet. He was wearing a plaid lumberjack's shirt with a yellow bow tie.

I'd walked rapidly past him, propelled by the angular momentum of my enormous backpack, when a sudden impulse made me apply the brakes and back up. He looked up and saw me standing there with my toes grazing the edge of his open instrument case and a folded dollar bill in my hand.

"My word," he said, craning at my pack. "You comin', or goin'?"

I told him everything. He rested the clarinet on his knees and looked into my eyes.

"I can see you have a beautiful heart," he said, and took my hand. "Your trip will be wonderful. You have my blessing."

I bent down as best I could and dropped the bill into his case. "If I get back safely," I promised him, "I'll come right back here and slip you a twenty."

"Never you mind that twenty. You just come back safe."

People hurtled by, their lives a blur.

"Play me something?"

"Oh, I will. You go on now, and don't worry about nuthin'. I will."

He played "Summertime" as I walked through the turnstile, the sweet, sad melody following me into the artificial cavern like distilled sunlight.

For all the rolling sweet oceans and burnt-caramel deserts, through all the songs and blessings still to come, there would never be a moment when I loved the world more. My journey began at that instant.

• 4 •

Gone

Coriola was waiting outside Burger King, braiding her hair. My catalog of emotions, like a lame thesaurus, could offer me nothing to define the moment, and I spent our final ten minutes together stroking the soft skin of her cheek and wishing that we were both the slightly different people for whom the relationship would have blossomed.

Dwayne's black Pathfinder swerved up to the curb, snapping the moment like a dry twig. There were quick, difficult good-byes, a final memory of Cori's breasts pressed against my chest, and a dizzy long slide down the wide glazed highway with the sun dropping slowly toward the sea.

o   o   o

After spending a night in Santa Barbara we gulped coffee and continued south, skirting miasmic LA. Dwayne, with the impulsive nonchalance of a man deciding to run out for some half-and-half, had agreed to drive us over the Mexican border. Sally sat between us, buttering bagels on her knee.

"Be nice to me today," she warned. "I have PMT."

"PMT? I thought it was PMS."

"We Australians aren't hysterical enough to call it a syndrome. It's just premenstrual tension."

But that deep hormonal gravity, that sense of a tidal pull, had us all in tow. The flow had begun. We were moving. We were on our way, beyond the long-familiar, entering a suddenly enormous world whose seismic vibrations were already shivering up our spines. Connected we were, and connected we would remain; and yet, strangely, the moment had the gut-churning flavor of free fall. We were Olympic high divers who, having bounced at the edge of the board, knew that we had committed ourselves for good. Our leap into the unknown, exhilarating and terrifying, would end in triumph or failure, but there was no turning back. Oakland, five hundred miles behind us, was twenty-five thousand miles away.

Bardo of the Prickly Pears

A quicksilver drive sucked us down Highway 10, into the southwestern reaches of winter Arizona. Hitting 85, we dropped dead south through the droll statuary of Organ Pipe Cactus National Monument. Here was True American Desert, the gorgeous filmic Gene Autry home on the range, where the sun sinks behind rusted buttes and hawks perch regally atop missile-high saguaros. In the Southwest, America retains its spirituality in spite of history; nothing can cheapen the mezcal piety of the sparse, unforgiving landscape. The sight of a little water becomes a religious experience; a lizard darting beneath the ocotillo is a haiku in motion.

We uttered our first true prayers, to the Virgen de Guadalupe, in a rustic one-room shrine on the highway shoulder just over the border. A Mexican gentleman stood in the dirt lot, filling his rattletrap pickup's tank with canned petrol. The fumes were a noxious sensory counterpoint to the amber foundry sunset over Sonora's charcoal hills. The man himself turned out to be a sweetheart, though, pulling us back into the shrine to show us the Virgin's busted pedestal and to point out her beautifully painted face and hands. We drove off into the fading light, wondering at exactly what point affluence kills spirituality.

o   o   o

This was Mexico: washboard roads, bottled water, fear of lettuce. Dwayne nodded off, bare feet pungent after three days in the same socks. His can of mace sat ominously on the night table.

The mace was one of several individually innocuous precautions that, taken together, sketched out a surprisingly sweeping paranoia on the part of our escort. We had already changed rooms three times, the first because the lock "looks like it's been fucked with," the second because the window ledge was leaping distance from a neighboring roof, and most recently when Dwayne realized there was no direct line of sight between the doorway and his car. The manageress referred to us, not affectionately, as *los locos*.

"This is Mexico, not Palm Springs," Dwayne said, ironically alluding to the nightmarish evening we had spent supping on frozen yoghurt beneath the sinister eye of a huge inflatable Santa. Palm Springs, absurd in holiday dress, where the authoritative snap of BMW door locks sucking shut had followed us down the street like a Greco-robotic chorus.

"Laugh at me all you want, but I'm not spending New Year's Eve filing a police report."

o   o   o

In point of fact we spent New Year's Eve in Guaymas. A police station would have been infinitely more entertaining.

It was one of those December thirty-firsts when you learn just how depressing New Year's Eve can be. Part of the problem was local good sense. Mexicans traditionally spend the last hours of the year with their families, handily eliminating the crushing pressure to find a good party. It is not until after midnight—long after—that they take to the bars, dancing and drinking 'til dawn.

We wandered the streets like desperados, searching for cold beers and a few warm tortillas. Absolutely nothing was open. Finally we were pointed down a side street where we spied, perched atop a ten-story building, one of those cheesy restaurants-with-a-view that are usually to be avoided at all costs.

This one was no exception. After a terrifying elevator ride to the summit, we emerged into an empty cafeteria awash in ultraviolet light that made the dandruff flakes on the shoulders of my fleece jacket twinkle like stars. The sulfur streetlights of Guaymas glowed through the steamed windows, punctuated by huge marquees advertising Corona beer and Bata shoes.

Just as our food arrived, a DJ in ruby-red shades and a barrister's wig materialized, taking a seat behind a cunningly hidden console. Acknowledging us with a nod, he flipped a switch. Within nanoseconds the entire restaurant was transformed into a gigantic subwoofer. I bit my hand to keep my teeth from rattling out of their moorings, watching helplessly as Dwayne lapsed slowly into catatonia. Sally, the only member of our entourage still capable of rational thought, scraped our supper into a doggy bag and directed a military-style evacuation. Minutes later we were back on the street, panting with relief.

Shadowy pelicans drifted above our heads, and a hazy moon branded the sky. We sat on a bench by the water, speechless, fishing gooey handfuls of *enchiladas con queso y frijoles* out of the soggy sack.

At quarter to midnight we climbed to the roof of our hotel. Guaymas frolicked with explosions. The night sky was illuminated with red and green Roman candles, the slow dance of descending flares, sparklers hurled from distant rooftops. Sirens wailed; Dwayne was sure he heard automatic weapons being fired. Terrified cats ran down the alleyway beside the Del Puerto, their stiff legs strobing beneath the streetlights. Suddenly it was the new year. We embraced among the skylights and rebar and water tanks, lit by the harsh Guaymas moon, avoiding any mention of omens.

Los Fugitivos

Dwayne dropped us off at the first-class bus station in Los Mochis, but not before we'd saddled him with a duck.

It was a monstrosity, a huge, grinning orange and yellow crepe waterfowl piñata we'd spied hanging from the ceiling of the single open shop on an otherwise blacked-out alley. I'd made Dwayne slam the Pathfinder into reverse and grind backward down the one-way street for a second look, which only confirmed my intuition that I'd found the ultimate farewell gift for Coriola.

Since we'd left San Francisco I'd known that a dramatic psychological gesture was needed: something to cut the cord of nostalgia that would otherwise tie Cori's memory to my receding fuselage like a string of Bud cans. Left to my own devices I'd never make it happen; I'm hopeless at ending relationships. The trick was to figure out a way for *Coriola herself* to do it. The instant I saw that absurd and humongous party favor, which would soon fill the back of Dwayne's 4WD and cause him unimagined grief at customs, I knew I'd hit pay dirt: a "Duck-duck," my ostensible alter ego, suitable for smashing into a thousand pieces.

Drive me out of your life once and for all, baby. Hit me upside the head with a bat.

Dwayne waited with the car while Sally and I bought tickets to the Distrito Federal. Our good-byes were brief. It was both sad and scary to see him go, to watch his Darth Vadermobile pull away from the curb and vanish into the unknown quantity of the Los Mochis night. Dwayne was on his own, off to face a new plate of worries in a world we were leaving behind at last. And that was exactly right: What Dwayne's departure meant was that the trip itself, *el viaje mismo*, the Actual Voyage, had begun. No more three-way check splits; no more easy-off easy-on gas stations; no more throw-your-stuff-in-the-back-and-let's-go. No more of those dreaded signs that seemed to materialize every fifty kilometers along Mexico 15: *Prepara Su Cuota*. The final toll had been paid. We were crossing the falls, on a tightrope. And our safety net, symbolized by the dark, droll and competent Mr. Newton, was gone.

But it was also a relief. The Pathfinder, for all its undeniable utility, had started to seem like something we were carrying around along with our huge packs and absurd armory of toiletries. It had to be fed, washed, insured, licensed, oiled and put to bed well within sight of its nervous master. It really was like a dog; Dwayne never looked more satisfied than after he'd pressed the button on his little car-alarm remote and heard the Pathfinder yelp its allegiance. Unfortunately the car was

also like a human infant, and addressing its many exigencies had consumed about 25 percent of our time.

Shedding that cybernetic second skin felt as good as taking off a
pair of clunky ice skates. If we'd left our backpacks behind as well, we'd
have felt light as air.

o   o   o

As Sally and I waited for our bus to arrive, I explained how I'd bought
the duck as a symbolic smashing of the neurotic ties linking me with
my ex-lover.

"That's great," she said, dusting motes of grime off her prized
Akubra. "After an intense breakup with my last boyfriend we did the
same thing."

"You bought each other duck piñatas?"

"We gave each other colonic irrigation treatments, to get rid of all
the shit."

o   o   o

Blue morning glories vivid against a tattered cornfield; a beheaded doll
waving to passing vehicles from the concave roof of a farmer's tin
shack; squashed iguanas lying like old handbags in the road. Aquamarine fields of maguey, the raw material of tequila, covered the Jalisco
hillsides like sea urchins, the military regularity of their planted rows a
disturbing sight after the chaotic desert.

The bus's video system offered *The Fugitive* (*El Fugitivo*), and I sat riveted during the terrifying bus crash scene as we careened along the
edges of steep embankments toward Mexico City.

My delight in the irony of the video presentation—akin to showing
Alien on the space shuttle—passed, and I began to feel an uncomfortable sense of identification with Dr. Richard Kimball. Sally and I had
been moving for five days straight, and the end was nowhere in sight.
An hour after hitting Mexico City we'd be rushing across town by sub-
way in a frantic race to catch the overnight bus to Oaxaca. This was a
pilgrimage? It was starting to feel more like the Paris-Dakar relay. The
big question, asked of myself in silence as we rolled toward dusk, was:
Am I running toward something, or away from something? *And why am
I running at all?* The true moments of our adventure, those worth
recording, would only come when we stopped.

I resolved to stop as soon as possible.

o   o   o

An eight-year-old girl perched her chin on the headrest of the seat in front of me. Our futile attempts to converse in Spanish soon gave way to primitive hand gestures. All over the world, it seems, bus travel is about playing with the eight-year-old in the seat in front of you. Silvia was a plump gem with precocious hazel eyes, immediately loyal, awkwardly affectionate. Despite my appalling incompetence with her native language, she never gave up. As so often happens, our mutual good intentions whelped a sort of telepathy that allowed us to communicate with each other.

We stopped for lunch in Tepic. Silvia took my hand and led me off the bus. Farmers and their wives were lined up along the roadside, selling big ripe strawberries that Sally and I desperately craved but didn't dare buy, since we had no way to wash them. Seconds before we were due to reboard, Silvia ran up with two large red berries, one in each open palm. It was an awkward moment—we couldn't possibly accept her little gift without breaking the prime directive of travel in Mexico—but I came up with enough vocabulary to at least be honest with her.

"*Imposible comer,*" I pronounced. "*Para nuestros estómagos, primero necesitamos lavarle.*"

Somehow Silvia got the gist of this, nodded ruefully, and hurried off. She showed up again two minutes later. The strawberries were dripping wet, "cleansed" with parasitic tap water. What could we do? Sally and I looked at each other with expressions of surrender and bit into the forbidden fruits.

We swallowed with effort. The conscientious Silvia had been more than thorough; she'd washed the fruit with shampoo.

• 5 •

One Hundred Nanoseconds of Solitude

To: **Allen Noren, O'Reilly & Associates**
From: **Jeff Greenwald**
Subject: **Big World/Oaxaca**

The warmth of this provincial capital radiates from the grills of the hotcake vendors, from the sunbaked walls of brilliantly painted buildings peeling and flaking in the Mexican sun, from the bighearted strangers who leap from Chevy pickup trucks to direct us to the *zócalo*. And it is the *zócalo* itself, the central community open-air plaza, that is the metaphorical heart of this magical city. Every Oaxaqueño, it seems, passes through the *zócalo* at least once a day—to read the paper, chat with friends, have a shoe shine—before spiraling back out toward work or home via the maze of immaculately swept avenues. The rejuvenating effect is palpable, even to a foreigner. Flowing in from the arterial streets like depleted corpuscles, Oaxaca's citizens rely on the zócalo for their social and spiritual refueling, their vivifying daily dose of community.

How do Americans survive without *zócalos?* How do we cope with the suffocating stresses of metropolitan life without an oxygenated pool of humanity to dip back into? The truth is, we don't.

Oaxaca is always a warm city, but this week even more than usual. Today, January 6, is the twelfth day of Christmas, also known as Los Reyes. The holiday commemorates the night when the three kings, or reyes, arrived at the infant Jesus' manger bearing exotic gifts. This evening the local children will place their shoes outside their bedroom doors, stuffed with notes—much like letters to Santa—telling the reyes what specific presents to bring (Jesus himself never had it so good). Toy stores stay open all night to satisfy these demands, and the narrow streets are clogged with desperate shoppers.

It's a fantastic time to be in Oaxaca, as colored lights blink in front of the ancient stone cathedral and the smells of baking bread, hot chocolate and honey-roasted nuts commingle with ozone and perfume. The broad plazas surrounding the *zócalo* are filled with an all-day carnival featuring Ninja Turtle balloons, local handicrafts, all manner of deep-fried foods, sweet stands swarming with drunken bees and hand-lettered stalls where squinting mestizos armed with hypodermic needles will engrave your name on a grain of rice—a feat of nano-engineering just as miraculous, at least to this beholder, as IBM spelling its corporate symbol out in magnetized iron atoms. Street musicians and beggars wander between tables at the open-air cafés facing the *zócalo,* palms out but not pushy, relying on the generosity of the season. They are seldom disappointed.

The great irony of this journey, which was not part of the original plan, is the dispatch you see before you now. Thanks to an ultralightweight computer, I now have the privilege (and burden) of remaining forever tethered to my electronic igloo back home. So while this overland voyage continues to remind me how enormous our home planet is, my fraternity of Internetted cybertuna—thanks to the miracles of the fax/modem—will never be more than a telephone jack away.

In theory.

In practice, it's a different story. Right now I'm in the tourism bureau's computer room, a half-block from the *zócalo*. Carnival rides spin outside the window, couples smooch beneath the rust-colored eaves of the cathedral and Sally, my irrepressible partner, is out drinking cold *cervezas* and watching folkloric dances as I hunt and peck my way through the electronic gate of this pesky assignment. I've been coming back to this office for the past two days in a continuing (and so far futile) attempt to connect with CompuServe in Mexico City. Linking with CompuServe in the Bay Area is not a viable option—the Mexican government enjoys a virtual monopoly on telephone service, and a fifteen-minute linkup would run me the price of a Chevy Nova. So I wait and write, wait and write, consumed by the sinking feeling that this unnerving pattern is bound to be repeated in Guatemala, Senegal, Turkey, Nepal. . . .

o   o   o

Two hours later. Suffice it to say that, despite efforts bordering on the heroic (or insane, if you want to be realistic), there will be no link with the electronic web tonight. Which just goes to show: The world isn't quite as small (yet) as I was afraid it might turn out to be after all. Listening to the unrequited gargle of the Mexico City telecom link as it failed to "recognize" my modem, I experienced a sense of informational isolation and electro-existential solitude rare in this hardwired age. Years of development, millions of dollars of elegant equipment, a cast of thousands, and I can't even log in. I guess we still haven't got the bugs ironed out of this global village business.

But if there's one thing I'm learning from this recent series of frustrations, it's that information operates by its own rules.

Take Oaxaca itself. Two thousand five hundred years ago, this region was the site of a thriving Zapotecan capital called Monte Alban, a monumental city set on a man-made mesa overlooking the entire Oaxaca Valley. During its two-millennia-long history (from about 500 B.C. to the fifteenth century A.D.) Monte Alban served, among other things, as the birthplace of both Mexican writing and a highly complex calendric system. The Zapotecs excelled in astronomy, ceramics and metalwork, and developed a sophisticated ritual and political structure. It is fair to say they presumed (not unreasonably, after the first awkward centuries) that their civilization—or at the very least, a cogent record of their history and achievements—would be around forever.

But the future, as usual, had other plans.

Yesterday afternoon Sally and I explored the broad, flat mesa, now a mammoth archaeological site heavy with naked stone stairways, round columns supporting the dusty sky and vast plazas overgrown with dry grass. Much of the architecture is beautifully preserved: an observatory oriented toward the magnetic pole; friezes of captured (and evidently cas-trated) enemy rulers; empty ball-game courts where copper-skinned ath-letes once competed, some say, for their lives.

Despite the evidence of these effortfully displaced stones, the culture that built Monte Alban, and all record of it, have all but vanished. It is an almost total enigma. Elaborate hieroglyphs appear in dark stone alley-ways, but no one can decipher their meaning. Archaeologists can only speculate on what occurred in the sweeping plazas, and why. Even the most commonplace details of life on Monte Alban—how the city was gov-erned, which gods the inhabitants believed in, how they entertained them-selves—are anybody's guess.

Beholding the ruins of this "eternal" Zapotecan civilization, I couldn't help but consider the vagaries of information. What lasts, and why? Our bold and cunning Neosilicate Age is less than fifty years old, but we're already audacious enough to imagine that, if we back up our files often enough, the megabytes we are so tirelessly generating will endure forever—pro-viding future archaeologists (God help them) with a seamless record.

I doubt it. The naked truth is that nothing lasts.

In October 1991, days after the deadly Oakland firestorm, I helped my friends Patrick and Sheila sift through the ashes of their incinerated home. The heat from the blaze forged from their lives a surreal ruin littered with oddly familiar icons—an imploded but otherwise intact lightbulb, flat as an idea balloon; a smooth red torpedo, once a can full of Lincoln pennies; a glossy aluminum pool, formerly a no-frost refrigerator.

Among the stray steel screws and bits of charred ceramic we found a clear, oblong marble, roughly the weight of an eight ball, lying beside a bare twisted U of flat, flesh-colored material. These two mysterious and elemental artifacts—variations on the theme of fused silica—were all that remained of their Macintosh computer.

The record of the Zapotecs, an amazing race who reigned over the Oaxaca Valley for more than fifty generations, was carved in stone. It is gone. What hope, I wonder, for these weightless electronic pulses, bleep-ing through the ether?

o   o   o

In a vestibule of the Oaxaca cathedral stands a statue of San Antonio de Pueda; Oaxaqueños pin medallions, photographs and charmlike metal milagros to his cloak to petition for miracles. Today a three-and-a-half-inch floppy disk hangs amid the offerings—giving new meaning to the concept of saving off-site.

Happy New Year, all. I'll connect again, in a week or two, from another corner of this big, warm, semi-wired world.

❡ ❡ ❡

Shooting Jacks with Jesus

In the late afternoon—from three or four until sunset—Oaxaca stands illuminated in an unearthly light that coaxes every angstrom from the vividly painted walls lining the narrow streets. Layered with paint, peeling like onions, they embody a local talent for leaving beautiful things alone. Walking among them is like staring at a Wayne Thiebaud painting until the forms disappear and you fathom the true genius of the colorist. On Oaxaca's streets the effect is reached without any trace of intention—although it seems impossible that the combinations and selections of hues and surfaces could be accidental. The faded, blistered walls, with their infinite shades of texture and color, are not framed by architectural "devices," exploited by trendy restaurants or coöpted in guidebooks. They're simply *there*, unself-conscious elements of the past wrapped within the present moment.

o o o

Two days before leaving Oaxaca, Sally and I took a room in the private home of a gracious Oaxaqueña named Señora Rosa Limon.

Señora Limon was the perfect *abuela,* a tiny, wiry woman who fed us elaborate breakfasts of jam and ham and listened, without comprehension but with evident delight, to our groggy dawn banter. Her house was simple but comfortable, lined with cabinets full of ceramic tchotchkes, paintings of *The Last Supper* and embroidered tapestries displaying desert pilgrims and their camels. A plastic Passion hung above the bed where Sally and I slept in false matrimony.

For the feast of Los Reyes, Señora Limon invited Fernando, her thirty-eight-year-old architect son. He arrived with his Hawaiian-born wife, Charlene, and their daughter, Luisa, a bold and frighteningly precocious eight-year-old who, missing her two front teeth, had perfected the tight-lipped and ironic smile of a scorned lover. As dictated by tradition we ate Rosca de los Reyes, a sweet, ring-shaped bread with a small plastic effigy of the infant Jesus baked inside. Luisa got the prize—a Cracker Jack version of Casper the Friendly Ghost—and ran off into the kitchen to play, using the baby Jesus as a jack.

During dinner Fernando talked about his work, and it was decided that Sally and I would meet the family the following day to look at his current project.

At four-thirty the next afternoon we joined Charlene and Luisa at La Niagara, the best of the dozen homemade ice cream stalls lining the broad cobblestone plaza by Our Lady of Solitude. I offered to stand Luisa ice cream.

"Not today," she deferred.

"What flavor?" I had literally not registered her words, so incredible was it to me that an eight-year-old would turn down ice cream.

"I said I don't want any," she repeated. "Can you see the shadows? Or the color of the sky? It's not an ice cream day."

It seemed like a perfect ice cream day to me.

"She gets like this," Charlene apologized. "Very willful."

Sally and I ordered nutmeg-flavored *helados* and wandered off for a quick look at the church. A host of life-size wooden angels, white as Nixon, loomed over the congregation. Their tiny wings struck me as absurd.

"They're completely impossible." I made Sally stop and look at what I was talking about. "All they've done is taken doves' wings and stuck them on people. It's too unrealistic; they could never fly."

"Bumblebees can't fly either," Sally informed me. "It's been shown to be aerodynamically impossible. Their wings are too small and their bodies are too round. Luckily, nobody told that to the bumblebees."

o   o   o

Charlene drove us to meet Fernando at the site of his latest commission. We wound along a narrow road and into the hills overlooking Oaxaca, finally arriving at a cul-de-sac where five separate homes faced a central court.

Fernando was waiting. He walked us through three of the units, explaining his philosophy of nesting. Above all, he felt, a home should never be boring. I was impressed by the novel confluence of angles, the curved hallways and his playful, contemporary use of light, space and Spanish tile. Sometimes his ideas worked and sometimes they didn't—the tiles in one kitchen were frankly garish, a bedroom ceiling was too low and one stairway was uncomfortably narrow. Fernando was aware of, though not obsessed with, his mistakes, an attitude I felt I could learn from.

I was also encouraged, in a selfish sort of way, by Fernando's admission that the day had been his worst in months. Everything had gone wrong. His workers had fought, a window had been shattered by the wind, the wrong tiles had arrived. His trials made me suspect that the nightmare I'd recently experienced with my computer was a function of some malign astronomical conjuction rather than a personal inability to master simple machines.

We wove downhill from San Filipe in the porous dusk. He drove like a maniac, headlights out. I'd noted this unsettling practice days before, driving with Dwayne and Sally down Mexico 15.

"I have to know," I asked 'Nando, "why Mexicans drive at night with no headlights."

"It's because we have bigger eyes."

o   o   o

We returned to the *centro* and, miraculously, found a place to park. It was quarter to nine, and the streets around the plaza were a riot of color and music. Thousands of people milled about, many holding balloons. Indians sold wooden combs, their kids sold Chiclets, and a middle-aged man walked around terrifying people with obnoxious paper pellets that exploded on contact with the ground.

We ordered beers and football-sized *tortas* and sat at an outdoor café, hypnotized by the relentless activity. Everyone in sight, from Fernando and Charlene to the bow-tied mariachis strolling between the café tables, felt like family. A wave of nostalgia overwhelmed me, inundating my sinuses.

"It doesn't get any better than this," I whispered to Sally.

She cast me a doubtful look. "Never? Nowhere?"

"It gets just about as good, but it doesn't get any better."

It was strange to feel so powerful a connection with a plaza in Mexico, but it was hardly surprising. I fully expected to find fragments of various homes—past, present and future—in various spots around the globe. Over a period of just a few days Oaxaca had shown me things both profound and compelling, and it did not seem impossible that this intense, intensely human city would be a factor, its weight yet unknown, in the variable equation called The Rest of My Life.

Sally and Luisa wandered off to the market to buy a bouquet for Rosa Limon. When they returned, Luisa put a carnation behind her ear and lay back on her father's lap. I was leaning across the table, drinking hot chocolate and talking to Charlene about our journey.

"You're our first favorite people on this trip," I confessed, and vowed to mention the family in my book.

Luisa sat bolt upright, her carnation flying off. "Leave me out of this," she declared. "I don't want to be a star. I don't want to be famous.

I don't care about any of that. When you're a star you have to be way up there." She pointed at the night sky, washed out by the glow of the carnival lights. "I like it right down here."

She retrieved her flower from the cobblestone sidewalk and settled back into 'Nando's arms with a sleepy smile.

• 6 •

The Ghost of Emiliano Zapata

All was not well in Mexico.

On New Year's Eve—while Dwayne, Sally and I were fleeing our Guaymas disco—the Zapatista Army of National Liberation (EZLN) had descended from the highlands in the southern state of Chiapas and seized the cities of Ococingo and San Cristóbal de las Casas. Founded in 1983, inspired by the Monkey Wrench Gang exploits of the early-twentieth-century freedom fighter Emiliano Zapata, the rebel army's display of "armed propaganda" was an effort to draw attention to the poverty and repression suffered by the largely Maya farming communities of Chiapas. Their plight was genuine; government economic incentives favoring cash crops like cattle and coffee had devastated the small holdings of subsistence farmers. Chiapas was the poorest state in Mexico, in dire need of new schools, roads and hospitals.

"We have nothing to lose," the EZLN declared on New Year's Day. "Absolutely nothing. No decent roof over our heads, no land, no work, poor health, no food, no education, and no right to freely and democratically choose our leaders."

The Mexican government responded to the uprising with gloves off. At least a thousand people had been killed in the region since the first of the year. Roads leading over the mountains into Chiapas had been sealed, and there were rumors of trouble on the Guatemalan border as well.

Sally and I boarded a bus to Tehuantepec. We had planned to travel from there over the mountains, through Tuxtla Gutiérrez and San Cristóbal, entering Guatemala on Mexico 190. With that route now closed we elected to hug the coast on Highway 200, crossing near Talismán instead.

I was keenly disappointed. Part of me, I admit it, bragged about wanting to get shot at, but when I tried to pin down which part it was I found no volunteers.

o   o   o

On the drive to Tehuantepec it was easy to see why Monte Alban had been left alone for two thousand years. The mountains south of Oaxaca are hell to navigate, relentlessly steep, covered with nasty erect cacti that countless snakes and scorpions call home. It's a rough mean holy land, that *istmo,* gnawing the southern bank of the Continental Divide: unforgiving, unpredictable and teeming with vultures. Still, brilliant yellow bushes flower amid the spines, and the dry mountain vista is inspiring in a squinty-eyed, melancholy way. It was a landscape we were happy to drive through.

I fell asleep, dreaming about my computer. Why hadn't I been able to link up with the net? I found the whole fiasco acutely depressing. Part of it was my old ghost self, clinging to America, reluctant to snip my umbilicus with a past that was still, presumably, my future. But a deeper element was my sudden loss of faith in the miracle, in the "sufficiently advanced technology" that futurist Arthur C. Clarke had promised would be "indistinguishable from magic."

"How can I believe in God," Woody Allen once asked, "when just last week I got my tongue caught in the roller of an electric typewriter?" And how could I believe in magic, when $5,000 worth of state-of-the-art hardware wouldn't even let me retrieve E-mail from my mother?

o   o   o

These were the first endless hours: Tehuantepec to Juchitán; Juchitán to Tonalá; Tonalá to Tapachula. Sometimes nothing happens. Sometimes you sit in the bus with your head sagging backward over the greasy headrest, or contorted against the window with your cheek sweating and the low sun tracing the capillaries at the back of your eye. *Home Alone* or a Mexican comedy rolls across the video screen, and once in a while you open an eye to see Cantinflas take a pratfall or Joe Pesci suffer a groin injury. Children invade the bus selling oranges, Chiclets, fluorescent-green soft drinks in plastic bags. Time passes.

o   o   o

The smell of sweet hot popcorn was the first thing we noticed about the border. We never found its source. A bridge over a small, trickling river separated Mexico from Guatemala. Garbage lay everywhere. A dozen men surrounded us in the lavender light, circling like lost spirits, eager to change our Mexican pesos into Guatemalan quetzales.

Sally handled the transaction, enthralled by the charisma of unfamiliar currency. "We're entering the only country in the world," she reported ecstatically, "where the money is named after a bird."

Before we knew it we were on another bus, a huge, poorly restored Greyhound destined to move far more slowly than anything we'd mounted before. It seemed at first a funky and amusing conveyance, with Madonna and Oakley Thermonuclear Protection stickers on the windows, but if we'd known in advance that it was compelled to stop for every man, woman, pig and chicken along the 150 miles of road between El Carmen and Guatemala City, we would've hitchhiked instead.

Our seats were next to the only windows on the bus that didn't open. We remained squashed in this sauna-on-wheels for the next seven hours—joined in turns by middle-aged Maya women wearing Patriot missile T-shirts, flat-nosed girls carrying baskets full of fried plantains, and screaming infants with increasingly soiled diapers. But a cool breeze blew through the open emergency escape hatches, and the winter sun climbed over a landscape that looked like the palette van Gogh had used to paint *Wheat Field with Crows*.

This was Guatemala.

The Paradise of Fire

The loneliest guy in Antigua, Guatemala, is not the the Maytag repairman; it's the guy who sells spare bulbs for turn signals.

We found ourselves in a city of intuitive driving, of unannounced turns and sudden stops, where pedestrians enjoy no right of way. It's a non-wheelchair-accessible town of jarring cobblestone streets and precipitous curbs, of protruding stone windowsills waiting to fracture a hip or abrade a scalp. The sidewalks are narrow; if two healthy people attempt to walk abreast, one is in constant danger of slamming into abutments while the other risks plunging off the curb and into the street far below. Antigua is a place where one navigates by an inner compass, oriented by the ominous volcano Agua that looms over the public parks and trendy neocolonial cafés like God's cigar: ready, at any moment, to kick a little ash.

It's a sweet but overpopular anachronism, Antigua, an ambiguous melting pot of *norte* and *centro* Americans, an empañada and Ray Ban paradise where gringos stroll the streets in rainbow-hued Guatemalan pantaloons and local teens terrorize the *parque central* in Rollerblades.

There's an air of collegiate unreality about the place, as if the entire town were an *escuela d'español,* a model village based on a language-school economy. The local people speak English slowly, patient with the pale and moneyed foreigners. No one gets bent out of shape when you ask for lawyers (*abogados*) on your sandwich or shyly confess that your bad Spanish makes you *embarazada* (pregnant).

We immediately felt we were on some kind of movie set. Every street was perfect, all the cafés perfect, the markets perfect, the children and Indians and even the banks, all perfect, everything in perfect order, the streets swept clean, no one throwing mean looks around. Safer than heaven. Maybe it's the volcano. Who can feel ill will toward his fellow man when the entire play could be canceled with a single divine hiccup? Religion, for all its good intentions, makes beasts out of men, but the prospect of imminent natural disaster is the world's greatest aphrodisiac.

o   o   o

Sally and I sat in the parque central, cursing money. Mexico had turned out to be far more expensive than we'd anticipated, while Guatemala, with its unexpected hordes of tourists, was only slightly less so. Sally was running well over her budget; and though I was able to help her out somewhat, I couldn't see moving from our modest hotel into a youth hostel or dorm.

We skipped dessert that evening and, on Saturday, I dropped by a local info-boutique to pick up an E-mail message. Carnival Cruise Lines had granted us a two-day passage aboard their luxury liner *Ecstasy.*

Though this meant a free return to the U.S. mainland, the news was bittersweet. The *Ecstasy* sailed from Cozumel to Miami on January 19. This gave us ten days to explore Guatemala, journey through Belize and make our way into the Yucatan. We would have preferred to stay in Guatemala longer—exploring the Maya ruins for a week, climbing Mount Agua under the full moon, making a side trip down to Honduras. But this journey was not about staying in places. This journey was about circling the world: tipping our hats here and there and moving onward, around, back to the starting point.

I spent Sunday morning alone in the park, watching the lovers and families and handicraft sellers, eating fried plantains, bending down to smell the roses. Tourists played Travel Scrabble and read Stephen King novels; a teenager circulated around the fountain, handing out flyers. No one seemed worried or out of place. Afterward I strolled through town and returned to our hotel. Sally lay in bed with her journal, a bottle of Liquid Paper by her side. She was the only person I'd ever met who, rather than cross things out, actually obliterated her handwritten mistakes with white ink. When I entered our room she was fanning the air with the open book, helping the paint dry before scribbling in a more appropriate word.

"Hey, Sal gal . . . . You don't have any plans for tomorrow, do you?"

"Not that I know of." She stopped fanning and blew on the page. "Are you saying I do now?"

"You betcha." I tossed a flyer onto the bed. "We're climbing a live volcano."

o　　　　o　　　　o

Halfway up the cone, wheezing with the altitude as we struggled up a seemingly endless incline of loose pumice and volcanic pebbles, it felt like a fool's errand; and as we approached the live caldera, a blackened maw spewing pus-colored smoke and sizzling ejecta, every bone in our bodies screamed at us to turn tail and run.

It was a silly place to be.

There was a terrifying explosion, and the ground shook like the soundtrack from *Jurassic Park.*

"*Why the fuck do people do this?!*" Sally screamed. She had stopped, briefly, to throw up, and stood hunched forward. Her Cro-Magnon appearance inspired a thought.

"*You know,*" I yelled back, "*the human fascination with pyrotechnics may carry over from a deep genetic memory of the days when we lived among giant reptiles, and volcanoes spewed fire into the skies. . . .*"

If there was something counterintuitive about our outing, my motives at least were clear. Any pilgrimage to honor the size of the world must include, I reasoned, a visit to a place where the Earth's crust is born. Well, here we were, about as welcome in this lithic forge as velociraptors in a maternity ward.

We reached a flat crest and walked the final hundred meters to the viewpoint. Along with us was Sebastian, a Dutch dentist on holiday from volunteer work in El Salvador. The people of his village, Sebastian told us, had not recognized the Earth when he'd shown them a photograph of it. On being informed, they had politely asked the doctor if he had taken the picture from the moon.

We sat in the lee of a gigantic boulder and watched our planet being formed. Stones the size of railroad cars boomed into the air, angled toward the north. They cooled as they fell, changing color, like autumn leaves burning black.

"It's beautiful," said Sally. And so it was.

It was a night of sparks: ejecta from the roaring volcano; the flashlights of other hikers moonwalking across the cone; Orion patrolling the sky. Guatemala's lights twinkled in the distance, and fireflies filled the jungle.

As we began our descent I tossed a paper prayer flag—a souvenir of my last trip to Tibet—into the wind. Tibet's unique brand of Buddhism took root when Padma Sambhava, a great Indian mystic, subdued the fierce elemental deities of that high plateau. Perhaps his mantra, carried halfway around the world, could calm Guatemala's fever as well.

Stoned Ponies

Lake Atitlán lies anywhere from two to five hours west of Antigua, depending on your bus. Sally and I had lunch in Panajachel—the fried-food paradise on the eastern edge of the lake—and took the next ferry toward San Pedro, a smaller village on the western shore. Our plan was to rent horses and ride them to Santiago, another lakeside town, reached by a twelve-kilometer path around the huge, coffee-covered volcano that towers above San Pedro and shares its name.

We sailed over the lake beneath the starlike sun. White villages climbed up from the water's edge, sprinkled across the hillsides like crystal salt. Atitlán is a bit like California's Lake Tahoe: a huge, deep caldera filled with freezing water and ringed by a nimbus of expensive homes. I studied Spanish verbs (*traigo, salgo, vengo*) as bolts of sunlight penetrated the clouds and illuminated the slopes of nearby volcanoes. The five cones surrounding Lake Atitlán are dormant, but the feeling around the lake is one of imminent change, an ambience heightened by the impossibly cultivated plots that hang like Christmas ornaments on the nearly vertical real estate.

The town of San Pedro swarms with bright and restless Lost Boys who specialize in attaching themselves to hapless gringos and serving, for an indeterminate tip, as guides. We hadn't been in San Pedro ten minutes when two of these professional truants—nine-year-old touts named Antonio and Juan—adopted us. Their English, while scant, was ambitious and elastic, and no obstacle short of red-hot lava would keep them from facilitating our goals. Sally called them *los lobos*.

They led us by hand down the main street, past talisman shops selling tall candles and haberdasheries displaying folded shirts hung upside down in the windows. We approached a small Evangelist church. Singing emanated from within. The boys opened the door, slipped inside and emerged half a minute later with a stunned caballero in tow.

Dressed in a starched pink shirt and still clasping his leather-bound hymnal, he introduced himself as Pedro.

"Desean ustedes caballos para la mañana?"

I nodded that we did. Pedro returned to the church, replaced the book and brought us down to his stables, where we agreed on a price: 65 quetzales, $11.50, per person, per horse. We would leave at six-thirty the next morning and arrive at Santiago by ten. Pedro would accompany us and take the horses back.

We tipped *los lobos* ten quetzales. Sally bought each boy a long beeswax candle to give to his mother. They pocketed the money and unrolled the candles, chewing the fragrant wax like fruit leather.

o   o   o

Sally and I woke early and watched the sun rise over Atitlán and distant Panajachel before setting off to find Pedro. We rendezvoused at a ramshackle café. Our caballero had brought two small, anxious horses, hardly the Spanish steeds I'd envisioned. The minute we saw them—not to mention Pedro's own lime-green mountain bike—we realized that our circuit around the volcano to Santiago would be less a heady gallop than a petting-zoo pony ride.

Despite the diminutive size and mincing gait of our mounts, it was initially an interesting ride, through rich coffee plantations and dried-up cornfields vivid as Oz scarecrows under the high-altitude sun. The roads were dusty, but the Maya sharecroppers strolling through them— clad in brilliantly embroidered calf-high pants, machetes hanging by their sides—were relaxed and friendly, always ready with a greeting and a good word.

As we progressed up the steep slopes of the volcano, Pedro spoke of the economic situation of the farmers around Atitlán. They live in conditions we often hear about secondhand but rarely witness personally. The price of Guatemalan coffee, Pedro told us as he shadowed our tip-toeing ponies on his bike (a far more sensible vehicle for the rocky trails than our own hesitant mounts), was at an all-time low of 60 quetzales for 100 kilograms. It seemed impossible: $10 U.S. for 220 pounds of picked coffee beans. Sally asked how much his mountain bike had cost, and he did the math in his head.

"Two thousand kilograms," he replied. "Used. A new one will be nearly twice that much."

I wondered if Pedro, who was thirty-six, owned any coffee fields himself.

"No. I own a small cornfield, two horses, a room that I let to three

Italian tourists, a wife, a brother, three children—ages seven, two and three months—one dog and a mountain bike."

We liked Pedro a great deal. He was an honest man, very warm-hearted, and when he realized that our alleged three-and-a-half-hour scramble to Santiago was going to take a minimum of five hours (not to mention the time it would take him to bring the horses back to San Pedro again), he uttered not a word of complaint.

We did; sore of knee, ankle and rump, unable to even canter the horses on the rocky road, we watched ruefully as heavily burdened pedestrians passed us easily. Pedro was also disappointed, for our agonies bode ill for his business future. The horse ride, he explained, was an activity he had hoped to market as an *aventura*. The morning was an experiment, a trial run to see if this kind of expedition was feasible for local tourism. We were proving, evidently, that it wasn't.

But the scenery was spectacular, and we were able to enjoy the fleeting notoriety of appearing, at least to the children of the small pueblos between San Pedro and Santiago, as saddle-sore demigods. Horses are rare around Atitlán; they are raised exclusively in San Pedro and neighboring Santa Cruz. Most of the kids we passed had seldom if ever seen a horse at close range before. Those who didn't flee in terror held their ground with saucer-eyed curiosity before zipping off into their haciendas to fetch their brothers and sisters while shrieking *"Caballo! Caballo!"* like manic Paul Reveres. I enjoyed the enormous prestige of a white mount, and few declarations have ever given me greater pleasure than the cry *"Un hombre encima un caballo blanco!!"* (A man on a white horse!!), shouted in awe by a troupe of thunderstruck teenage girls. How I longed to live that myth; how fortunate that they did not look too closely.

o   o   o

It was well past noon when we slouched into Santiago, ragged equestrian dust bunnies. We had filtered, through our hair and lungs, the dust churned up by every vehicle plying the final five kilometers of road into Santiago. Had I been a bread truck or a Grumman van, I would've bet my last quetzal that someone would have scrawled *Lavame* (Wash me) straight across my face.

By the time we arrived back in Antigua the laundromat was closed. We set off for dinner, shamefaced, in short shorts and sandals, feeling as out of place on those modest and God-fearing streets as nudists in Teheran.

A Day at the Ruins

The overland journey from Guatemala City to the Maya monuments at Tikal was pure hell. We sat for twelve solid hours, cramped into bite-size seats above the naked rear axle of an ancient, lightless, fart-filled second-class bus as it churned up clouds of dust over unpaved lunar roads. The three children seated behind us, squirming like feral mice on the oblivious laps of their snoozing parents, hacked with tubercular frenzy onto the backs of our heads.

"It's good practice," Sally advised me.

I reluctantly took her point. Traveling this way—hopping from one town to the next, sleeping on buses, our pockets stuffed with orange peels, luggage receipts and used tissue—was the ultimate meditation. There was nothing to hold on to. The illusory carpet called stable ground was yanked from beneath us, leaving nothing for the teetering mind to seize upon. Much as Zen students are presented with ambiguous koans, which unbalance linear thinking long enough for a sudden satori to slip in, so did our relentless itinerary confound our sleep-deprived minds in a fashion that might ultimately prove enlightening. More likely, I thought, we would go mad.

Once in the Parque Nacional Tikal, we mustered the energy to eat a decent breakfast. It was pouring rain, and lightning flashed in the green sky. We paid our bill, took a room at the inn, unpacked our umbrellas and wandered off into the saturated subtropical rain forest to see exactly what these Maya chaps had put together.

The weather cleared. We climbed to the summit of Temple II and peered out over the Great Plaza, imagining what it must have felt like to be a human sacrifice. It was amazing to consider that the Maya, sensitive architects of stone and time, spent long, noisy evenings tearing out the beating hearts of enemy warriors. Their abominations, ostensibly staged to keep the sun rising on schedule, occurred at roughly the same time that Buddhist sutras were spreading through China and into Tibet. I found it phenomenal that two strains of humanity, cut of the same genetic cloth, could handle the heart so differently.

Tikal was overwhelming. Its dense canopy of jungle and steep stepped pyramids suggested a lost world, but it failed to awaken my sense of longing or nostalgia. I have no cultural sympathy nor feeling of romanticism toward any race that sacrificed human beings; it is the most sociopathic practice imaginable, unknown among even the most vicious animals. Despite years of conditioning in political correctness I felt genuinely grateful toward the Catholic missionaries who had put a stop to it.

We forged deeper into the jungle, locating the gigantic hulk of Temple IV by late afternoon. The climb to the overlook was harrowing, up makeshift ladders and across slick stone patios, but when we arrived the entire jungle stretched beneath us: a green shag carpet tipped with gold. Parrots squawked and monkeys screamed, rattling leaves in the dense canopy below.

"It's a dick thing," Sally explained, referring to the monkeys, or the temple, or both.

We had dinner that evening with Roxy Ortiz, a moon-faced, half-Maya guide who knew the ruins, and the region, inside out. Human sacrifice came up, followed by a discussion of how the abuse of power led to the fall of Maya civilization.

"It was another classic case of ruling-class excesses bleeding a culture dry," Roxy asserted, drinking beer from a can. "That's what the archaeologists say. The Maya were relatively peaceful during their early period. The human sacrifices—and by the end there were hundreds, maybe thousands of them a month—were a response to population pressure, and a lack of nonrenewable resources. After a while no amount of warfare could sustain Tikal and the other cities, so people started drifting away. And the jungle drifted in . . ."

It was all highly theoretical; we know less about the Maya than we know about ancient Egyptians. After a few beers I found myself rethinking the demise of the once-great civilization, and willing to share my own harebrained theory with all present.

"We may never really know what the Maya were about, or what caused their downfall," I began. "It's fashionable to believe that war and ecocide drove them under. But what if it wasn't that way at all? What if classical Maya history ended, not through violence, but with the sudden emergence of a charismatic leader who preached a new, pacifist philosophy? It happened in India; why not here? Maybe there was someone, a forgotten Maya 'Buddha,' who rendered the whole militaristic structure of the society obsolete. . . ."

Roxy was dubious. "I've heard crazier ideas," she said, shrugging, "but not a lot. If that happened, why didn't they build new temples? Why aren't there images of this guy?"

"Who knows? Maybe they'd already run out of money. Maybe he—or she—forbade them to make images. Buddha did. . . ."

"That's right." Sally had hold of it now. "Try to imagine what archaeologists in the distant future would make of western culture. The only things that would survive a cataclysmic disaster would be our heavy weapons and huge buildings. The archaeologists would guess we were a culture that prized art, but they'd probably think that we were basically warlike savages who built weapons of mass destruction, systematically destroyed the environment and worshiped a great god called Coca-Cola.

"Coca-Cola." She rolled it around in her mouth. "It's oddly Maya-sounding, actually."

The Burning Bush

Cristo Negro is the patron saint of Flores, an island-village rising from the waters of Lago Petén Itzá. Recent floods had swollen the lagoon, devastating nearby island communities; Flores itself was ringed by a barnacled nimbus of submerged buildings through which fish and sunlight freely streamed.

The Festival of the Black Christ, held in the cathedral courtyard of Flores, was a carnival the likes of which one might have seen in New Jersey in the 1930s: hand-spun cotton candy, popgun shooting galleries and kids angling for flat wooden fish with prize numbers etched onto their bellies. The women were dressed in high heels and garish Sunday outfits that would have looked trashy and suggestive in any American city but which made the local girls, pacing self-consciously amid the booths, appear sweet and innocent—like tropical birds arrayed for a courtship ritual, feathered in iridescent and exciting costumes of which they are vaguely but deliciously aware.

We reached the island by crossing a narrow causeway from San Benito—a drab interchange from which our minibus to Belize City would depart the next morning—and arrived in time for the evening procession. Twelve able-bodied men strained beneath a heavy wooden palanquin, bearing the Black Christ through the township's narrow streets. They were preceded by bandoliers of deafening firecrackers and followed by a brass band composed of clarinets, tubas, saxophones and drums. The melody they played was both bone-jarring and eerily mournful, a funeral dirge with a hint of Sousa. The musicians read from photocopied scores, attached with clothespins to the backs of the men walking before them.

After the parade Sally and I returned to the fiesta, where food was cheap and plentiful. We'd bought two tall candles but arrived at the cathedral to find the doors being locked and bolted.

"*Revuelvan a las ocho*," we were advised. The church would reopen at eight.

It was six-thirty. We spent the next ninety minutes people watching, chowing down on barbecued chicken and trying, without success, to win big stuffed snakes.

o   o   o

The cathedral was still locked at eight, though a crowd was forming in the plaza below the entrance. Worshipers were gathering at the foot of the broad stone steps, admiring an artificial tree. The "tree" was more than twenty feet high and constructed of four long wooden poles. Halfway up, the poles bent outward, forming four equally long "branches." Thick red bunting ribboned the trunk, and strangely shaped ornaments hung from the four limbs above. It took me a couple of minutes to realize that the "fruits" were actually fireworks—rockets and pinwheels and Roman candles—and that the tree's red bunting was a fuse made of thousands of firecrackers.

By now hundreds of people had swarmed into the plaza, creating a huge doughnut with the tree in its center. Sally and I joined the crowd on the steps—twenty feet from ground zero—but were warned back by a stout Guatemalan policeman with a graying mustache. I believe that he saved our lives. . . .

The fuse was lit. The bandolier exploded into life, and I clamped my hands over my ears. After five full minutes of relentless explosions, the ribbon of firecrackers exhausted itself. There was a split second of dead silence, followed by a bright, whistling fizzle as another fuse ignited. A cord of sparks raced around the tree—and all hell broke loose.

A hundred rockets ignited at once, hurling fireballs in every direction. The crowd roared and surged backward in animal panic, fleeing toward the naked stone walls of the cathedral. I hit the ground, covering my head as flaming meteors and photon torpedoes bombarded the stucco walls above me. A mongrel dog buried itself beneath my armpit. The air was thick with smoke, children were shrieking, and I felt the glorious rush of knowing that where we were, that precise spot at that exact moment, was unlike any other spot or moment on the planet Earth.

I rose to my feet with effort. My sandals had slipped off during the melee, but a kind soul had set them against a nearby wall. I also found Sally, smoking a cigarette in the postcoital lassitude of the bombed-out plaza. Women were weeping, children collected plastic shrapnel, and wisps of gunpowder-flavored smoke hung like pungent phantoms in the still night air. There was a sharp smell of scorched hair.

"How you doing?" She didn't answer. "Sal, are you all right?"

"It's funny," she said, looking elsewhere. "In the midst of all that noise, all I could really think about was India. I hadn't realized how much I miss Papaji. The silence around him."

I wasn't sure what this required. "We'll be there by spring."

"I know." She dropped her cigarette and ground it underfoot. "It seems like a long time, that's all."

The cathedral was open. We went inside and lit candles, our

thoughts on the journey ahead of us. Sally prayed for patience, and manna from Heaven; I wished for our safety, and the strength to find my Promised Land.

• 7 •

To: **Allen Noren, O'Reilly & Associates**
From: **Jeff Greenwald, The Gulf of Mexico**
Subject: **Big World/The Caribbean**

The *Ecstasy* is the sort of place that makes us feel like aliens from Aldebaran, sent to the Sol system to study the bizarre behavior of Earthlings. It's an unsettling feeling, composed of two parts: a professional desire to understand the outlandish creatures surrounding us, and a deep and abiding relief that we are not of the same species.

Greetings, then, from one of the more unlikely oases on this Big World. I call it . . .

The Neon Bardo

But we are, of course . . . Earthlings, that is . . . Sally and I boarded the tender in Cozumel along with everyone else, piling onto the huge flat ferry that would carry us to the anchored *Ecstasy,* Carnival Cruise Lines' nine-hundred-foot, seventy-thousand-ton Coney Island hot dog, plying the Caribbean from Miami to Mexico and back again. Nonetheless, despite our undeniable genetic link with the assembled company, something about the scene immediately brought out the alien anthropologist within. The first question Sally and I asked each other on finding ourselves surrounded by these docile, overweight creatures, was: *What do all of these humans have in common?*

The answer, of course, was an irrepressible addiction to Hard Rock Café T-shirts. They are the costume of choice when Middle America lets its hair down, a variety of fashion hamburger whose sales, like McDonald's, must number by now in the hundred-millions.

Sally and I have been on this mammoth ship for exactly thirty-six hours, boarding in Cozumel after a lightning journey through Belize. We spent three days in that washed-out Caribbean paradise, two nonhoneymooners tucked into a beach bungalow on Corker Caye beneath the staccato rhythm of raindrops on palm fronds and the somewhat less soporific sound of Ignacio's TV. Ignacio, proprietor of our beach bungalow compound, was a man of few words and an infamous temper. His eyes bulged belligerently behind thick glasses as he hammered a freshly painted sign to the end of his collapsing pier:

FOR IGNACIO GUESTS ONLY!
IF ANYONE ELSE SWIMS HERE I, IGNACIO,
WILL CHASE OR DRIVE YOU AWAY.

Our first morning on the caye, after a terrifyingly stormy night, we were awakened by the thunder of Ignacio's fist upon our door.

"Hello?! Hello!!" Silence. *"Yes, yes! Wake up! Are you from the States?"* We made noises indicating weary reluctance. *"Wake up! There's been a tremendous earthquake in California!"*

We spent the next hour sitting in the cluttered living room of Ignacio's stilted beach house, watching CNN satellite footage of burning buildings, collapsed bridges, water geysers and neighborhoods aflame. No matter how big the world may be physically—and it already seems unmanageably huge from my point of view—information is forever at our fingertips. We're wired to disaster, worldwide.

The following afternoon the sky cleared, and we were able to hire a boat and go snorkeling on the local reef. I was drifting languidly above a mountain of coral when the tide suddenly ebbed, leaving me suspended in midair above a hump of razor-sharp exoskeletons. Had there been a camera I'd have shot the audience a wry glance; instead I instinctively arched my back and stiffened. The wash dragged me across the reef belly first, leaving long, bloody welts across my middle. I swam back to our dive boat without flailing, an eye on the reef shark wrinkling her nose a few meters below. . . .

o   o   o

. . . which explains my current posture. At present I'm sitting ramrod-straight behind a faux-antique desk in the *Ecstasy's* so-called Explorers' Club. I cannot bend. Directly in front of me is a window, through which the sky and ocean are changing from Bronx Cement to British Charcoal (colors from Crayola's new Millennia Edition). The rainy season is still months away, but nobody told the sky; a gigantic storm front clings to the Eastern Seaboard, a gray skid mark stretching from Manhattan to Puerto Cortés, Honduras. My heart goes out to our 2,094 fellow passengers, who booked this five-day cruise hoping to enjoy the sun and water sports theoretically endemic to the Caribbean. Except for one day—in Cozumel—the *Ecstasy* hasn't even been allowed to anchor. Key West was a total wash-out, forcing this handsome ark of pleasure seekers to find their fun in shipboard activities.

Fortunately this is not a problem. The *Ecstasy* is nothing less than a floating Las Vegas, loose on the seven seas. Walking onto this ship, after weeks of busing and riding horses through the small towns of Latin America, was like having a jet engine ignite under my ass. Only the most shamelessly mixed metaphors can do it justice: It's like being stuck in the guts of a kaleidoscope, trapped in a blinding blast furnace of colors and sounds, lost amid acres of mirrored glass. Plush theaters, a gigantic casino, two brass and marble dining halls and five floors of bars, grills and discotheques fill the decks. Neon-girdled elevators ascend through a vast open atrium like *Body Snatcher* pods.

Nor has the question of food been overlooked. There are at least six feeding frenzies a day—beginning with Early Risers' Breakfast and ending, believe it or not, with a 1:30 a.m. Pizza Buffet (fifteen varieties). The ship set sail bearing 10,000 pounds of beef, 1,000 gallons of ice cream and 6,000 pounds of fresh seafood. There is enough cheese to entomb the entire staff of the American Heart Association beneath thirty-seven feet of cholesterol.

Dinner—tightly scheduled between dance programs, comedy acts, talent shows, trapshooting and the celebrated Knobby Knees contest—is a Bacchanalian ritual. Any number of appetizers, main courses and desserts are offered. You can have one or two; you can order all six. We wallow in culinary decadence unimagined, I'm certain, by 99.999 percent of the planet's population. It's not unusual to see each of one's co-diners—we're seated at a table for ten—call for Norwegian smoked salmon, escargots in garlic butter, strawberry soup and lemon-marinated asparagus and then, having devoured these starters, order four separate entrées. (Last night it was grilled tiger prawns, orange-marinated duck, pesto-shiitake lasagna and veal stroganoff.) Then comes dessert, and devil take the hindmost. No one spoils the fun, citing starvation in Bosnia; there is no finger wagging to forbid departure for the shopping arcade or blackjack table "until you finish everything on your plate." The *Ecstasy* is an oasis from responsibility, duty-free decadence afloat, and nearly all our fellow passengers seem lost in a hyperconsumeristic wet dream.

Our own dining companions include Cindy and Mike, from North Carolina. Cindy and Mike are both twenty; they went to high school together. He was the quarterback, she the homecoming queen. Both resemble products from the Barbie/Ken catalog. Over the past five days—since boarding the ship in Miami—they have spent exactly $387 on alcoholic beverages.

I might also mention Seth and Jill, another couple in whom Sally and I have taken an anthropological interest. Seth—who looks a bit like the Professor on *Gilligan's Island*—is a former Marine. Two weeks after he left the armed forces he enrolled himself at the Art Institute of Chicago, where he studies painting and contemporary sculpture. Reserved but articulate, he leans slightly over the round table to evaluate Christo's plan to wrap the Reichstag, or offer sly commentary on the latest Jeff Koons scandal. His companion, a chunky blonde in heavy makeup, listens impatiently, punching him in the arm and stealing french fries off his plate. *The Moon and Sixpence* comes up; Jill rolls her eyes.

"The last book I read," she boasts, "was *Oprah*. And I finished it."

Seth pets her, enraptured. "That's not the only book you read, sweetheart."

"Oh, that's right. I also read *Six Habits of Highly Effective People.* It was good."

"*Seven* habits, honey."

"Shut up!" Punch.

Go figure.

o   o   o

In some respects, the *Ecstasy* much resembles a high-budget Broadway set. The architectural leitmotif of the ship is "A City at Sea," and this theme may be followed through the dozens of micro-environments on board. Each, with varying degrees of success, attempts to portray the archetype of a particular metropolitan mood or era. There is the Chinatown Lounge, with its crimson chairs, yin-yang dance floor, huge Chinese lanterns and bok choy delivery truck recessed into the wall. There is the Stripes discotheque, a dizzying John Deere yellow-and-black-striped cave that looks, notes Sally, "like a traffic school nightmare"; there is the Blue Sapphire Lounge, the ship's main auditorium, with its pink marble tables, glittering curtains and plush couches; and there is the inevitable Neon Bar, an epileptic lightfest featuring pulsing electric signs, fluorescent swizzle sticks and a raised, revolving baby grand piano upon whose keys the fabulous Tony hammers contemporary hits like "Piano Man" and "Bad, Bad Leroy Brown."

Finally there is the Explorers' Club, the richly paneled room in which I now sit: president, treasurer and secretary. The Explorers' Club is as kitschy as any other place on the ship, but it's kitsch I can live with—leather armchairs, porthole paintings of schooners at sea and a well-appointed library. It is a measure of Carnival's confidence in its new ship, launched two years ago, that the volume most conspicuously displayed in the central glass showcase of the Explorers' Club is not a first edition of *Captains Courageous;* it's *The Titanic: An Illustrated History.* This bit of bravado is belied, however, by the cabinet on the starboard wall, filled to capacity with New American Bibles.

A twenty-minute tape loop of classical Muzak—bits of Tchaikovsky, Rimsky-Korsakov, Borodin and Debussy—filters through the speakers, whiting out the chaos emanating from the nearby dining hall. But the pièce de résistance of the Explorers' Club is a gigantic world globe. Six feet in diameter, it portrays the continents in stunning relief . . . and gives Sally and me a gulping sense of how pitifully short a distance we have come, and how incredibly far we have yet to go. It is my first true indication, at an approximately 1:1,000,000 scale, of the size of the world—and it scares the shit out of me.

o   o   o

At precisely 15:30 this afternoon, Sally and I were taken for a bridge-to-bilge tour of ship's operations by Ron Ness, the *Ecstasy's* capable and engaging Hotel Manager. It's his responsibility to supervise the entire staff: 904 employees. That kind of position requires a very specific personality, and I knew right away that Ness was the kind of guy who could get along with anybody—even me.

Over the next three hours we explored the secret life of this ship. During that time my sense of where I was—of what kind of place this really is—forever changed. Standing on the bridge with Ness, Sally and Vittorio Sartori, the sixty-five-year-old Italian salt who serves as master of this vessel, I was astonished by how much effort and technology it takes to drive this vehicle, bolt upright, through the sea. Shopping for suntan lotion in the Grand Atrium, dizzied by the roulette wheels and arteries of fuchsia neon, your garden-variety passenger is blissfully unaware, but it's true: the *Ecstasy,* despite being groomed like a poodle and painted like a whore, is a goddess of a ship. An exquisitely maneuverable monster, she slices past Cuba under 64,000 horsepower. There are three thrusters below the helm and three aft, allowing Captain Sartori to turn on a dime. Two enormous propellers, cast in Holland, drive the vessel through the night at a whisper-quiet 21 knots.

Captain Sartori was a lean and erect man with a white-pepper beard. He stank so richly of garlic that, halfway into our conversation, he felt compelled to tell us why.

"When I am sixteen," he began in halting English, "I lie about my age so I can fight against Germans. In 1944 I get captured; I am young man so the Germans use me as courier, carrying machinery parts for cars and tanks along the side of a deep trench. One day while I am doing this, I drops one of the gears I am carrying. It fall into the trench! I chase after it, and when I comes up I am surprised: No one even noticed. This gives me an idea and, a few weeks later, I drops another gear—this one, on purpose! So then I runs through the trench, and when I crawl out I runs to a village. There is a farmhouse in the village, and I go inside. The place is loaded with garlic; there are many tons of it in open wooden crates.

"A few hours later the Germans notice that I am missing. They sends a patrol after me. As I hear them coming, I dive into one of the crates and hides myself away. The troops come in and, after questioning the farmer, they sticks their bayonets into the crates. I am buried deep inside, and the bayonets do not touch me—but much garlic is chopped this way.

"When the patrol leaves, I come out. From head to foot I smells like the garlic. At that minute, and forever, this is always the sweet smell of freedom for me.

"I loves the garlic," he said with real reverence. "Even I would eat it a hundred times a day, I would never get tired of it."

o   o   o

Ness continued our tour. We stood beneath the towering tanks of the *Ecstasy*'s seething reverse osmosis plant, capable of transforming a thousand tons of ocean brine into pure drinking water each day. We toured the maze of her computerized engine room, where 6 megawatts of raw electric spunk—produced by roaring generators the size of Amish barns—power everything from the main propellers to the Neon Bar's slot machines. And we visited her kitchens: polished chrome factories where tons of butter, sugar, flour and milk are kneaded, baked, toasted and sliced by a vast corps of Indian and Mexican waiters who race through electric revolving doors with towers of trays balanced on their shoulders. It was an eye-opening exhibition, and it made all the other activity aboard the ship—the drinking, gambling and gut stuffing—seem unreal by comparison.

Unreal, also, the quick, invisible flow of information originating in this tiny OmniBook and evaporating into the ether like the memory of Samsara perfume. For weeks now I've been in love with tinyness, the sexy superportability of high technology. It was sobering, even inspiring, to stand upright in the bowels of this vast steel beast, watching her pistons pound. Living and working in the global village, enmeshed in its spidery web, we tend to forget the beauty of size.

Back in the Explorers' Club, mincing away on the keyboard, I peer out the window, watching the dark ocean rush by. And I recognize myself—

my tiny, information-packed body—as a pulse among pulses, surrounded
by the awesome gigantic hardware of Earth.

o   o   o

Tomorrow morning we'll alight in Miami, a city I fear far more than Oakland. Then up to New York and—if all goes well—onward to Senegal. No
airplanes; no airports. Having described a gigantic U from California down
to Guatemala and back up again, we will at last set our bearings east.

• 8 •

The Silver Star

I pressed the recline button and dozed off, feet up, to the microchippy
sound of a kid playing with an electronic book. Sally of the swollen
glands and aching wisdom teeth snoozed as well, making up for lost
time. It had been nothing but lost time since the *Ecstasy* had maneu-
vered into a Miami berth, her aft thrusters rattling us awake with the
sound of a thousand mountain goats prancing down a hill of recycled
Pepsi cans. . . .

o   o   o

Miami tripped by like a punctuation mark. After a brief debate about
whether to hitch up the coast—reports of foul weather notwithstanding—Sally and I bought tickets for the Amtrak *Silver Star* and descended
into Industrial Miami in search of lunch. We stopped in the first place
we saw: a Cuban greasy spoon featuring *cubanos, empañadas* and *menudo*.
I ordered a chicken cutlet sandwich. It came big and greasy, smothered
in onions and limp potato sticks, the puck of chicken sliding off its saturated bun. A large man at a small table stuck a couple of quarters in
the jukebox and played his favorite Beny More hit: "Y Hoy Como Ayer."

"Today's just the same as yesterday. . . ."

And so it was. It was outlandish to be back in the States, surrounded
by the familiar lunacy we had ostensibly left behind four weeks earlier.
There was something decidedly tail-between-the-legs about it. What

would Geoffrey Hill make of this, I wondered. It was as if Odysseus, having departed Ithaca for the Trojan Wars, showed up back on his wife's doorstep a month later claiming to have forgotten his umbrella.

But the return to my native soil also presented an unusual opportunity. The goal of all travel, the cliché goes, is to return to the place one has started from, seeing it through fresh eyes. Here was a chance for the East Coast, where I had spent the first half of my life, to be included within my kora. How I chose to experience it—as another point on my pilgrimage or as an awkward retreat—was entirely up to me.

o   o   o

Another day of eating miles, seeing the world through a window. Sally offered me a Chips Ahoy!, along with her latest take on the pilgrimage.

"I've decided that you and I are actually standing still," she said. "The world is just spinning by underneath us."

As I lay back in my seat and listened to the bleeps and whistles, the dolphinlike squeals of what passed for reading in the 1990s, my mind wandered back to the woman beside me. I thought about how much I once loved her; about how we'd met, and how we'd fallen in love. I thought about that afternoon at Point Reyes, when I told her how much I'd love to kiss her breasts, and she'd sat up silently and pulled her T-shirt over her shoulders and lay back on the sand. We'd spent that summer like a single organism, laughing at nothing, reading poetry to each other, cavorting like puppies on the beach. I thought all the way up until August, until the night before Coriola came back from India and I stayed up all night drinking ice-cold vodka and wondering what I'd tell her, wondering what I wanted, wondering whom I loved.

When it was all said and done, when all the guilty dues had been paid and all the feelings that could be squashed and dismantled were laid in their respective junk piles, the answer seemed to be, no one. Least of all myself.

That was ages ago. Sally and I hadn't made love, or even kissed, for more than seventeen months. We traveled together like business acquaintances, rarely touching, an awkward and unspoken vacuum muting the sounds between us. Three days, five days, it might have been a year ago, I sat on the bus from Tikal to Playa del Carmen and shivered, my coral-inflicted belly wounds aching, rain assaulting the window as over-amped air-conditioning blasted frigid air through the already chilly bus. Hugging myself for warmth, and wishing, wishing, wishing, that I had had the sense to travel with someone who would wrap her arms around me when I was cold.

o   o   o

In the lounge car I confronted a dismal collection of featureless tables and tin ashtrays. The car was half nonsmoking, a cynical regulation which assured that the entire car forged along in a cloud of Chesterfield smoke. My eyes watered; my throat burned. But there was a table and the sense of a workplace. I opened my computer.

Fifteen minutes later the seat across the table creaked, and I looked up from my writing to see a ruddy-faced, curly-haired man bearing a striking resemblance to Tom Selleck.

"Whatcha doin' there?" When I told him, he bought me a beer and ordered a rum and Coke for himself.

His name was Ted. He was thirty-nine, and he knew a lot about arches.

"You seen the Gateway Arch? In St. Louis?"

I told him I'd seen pictures of it.

"Okay. When they built the two sides of that thing and brought them together, they were *one-sixteenth of an inch apart*. Hell, they couldn't do that today." He polished off his drink. "Today a half-inch, an inch, no one gives a shit anymore."

Ted worked in high-rise construction, hundreds of feet in the air, grabbing the ends of I beams as they spun toward him on the ends of steel cables and securing the massive limbs with rivets and compressed air.

"It's like walking on the ground." He said it without vanity. "If it's not, you've got no business being up there."

I bought the next round. When I returned to the table he'd taken off his jean jacket, revealing the gold chain around his meaty neck. He picked up his thread without preamble.

"I'll tell you something. My father was an ironworker too. One time, on a site in Trenton, he fell off a beam. Dropped twenty-seven stories, and landed upright in a mountain of sand. Both legs snapped like toothpicks, but he lived to tell the tale."

"What kind of shape are his legs in?"

"Oh, he limps, he limps. He's about two inches shorter than he was. But he knew what he had to do as he was falling, and he did it. Pushed away from the building, and turned himself to land on his feet so he could roll with the fall. But instead of hitting the ground he hit sand. There was nothing to roll with; he just sank."

"They must take pretty good care of him after something like that."

"Hell, no. He's in Vegas, working on a new high-rise."

Ted told me that he could make $14 an hour in Florida, $25 in Chicago. It sounded low to me, considering the risk.

"You ever think of doing anything else?"

"I've tried," he said, looking weary. "But this is what I do."

Ted gave me his rap. He was heading up to Orlando to see his girl-friend. She was a cop. He'd been divorced for three years, had joint custody of a six-year-old daughter. During Reagan's first term he'd done two years for cocaine; sale or possession, he didn't say. The more we talked, and the more rum he put down, the more I suspected he was subtly reinventing his personality to suit our encounter.

When drink made him insufferable I moved to the smoking side of the car. Sally was immersed in conversation with Cyan, a tall Scottish redhead who occupied the seat in front of ours. Her silky Highlands beauty purred against my lap, and watching her green eyes, I found myself drowning, losing my grip on the familiar universe like a ship-wrecked sailor surrendering to the sea.

She was in the middle of a story about how her petition to end an abusive marriage had been denied by the Presbyterian Church.

"I spent years working with preschoolers, teaching them Bible stories and mythology, pouring everything I had into the church while my marriage—and my life—fell apart. Then, one night, I dreamed that a figure approached me. She had a radiant aura, but fierce, fiery eyes. I was absolutely terrified. I was sure she was a kind of dark angel, and called out to God to protect me. But no one answered—and as the being came closer I saw that she looked exactly like me. She wrestled me to the ground, and held me there."

When she woke up the next morning, Cyan understood the meaning of the dream. She decided to end her marriage immediately, with or without the church's blessing. She did so without, and the Presbyterians excommunicated her. Since the church refused to recognize the divorce, her new fiancé—another Presbyterian, whom she'd met at one of the church functions—was excommunicated as well, for adultery.

"Now I'm a born-again pagan," she remarked. To prove this, she opened her suitcase. It was packed with texts on herbalism, Celtic mysticism, Chinese reflexology, astrology, goddess worship and Tantra. "I'll read them, too." She slapped the bag shut. "After years of begging the church to liberate me, I finally wised up. The only one pinning me down was myself."

My Time in Eden

I was bounced from an illicit double-seat arrangement in the middle of the night by an enormous woman of color and found myself creeping—sleeping bag and shoes in hand—back to my assigned spot. But I found

it impossible to get comfortable and spent the night tossing and turning, aching and itching, wondering what the hell I was thinking when I
volunteered to take buses and trains around the world.

We rolled through iced bare forests, over edge-frozen streams, past
old hick North Carolina towns full of brick buildings with fading tobacco signs painted on their otherwise featureless flanks. I thought
about the forests I grew up with on Plainview, Long Island—and about
the gigantic elm, a block and a half away, that we called the Grandmother Tree.

As the years passed, and more and more of the local woods were
mowed down for developments, the Grandmother Tree somehow sur-
vived. With its dense, opaque canopy and whiskey-barrel trunk, it became the refuge for all the neighborhood birds and squirrels,
butterflies and bugs. It was my refuge, too. When I entered fifth grade,
after enduring hours of academic frustration and social ridicule at the
hands of my classmates, I'd steal off to the little woods on Elm Street—
they actually named streets after trees that were on them back then—
and sit underneath the huge boughs, reading science fiction books. My
brother, Jordan, a precocious seven, would grab his bug-collecting jar
and join me. In mid-spring the clamor from the tree was so loud that
even reading was impossible. All I could do was sit and stare upward,
listening for the moments of silence that, when I found them between
the ebbs and swells of noise, contained a message for my ears alone.

By my first year of junior high nearly all the woods in Plainview were
gone. The lot containing the Grandmother Tree stood alone, bordered
on the right by an old house that used to be a stable, and on the left by
a new two-story job owned by a Mr. Montelbaum.

My mother told me about Montelbaum. He'd been in a concentration camp when he was a teenager and had fled to America in his twenties. Now he was a real estate developer. Montelbaum owned all the
property along Elm Street. He'd bought up the forest and, over the previous five years, put in all the new homes. It seemed incredible to me
that he hadn't left any forest at all. Escaping to the woods—reading *A
Fall of Moondust*, building tree forts and playing elaborate war games
with my brother—was my only real encounter with the Great Outdoors.
It was inconceivable that one man with some money could so decimate
the geography that had filled the map of my youth.

In the early spring of 1967, when the last signs of snow had melted
from the bushes, Jordan and I slapped together a couple of sandwiches
and headed for the Grandmother Tree.

The lot was completely cleared. A yellow bulldozer was parked on
the site, its tracks deep and dry in the soil. The devastation must have

occurred weeks earlier, for the branches and sticks of the giant elm had vanished without a trace. Even the stump, which must have been enormous, was gone. Not even a crater remained.

It felt like walking through the ruins of Hiroshima. There were no other trees for blocks around. We had no idea where the birds and animals who had fled to the Grandmother Tree had gone, but it was easy to imagine what the scene must have been like as their nests were destroyed. A few of them might have gotten away all right; others were undoubtedly killed, crushed beneath the treads of the earthmoving machinery.

I returned home in a daze, reeling with the most intense anger I had ever experienced. It occurred to me that not only did those animals have as much a right to live where they wished as Montelbaum did, but that Montelbaum's single human life was not necessarily worth any more, on balance, than the lives of the thousands of creatures he had destroyed.

And so I wrote the developer a note.

"It would have been a better thing for you to have died in the concentration camp," I wrote, "than to have lived to kill thousands of our neighborhood animals by destroying their last natural home."

I signed it and dropped it in his mailbox.

To this day I cannot imagine how my parents must have reacted when Montelbaum's wife brought the note around. Her husband, she said, could not come personally; he could not even leave the house, for fear of what he might do.

Nor can I remember how my parents dealt with me, except for the demand that I write an apology and deliver it to the man immediately. I refused. A radical streak in me felt absolute confidence in my actions and recognized what I had done—or, at the very least, the overwhelming rage I felt—as a presentiment of my future relationship with the world.

By the following summer, a three-story home with a built-in swimming pool sat on the lot where the Grandmother Tree had lived. Montelbaum and his family sold their smaller house next door and moved into it. The man never spoke to me, or even glanced at me after that. He would cross the street if I was walking toward him—for fear, ostensibly, of what he might do.

My brother, always well disguised, made a special point of trick-or-treating at Montelbaum's house on Halloween, returning home afterward to display the ostentatious sweets that our local speculator distributed, as compensation for our forest, to the neighborhood kids.

o   o   o

We crossed Virginia. Snow was everywhere now, a fine flour between the trees, talcum on the edges of the tracks. Small lakes and narrow rivers lay frozen. The bare branches held a beauty so primal and nostalgic that I was frightened to give it full sway. It had been twenty years since I'd lived in this cold, chaste environment; two decades since I had thrown my own books into a backpack and set out, with a dime bag of grass and my stuffed snake, for California. I missed the person I had been at nineteen: the excitability, the reckless creativity, the courage to wrestle with angels.

The flight from my adolescent winter, that rush into bloom, had happened half a lifetime ago. Crawling up the Eastern Seaboard on Amtrak's *Silver Star,* dreaming of fur-mitt massages and amazed oral sex with my first girlfriend on Long Island ("I know how to fix your wagon," she'd giggled, sliding her slim naked body down under the sheets), I found myself longing for sweetness and unpredictability, for the sense of possibility that had once expanded away from me in all directions like the skin of a dirigible.

• 9 •

The Bardo of Fried Egg Sandwiches

If a cow took Pepto-Bismol, would it coat all her stomachs?

The graffito, writ upon a gray gate above a graying drift of snow, stopped me in my tracks. It was scrawled obliquely, almost desperately, as if a dying man who just happened to have a purple Magic Marker in his hand had struggled to the nearest available surface and inscribed, with his last burst of strength, this riddle for the citizens of Chelsea.

There were so many things to think about in New York City.

Fortunately, finding a place to stay hadn't been one of them. My Oakland subtenant, a video artist named Matthew who was moving to the Bay Area from Manhattan, had given us the number of his friend Stewy Shamus, a radio producer who had established himself in the New York art scene with a series of collaged dance mixes based on the predawn ululations of TriBeCa garbagemen. The cuts had proved so popular on the New York rave circuit that Shamus was now cutting an album in LA. Any friend of Matt's was a friend of Stewy's, sight unseen, and Sally and I picked up the keys to Shamus's Chelsea loft at the Korean ginseng outlet half a block away.

It was the coldest winter in New York in recorded history. Much of the Hudson River had frozen solid, and a startled white-tailed deer, marooned on the ice of that famous waterway, stared at me from the front page of the *New York Post*. Its expression seemed to capture the sense of betrayal felt by all New Yorkers. The fact that global warming could produce Spandex-melting summers was well understood; but no one had expected the flip side of the coin to be this new Ice Age, through which snowplows and salt spreaders lumbered like woolly mammoths amid the dying cicada song of a million frigid engines.

o　　　o　　　o

Contrary to popular wisdom, New York is the friendliest city on Earth. The ultracold weather intensified this spirit, providing Gotham's buffeted denizens with an excuse for the spontaneous bonhomie that one finds in West Coast cities after a major quake.

The short-order cook at Hamid's New York Buffet Deli knew all about boats. It didn't take nuthin' to get him started.

"Yiz all know the difference between a boat and a ship, don'tcha?"

I drew in a breath to respond but realized I couldn't. "No. What's the difference?"

"Okay. The difference is this: *A boat can fit on a ship.* You got that? A ship can carry boats, but a boat can't carry ships. Think about it."

I did. "So is a yacht a boat or a ship?"

"What are you, a wise guy? If it's got lifeboats on it, it's a ship. If it's loaded onto a ship, it's a boat. Simple."

He looked like my platonic ideal of a messman: surprisingly tall, because he was fat, and surprisingly fat, because he was tall. "I was fifteen years in the Merchant Marine." He flipped my egg into the air. It turned over a few times and slapped back onto the grill like a cheek of abalone. "You been on a ship before?"

"Never," I said. "Sailboats, ferries, a Caribbean cruise ship, but never a *ship* ship."

"Problem is, this weather. North Atlantic's a bitch in the winter, and this is the worst winter in what, fifty years? You might be in for some real rock 'n' roll. Twenty-, thirty-, forty-foot waves."

"We're sailing to Africa, not Rotterdam. It'll be more like the Central Atlantic."

"Give me one egg, give me two/In a skillet, in a shoe . . ." He lathered a kaiser roll as he sang. "Africa. Never been there. Mustard?"

"Just mayo. Me neither. You think the seas'll be rough that far south?"

He shrugged. "Never can tell. Cheese?" I nodded. "Not too bad, probably. But I tell ya what; if yiz start feeling seasick, first thing is, you whack a lemon under your nose. A lemon, orange, anything citrus. Don't ask me why, but it works."

"No kidding? Thanks a lot. Hey, sorry—that's to go."

o   o   o

Chelsea was a greased chute, weeks of snow packed and frozen into a porpoise-gray permafrost that presented nearly frictionless footing. I skied cautiously between WALK and DON'T WALK, a last-minute shopping list tucked into the flap of my hat:

> underpants
> earplugs
> AA batteries
> Altoids
> chocolate
> diskettes!!
> Chivas for Captain (or cognac??)
> Scotch
> saxophone

The truth was I didn't think I had the guts to buy a saxophone, but I liked the way it looked on my list. Yet somewhere in my mind's eye this was a legitimate fantasy, a best-case projection of my near-future self, cruising at 18 knots through the horse latitudes, braying *All the Things You Are* into the tape loop of the horizon as gulls swooped overhead. In point of fact I'd be lucky to master a basic F scale during the ten or eleven days it would take us to reach Senegal; a keener prescience would have seen me puking into the bell.

But it was more than an urge to woo Hillary Clinton that finally made me carom off the trash basket at Twelfth and Broadway and through the entrance of Bongo Music. It was the realization that, regardless of any literary "growth" in store for me during my pending odyssey, I was under a strict ontological obligation to return home a changed person—a New Man. The appeal of my intraretinal image of myself playing the sax, bent backward in the classic hyperbolic arc, was that it was the image of a *me* I didn't know yet: someone who could surprise himself with hitherto-unimagined natural talents. A man who could entertain people without talking. A man who could breathe. . . . For just as smokers suck their cigarettes in a paradoxical effort to draw more oxygen into their lungs, so I envisioned myself drawing divine atmospheric sustenance from a relationship with the duck neck, mouth-piece and reed—as if my real need were not for a musical instrument at all, but a snorkel.

"No food in the store, please . . ." That bored lugubrious New York voice, so reminiscent of the way operators sounded before AT&T merci-fully automated them. A quick glance at the sole proprietor revealed coal-black eyes between a graying beard and a crimson Santa's cap, as out of place on that Hebraic head as a fannypack on a crucifix.

"Unh?—sorry—"

I tossed the chomped pickle back into the white waxed paper bag and, aware that I'd already lost all my potential credibility, drove di-rectly to the point.

"I'm looking for a sax," I said, exuding pickle breath.

"Okay. Soprano, alto, tenor, bass . . . ?"

"Alto. . . . Or tenor."

His eyes narrowed. "How much you looking to spend?"

This was something I hadn't considered. "I don't know, frankly. Three, four hundred dollars?" It came out like a plea.

"Okay." Santa walked over, placed his hand on my shoulder and steered me toward the door. "What you want to do is go outside, make a left, and grab a cab up to Thirty-fourth Street. You'll see the place on the corner. Right next to Macy's. You can't miss it."

"Another music store?"

"No, *Toys 'R' Us*. They might have something around your price range. You want a real sax, you're gonna spend real money. We're talk-ing eight hundred, a thousand bucks."

This was sobering news. "How about something used?"

"We do get used horns sometimes, but they go fast. What I *can* do is, if you leave your number, I can *try* to give you a call when . . ."

"No . . . no, thanks. I'm leaving town tomorrow. Anyplace else I might check?"

"You can hit the pawnshops. But I'll tell you something: Buying a used sax isn't like buying a used toaster. You've got to know what you're looking for. A loose fitting, a missing pad, you could be talking big bucks."

I left the heated store and reemerged into the frigid air, my saxo-phone fantasy steaming into oblivion like moisture off a nuked potato knish. January in Manhattan is brutal, clipped; even the late morning felt like cadaverous dusk. After I'd spent thirty seconds in purely seden-tary activity, contemplating my fate on the icy sidewalk, my face was as numb and slick as a chrome fender.

So the sax was out. But the prospect of the next day's voyage, and the empty days at sea, still loomed large before me. I needed something, anything, to fill the hours, to stave off the inevitable confrontation between my loosely caged inner demons who—ill-mannered tots that they were—would howl and slash one another to bloody bits if I failed to placate them with a distracting toy.

What else, I wondered, was there? What long-term self-improvement goal, besides the epiphanic saxophone, could see me through my ten days across the Atlantic?

Two hours later I was mounting the steps back to Shamus's lavish apartment, whiskey bottles and sundries in my daypack, and a PC software release of *Mavis Beacon Teaches Typing!* under my arm.

Gesture and Pose

To Sally, the aggressive crowd of Cubist, Fauvist, Surrealist, Purist, Pop, Primitive, Realist, Impressionist and Abstract Expressionist paintings packed into the Museum of Modern Art—as if the works themselves were refugees from the inhuman cold—were abstractions of abstractions, a transparent display put on by the more animated display called humanity.

In this respect we differed dramatically.

"Look at this." I dragged her up the escalators and through the galleries until we stood before *Starry Night.* The ghostly cypresses, the tortured yin-yang, the eternal poetic angst, sucked me in like a whirlpool, and I stared in awe.

"It always astonishes me to imagine that van Gogh himself stood as close to this canvas as we are; that he reached out with his brush from the same distance, the same relative position that you and I now inhabit. He was right here"—I stamped my foot—"living, breathing, painting for no one but his brother and himself. One hundred years ago Vincent van Gogh stood here, and everything in his soul reached out to touch that canvas."

She nodded, staring, and gamely allowed herself to be led past the Gauguins, around the Brancusis and amongst Monet's water lilies. We huffed and puffed at Calder's mobile, making the flurry of white disks dance and seesaw. At length we separated; I to gawk at the sexy roadsters in the Gallery of Architecture and Design, she to explore the photography exhibit a floor below.

Half an hour later I found her on a low marble bench, thumbing listlessly through a pamphlet entitled "Gesture and Pose: Twentieth-Century Photographs from the Collection." She was wearing her glasses; it took me a few seconds to realize she was teary-eyed.

"Are you all right?"

"I don't understand what I'm doing here," she responded slowly. "I should be sitting at the Master's feet."

I sat down beside her, hands flat on the cool marble. My heart was aching. "If you really feel that way," I said, "why don't you just go on to India? There's no point in your continuing with me if you're miserable, or if you want to be someplace else. You're not interested in any of this stuff"—my gesture scooped up a century of painting and sculpture— "and, frankly, it makes me feel like shit to think I'm the only thing standing between you and your guru."

I tried to sound compassionate, but it was hard to keep an edge out of my voice. While it was impossible to be angry at Sally for discovering what she really wanted, I felt poorly served by the gods. All the effort I'd put into finding a traveling companion, all the luck and enthusiasm we'd felt embarking on this grand voyage together, all the fortune cookies we'd cracked open with conspiratorial delight, suddenly seemed a dead end, a cosmic joke.

We weren't working. Our ways of being curious about the world were too different. There would be art galleries in Senegal, and Sally wouldn't be interested in them either; nor in the museums of Europe, or the minarets of Turkey. Until we were in a situation where she could address her spiritual needs—and God only knew when that would be— she would feel restless and dissatisfied.

"While you were out shopping yesterday," she said, "I saw a travel agent. He offered me a one-way ticket to Bombay, via London, for six hundred dollars."

"When?"

"The day after tomorrow."

My breath hissed out slowly, as if I were inflating a balloon. "Is that what you want to do?"

"I don't know." She let herself sag against me. "Sometimes it is. I can't help it. All this running around, seeing this, seeing that; I don't see the point of it, at least for myself. I'm sorry." I felt her shake her head; she was weeping now.

"I've only got two thousand dollars left, but that's not the problem. We could work around that somehow. The truth is that I'm just not having much fun. Maybe it's me, or maybe it's us, but I thought I'd enjoy it more. All I can say is that it's hard for me to imagine being any-place right now except in Lucknow, with Papaji."

"So what stopped you from buying the ticket?"

She sat up and faced me directly. "I won't abandon you. I commit-ted myself to making this trip, and I'm not a quitter. Even though everything I say about Papaji is true, I won't walk out on you. I'll stay on until my money runs out—and we'll take it from there."

"When do you have to buy the ticket?"

"Up until the morning of the flight."

We sat in silence. My mind and my heart were a morass of conflicting emotions. There had been times over the past month, it was true, when I had wondered, not without longing, what it would be like to be making the voyage alone. Part of me wanted to be completely open to those chance encounters, those wild romantic trysts that had made my earlier trips steam like a kettle of bouillabaisse. The reality, though, was that if Sally left me I'd be spending most of my time *alone* alone: riding buses alone, eating dinner alone, sleeping alone in double beds. This was a condition I had striven mightily to avoid, and the prospect held no more appeal for me on the winter streets of New York than it had when I'd filed my reckless Personals ad.

I kept my hands on my knees and turned my upper body toward Sally. "What do you want to do?"

"I don't know."

o   o   o

Central Park in late January has the postnuclear docility of a high school at dusk, or of Carnegie Hall an hour after Pavarotti has sung and a few sweepers and germs are the only living things circulating among the discarded playbills, ticket stubs and Ricola wrappers.

We crunched past empty playgrounds, their iced metal bars deadly to the tongue. The Central Park Zoo, animals hidden away, looked like a theme park on the moon. Central Park in winter is an empty popcorn bag, a broken twig, a lost mitten. All the green benches were empty. A red squirrel, the eternal denizen of this model urban wilderness, approached us in its winter coat and assumed the position.

"The only New Yorker," observed Sally, "allowed to wear fur."

We emerged near the Plaza, with its hansom cabs and slush-stained yellow taxis. I looked up at the park-facing rooms and for a long and painful moment wished that we were lovers again.

"That looks like fun," Sally said. I glanced at her hopefully, but she'd meant the cabs. She stopped to stroke an equine nose. "Poor little horse—you must be so cold . . . I wish I had an apple to give you . . ." Horse and driver waited patiently, conversant with the routine.

In an hour or two we'd need to catch the Metro North up to Croton-Harmon: dinner with my mother. To kill time we slipped into Bloomingdale's. The store was in the hysterical throes of its post-Christmas–pre-spring feeding frenzy. Handbags clicking open and shut like snapping fingers, registers spitting receipts with the rhythm of grating carrots, and the dance-floor shuffle of money on the move combined to create a dense aura of wholesome New York happiness. We did not shop so much as absorb the scene, stashing it away in squirrel-like fashion for the days when, alone at sea or deep in the Sahara, we would refer back to it as a gnomon of distance: a radar blip marking the most extreme edge of our American experience.

A Deconstructionist Diversion

A year before, when I'd been shopping the proposal for this book to literary agencies in Manhattan, I'd had three bites: one from an agent who admired the concept and thought she could get me a halfway-decent advance; another from an agent who thought she could do even better than that; and a third from an agent who didn't know how much she could get, but called me back a week after my visit to tell me that she didn't like my writing, she *loved* my writing (italics hers), she thought I was *fabulous* and would *love* to represent me. I was naturally suspicious of this character, until Sally put in her two cents.

"Fuck the money," she declared with customary economy. "Go with the one who believes in you." And I did.

Now I sat across from this woman in Pablo Shankar's, the current front-runner in New York's ongoing pageant of luncheon hot spots, charting the stars through the stem of my third Bombay Sapphire martini.

"I can't believe you spent an *entire day* going to museums. I can't believe it. I can. Not. Believe it." Blonde and petite, she reminded me at that moment of a small and fragile shorebird. "I am *soooo* jealous. Do you know the last time I went to a museum—any museum—in this city? I'm not joking. Ask me when."

"Jane?" The requisite pause. "When was the last time you went to a museum—*any* museum—in this city?"

"Three years ago. Georgia O'Keeffe at the Met."

"That was five years ago."

"Oh my God." She dropped the subject, leaned over and clinked my glass. Our food arrived—tandoori chicken in mole sauce, accompanied by mesquite-grilled *paneer*—and she shook out her napkin. There was a momentary silence.

"Jane?"

"Mmmhnn?"

"What if nothing happens?"

She set down her fork. "What are you talking about?"

"What if nothing happens? I mean, okay, I'm going off on this big trip, I have a book contract, and the assumption is I'll have loads of great adventures and write a spellbinding tale of peril and romance. But suppose it doesn't turn out that way? I read some *National Lampoon* thing once, a parody of the future, where scientists learn how to communicate with dolphins, but all the dolphins want to talk about is what they ate for lunch. Honestly, the same thing could happen to me."

"Honey, if you meet talking dolphins your future is *rosy*."

"You know what I mean. I've gone on trips and written about them afterward, because they were terrific—but I've never gone off on a trip knowing that it had to be terrific in advance. All I'm saying is, you can't predict these things. No one can."

"Jeffrey. Jeffrey, Jeffrey, Jeffrey." There it was: my name in print. "This is what I *love* about you. You will bitch, you will moan, you will *kvetch* and complain. Then you will come back and write these people a *great* book."

And as she said the words I realized it was not my agent, or my mother, or even Blake speaking. It was Don Corleone, making me an offer I dared not refuse.

The *Ursus Delmas*

On the morning of January 27, Sally and I shouldered our packs and took the R train from Twenty-third and Broadway to Court Street in Brooklyn. We caught a gypsy cab to the Red Hook district. After some finagling our driver was permitted to take us right up to the dock where the *Ursus Delmas* was moored.

The *Ursus Delmas* was a working vessel, shipping cargo between the United States and Africa. Sally and I would be her only passengers. She was carrying three Mack dump trucks, two bulldozers, a big white water truck, loads of lumber, PVC pipe and any number of those huge yellow, blue and green 8-by-8-by-20-foot containers that one sees passing by on trains or sitting in gigantic anonymity in equally anonymous and gigantic freight yards. What they contained was anybody's guess.

Sally's decision to continue—made, after a sleepless night, during our traditional breakfast at Hamid's—was untroubled but qualified. Since Delmas Shipping Lines had offered us transatlantic passage for a song, it made sense for her to carry on at least as far as Senegal. She would check out the plane fares in Dakar and fly on to India from there. Her compromise suited me as well, since the long ocean crossing would probably be terminally dull without her.

Ernesto "Ernie" Sandoval, the first mate, met us at the foot of a precarious gangway. A slim, slightly hunched Filipino with dark eyes and a hangdog expression, he led us into the ship's superstructure and up several flights of steep metal steps to C deck. We shed our packs in the hallway, and were ushered into the captain's ready room.

The master of the *Ursus* was Elmar Wöhlgemuth, a paunchy, middle-aged German who looked, Sally noted, like a retired Macy's Santa. I was reminded of Geppetto, but with a melancholy streak; as if we'd come across the woodworker late in life, after Pinocchio had moved out, married and settled in some distant city.

Wöhlgemuth greeted us with enthusiasm and took pains describing his ship and our route. The *Ursus* was a relatively small containership, 438 feet at her longest beam, launched in April 1983. Half the size of the arrogant *Ecstasy*, she was capable of about three-quarters the speed, some 16 knots. At that rate—burning twenty-three metric tons of fuel per day—it would take her about ten days to cross the Atlantic, from Brooklyn to Dakar.

The captain spread a pilot's chart of the North Atlantic across his desk. We studied the various options. Most ships crossing the Atlantic take great-circle routes, calculated to save time and fuel, but Wöhlgemuth eschewed those conveniences.

"I always go direct," he said, tracing his finger along a beeline linking New York Harbor to Cape Verde. "Only direct. Yah, yah. Look here." He tapped the upper North Atlantic, where the routes linking America's Eastern Seaboard to the major European ports cross turbulent seas. "The great-circle route takes you right through fifty-foot swells, very bad weather. This route here"—again he crossed the ocean with a straight shot—"is sixty miles longer. That's four hours extra, yah, but it keeps you farther south, and out of the worst swells. So. I always go direct. You see? Always direct."

My cabin was larger than the room Sally and I shared on the *Ecstasy* and, compared with my worst-case scenario, almost luxurious. There was a table, a built-in couch, a desk, two closets, two bunk beds, and a full bathroom with a strong shower. The decor was wood-grain Formica, chipped around the edges, with cut-rate curtains and upholstery. It was very much like the kind of dormitory room you'd find at a low-priced student housing development in the late seventies. Still, for all the artificial wood grain, there was something authentic about it, something that our room on the *Ecstasy*, for all its designer lamp shades and monogrammed towels, lacked. The *Ursus* was a ship, built for shipping, and had circled the world loading and delivering cargo. Any attempt by the *Ursus* to accommodate passengers was merely an afterthought, a thin veneer of creature comforts that did nothing to conceal its true mission.

We followed Ernie down two flights to Sally's quarters on A deck, portside.

If my room was luxurious, Sally's was the Plaza Suite. We beheld a big living room with a free-standing table and a minifridge, two picture windows and an adjoining bedroom with two roomy cots.

"We give the best to the lady," the captain chortled as Ernie nodded. "Yah, yah, always the best to the ladies." I seethed quietly in a corner.

Our sailing time, originally three in the afternoon, had been moved to five, six and finally eight. I decided to brave the icy weather and make my way to the Red Hook Market, half a mile away. After an hour of moonwalking down ice-slicked streets I returned, numb of face, with the following supplies:

> 1 bag Ruffles potato chips
> 1 box hard pretzels
> 8 Mars Bars
> 1 package Stella D'Oro Swiss Fudge cookies
> 1 tin honey-roasted peanuts
> 2 bags M&Ms
> 2 bags tortilla chips
> 1 jar jalapeño salsa
> 2 bottles iced cappuccino

Added to our existing stash of a liter of Johnnie Walker Red, one tin of Altoid Curiously Strong Peppermints and a one-pound box of Andes *crème de menthe* thins, these provisions effectively assuaged our fears of dying from snack deficiency.

o   o   o

Red Hook port by night was just short of surreal. Twenty- and forty-foot containers stood arrayed like gigantic building blocks, yellow, blue and rust-red beneath high halogen lamps. The air was filled with icy mist. Beyond loomed the Battery, a cliff of foggy cold light. There was no one around but me, carrying my ridiculous sagging snack sack along the frozen ground, surrounded by mammoth crates and the huddled boroughs. My breath steamed in the air. A few yards away the *Ursus Delmas* lay dormant, gathering its strength.

I stood still. It was Thursday evening. Across the East River, all over New York, the fate of the world was being decided. Millions of dollars were changing hands. Symphonies were playing, parties were steaming the windows of penthouse suites, take-out Chinese was being sorted into waxed containers, padded with inadequate numbers of napkins and bagged for delivery to lofts in SoHo, TriBeCa, the East Village. I'd just spent three days on those luminous streets, wishing to God I'd had the guts or bravado to storm out my younger years in the only place that really mattered. To make my name in New York City, the literary launchpad from which any destination is possible. That very morning, stomping through the sludge, the thought had caused me pain.

But that final American evening, standing alone in the icy sodium cold, a white cargo ship waiting to carry me off to West Africa, my eyes opened. I realized how many of the warm, brilliant people in that frigid, dreary city, consumed by careers and despairing of escape, would trade everything to be standing where I now stood. At that moment New Yorkers seemed the most beautiful and the saddest creatures on Earth—rare, gorgeous tigers whose cunning and ferocity had required the construction of an impenetrable cage.

Here, at last, was the reason I had returned to New York.

I turned my gaze from the illuminated towers and concentrated on the slippery gangplank.

· 10 ·

The Bardo of Rock 'n' Roll

I woke up at six-forty Friday morning and, with considerable bravado, shaved and showered. We were in good rough waters. The lethal low-pressure system that had kept the Eastern Seaboard in subzero temperatures was churning up the sea. We bounced through twenty-foot swells, rocking dizzily. I popped a motion-sickness pill and made my way down to breakfast.

My cabin was on C deck, the mess on deck 1. To get from my bunk to breakfast required entering the ship's central staircase and descending four flights. For some reason—the enclosed space, the spiral design or the very idea of going up or down in a sea with its own up-down agenda—the stairway proved completely discombobulating. I emerged drained and sweating, fighting back waves of nausea that barely subsided as I sat down with Captain Wöhlgemuth and Karsten Zschoche, the chief engineer.

Sally arrived in no better condition. We ate a very light breakfast, after which I accompanied Sally back to her room. She ran into the head, became violently sick, collapsed into a bunk and went out like a light. I returned with great effort to my room—a feat equivalent to climbing a ladder inside a high-speed elevator that is bouncing unpredictably between floors—threw open the door, fell backward onto my couch and fell fast asleep.

When I opened my eyes it was noon: lunchtime. The room was a carousel, a seesaw, a raft. Everything in my body told me not to stand, let alone move, but aside from being ravenously hungry I feared committing a fatal broach of ship's etiquette. I descended to the mess.

Sally was absent. I made up my mind to eat something and began, very slowly, with soup, followed by a plank of dry Jewish rye bread and the sort of ugly, colorless salad I thought United Airlines owned the patent on. I ate some rice and drank half a glass of milk.

The captain inaugurated a polite conversation about seasickness as a phenomenon.

"It's not the stomach," Wöhlgemuth explained. "It has nothing to do with the stomach. The stomach may be perfectly fine. It is only the ear, the canals in the inner ear, that become confused. They tell the brain that the body is not in balance. And so you spit."

"But why should being unbalanced make your brain tell you to throw up?"

Wöhlgemuth shrugged. "Yah, yah, yah. Nobody knows. For some reason. I don't know."

It was something to think about while I decided if I could move. The fact was I didn't dare. Joel, the messman, noticed my plight and approached me with his minimal English.

"Not feel good? Better take little whiskey."

"No. . . . ugh . . ." The thought alone almost pushed me over the edge.

"Okay. Tea?"

"Yes, please. Tea sounds wonderful."

Joel brought tea. I drank a little and had a few grapes. The last one went down a little funny, and I realized why: It was fighting oncoming traffic.

"JOEL!!" The messman ran over. "I need a bucket."

He looked at me quizzically, ran back into the kitchen, and returned, years later, it seemed, with a hand towel. For a moment I stared at it in wonder, unable to imagine that my message had not come across. Had he totally misread my plight? Was this a receiving blanket of some kind? Was it the Filipino custom to throw up into a towel? Or was I expected, as per the captain's quaint phrase, to merely "spit"?

"A bucket! A pail!" I cried, adding with my last breath, "I'm going to be sick. . . ."

Joel stood nodding, his face a mask of concentration. Finally, recalling my younger days as a charades whiz, I tilted my head back and pantomimed a geyser. At this the messman ran off again. I was terrified he'd return with a pair of binoculars, for whale watching, but he reappeared on the double carrying a two-quart saucepan. This was more like it. I grabbed it, spat, and rested in blissful peace with my face ensconced in its cool aluminum maw before daring to raise my head again. Joel, gentleman and saint, removed the saucepan for cleaning and, ostensibly, cooking. I rinsed out my mouth and prepared to ascend the monstrous stairway again.

As I stood up, Joel returned with an orange rind. "You smell this," he said. "Make feel better." Of course; this was the very tactic that my fried egg flipper had endorsed.

I kept the rind clamped over my face as I reentered my cabin. During lunchtime it had become a chaotic venue. My toiletry kit had flown from my desk, and the floor was littered with razors, earplugs, antibiotic cream, condoms, Wet Naps, and keys. Bottles of Guinness and iced cappuccino, along with two glasses, rolled around on the carpet like drunken pill bugs. The drawers of my desk were open, my chair had toppled over backward, and my toothpaste and shampoo were sloshing about in the toilet bowl like toy boats. I groaned deeply, lay down on the couch with the orange peel over my face and fell unconscious.

I was awakened by a gentle knocking at my door. Ernie Sandoval, the doe-eyed first mate, was peering into the room.

"Dinner," he announced.

"I can't move."

"I think you better eat something." Ernie had spent twenty years at sea; his English was excellent, and he had the kind of compassion that informed you, subtly, that he knew the meaning of suffering. "Some chicken porridge, and rice," he offered. "And a Coca-Cola. Can you eat? I think better you try."

I agreed, and drifted off again. Presently the door opened, and Ernie set a tray on the table just above my head. An hour later—maybe it was two—the ship pitched mightily. I was jarred from my slumber as the tray and all its contents crashed onto my cabin floor.

This was the limit. For a brief but thrilling moment I considered jumping ship and swimming toward Bermuda; it couldn't have been more than three hundred miles away. Ultimately I dragged myself to my feet. I did what I could to clean up the mess, then set the tray by my door and steeled myself. I would suffer, yes, but not alone. An agonizing minute later I was in the stairwell, at Sally's door, swaying sickly in her room. She was sitting on her couch.

"Hello," she said brightly. "I'm actually feeling quite good. I've been reading, and meditating, and sleeping, and then getting up to do a little reading again . . ."

I stared about in amazement. She had managed, incredibly, to fill three liter bottles with purified water, disassemble our complicated filter, cloister away all her stray belongings, read several chapters of a dense tome by Sri Nisagadartha Swami and rid her yachtlike suite of nearly all the clanking, bashing and clonking noises that continued to fill mine with the din of the Notre Dame belfry.

I hated her then, but not enough to keep me from gulping down a full liter of the water she had so painstakingly purified. My thirst quenched, I collapsed uselessly onto her spare cot, fully clothed.

"You'll get used to it," she assured me. "In a day or two we'll be laughing about this."

"Will I?" It was 10:00 P.M., our first evening aboard the *Ursus*, and I had more pressing questions on my mind. "What do you think it would cost," I asked, "to have a helicopter pick us up at sea?"

o   o   o

Saturday dinner was the first meal I ate with good appetite. Sally was absent. The captain and I spoke about the early explorers: men like Henry the Navigator, Vasco da Gama and Magellan, who had set off into the unknown in ships smaller than the *Ursus*'s superstructure.

"And not just small," Wöhlgemuth reminded me. "They carried horses, and pigs, and chickens, and a crew of nearly two hundred! Under sail!"

I thought of those miserable conscripts, and of how seasick they must have been in the ships we've glorified in history—the *Pinta*, the *Nina*, the *Santa Maria*. Hundreds of vomiting convicts and a captain who didn't know where the hell he was going but had a crazy idea there was something out there. And they did it. They made it. Months at sea! It was a staggering thought.

We moved backward from there, all the way back to the Polynesians, the first and possibly the greatest navigators of all, with their stick-and-seashell maps and dugout canoes, setting off on the limitless ocean for voyages from which they might never return. For it wasn't until the Middle Ages, and the days of Henry the Navigator, that ships were built that could sail *against* the wind and return home under the same currents that had carried them away.

After dinner I made my way to Sally's cabin and picked up *The Great Gatsby*. It was a relief to find I could read despite the constant rocking of the ship. I read the first chapters like lightning, and a few more than that, and when I reached page 60 it appeared I was already halfway through the book. Could it be? I glanced at the final page. Odd; 195.

That would put the halfway point at more like page 100 . . . so how could I . . . *Oh no.* I thumbed rapidly through the pages. Forty pages missing! Damn Charles Scribner and all his sons!

I read on, watching the massive misprint race toward me like a shock wave. Finally I tossed the thing into a wastebasket.

Sally plucked it out.

"Are you reading for the *writing*," she asked archly, "or for the *story?* If you're reading for the pure enjoyment of his style, I really don't see what difference it makes if a few pages are missing." She set upon the novel herself, abandoning for the evening her works of eastern religion and philosophy.

I looked out the window. It had taken me a couple of days, but I was beginning to understand something: We were in the middle of the Atlantic Ocean. There was nothing but ocean, and more ocean, for hundreds of miles in every direction. We were alone, a tiny ship with twenty people and tons of anonymous cargo, out in the middle of the rolling sea, tethered to civilization by a navigational satellite and a few paper charts. This was awesome. This was new. This was scary, if I decided to think about it that way.

I decided not to, and crawled into bed. I read for a while, dozed, read, dozed. I was awakened a final time by Sally's snort of frustration, followed by the impact of *The Great Gatsby* striking the cabin wall.

34°50'N x 57°47'W

The next morning, standing by the rail outside on C deck, I saw the first sign of life beyond the *Ursus* herself: a big yellow sea sponge floating on the surface, followed by a tangle of kelp. The sight filled me with nostalgia, and I understood for the first time why Russian cosmonauts, confined for months aboard their *Mir* space station, race down to the hydroponics lab every day to visit their yeast cultures.

The wind whipped through my parka, making it billow like a spinnaker. Gunmetal ocean lay in every direction, to every point of the compass. For an instant there was a tightening in my gut, a taste of agoraphobia, and I felt real fear: Anything could rise from those depths. *Or from mine* . . . But the panic passed quickly. This was, after all, what I had come here for—a taste of true emptiness.

And yet it was not empty at all. There was a universe beneath our hull, cool and dark, full of fish and mermaids and monsters. What would it be like, I wondered, to be utterly alone, truly alone, like those wild few who've crossed the ocean in sailboats, rowboats and rafts? Did it take courage, or insanity? But I knew, looking toward the horizon, that what it took was an obsessive love. I understood that it is possible to love the sea that much: to love it as much as a woman, or money, or heroin.

o   o   o

The first mate joined us after lunch, and spoke about his life.

Despite the impression gleaned from a glimpse into his quarters—a shrine to the female breast, celebrated in dozens of glossy centerfolds—Ernesto Sandoval was decent and disarmingly direct.

Ernie was forty-two; he had been at sea for twenty-three years. His slightly oblong head seemed to account for half his height, like a character from *Miss Peach*. The rest of his body was compressed into a lean, efficient bundle. Ernie grew up on the Philippine island of Cuyo, the youngest of three children. His father died when he was small, and his mother struggled to feed the family. She received considerable help from Ernie's elder sister, Maria, but that arrangement ended when Maria was gunned down by a jealous suitor.

"There is no justice in the Philippines," Ernie said bitterly. "The boyfriend paid off the right people, and never even went to jail."

Ernie sold newspapers and worked as a shoe-shine boy to make ends meet. Throughout high school he entertained fantasies of revenge—of killing the man who had murdered his sister—but ultimately realized that the best thing he could do was study hard and find a career. His second sister, a waitress, paid his way through nautical school.

"I worked as a stevedore, too, after school. It was hard work. There were no forklifts in the area where we lived; we had to carry the heavy things by ourselves."

In the late 1960s and early 1970s, life in the Merchant Marine was different.

"The old motto of a girl in every port was true." Ernie laughed. "But AIDS has changed all that." The other big change was in navigation. "Back then we would navigate only by celestial means. If it was bad weather we did dead reckoning, or we'd use a radio beacon if we were close to one. Even now," he said, "you have to know how to use celestial navigation. What if the information from the satellite fails, or if there is some electrical problem?"

Later that afternoon he brought me out onto the bridge deck and taught me how to use a sextant.

"It's all in the wrist." He swept the instrument to and fro, finding the horizon within its mirrors. "You can know all the calculations, but if you can't get the tangencies right they are of no use at all."

We took a reading off the sun, already low on the horizon and partially obscured by clouds. We then matched the angle on the sextant to Greenwich Mean Time, correcting for the time it took us to return indoors and check the clock. What followed was a mind-numbing romp through text after text of azimuths, angles, declinations and corrections, more confusing than anything I had experienced in calculus. When all the calculations were complete, Ernie showed me the result: The position I had "shot" was about twelve miles off our satellite-endorsed location.

"Not bad." He nodded approvingly. "Back in nautical school, students first learning the sextant would sometimes find their ship in the middle of the Sahara."

There is no retirement policy in the Philippines. Ernie will have to continue working until he has saved enough money to support his wife and their four children: a daughter of fifteen; a twelve-year-old son, another daughter, nine; and an infant boy.

A current of sadness and solitude flowed from Sandoval as he spoke of his family.

"I have never seen my wife fully pregnant," he confessed. "I have never been at home when she has given birth. She will be at one month or two when I leave; when I come home, a year later, my child is already months old. The next time, over a year old."

"I'm curious to know," I said, "why you decided on a career at sea. You must have known it would take you far away from home. . ."

"When I was a young man I wanted to travel everywhere, see the world, meet different people." He sighed. "But it is not so interesting anymore—and now it's too late to change." He set the sextant gently back into its case. "I think it's good for the young men, this business. For the family man, maybe not so good."

The Paradise of Wind Roses

To: **Allen Noren, O'Reilly & Associates**
From: **Jeff Greenwald**
Subject: **Big World/Aboard the *Ursus Delmas***

> *That pure land ahead of us*
> *where flowers ceaselessly bloom . . .*
> —Rainer Maria Rilke

It's a lousy, stinking cliché, but I'll say it anyway: The sea is like glass.
    But what glass! Not the cheap, pathetic panes that screen out rain and

mosquitoes and ultraviolet light; not even fine lead crystal, or prism, or quartz. The *Ursus Delmas* is surrounded by an ocean of elemental glass, the deep volcanic runoff of the primordial atmosphere. It is jet-black, protean, an ever-changing fluid that seems infinitely dense. Its weight is unimaginable. Seen from the safety of C deck, it resembles a shifting plane of Stone Age obsidian, ready to be chipped and flaked into primitive tools: axes, knives, arrowheads, scrapers for skinning wild animals and working their hides. Sometimes it appears frozen—and for a microcosmic second the entire ocean hangs motionless around us, tipped with razor-sharp blades. At moments like this I want to vault over the rail and walk alone among those amazing formations until the ship is out of sight and the eerie black horizon stretches around me like a priest's collar.

At other times the ocean, which descends more than two thousand fathoms beneath our hull, appears as clear as a Gypsy's ball, and if I stare unblinking through the surface I can observe its most profound depths: past the domain of the currents; past the point where color dissolves; beyond the realm of light altogether.

I can see down to the unmarked highways where caravans of gigantic blind predators glide by and, after they pass, down farther still, into the deepest canyons of the sea—the kingdom of illuminated creatures, sacred snake gods and steaming sulfur vents twisting cords of vaporized magma into the diamond-dense water. And then, damn it all, I feel the hands gripping my ankles, pulling me back toward reality as I tip dreamily over the rail. . . .

Sally is on the deck behind me, smoking a Benson and Hedges.

"The sea is like glass," she remarks.

⚡   ⚡   ⚡

Groundhog Day

Karsten Zschoche leaned over his salad, reading a fax. The subject looked interesting: stowaways.

"Do you ever get any on this ship?" I poured myself a bowl of cornflakes, slicing a green banana into the mix.

"You don't know?" Zschoche looked at me in surprise. "We have one just now."

"There's a stowaway on this ship?" Sally was incredulous. I took one look at the chief engineer's droll expression and assumed he was joking. But he continued on, quite serious.

"Yah, yah, yah. There were two stowaways on board. From Ghana. We found them on the way to Houston. One of them had a passport and was flown home from the States. The other had no documents, so he was not permitted to land in the U.S. We must take him back to Ghana."

"Can we talk with him?" Sally asked.

I was horrified by the naïveté of her question. The man was a prisoner; he could be ruthless, dangerous. "Of course not," I muttered, kicking her under the table.

"Sure," said Zschoche. "I don't see why not."

"How old is he?"

"Young. They were just boys, looking for some adventure."

"So what will happen to him when he's returned to Ghana?" Sally, to my amazement, had pulled over the meat tray and was wrestling a steak the size of a catcher's mitt onto her plate.

"He will go to jail. I hope they put both of them in jail for at least ten years."

It seemed a rather high price to pay for stowing away aboard a cargo ship, and an utterly preposterous penalty for two boys looking for adventure.

I asked if they spoke English. Zschoche nodded.

"I think so, yes. Ghana was a British colony. Certainly they will speak English."

o   o   o

Wöhlgemuth also spoke with us about the stowaway. He was no boy at all, the captain said, but a man in his early thirties.

"How did you find him?"

The captain looked up from his stew with raised eyebrows. "After five days they must come knocking! It is sixteen days from the Ivory Coast to Houston. You need much food and water for such a crossing."

Africans will often hide in cargo containers, the captain explained, locked away in total darkness until the ship reaches port. Other refugees squirrel themselves away in the cargo itself, squeezed between sheets of lumber or in pipes. Customs requires that each container be examined before it is closed, then sealed with a bond of plastic. The fact that the two stowaways from Ghana were in a sealed container meant that someone in the port itself had been in cahoots with them.

"Still," Wöhlgemuth said, "we were lucky to have only two. Our sister ship—the *Sirius Delmas*—also left Africa, and a few days later the captain discovered thirty-five stowaways on board." All had to be fed and sheltered, an obligation that put tremendous pressure on the ship's resources and crew. Locating stowaways is the captain's responsibility, and repatriation—which can cost thousands of dollars—is the ship's liability.

The captain agreed to let us meet the stowaway but cautioned us. "You never know what these people will do. They might try to hijack the ship. They might break things, or set the ship on fire. They might try to take a hostage. Yah, yah. All these things have happened! You don't know what they will do if they are desperate."

o   o   o

The stowaway's name was Fred. He looked tired, unhappy and ill prepared for guests. His appearance surprised us. I couldn't tell you what we were expecting, but it wasn't a tall black man with dreadlocks, wearing a purple Hawaiian shirt and a glass bead necklace. He looked like he could have walked right out of a Berkeley dance club.

Ernie and the captain sat with us, a fact that must have contributed to the stowaway's reserve. He communicated in the barest whisper, wringing together hands with long fingers and beautifully manicured nails. His left ear was pierced with two small studs; he wore a bronze bracelet on his wrist and a few small gold rings on his left hand.

Though Fred was a good-looking man, we saw him at his worst: frightened and despairing, having failed in a dangerous bid for freedom. The irony of the situation was that Ghana, his home, was considered one of the most democratic nations in Africa. Fred could not shed any light on his life in Ghana or on why he had run away, leaving a wife and three children behind.

The encounter left me feeling strangely guilty, like a voyeur who discovers that the neighbor who always forgets to pull her shade down has Alzheimer's.

"I guess I was expecting some kind of radical activist," Sally said as we commiserated afterward. "Someone who would mount an impassioned and irresistible plea for freedom."

What we saw instead was a lonely and uneducated man who had hoped, naïvely, to run off to America and make a living playing soccer— the only skill he had learned in his village.

Slouching Toward Senegal

The *Ursus,* hampered by winds, crept toward the Tropic of Cancer, its progress evidenced by a slow pitch that kept us in a mild but wearisome state of nausea.

I am a traveler in search of travel, I had written in my proposal. Eat it up, kid, I told myself. This is what you wanted. This is travel, the old-fashioned way. Tourism á la Noah. Every inch of the distance between New York and Africa passed beneath our increasingly flabby butts as we plowed ahead at a snail's pace, towing our cargo beneath billowing cumulus clouds.

We were past the days of novelty or humor. Sally and I became utterly lethargic, unable to either read or write, consumed by a boredom so intense it was almost a spiritual experience. By day we ate, slept or stared at the carpet with intense interest. At dinner I gnashed my teeth to behold the identical cello-wrapped salad of wilting iceberg lettuce, sliced tomato and pulverized carrot that we were served meal after meal, to the accompaniment of Thousand Islands dressing. Afterward we watched action-packed double features, *Cliffhanger* on the heels of *The Fugitive,* glancing up at the wall clock to find, much to our amazement, that time was passing after all.

o   o   o

The high point of our penultimate evening on board was a bottle of Mateus, offered to us by Pablo, a twenty-three-year-old seaman with a desperate crush on Sally. As we drank together in Ernie's cabin Pablo explained, with no little sarcasm, how so many Filipinos found their way onto the open seas.

"It's an ad," he said, nodding. "'See the World—for Free!' It's posted everywhere. You'd be amazed at how many Filipinos—kids, like me when I started—find it irresistible."

"And it isn't even nearly true," Ernie lamented. "I've been in New York four times, and I've never even set foot on Manhattan." He had seen the Statue of Liberty, however—through binoculars.

Both Pablo and Ernie agreed that, though the pay was good and Delmas treated its sailors well, being at sea is often like being in prison. This was literally true for Ernie during his second year behind the mast. The company he was working for went bankrupt while his ship was anchored off the coast of India, and a huge legal battle ensued. The seamen—Ernie among them—were confined to the port of Calcutta for an entire year, forbidden to leave the vessel. They fished for their supper, lived in the same clothes and hired locals to bring fresh water. At last the ship was sold and the crew paid off. The experience gave Ernie the advantage of experiencing the worst possible thing (next to sinking, of course) that can happen to a ship at sea.

"Nowadays, before I get on any ship, I check the company books," he said. "If they're behind on their payments to the crew, forget it. I won't even board."

Tropic of Cancer

After a few glasses of wine Sally and I returned to her room, sat down together and uncaged the confrontation we'd been holding at bay for weeks. Some of our problems, we agreed, stemmed from what she called mutual patronization: I patronized Sally by flaunting my "superior" experience in the material world, while she excelled in making me feel about as spiritually evolved as a sea slug.

"This isn't the way I remember us," she sighed, avoiding my eyes. It was the truth. It was as if the magnetism that had bonded for the past year had suddenly reversed polarity, causing us to repel at every contact.

After our discussion I fell asleep, sinking into a vivid nightmare about an alien invasion. Brooklyn was rocked by fires and earthquakes as huge flying saucers soared above the burning horizon. I wondered if anyone could hear my desperate cries for help.

"You scared the shit out of me," Sally confirmed the next morning. "You were yelling and moaning, lowing like a cow. I thought that you were possessed, or that the ship was sinking, or both."

o   o   o

During our final day at sea I fell into a deeply depressed state. I was tired of traveling, despite the fact that we hadn't really moved at all for the past ten days. I dreaded being alone, dreaded schlepping my Endless Journey from bus to train to boat to taxi. Part of me wanted more than anything to throw the whole thing over and catch the next airplane—anywhere.

What would it take for me to regain my love of life, of adventure? How could I break free of my self-imposed restrictions? Perhaps that, as Geoffrey Hill had sugggested, was what this pilgrimage was really about: a private journey to reclaim the dormant parts of myself. To find a fire, even a small fire, and fan it. Viewed from that perspective, it made perfect sense that I must continue on from Africa alone, for there were no embers burning with Sally.

o   o   o

That night, I dreamed I was on an island. As I was strolling past the tables along a shaded beachside walk, I recognized with astonishment a familiar face. It was my brother, Jordan.

"So this is where you've gone off to," I exclaimed as he rose, laughing, to greet me.

In his dream avatar Jordan was a prolific and imaginative painter, specializing in lush, luminous canvases thick with tropical color. He invited me to attend a huge banquet—part of an island-wide cultural festival—to be held in his honor. My mother and sister would be there, too. But I didn't want to go; I wanted Jordan to myself.

"Why not?" he agreed. And added, drolly, "I won't be missed. . . ."

I climbed onto the back of his motorcycle and put my hands on his shoulders. I had to lean over to see. Though three years younger, Jord was taller than I, and had always been more athletic. We explored his island together. It was a quaint, breezy place with Mediterranean architecture, simple food and friendly natives. My brother owned a large, open studio, and his brilliant murals stretched across the walls. The room overlooked the sea.

I woke up feeling refreshed, despite a bittersweet melancholy. It was wonderful and strange to have spent the night with my brother; his adventures always inspired me. But such meetings with him were rare. In the waking world, Jordan was dead. He had killed himself with a pistol four years before.

The Paradise of Large Brown Birds

We were entering a place where the back of one's throat is forever dry, one of the regions that, viewed from space, give the appearance of being under a perpetual Venusian cloud.

Dakar lay on the horizon, an angular khaki smudge. Weird brown birds, semi-pelicans with short broad beaks, farmed the sea in our wake. We passed Ile de Gorée, the former slave-trading island and the first European settlement off the west coast of Africa.

And there it was: Africa. *Africa.* We stood on deck, feeling the warm air against our faces, smelling land. Smelling Africa.

It smelled like smoke, wood fires, exhaust and exhaustion, turbans, camel shit and cheap cigarettes, human bodies, sandalwood and knock-off European cologne. It smelled like butane and diesel, roast chicken, rotting bananas, soiled underwear, goats, coffee and bitter chocolate. I stood on the observation deck, dancing in circles with my arms in the air.

A tugboat pulled up alongside the *Ursus,* and a native pilot climbed aboard. Sally joined me with our two cold bottled cappuccinos in her hand.

"To the end of our second leg."

"To the end of our second leg."

"To having crossed the Atlantic in a fucking cargo ship."

"To having crossed the fucking Atlantic in a cargo ship."

An echo of our jubilation came from the bridge below as the captain, pilot and navigator guided the *Ursus Delmas* into the port of Dakar.

"Starboard ten . . ."

"Starboard ten."

"Steady . . ."

"Steady!"

"Stop engine . . ."

"Stop engine."

Dakar's musky scent made my heart pound in my chest. I swallowed the last sweet frothy gulp of my American cappuccino, whispered a prayer toward the east and prepared to arrive in Africa.

• 11 •

The Paradise of Pheromones

We spent five days and nights in Dakar, searching for music and wrestling with the logistics of escape.

Built on a fractal peninsula scratching the Atlantic, Dakar is a schizy, frantic and often unnerving metropolis where French manners meet African funk. It's a city where you can have fresh-baked croissants for breakfast and *yassa thiof* for dinner; a place where Muslims spread their prayer mats out on the sidewalks at the stroke of noon and *borro-burros*—traditional pharmacists—hawk iguana heads and monkey paws on blue plastic tarps. Blind beggars pace the sidewalks chanting verses from the Koran, while musicians like Youssou N'Dour and Baba Maal keep the nightclubs alive til dawn.

Our original idea had been to spend ten days in Senegal, journey east to Mali and then steer due north: through Gao and into Algeria. We would cross the Sahara and emerge at Algiers, from which point we'd catch a ship to Italy or southern Turkey.

The plan fell apart our second day in Dakar when, just outside the American embassy compound on Rue Jules XXIII, we met two consular officers.

They bore sobering news. The trans-Saharan passage—fifteen hundred miles, from Gao to Algiers—had become extremely dangerous. Islamic fundamentalist rebels were murdering foreigners and stealing their vehicles (or just stealing their vehicles and leaving the owners by the roadside, which amounted to much the same thing). Their nefarious activities had spilled into northern Mali, and it was now considered unsafe to travel overland even as far north as Timbuktu without a military escort.

The preferred overland route, they told us, was the one that followed the West African coastline: up into Mauritania and through Western Sahara into Morocco.

I was astonished to learn this.

"From what we've heard," I said, "no one's allowed to travel from Mauritania into Morocco. The entire region is supposedly at war."

"Yes, that's basically true." The consul's face was beet-red; how anyone could wear a three-piece suit in the solarium heat was beyond me. "But it's not affecting the whole region. Most of the rebel activity is contained. The only real problem is that twenty-seven kilometers of the stretch is mined. You'd need to get permits, and go with soldiers who are familiar with the territory. It's basically a Yellow Brick Road situation. As long as you stay on the prescribed route you're safe, but the minute you take a detour. . . ."

The situation was complicated by a bit of intelligence gleaned by Sally the previous afternoon. We had arrived in Senegal, luck would have it, the very week that the West African franc was devalued by 50 percent. The one-way airfare between Dakar and Bombay was $819—*for the next forty-eight hours only*. Following that it would increase by $500. She thus found herself up against the same horns she'd faced in New York: the dilemma of an immediate decision.

That evening we planted ourselves in Le Ponty, a semi-sleazy hangout where French expats hustled and were hustled by anorexic prostitutes. Sally ordered two industrial-size Flag lagers as a five-piece band navigated a repertoire of African and American pop. A six-year-old girl was playing electric bass.

"Are you sorry you didn't leave from New York?"

She shrugged. "There's no use regretting the past. The only question now is if it makes sense for me to leave after spending only three days in Africa."

"Do you think you'll ever come this way again?"

"Never." She stood up, walked to the bar and returned with a wedge of lime, which she forced down the throat of her bottle. "You still plan to go to Mali, don't you?"

"Absolutely. I want to leave as soon as possible. It's getting hotter every day, and I'll have to come back to Dakar anyhow."

Sally peeled the label off her beer. The band launched into a plinkety cover of "Hotel California."

"I'll come with you," she said. I expected a caveat of some kind. None was forthcoming. "I'm literally sick of dealing with this issue. Thinking about it makes me want to throw up. We both know I want to be with Papaji, but that's simply not feasible in the unfolding of this moment. And it's idiotic to give up my only chance to visit these African cultures. So if it's okay with you, let's drop it for now."

"What about the money situation?"

"I've still got enough to last me a couple of months if things stay cheap. In Morocco, or maybe in Greece, you can lend me what I need to fly ahead to India. If you're comfortable with that. If not, so be it. I'll deal with it when the time comes. Agreed?"

I pondered this in silence. There was no question that part of me, angst be damned, had been hoping Sally would fly. I was craving the bittersweet medicine of solo travel, and the tough calls it would require. Sally's decision left me treading water in an emotional maelstrom, wondering if I was getting what I wanted after all, damning my own gutlessness, her protracted indecision, the fates that had thrown us together in the first place.

My God, we had had so much fun once. It had seemed we could never exhaust, in one or a hundred lifetimes, the thrill of each other's wit and company. When did we lose interest in treasuring the discovery of who the other was inside? When did love become familiarity, and familiarity contempt? When did my theatrical, semi-serious whining stop amusing her, and her own spiritual radiance become critical and trite to me? When did we stop being supportive and inspiring for one another? Would it, could it, ever begin again?

The entire process had been a lesson in being careful what you wished for.

"Agreed," I said. We clinked our bottles, drained them and walked back to our hotel across the raggedy scrub of the Place de l'Indépendance.

Along the way we ran into Mballo, a freelance photographer who made his rent shooting the peacocked clientele of Dakar's nightclub scene. Hyped and wiry, an ancient Petri slung over his shoulder on a guitar strap, Mballo thrust a tubular copy of *Le Soleil* into my chest.

"Good evening, mon. You reading French?" I unrolled the paper and scanned the front page under the street lamps, but Mballo leaned into me and flipped ahead. "You and your lady might care to check out this scene tomorrow, maybe it's something interesting for you. I think so, I think so ... *moment* ... *voilà.*"

He tapped his finger on the top of page 7, and I read the headline:

"Premier 'Rave' en Dakar."

I'd been to raves in the States; they weren't the sort of event one advertised in the newspapers. The digital-era answer to the acid tests of the 1960s, the raves I'd attended had featured super-amped, pulse-pounding house music and Ecstasy—or 3,4-methylenedioxymethamphetamine (MDMA)—as the recreational drug of choice. The effect of Ecstasy is comparable to the feeling one might enjoy while making passionate love to a woman made entirely of chocolate mousse.

The article piqued my interest. The location it suggested for the event was unclear, however, and my attempts to get further information by calling *Le Soleil* led nowhere. Dakar is probably the only city in the world where, instead of a busy signal, you often get a scratchy Afro-pop recording, backed by a kola-nut voice that apologizes, in melodic French, for your call's delay.

At ten the following night Sally and I hired a taxi and set out in search of the event.

We were joined by two friends: Pierre, a French volunteer doing two years of foreign service in Dakar, and Mohammed, a tall Senegalese sculptor who hewed rough tribal figures out of granite on the rocky beach behind the Sofitel Teranga's huge swimming pool. Together we motored toward the outskirts of Dakar, a neo-industrial wilderness bearing a discomforting resemblance to downtown LA.

Finding the location of the rave proved difficult. We drove in huge circles for nearly half an hour, finally spiraling inward toward a vast walled compound. A handful of gendarmes stood guard by the entrance, clutching automatic weapons. I doubted this was the place.

Mohammed insisted, however, that it was. The terrifying military edifice apparently concealed a huge amphitheater. He jumped out of the taxi and approached the guards. A lively dialogue ensued, at the conclusion of which our artist in residence returned to the taxi shaking his head. He gave us the goods in French.

"This is certainly the place," he said. "But the rave is not to be."

"What happened?"

"There was a lack of harmony about the finances, so it was canceled."

"Welcome," Pierre breathed, "to Africa."

"But I have good news as well."

"*Oui?*"

"The guard on the left is the nephew of my brother's best man's co-worker. He advises us that Youssou N'Dour will play tonight at the Thiossanne—his private club on Route de Ouakam."

o   o   o

In East Africa you've got giraffes and lions; in West Africa the draw is the beat. Afro-pop was born at the turn of the century, when the French colonial era brought the language of ballad-based music to the region. The fresh, melodic style, along with an influx of new instruments—guitars, saxophones, even accordions—gave birth to an irresistible sound that the Lonely Planet guide describes as "an incredible mishmash of traditional, Latin and Black American music with elements of American jazz and rock." N'Dour, one of the true Afro-pop superstars, calls his music *mbalax,* the Wolof term for a highly percussive sound dominated by the goat-skinned *sabar* drum.

The show started at one in the morning. Youssou and his Super Etoiles took the stage by storm, waltzing out to loud applause, and by the time the band played its first measure, the dance floor was so crowded that a lobbed Ping-Pong ball wouldn't have hit the ground.

Sometimes you know you're in Senegal. It doesn't take much. The clues are often subliminal, subtle to the point of being intuitive. The way a red spotlight refracts through a Flag beer bottle; the smell of local tobacco and cologne; the background conversation in French and Wolof, commingled with the otherworldly rhythm of African feet orbiting the room. I looked around and, for a split second, felt the conditioned unease of being one of three white faces among hundreds of black people. Black faces; black lips; tall black women with tightly braided hair; the spicy, treelike fragrance that black people have.

The weird thing about watching the Senegalese dance is that, viewed from above, it looks like nobody is moving. All one can see is a densely packed room of blasé heads and faces—bobbing slightly, perhaps, but by and large as nonchalant as a roomful of people awaiting the results of their civil service exams.

When I hit the dance floor I realized why: All the action is taking place *below the waist.* From the belt line down, the Thiossanne was writhing like a snake pit, an X-rated pelvic paradise of mutual assured fertility. The women rolled back their eyes, running long fingers across their breasts and down between their legs; the men pinched at their crotches and hiked their belt buckles, easing a mythical confinement. No one was smiling. No one, of course, except Youssou N'Dour, who swayed upon the stage in a broad red tie and Panama hat, belting out rhythms like a caller at an orgy.

I was suddenly glad the rave had been canceled. If this was how West Africans behaved on beer and cocktails, adding Ecstasy to the mix would've caused a meltdown that made Chernobyl look like spilled milk.

A smoldering cigarette drooling ash . . . beams of purple light raking through the smoke . . . black waiters in fluorescing white suits . . . Mohammed's Cheshire cat smile . . . my alcohol-addled brain became a repository of snapshots, disconnected in time and space. A princely looking black man led Sally back to the table, offering the ultimate tribute: "You dance like a Senegalese." And toward the end of the long night I registered the remarkable *nonthreateningness* of it all. Our initial awareness of being the only whites in a nightclub packed with Africans had dissolved, leaving only our pheromones. There had been no edge at all, no trace of the tension I felt on the streets of Oakland.

"*Bien sûr,*" Mohammed nodded when I mentioned this in the taxi home. "You are among people who have never been slaves."

A Brief History of Hell

Mohammed's comment had struck a nerve, serving as a wake-up call about exactly where on Earth we were. The black Africans we saw on the streets of Dakar were survivors: the people whose families had not been hustled into wooden ships and hauled across the Atlantic to slavery in Brazil and the Americas.

The next afternoon I left Sally to her writing and caught the ferry to Ile de Gorée, the rocky offshore island from which captured slaves were transported off the African continent. During the half-hour journey I watched the island approach with a sense of dark irony. Sally and I had had a tough time finding a boat to West Africa, all right—but 150 years ago, securing passage from Latin America to Senegal would have been the easiest thing in the world.

Today Gorée is a tourist spot, its flowered paths and colonial architecture—once the property of wealthy slave-traders—preserved for posterity. The old *castel,* with its impenetrable ballustrades, has fallen to picnickers, drum makers and visiting marabouts, Islamic holy men. Half-naked children run through overgrown lots, hollering at the local dogs. Fish and chips are served by the landing.

I walked up a cobblestone street and found the thick wooden entrance to the Maison des Esclaves—the Slave House—built by the Portuguese in 1530 and renovated by the Dutch in 1776. Until it closed down in 1848, the Slave House was the last glimpse of Africa seen by countless men, women and children. The structure is now a museum, and guided tours are conducted around this black African Auschwitz.

"Slaves were sold by the ton—not by the man—and stored in these rooms until picked up by ships." Joseph N'Diaye, the stern, gray-haired *conservateur,* led me into one of the cold stone cells. I stooped in beneath the damp ceiling. The area was smaller than my kitchen. Small vents, through which excrement and vomit were hosed out, opened from the floor into the pounding sea.

"Two hundred people were kept in this room, sometimes for months at a time. The fact that these conditions were inhuman, *beyond* inhuman, bespoke their status as cargo, plain and simple. Though millions were transshipped from this place, we estimate that another six million died—from disease, infection, starvation, or drowning at sea."

Before leaving the Slave House, I stopped into N'Diaye's office. Hanging amid the shackles, branding irons and diagrams of ship-loading schemes—the slaves were packed into the hull head to foot, literally like sardines—were emotional statements by African Americans who had visited the monument. Witnesses included activist Angela Davis, then Democratic party chairman Ron Brown and actor Danny Glover. In the center hung a photograph of Nelson Mandela, who visited the Maison shortly after his own release from prison. His bowed head and agonized expression spoke more eloquently than any words, and I found myself moved to tears.

The most disturbing sight of all, though, was housed in the Musée Historique, a converted fort half a kilometer north of the ferry dock. Amid glass-encased relics of Senegalese history and independence, I found a large mural depicting the slave trade in action.

The painting revealed, without excuse or apology, a piece of history I had not known. It was the warring black Africans themselves who "harvested" this human bounty from rival tribes and kingdoms, selling their captives off to Arabian and European traders for handsome profits.

Later on, referring to an article on the slave trade written for *National Geographic,* I confirmed my observation. As many as 80 percent of the slaves were taken in tribal wars. The slave trade, a gold mine for the Europeans, Arabs and Americans, depended on black complicity to survive. There were very few black leaders indeed—with the heroic exception of a Sierra Leonean freedom fighter named Tomba—who tried to fight the tide.

Wet Wear

The 750-mile journey between the capital cities of Dakar, Senegal and Bamako, Mali, takes at least thirty hours. Travelers we'd met in Dakar had spoken of nightmarish delays and two-day passages, but we seemed to be running on schedule. We'd boarded from Dakar's rococo train station at ten in the morning, taking our assigned seats while an endless caravan of small-goods vendors squeezed by. It was a bazaar on the hoof; green bananas, kola nuts, plastic pails and cotton scarves were waved in front of our faces as we tried, without success, to make ourselves comfortable.

A man walked by with a wooden pallet full of pharmaceuticals: nasal spray, painkillers, remedies for the runs.

"They're probably selling this stuff because we're going to need it," observed Sally.

"That's a frightening thought."

One never says "no" to vendors in West Africa. To do so is to reject both the person and his or her livelihood, a cruel and demeaning insult. Instead one uses the phrase *la prochaine fois,* a French expression meaning "next time." This white lie conveys the idea that you've seen the offered goods, deeply admire them and are simply waiting for the most opportune moment to buy.

I stopped the medicine man and asked if he had anything for sleeping. He laughed heartily, clasped my hand and shook his head.

The most essential commodity, we soon learned, was the ubiquitous cotton scarf. February was the height of the harmattan—the annual West African dust storm—and within minutes of our departure from Dakar the train was immersed in huge pink clouds that swarmed through the ill-fitted windows. The dry Saharan breath steamed on our necks, infiltrated our food bags, powdered our hair. Restless children busied themselves in the surrounding seats, fishing boogers the size of trout from their nostrils.

The journey began with a holiday air. Our car was full of lively Bambaras, stately Wolofs and beautifully dressed women whose bodies moved fluidly under brilliant print gowns. Sally and I were ravenous, having skipped breakfast, and we raced against the clock by jumping off the train as it pulled into small village stations and sleuthing among the vendors—who descended on the train with baskets of everything from small sweet muffins to fried fish stacked on their heads—to find snacks that seemed tasty and safe.

I darted off in Kaolack and reboarded with two fresh, crisp baguettes and four eggs. Sally eyed them dubiously.

"Hard-boiled eggs are always safe," I reassured her.

"How do you know they're hard-boiled?"

I rolled my eyes. "Of course they're hard-boiled." I grabbed one from her and cracked it on the top of my head.

Half an hour later, braced against me in the waterless bathroom, she had managed to sponge about 80 percent of the gooey albumen off my neck and shoulders.

"Well," I said sheepishly, "they're *supposed* to be hard-boiled. . . ."

Dry Goods

The Dakar-Bamako Express rumbled on through a parched landscape scattered with thatched-hut villages. Everything seemed to be made of dirt and straw. Horse-drawn carts rolled down dirt roads, and bare-limbed baobabs rose from the earth like raw dendrites. Little black boys tended flocks of goats, waving wildly as we passed. Brilliant blue king-fishers perched regally in the trees. I stood by the open door of the train car, palm against a wall, watching Africa pass. When I looked down I saw a little girl with cornrowed braids and huge brown eyes watching me intensely. I returned her gaze, but she stared back unblinking.

The day passed. I read the *International Herald Tribune,* devouring every article, nudging Sally to tell her about the widespread support the Zapatistas had won among the farmers in Chiapas. I read of the agony in Sarajevo, the desperation in still-trembling LA, and of the new French francs, made of fiber, that shrunk if you washed them.

Dusk approached, marking the first evening of Ramadan. Many Muslims, commemorating the revelation of the Koran to their prophet, Mohammed, would soon begin their monthlong fast. Neither food nor water would pass their lips during the daylight hours, though the nights would bring banquets and celebrations. As the sun touched the horizon, a tall, elderly man with one cataracted eye made his way into the small oasis of space in front of the bathroom door and spread out his woven prayer mat. The sight made me think back on something that Sally had said a few hours earlier: "In Africa, the only thing that happens on time are the prayers."

The air was thick, toasted with a nutty flavor that filled the back of my throat. I stared out at the darkening landscape, free of expectation or anxiety, lost at last in the erotic rhythm of travel, the train rocking beneath me like a familiar lover, the pungent human smells unavoid-able, breathing the overbreathed air and drinking an orange Fanta. The train's horn, oddly musical, sounded through the trees like a bass kalimba.

And I asked myself: *Are you happy now? Jeff, are you happy now?* As if that self, that Jeff, were a separate identity, a fiercely obsessive and anx-ious personality that inserted itself between my moment-to-moment experiences of the world at large and my deeper contentment. As if Jeff and all his nicknames were no more than a snag in this gorgeous weave of unfolding landscape and presence, a Jack of Hearts lying facedown in the Anoma River, a pair of dark glasses to protect me from the sun.

Are you happy now? I inquired of this person who was so hard to please; of this compulsively self-critical person who got so pissed off at himself over a clumsily missed bus connection that he had wandered around the streets of Dakar dizzy with self-loathing. *Are you happy now, traveling like this, this rhythm under your feet, the smelly toilet a few steps away, a tubercular Muslim praying and coughing by your feet, dry Africa rolling by? Is this what it takes to make you happy?*

Yes. Yes, it was.

o   o   o

It was one of those nights when you don't sleep but things happen that make you feel you're dreaming anyway; dreaming, or caught in some Kafkaesque drama. The car was filled with crying children, loud people, cigarette smoke. We stopped frequently as we approached the Malian border. Our passports were collected around midnight; at two or so the train ground noisily to a halt, and several of my African neighbors shook me awake, explaining that Sally and I had to disembark, go to the police post and retrieve our documents. I staggered out bleary-eyed, my skin covered with dust, my voice a dry whisper.

It was an odd scene: stars overhead, thousands of people squatting over braziers in the dull half-light, the huge smoking trains, the constant overloud banter of Wolof and Bambara. "Market voices," Pierre had called them. It was true. The people of West Africa seemed incredibly loud and aggressive, regardless of the circumstances.

Around a corner, an official sat at a wooden table heaped with passports. He was surrounded by a semicircle of several hundred men (funny, it was all men, except for Sally and a few other foreigners) who pressed in on him as he called out names. Eerily, it felt almost like we were for sale; I got a nightmarish flash of Africa centuries back and tasted the barest hint of what it might have been like to be a commodity at a slave auction.

We had expected to wait at least an hour, but after five minutes I was tugged toward the table by a smiling African man. The official was jotting some lines in a big red ledger. My sudden escort held up a passport and showed me the picture. He addressed me in French.

"Do you know this man?"

I squinted. The man in the photo was young, healthy-looking, freshly shaved and alert, smiling unself-consciously into the camera. He might have been my son.

"*C'est moi,*" I admitted. And added in response to their disbelieving stares: "*Avant le train.*"

o   o   o

I awoke at precisely seven to the calls of a boy selling medicinal sticks called *sump*. Used especially during Ramadan, they recall the method by which Mohammed kept his teeth clean during his monthlong hejira in the desert.

The sun was a desiccated yolk over the horizon, risen some time before and now just barely visible through the harmattan haze. At Kalé I got off the train and bought a cup full of water from a little girl. She poured it slowly into my palms. I washed the dust off my face and neck and out of my stinging eyes, and looked at Mali.

• 12 •

Valentine's Day

The Mercedes-Benz bus from Bamako to Mopti was a half-blind dog, one headlamp gone, the rooftop luggage racks webbed with frayed hempen rope. Its red velour seats, side levers to the contrary notwithstanding, did not budge. The round plastic cap that had once covered the middle of the steering wheel was gone, and the shallow well overflowed with coins, screws, double-edged razor blades and kola nuts. Each of the fly windows was emblazoned with a stick-on decal of Madonna, blowing kisses to Allah.

We had elected to leave Bamako for Mopti immediately, rather than spend another night at the M/S Hotel, where our floor served as the subwoofer for the downstairs discotheque.

The market in Bamako had been wonderful, a kaleidoscope of mud-print textiles and balloon-tire bicycles, amber beads and silver beads and lapis and bone beads, beads made from gourds and shells and bark and clay. There were booths selling frankincense and myrrh, shelves packed with tiny bottles full of exotic scents, woven silk prayer mats, holy Korans, batiks and embroidery. I fell in love with the light: the way it dripped in through the faded awnings and the pieces of rag hung up to foil the fierce African sun; how it jittered off the half-century-old silver 20-franc coins and threw fish-eye patterns on the ceiling; the way it passed through colored bottles and glass beads and bolts of embroidered silk, reflecting off the blue turbans of the legendary "Men of the Desert."

It was among these narrow alleys of decals and fried fish, of color and smoke, that we ran into Shoshana, Kristen and Galandou.

Shoshana and Kristen were Peace Corps volunteers, halfway into their two-year tours of duty. Both were stationed in remote jungle villages in Guinea-Bissau, a tiny plug of a country squeezed between southern Senegal and Guinea. Shoshana, a tall, zaftig woman with thick glasses and muscular, unshaven legs, worked in a primary care clinic. She was coltish and shy, excited by the opportunity to engage with us but reluctant to part with the quiet self-reliance one gains after six months in the bush. Kristen was an English teacher, blond and fair-skinned and far more animated. She shared her village hut with Galandou, an agricultural adviser from Gambia. Their love affair was more awkward for him than for her, and though he didn't resist her public displays of affection, he was visibly aware of being the focus of incredulous attention among his fellow Africans.

American Peace Corps volunteers have got to be the most dedicated, effective and underpaid players in the multibillion-dollar foreign aid industry. Each receives a tiny living stipend, calculated to place them on a financial par with their usually impoverished host villagers. Back in the 1970s, a separate $125-a-month "readjustment allowance"—paid into a bank account back in the States and released at the conclusion of their tour—amounted to a handsome nest egg when they returned, culture-shocked and hosting any number of exotic parasites, to their native soil. Twenty years later, this monthly allowance has increased by only $75.

Volunteers remain in their isolated villages forty-nine weeks of the year. Kristen, Galandou and Shoshana had decided to take their twenty-four days of vacation together, in Mali. Once we arrived in the trans-Saharan town of Mopti—an overnight bus ride from Bamako—they'd drop their packs at the Peace Corps transit house, an unpresuming crash pad for visiting and local volunteers. Sally and I could join them there, space permitting.

As the bus bucked along pitted roads, Kristen and I found ourselves on the topic of interracial—and in her case cross-cultural—sex.

"African men are surprised," she said, "by how responsive western women are. I mean, we actually enjoy it."

"That's unusual?"

Kristen shrugged. "Well, it makes a difference, having a clitoris."

I was shocked, harboring the misconception that clitorectomy was limited to a few very primitive and secluded tribal areas. Not so, Kristen informed me. It's endemic throughout West Africa.

"Most Muslim women in Senegal, Mali, Guinea-Bissau and the Gambia have it done." She leaned back against Galandou, who seemed imperturbed by our conversation. "They claim it's Koranic law, but I think it's another one of those situations where Islam has been conveniently reinterpreted to jibe with local customs."

Shoshana, peeling an orange in the seat behind me, leaned into the aisle. "It still serves as the right of passage for almost all local women." She added cynically, "And unlike with the boys, who get circumcized when they're seven or eight, there's no princely ceremony for the two-year-old girls. They're totally traumatized by it. Also, there aren't any local health care workers coming in—like they do for the boys—to see that everyone is up-to-date on their tetanus shots."

Kristen and Shoshana ran through the scare tactics used to perpetuate clitorectomy. African women are taught to believe, for example, that without it their babies will not be able to emerge through the cervix successfully, or that if they do they will be retarded or deformed. Mostly, though, what keeps the practice going is peer pressure: an overarching need to conform and thus be accepted. In small villages, such pressure is virtually indomitable. It is the women themselves, Kristen had observed, who are the staunchest defenders of the practice.

"Tell them what happened to you," Shoshana urged. She handed around kidney-shaped wedges of fruit.

"Okay. Before Galandou and I were living together, I was staying in a room in this one family's hut. After I'd been there about four months, they asked me to be the namesake—godmother—of their daughter. Partly, really, it was a bullshit thing for them to do; it was totally untraditional, and we weren't even close, but it was mega high status for them to have a white namesake. And I couldn't refuse, really, since I was staying with them and didn't have an excuse.

"So I said yes, right? Well, two months later they inform me that it's time for their daughter's circumcision ceremony—and that the namesake is supposed to pay."

Sally's hand went up to her mouth; Kristen leaned forward. "As you can imagine, I went nuts. No way was I even going to be present to watch a little girl get her clitoris cut off, let alone *pay* for the ceremony. I was totally outraged and confused. So I had one friend in the village, and I asked her what to do. She said that if I refused, the entire family would be completely humiliated, that the girl would miss the ceremony, and that for the rest of her life she'd be a laughingstock and a scandal."

"So did you pay for it?"

Kristen nodded. "I had to. The alternative would have been to pack up and leave—which wouldn't have accomplished anything, except that my family would have been socially screwed and all my students would have been left out in the cold. I paid, and I was there while it happened."

"But it's different in different places, right?" Sally needed some reassurance. "I've heard that usually they just take the clitoris, and leave the labia minora and . . ."

Kristen preempted her. "There was nothing left but a hole."

"It's so fucking . . . *misguided*," Sally said. "You'd think that people with so much time on their hands—I mean, there are huge chunks of time when the villagers do virtually nothing—would prefer living in a society which cultivated sex, and sexual technique, as an enjoyable and creative way to pass those long hot afternoons."

"Forget it," Shoshana said. "In the societies where female circumcision is practiced, women don't participate in sex at all, at least not in the way we think of it. For the men it's a basic bodily function that needs to be relieved—like taking a leak. Wham, bam, and not even a 'thank you, ma'am.'"

We stopped for gas. A chorus line of hawkers infiltrated the bus selling gateaux and bananas. They piled on, singing their sales pitches and left in obedient silence as our driver reboarded. An hour or so later we pulled over again. A dozen elderly Muslim passengers filed out, spread their woven cane prayer mats on the dirty ground and faced east, away from the crescent moon. It was around 9:00 P.M.

I looked out the window at the tired village we had entered. Adobe buildings stood surrounded by sand and scrub, a few anemic buffalo, a broken-down Peugeot truck. Sally was right: Here was a place where people had nowhere else to go, nothing to do. They could be practicing Tantra and sexual yoga, becoming world-renowned masters of love. Instead they were snipping clits off little girls. People, I reflected, have an extraordinary capacity for self-inflicted suffering. I stared out the bus window at the Muslims, bare-kneed upon their thin mats on the rocky, unkind ground, and thought about our compact inflatable mattresses.

"You know," I mused, "Therm-a-Rest could make a real killing by producing self-inflating prayer mats. . . ."

"With pictures of Mecca printed on them," Sally added enthusiastically. "That is a *fantastic* idea."

"They'd sell in Africa, the Middle East, Iran, India, Indonesia . . ." The global marketability of the scheme overwhelmed me. "I tell you, as soon as we get back to the U.S., I'm going to ask the corporation for the African franchise. Within two years I'll be a millionaire—*guaranteed.*"

Shoshana leaned over the back of my seat. "And what will you do with the money?"

"I'll devote my life to eradicating female circumcision. I'll start a pro-sex movement instead. By the time I'm done there'll be a copy of the *Kama Sutra* in every village hut—right next to the Koran."

Kristen laughed. "Is that how you'd like to be remembered? As the man who brought Therm-a-Rest prayer mats to Islam and got rid of clitorectomies?"

"I can imagine no prouder epitaph."

"I'll be your partner," Sally volunteered. "I could use the money. And I could certainly get behind the cause. . . ."

o   o   o

We stopped in Sévou for a late-night dinner. When we got back on the bus I ate a few squares of waxy chocolate, moved into the adjoining seat and slept.

My rest was short-lived. At about 1:00 A.M. I was awakened by a cacophony of banging and clanking—the familiar tune of engine work. Calls for wrenches, in French, penetrated the stifling night air: *"Donnez-moi le 8.5 . . . non . . . c'est petit . . . donnez-moi le 9 . . . oui. . . ."*

We'd blown our clutch; the transmission lay in ruins. I slumped down, wondering if we'd move before daybreak. By two-fifteen, amazingly, we were on our way—only to coast to a stop again thirty minutes later. The hours until dawn witnessed an unending series of jarring mechanical breakdowns, followed by barked French orders and noisy scrambling under the hood.

But West Africa is not a land of complainers. It is the *Ça va bien* bardo, where everything is always all right, and never is heard a discouraging word. Whatever the trouble, it's handshakes and smiles all around.

"Ça va? Ça va bien?"

"Bon, bon!"

"Eko kah nee wah??"

"M'ba, m'ba!!"

Everything's fine? Everything's fine! Everything's always fine, even when it isn't fine. *Especially* when it isn't fine.

The Bardo of Bozos

Mopti gives the impression of having risen from the desert spontaneously, much like those Magic Crystals that, placed in fishbowls, grow into colorful, sharp protuberances. The difference is that in Mopti everything is colorless and essentially flat—apart from the Sudanese-style Grande Mosquée, a pointy-roofed, mud-brick oddity rising from the center of Old Town, across the swamp.

The heat was terrific. We arrived past noon and walked through the streets dogged by touts and begging children, our dust-covered back-packs leaving bands of sweat around our shoulders. Kristen, Shoshana and Galandou spoke fluent Fulani, and we were directed to a worn wooden stairway that climbed to the second floor of a building behind the open-air market. At the head of the stairs a patched screen door creaked open, admitting us into the transit house. It was comfortable and simple, with a kitchen, storeroom, shower, toilet and large dormitory. Fans whirred overhead, stirring the mosquito netting that hung above the beds like dirty bandages. We dropped our packs onto empty cots, took turns showering and napped.

In the late afternoon we rose from our mattresses and walked down to the banks of the Niger River. The sun showed its disk reluctantly, casting an almost shadowless light onto the long painted canoes snouting onto the Niger's eastern bank.

There was a market along the beach, the tent poles of the merchants anchored in the empty cylinders of engine blocks half-buried in the sand. Afro-pop blared from naked speaker cones nailed above bins of cassette tapes. Bowls and ladles shaped from gourds overflowed with clove necklaces, dried fish and roasted groundnuts. Salt sellers from the Sahara, down to the big city from Timbuktu, squatted near the breakwater wrapped in turbans. Their cargo, like tea or hashish, was sold in a variety of grades and configurations: raw chunks, round rods and thick, translucent sheets that looked exactly like unpolished slabs of Piraean marble.

On the far side of the Niger lay Kakalodaga, a settlement of grass huts inhabited by fishermen and villagers of the Bozo tribe. We decided to hire a dugout to take us onto the Niger; not to get to the other side, necessarily, but to have a closer look at river life and to pass the last, coolest hours of our long, hot day in comfort.

Finding a canoe was a cinch. The most infinitesimal show of interest in any commericial enterprise is met with immediate attention in Africa. The merest glance, the slightest turn of our heads toward the riverside, and we were instantly accosted by a boatman—or, if not a boatman himself, a self-appointed "agent."

Bargaining in Mali is quick and dirty. The agent began by demanding 3,000 francs but immediately agreed upon 2,000, finally hollering out "Okay, okay, fifteen hundred!" as we turned to walk away. We ultimately settled on 500 francs—$2 U.S.—for thirty minutes on the river. He led us toward a rather flimsy-looking dugout canoe, manned by a ten-year-old whose muscled forearms made Popeye look like Uriah Heep. The boy bent over the canoe, bailed out an alarming quantity of water and motioned us in.

The Niger was brown and very calm, and as soon as we left Mopti we felt as if we'd entered a world apart. Narrow boats loaded with local passengers and miscellaneous cargo plied the river, slicing across our path. On the far shore, the huts of the Bozo resembled weathered haystacks.

Despite our protests, our boat driver landed on the beach. I hopped off the skiff and wandered along through the small, poor village, nodding to the men squatting by their fishing tackle. They nodded back, amused. Naked boys ran along the shore, playing amid piles of garbage that consisted, as trash does in many undeveloped countries, of discarded water bottles, spent batteries and blue plastic bags.

I wondered if Sally was happy, if there was anything to interest her here. The very fact that we had reached this place at all was enough for me. It was thrilling to realize that an unbroken path connected my fourplex in Oakland with the Bozo shore. Oaxaca to Atitlán, New York to Dakar; all the points between my home and Mopti were physically linked, part of the same world. These people weren't just Bozos—they were my neighbors.

I found Sally by the waterfront. She was holding a naked boy by the ankles and spinning him around in a dizzying orbit. A circle of kids surrounded her, shrieking with glee and clamoring to be next as her bug-eyed victim, his arms extended like Superman's, plowed into the beach. As I approached Sally she fell on her ass, winded and sweating, a laughing white angel in the filthy sand.

o   o   o

By the time we crossed back to Mopti, angling into our berth after scooting beneath the prows of larger fishing boats, it was nearly dusk. The sun had virtually given up on the idea of providing light and shone glumly, like a nearly expired flashlight, on the whitewashed walls of Le Bozo Bar.

It is imperative to watch the sunset over the Niger River from the Bozo Bar; it says as much in the guidebooks. The five of us walked along the beach toward the restaurant's whitewashed patio, tailed by a local tout.

I mean no disrespect to the proud Bozo people but, speaking strictly from a western perspective, never was a bar more aptly named. The place was full of beefy, red-faced tourists, drinking, chain-smoking and snapping pictures of the endless procession of touts, guides and postcard sellers who buzzed about their heads.

A waiter brought Castel beers, and Galandou raised his glass.

"I am Galandou Ba," he announced solemnly, "and you are my brothers and sisters."

"We are brother and sister," Shoshana responded.

"To Shoshana Ba," Galandou toasted. "And Kristen Ba. To Jeffrey and Sally Ba. We are all Bas."

"We are all Bas," we repeated, touching our glasses to his.

I paid for another round. We drank them slowly as the sun evaporated into the haze.

o   o   o

We ate dinner at the Restaurant Sigui. The menu, like many menus in West Africa, included a puzzling repertoire of Southeast Asian dishes: *salade viet-namienne, riz viet-namien, rouleau printemps, poulet à la vermicelli* and *capitaine saigonnais*. I had yet to see a single Vietnamese in Senegal or Mali, and aside from radio broadcasts about the war—a good twenty years earlier—I could not imagine how word of that distant country, let alone its cuisine, ever reached Mopti.

The moon glowed low over the river. Lizards, scampering through the tree branches above, shat on our table. The food was bland, but we ate to the hypnotic musical accompaniment of Mamoukonake Daxo, a Bozo guitarist and harmonica player who knew all the local blues. I stayed at the Sigui and listened to him long after Sally and our friends had gone, sitting in the webbed lawn chair just to his right, buying him drinks, watching the crescent moon follow the sun into the all-consuming harmattan.

o   o   o

Mopti at dawn: the Old Town. I crossed the dike at about six-thirty and walked toward the Grande Mosquée, a fluted and almost windowless edifice that resembled an Addams family sandcastle. The sun hung above the band of dust on the horizon, rising above the simple mud-brick dwellings of the quarter, gaining brightness slowly. There was a sense of dusk rather than dawn in the air, but the illusion would fade within a few hours—when the roasting heat of mid-morning came into its own.

After an embarrassing faux pas at the mosque—I wandered blithely in, sandals on, and was promptly ejected by a furious mullah whom no amount of *ça-va-bien*-ing would calm—I left the main road and wandered into the maze of side streets. The lanes and houses were a monochrome beige. Goats stood tied alongside doorways; women pounded grain in stone mortars; blind men wearing knitted skullcaps sat with their canes by the sides of the road, collecting coins in smooth gourds or in the folds of their pale blue caftans.

At about eight I ran into Shoshana, who was leaving the Old Town after being blissfully lost for some hours. She cut a beautiful figure in her long skirt, and I longed to lead her away, remove her loose blouse and make love to her to the sounds of animals and children and stone against stone. We spoke briefly, but I continued on alone. I felt certain that here, as in Nepal, the solitary wanderer would inevitably encounter scenes and situations divinely tuned toward one's private conception of magic.

I found a group of five children playing drums on a street corner. The lead percussionist—a boy no older than eight—had engineered an amazing trap set. His drums were a collection of vegetable cans, the high-top cymbal a couple of broad tin lids joined by a nail. He was superb; adults were leaning out their windows up and down the narrow street to watch him play. Another boy sat on the curb, beating out an irresistible rhythm on an overturned plastic jerry can. The three others, younger still, danced and clapped, their bare feet stamping in the dust.

I stood there a long while and took some pictures. The children never broke their rhythm or concentration but played on, smiling yet dead serious, motivated by a deep sense of purpose.

o   o   o

We were close, tantalyzingly close, to Timbuktu, every traveler's idea of the edge of the galaxy. From August to December it's possible to catch a ferry to the famous oasis, but in February the river is too low. Since the overland route was reportedly under seige, our Peace Corps pals decided to fly there—an option Sally and I didn't have. We opted instead for a four-day excursion to Dogon country: a rocky region inhabited by animistic cliff-dwellers.

Two days later we stowed our Endless Journeys in the transit house, loaded a small amount of gear into our daypacks, and set off.

• 13 •

To: **Allen Noren, O'Reilly & Associates**
From: **Jeff Greenwald, West Africa**
Subject: **Big World/Dogon Country, Mali**

I type these words in Dakar, slurping a pineapple soda in the midafternoon. Anyone with any sense has closed up shop for the African siesta. I'm dead tired, have gone without any sleep for two nights. Got back to Senegal early this morning, after a total of eight days in Mali: an eye-opening but torturous side trip to a roasting, dusty land fraught with transportation nightmares. Every single vehicle we hired broke down, with the sole exception of a horse-drawn cart.

It seems like ages since my last dispatch. The African sun has a way of softening time like taffy. Events and obligations yawn into the distance, inscrutable as the dust-colored horizon, with no discernible beginning and no imaginable end.

We are here and it is now. Beyond that, all human knowledge is moonshine.

I can't remember who said that, but it certainly applies to life on this continent. West Africa is a land where the future can be generalized into two distinct epochs: *maintenant* and *demain. Maintenant* (right away in French) can mean any time from this instant until two or three days hence. *Demain,* tomorrow, means any time between two or three days from now and the eventual heat death of the sun.

But the western mind is a force to be reckoned with; it struggles out of this stupor like Superman crawling away from a pocketful of Kryptonite. And so, while the rest of greater Dakar is peacefully napping, I comb the streets on what may be a fool's errand, seeking a thread of the global electronic web that, when plucked, will vibrate all the way to California, carrying the pulses of this latest installment:

The Unbearable Lightness of Data

It's funny how *weightless* information is. I've been thinking about that a lot lately, as I carry my OmniBook around the world. I'm constantly amazed by the fact that cramming it with words—even big words like *circumambulation*—doesn't make it any heavier.

Or does it? Perhaps information, like time, becomes heavy in a relativistic sense. My notebook computer may weigh measurably more to an outside observer, for example, to whom this information is new, than to myself, whose thoughts, inspirations and peripatetic ejaculations have been downloaded into it, creating a kind of zero-sum balance.

I'll leave the hard science behind that theory to better minds. Suffice it to say that the less information weighs, the happier I am. You'd feel the same way if you'd carried your PC to Dogon country. . . .

The Dogon are a tribe of black Africans who, escaping Muslin oppression, fled to the Bandiagara cliffs of south-central Mali more than eleven centuries ago. They evicted the Telem—pygmylike hunter-gatherers who'd been there since Noah was in Pampers—and occupied their dwellings. It was those remarkable homes, virtually unchanged for nearly a millennium, that Sally and I had come to see: They are among the most fascinating sights of West Africa.

Built on precarious ledges along a high sandstone escarpment that runs for sixty miles across the parched Malian savanna, the Dogon villages are living versions of the abandoned American Indian settlements at Canyon de Chelly. A miracle of architecture, totally organic, the villages seem to grow out of the cliff like cubist mushrooms: stark, spontaneous habitations made of the exact stuff they're sitting on.

o　　　　o　　　　o

Dogon country is remote. Let me tell you how we got there: a train from Dakar to Bamako, the capital of Mali (thirty-five hours); a bus from Bamako to Mopti (sixteen hours); a bush taxi (a covered pickup truck with twenty-two people stuffed into the back) from Mopti to Bankas (six hours) and a horse-drawn cart from Bankas to Endee, the first village along the escarpment (two and a half hours). Maybe all that explains why, even though Dogon country is the most popular tourist attraction in Mali, it sees fewer than a thousand visitors a year.

Finding a guide was no problem. Back in Mopti, the Peace Corps volunteers had recommended a man named Elijah. No one called him this, however. His nom de plume, inspired by an uncanny resemblance, was Bill Cosby. There was a problem, though: Every other guide and tout in Mopti was now calling himself Bill Cosby. To solve this dilemma the PCVs had provided the "real" Bill Cosby—a twenty-one-year-old from Timbuktu—with a password. When we were introduced to the man, I duly requested the confirmation.

He leaned over, put a hand on my shoulder and sang into my ear:

> *"Hey, hey, we're the Monkees*
> *And people say we monkey around*
> *But we're too busy singing*
> *To put anybody down. "*

"You're hired," I replied.

Our bush taxi broke down in the scrubby Sahel desert halfway between Mopti and Bankas. While we waited in the sparse shade of a little tree we witnessed the worst sight one can expect to see in the Sahara: our car's engine being hoisted in its entirety from the hood by ten male pasengers, who set it on the spare tire and proceeded, bolt by bolt, to disassemble it. The situation seemed desperate, but Sally remained unperturbed.

"Thank God for *anitcha,"* she reminded me: impermanence. Sure enough, we were eventually able to flag down a pickup truck that took the three of us on to Bankas.

It was a flat, almost featureless town that seemed to be waiting for a second coat. We walked into an adobe-walled encampment as dusk fell. A cotton sheet had been hung between two volleyball net poles, and a kung fu movie blared at the evening star. After eating a dinner of chicken stew and Coca-Cola ("The astonishing availability of it!" as James Joyce once remarked of masturbation), we loaded our gear onto a mule-drawn cart and set off for Endee, fifteen kilometers away.

The crescent moon set in the west, grinning beneath the skid mark of the Milky Way, and baobab trees stood like giant ginger roots along the rough dirt track. The edge of the world loomed ahead of us, never more than a hundred meters away. As Sally and I chortled about how remote our location seemed, Bill switched on a transistor radio and pulled in a Moroccan rock 'n' roll station. It was an astonishing reminder that, even out in the middle of the Sahara, radio waves knit the air. Coca-Cola, kung fu movies and "Hotel California": These are ubiquitous in the twentieth century.

We passed a dark Sudanese mosque where dozens of Dogon Muslims in glowing djellabas intoned their Ramadan prayers beneath the moonlight. As we approached Endee, the ritual greetings began.

"Aamadjeri?"

"Poi . . ."

"Su . . ."

Bill directed us to the local chieftan's home, where we climbed a precarious stepladder, hewn out of a twisted tree trunk, to the roof. There, amid the sound of braying donkeys, crying babies, baaing goats and boasting roosters, we inflated our mattresses, wrapped ourselves in sheets and tried to sleep. But the wind came up, carrying fine red dust, the air chilled down, and we spent most of the night tossing and turning, waking up every half hour to look at the barely shifted stars.

At quarter to seven the sky turned orange. We rose in an isolated mud-walled village full of donkeys, guinea fowl, half-naked women and totally naked children chasing hoops through the dirt. Everything we owned, our skin and hair and pillows, was covered with powdery fine dust. Our eyes were cemented shut. My tongue felt like the thumb of a pitcher's mitt.

After a breakfast of Nescafé we packed up, presented the chief with a gift of kola nuts and set off for the next village. I did most of the walking alone, sweating, singing Elvis Costello songs to myself until the phenomenal cliff dwellings of Tele loomed in the cliff sides above the road.

o   o   o

The Dogon don't actually live in the cliff-hanging villages, as did the previous tenants. The reason is obvious: They'd whack their heads. The Telem were quasi-Pygmies, and their doors and ceilings are too low. The Dogon settlements, with their wells and livestock pens, lay below, a short walk from the base of the sheer cliffs. But the dizzy Telem villages are still in full-time use. Their straw-roofed huts are used for storing millet (the essential grain of the Dogon), and their squat apartments serve as the sequestered home of each village's elderly *hogon,* the local patriarch. This old man, selected by lottery, serves as a kind of medicine man and as a de facto godfather to the village boys.

After lunch, while Sally rested, I hiked up to the cliff dwellings above Tele with Bill. The granaries were empty, since it had been a poor year. Bill pointed out row upon row of bleached monkey skulls, recessed into the wall above the hogon's residence. The hogon himself, Bill explained, was absent; he had severe liver problems and was confined to the hospital in Bankas. I sympathized with the hogon—it must be terrible to be selected at random, removed from village life and forced to live out your "golden years" in a tiny hut on a high cliff ledge. Who could blame him for drinking?

The cliff dwellings provided a sweeping vista over the inhospitable terrain. Tele, molded from the desert itself, sprawled like a resilient virus below the cliff. Beyond it lay scrubby desert, hazy, with no discernible line between horizon and sky.

We descended to find Sally playing patty-cake with the local girls, who had caught on fast and were already defeating their teacher at her own game. I stopped short and focused my ears, trying to distinguish among the riot of village sounds. I heard the rhythmic pounding of millet; a child beating a tom-tom; at least three crying infants; a donkey braying; Dogon elders in conversation; Sally's patty-cake game; laughter; and, threading through it all, the eerie melodic wail of a wooden whistle. Tele felt like a living organism, complete and self-sufficient; remote, yet so familiarly *human* that I was momentarily unbalanced.

For a fleeting instant the world seemed of a single piece, with every individual distinctly and uniquely connected. Our sense of separation from each other, I realized, is only a function of relative distance. Someday—when we become aware of the thousands of other inhabited worlds—we will realize how much a village this planet of ours really is.

o   o   o

We swallowed some *chakalow*—millet beer—at the chief hunter's house and continued on, following the escarpment southwest to Kani-Kombole. We approached just before sunset, veering off the dirt track into an encampment not far from the village pump.

A guinea fowl was running around the compound when we arrived, but within minutes it lay dead, its neck broken, across the lap of an eight-year-old boy. As he plucked and butchered the bird, Bill and I lay flat on our backs on a straw mat beneath the sky. It was a cool evening. The moon was perfect, and ghostly rhythms seemed to emanate from the monolithic escarpment rising above us.

"Hey, Bill—have you ever seen the moon close up?"

"No, no. I never saw this thing."

I pulled my binoculars out of my daypack, focused them and handed them over to our guide. It took him a few minutes to adjust and bring the moon into view, but once he did he gasped.

"This . . . this is *awesome*," he whispered. It was not a word I had heard him use before.

For the next half hour I shared what little I knew of the moon: its creation, its effect on the tides and the six successful manned landing expeditions—all of them completed before Elijah was born—to its stark, lifeless surface. After a while Sally joined us, and we told him a few things about the stars. Bill Cosby, *né* Elijah, lay unmoving, binoculars pointed heavenward, exploring the craters and seas of the moon, the huge red eye of Betelgeuse, the myriad stars and dull fuzzy nebulae. He already knew the Milky Way—*la voie lactée*—but had not been aware that it was an edge-on view of our very own galaxy, hosting a million other suns.

We did not know how prepared Bill's neurons were to grasp the astrophysical basics we had taught him: "dark" matter, cosmic strings, the Big Bang. We did not know how much of our intelligence he would retain, or how much would be reshaped by his own imagination and expectations of what the universe should be. For the one thing we had learned, listening to his radio in the apparently empty wastes of the Sahel, was that information is weightless. It wriggles through the ether, a will-o'-the-wisp. And finally, when there is nothing to receive it, it simply evaporates.

Information evaporates . . . and mythology remains.

I write those words thinking specifically of the Dogon and their utterly astounding mythology—the informational roots of which have long ago dissipated into the ether (for no one knows, really, where the Dogon lived before they usurped the Bandiagara cliffs). The mystery behind Dogon cosmology is so compelling, in fact, that once I had read of it in *The Rough Guide to West Africa* I could think of little else.

The most elaborate celebration of the Dogon people is called the Sigui Festival. It is not an annual event; the feast takes place only once every fifty years. And the cycle of this celebration—according to ancient oral teachings, passed down through innumerable generations of Dogon—is precisely timed to match the orbital period of a specific heavenly body.

But it was neither the sun, moon nor any of the known planets that inspired the Dogon. Their ancients scheduled the Sigui Festival to coincide with the cycle of an "infinitely heavy" yet "invisible" star called Po Tolo, in orbit around the brilliant Dog Star, Sirius.

The ancient Dogon had no way of discovering, as an American astronomer did with a twenty-one-inch telescope in the 1860s, that there is indeed a star in orbit around Sirius. Nor did they have the means to determine that this star is a tiny white dwarf, more than fifty thousand times heavier than its neighbor. Nor could the Dogon have deduced, by any logic known to us, that the rotation of this "invisible" star—now listed as Sirius ß—is precisely 50.4 years.

⚡   ⚡   ⚡

· 14 ·

The Man Who Wired Africa

How long can saliva collect in the human mouth before it needs to be swallowed or spat?

I contemplated this riddle as a taxi chauffeured me to the Pan-African News Agency headquarters in Faan, a ritzy Dakar suburb where the ambassadors sleep. The driver leaned out the window at odd intervals to expel—with a characteristic *tsck* that I'd been hearing since the new moon nearly two weeks ago—his own forbidden spit. Devout Muslims are forbidden from eating or drinking during the month-long Ramadan fast, and one's own saliva is considered, strangely, water. People actually die of dehydration during the fast; a small price to pay, I supposed, for rebirth in Paradise.

o   o   o

Babacar Fall was a tall, intense man of forty-two with almond eyes and a wiry beard. Educated in Dakar, Montreal and the Sorbonne, he was fluent in six languages. A thickly flagged copy of Howard Rheingold's *Virtual Community,* sitting on his office table, confirmed my intuition that he'd be an interesting study for *Wired.*

The Pan-African News Agency, Fall explained, had been launched in 1979. Its mandate was to gather news at the local and continental levels and distribute it among African nations and throughout the world. "PANA filed its first dispatch in eighty-three," he said, "but the agency's success was short-lived. Political interference compromised its credibility, and the product could not be used."

In 1991, Senegal's state telecommunications utility shut down PANA for nonpayment of bills. That same year, Fall—then heading UNESCO's African Communication Projects office in Paris—was asked to lead a team of experts charged with developing the agency's recovery plan.

"Forty-eight of the fifty-two African nations now belong to PANA." Fall poured me a cup of tea and freshened his own. "But most of them are using radio receiving stations, which depend on the weather. Tropical storms and sandstorms can totally screw up transmission. Africa," he sighed, "has two weaknesses: the Equator and the Sahara. So we get both kinds of storms."

Bad phone lines were another problem bedeviling PANA in its attempt to become a credible media source. "It can take an entire *day* to reach another African country by phone," Fall explained. "And where good lines are available, the price is prohibitively expensive." Telecom in Africa is so bad, in fact, that some stations still rely on a time-tested dinosaur: the telegraph.

His solution envisioned linking the main news agencies in Africa through satellite systems—a move that would cut PANA's operating costs in half. "But to gather and collect information from all our African bureaus," he pointed out, "and to transmit them worldwide, we need a *two-way* link. We need the Internet."

Fall's dream of a wired Africa was realized—partially—when a Dakar-based French research company provided PANA with a basic Internet link. It was a start, but it wasn't enough.

"When you have news, it burns your hands. You've got to get it on-line very, very quickly. We want more than just a link; we want to be *the* electronic center for African media. We want to become an Internet node."

An expensive ambition, but Fall seemed certain that the agency's volume of news could support the expense. His convictions were echoed by PANA's marketing chief, who'd just returned from the United States. More than 300 black media sources and African-American support organizations in America and the Caribbean, he reported, were ready and waiting to buy PANA's output.

But Babacar Fall's personal vision had less to do with late-breaking news and World Cup scores than with the larger issue of African development. Aid projects on the continent have a history of expensive failure; the primary reason, Fall theorized, has been the dismal state of African communications.

"You can't treat people like cattle," he stated imperatively. "You have to communicate *with* them, not *at* them. For twenty years, the priorities in Africa have included agriculture, health and the environment. *Yes*. But none of these can succeed without communication. You can't develop agriculture if you can't contact farmers in rural areas. You can't improve health if people aren't informed about major epidemics like AIDS. You can't protect the environment if you can't communicate with the people who are placing it in danger! The industrial countries have spent billions of dollars here, trying to develop agriculture, change health conditions and fight problems like pollution and desertification. Nearly all of these programs have failed. Finally, we understand why: *There is no way to develop a country if the people cannot participate.*"

Fall peered into his empty teacup as if reading the leaves. Then he made what I considered a revolutionary declaration.

"In my opinion," he said, "the main obstacle to effective development has been the statement 'We have to feed the people first.' After all, who can withhold food? But if you want the people to feed themselves, you have to have a different view."

He gave me an appraising look and popped his toughest question. "Okay. Let's say you're a development agency. You go into a small village. People are hungry. Is the priority setting up an electronic mailbox . . . or airlifting in a hundred kilograms of corn?"

I said nothing. Fall nodded his head.

"What we have learned here, over the past twenty years, is that the electronic mailbox may well be the priority."

Stalking the Wild Juju

The Dakar Sally and I had returned to was utterly different from the one we had left only nine days before.

The harmattan was ending. Mornings were clear and deliciously cool. The ocean gleamed like a worn buffalo nickel outside our hotel window, tiny boats cleaving its surface like rusty X-acto blades. We breakfasted on croissants and caught a taxi to the Mauritanian consulate, located near the PANA offices in Faan. An hour later we exited through a grimy, mosquito-infested garage, the coveted visas indelibly stamped in our passports.

As we stepped onto the sidewalk, a man hailed us from the window of a silver sedan. This was Malang Dippa, our guide from Top Tours Senegal. We strolled up to meet him, astounded by his punctuality, and hopped into the car for our first full day of visiting traditional *juju* makers, herbalists and healers.

Our first stop was a street corner somewhere on the outskirts of Dakar. A few middle-aged men sat by the roadway on blue plastic tarpulins, surrounded by neat piles of jujus (or *gris-gris, mojos* or talismans, as you prefer) and the raw ingredients for making many, many more. These men, Malang explained, were *borro-borros*, Africa's traditional pharmacists.

Their pharmacopoeia was unnerving; the sort of stuff you might see if *The Silence of the Lambs* had been a *National Geographic* special. There were stacks of skins and hides, including iguana, beaver, monkey and crocodile. There were lizard heads, monkeys' paws, bird brains, goat jaws and any number of rat and other rodent skulls. I noted a bottle full of small teeth, a sheaf of porcupine quills, empty turtle shells, and a pile of hawk wings (not feathers, mind you, but whole wings). Malang picked up a hollow conical antelope horn and examined it closely.

"These horns are filled with medicines," he stated, "and tied about the waists of women as they deliver. They are then put around their baby's wrist, for protection."

A tall Fulani with a high forehead, Malang had been born in Senegal's southern Casmance region in 1954. Just four days my junior, he possessed a sharp intellect, a keen sense of humor and a profound, contagious respect for the powers of traditional medicine. He was also a devout Muslim, and fasted during the entire time we were together.

The jujus were simple but wonderfully aesthetic. Each held different ingredients, had a different shape and a unique purpose. *Nissi binno*, a cow's horn wrapped in a cloth sheath and decorated with small white cowrie shells, offered protection for one's living compound. Placed in a hole, it warded evil spirits away from children. There was the *numba*, a belt for protection against assault, and *taffo*—amulets worn by wrestlers to "bring down the adversary." *Sadji binno,* a goat horn wrapped in red cloth, was handy for attracting business.

Malang showed us purple and white packets for children's headaches and other colorful talismans assuring fame, success on school exams or invulnerability to gossip. My personal favorite was a multicolored firecracker-shaped lozenge with a tiny brush of hyena hair protruding like a fuse from the end.

"This is meant to be worn inside the waistband of a man's pants," Malang informed us. "The sole function of this talisman is to get people to like you."

"Dale Carnegie's secret," I quipped, "revealed at last."

"And if you light the fuse," Sally whispered, "it lets you sing like Michael Jackson."

Malang paid for a nissi binno and tucked it into his pocket. "All of these amulets contain secret words and passages from the Holy Koran. The borro-borro's tradition is a marriage of ancient animist practices and the more recent arrival of Islam."

"But how do they work?" asked Sally. "Are they medicinal, or a kind of portable 'spell'?"

"It is all in the mind," Malang nodded, hitching his shirt to reveal a round leather belt festooned with amulets. "It is always in the mind."

o   o   o

There is a customary method for obtaining jujus. One brings one's problems to the village marabout, or Islamic scholar/priest, who inscribes a passage from the Koran on a piece of paper. The marabout also lists the specific ingredients that must be sprinkled into the amulet. One then goes to a borro-borro to fill the prescription. The amulet(s) are finally brought to a *cordonnier,* and sewn into a durable leather sheath. Each leather has a different quality. Iguana brings good luck, red monkey hide assures fame and porcupine skin protects one from enemies.

Malang took us up a filthy alley to visit one of these cordonniers. A poor man with a beautiful smile (he looked like an African version of the Dalai Lama), the leatherworker had occupied the same tiny streetside stall for fourteen years.

"He is a wise man," Malang said reverently, "because he is old. But his knowledge is all coming from mouth to mouth. When this man dies . . . well, it will be like a great library in Europe burning down."

o   o   o

After a spicy dinner back in town, Sally and I bought cups of strawberry sorbet and wandered down Avenue Pompidou. An old griot leaned against a building, a weathered *kora* by his side. I asked him for a song. He attached a metal buzz rattle to the instrument's bridge and plucked away, his joyful ballad a surreal counterpoint to the evening traffic. An old woman selling cassava roots in a straw basket joined us. I gave her my strawberry sorbet and chewed a handful of Pepto-Bismol tablets as she danced on the sidewalk with the basket balanced on her head. It was disconcerting how out of place they looked—the griot and cassava seller—on the empty urban sidewalk of their own country.

Black Tongue Blues

I woke up the next morning with a black tongue: not the sort of thing one wanted to write home about. I managed to brush most of it clean, but the back portion—the part that makes you gag if you touch it— remained a matte jasper, as if I'd dreamed of Catherine Deneuve and spent a wild night sucking on her shoe.

It was an inauspicious start to our second day of visiting Dakar's traditional healers. I wondered, briefly, if any of the places or people we'd visited the previous afternoon were responsible, directly or indirectly, for the weird malaise.

To make matters worse, there were two faxes under our door. The first was from Wilderness Travel, in Berkeley. Due to expenses beyond their control, the expedition company informed me, they would be forced to raise the cost of my joining their Mount Kailas expedition— from zero to $3,500. Sally's share would be at least $4,000, an impossible sum. The sharp central focus of our trip, I realized, was rapidly blurring.

The second fax was from Matthew, my subtenant in Oakland. A letter had arrived from the Iranian embassy in Washington. My request for a visa to cross Iran—absolutely essential if I hoped to visit Turkey and reach Nepal in time for the Kailas expedition at all—had been denied.

"Called up and spoke to the guy in D.C.," Matt had added at the bottom of the official letter. *"He suggested you try again at the consulate in Istanbul."*

The morning was a low point for me, and my black tongue was an evident symptom. I seemed to be bottom feeding in general, coasting along the sulfur vents of a suboceanic depression.

I wanted to spend days on end sleeping. I wanted to spend the morning drinking coffee, eating onion bagels and reading newspaper stories about more courageous people. I wanted to be pulled back into the bedroom for a deep brunch. I wanted to shop in a place where the prices were fixed. I wanted . . .

I glanced once more at my tongue, located mercilessly at the front of my face, and went into the bathroom to gargle again—this time with Johnnie Walker Red. Take that, you fungal fuckers!

o   o   o

The highlights of Black Tongue Day were our intimate meetings with three very different spiritualists.

Our first encounter was with Younouss Koly, a marabout who lived in a compound in the nearby village of Thiès. We found him in his tiny meditation room, sitting on an elaborate prayer mat. He rose to greet us, a rosary in his hand. Dressed in an iridescent blue caftan with swirling white trim, Koly radiated inner calm. His unlined face was as beatific as a buddha's, and I felt a wave of well-being wash over me in his presence.

Marabouts like Koly may either inherit or earn their positions. Though healing techniques vary, most of them create magical potions by first writing words from the Koran onto oval-shaped wooden slates. After intoning various prayers they wash off the ink, pour the solution into a bottle and bathe their "patients" with it. The elixir can cure women of infertility, ease depression and erase criminal sentences.

"A single word of the Koran, dropped like medicine under a criminal's tongue, can be enough to make the jailers open the cell doors and set him free," Koly confirmed.

I was dubious. "I really don't see how that's possible."

Koly motioned to the corner containing his marabout paraphernalia. "If you can stay a moment, I will show you."

Malang, Sally and I sat on the prayer mat as Koly demonstrated his spell-brewing technique. After he had inscribed a prayer on his slate, doused it with purified water and funneled the liquid into a vial, he offered me a sip. No sooner had I swallowed the drops than a strange and inexplicable thing happened: For the first time in months, I felt absolutely relaxed. After sitting on the edge of Koly's small cot I slid off my sandals and, without preamble or permission, lay down for a nap.

When I opened my eyes some fifteen minutes later, Koly and Malang were standing together in the narrow doorway, whispering intently and holding hands. Sally was outside, laughing with the local children. I sat up, feeling rejuvenated and completely refreshed. Koly glanced at me across the dim room, his teeth gleaming like a Fruit-of-the-Loom T-shirt under black light. I approached him sheepishly.

"I wonder if I might ask you," I inquired of the marabout, "the secret of life?"

Koly threw back his head and laughed. "In Islam," he said, "the idea is to enjoy yourself. When you die, nothing is lost if you have lived well and enjoyed fine food, good clothes and dear friends."

"Is that all?"

"That is all."

It wasn't the Islam I knew from the headlines, but in an African context it made perfect sense. The Senegalese, blending the gospels of Jesus and Mohammed with their ancient tribal beliefs, had composed a spiritual dance mix as all-embracing as their music.

Though our meeting was brief, it touched me deeply. Malang, evidently, felt the same way. As we were preparing to leave he held Koly by the shoulders and peered into the marabout's eyes with supernatural intensity. "After one meeting with this man," he said with complete sincerity, "he has become my brother."

o   o   o

We drove toward our next encounter—a "future-telling woman"—while Sally grilled Malang about female circumcision.

"Yes, it is done here as well." Malang showed no squeamishness around the subject. "Nearly all women undergo this rite, when they are little girls."

Sally pressed on. "What I don't understand is why it's considered to be part of Islam. I can't believe that the Koran actually instructs men to cut off girls' sexual organs."

"No, not directly. But Islam, you see, is one of the first religions to truly acknowledge that the woman experiences sexual pleasure as intensely as the man. If certain parts are removed, it will deaden those sensations. Frankly, it is a method of limiting and controlling her sexual behavior. With the most sensitive sexual organ removed, she no longer feels the sexual drive while walking, crossing her legs or touching herself. Sex and any sexual feeling are then bound exclusively with marriage, so that the only man she will feel anything for is her husband. She will be faithful. When she makes love it will be only for love—with her husband."

"Is it true? Are circumcized women always faithful?"

"Sometimes not. They are sometimes very wild."

"I guess the theory needs some work." Sally fell back in the car seat, reluctant to cross the line that would make Malang—frank, generous Malang—the enemy.

The future teller was named N'Deye Sydibe. I had never seen a more charismatic human being. She rolled her eyes, whacked her knees, slapped her forehead and rocked backward, forward and from side to side as she kept up a running stream of banter. When she looked serious, the room fell silent; when she laughed, it was impossible to keep a straight face. She shook her twenty cowries, tossed them onto the black-and-white tiled linoleum floor of the bedroom and read in them my fate—the gist of which was that my mother loved me very much, but I should become a doctor.

"I'll be forty next month," I laughed. "A little late for all that now . . ."

"It is never too late," she solemnly declared, "to do what Allah has decreed for you."

o   o   o

Later that afternoon we reached the village of M'Bour and dropped in on Fat Seck, a well-known African priestess. Wizened and imposing, she was as close as we had come to seeing a witch doctor. Seck was attired in a beautiful purple gown, with blue rubber thongs on her feet. Her lower lip jutted out, and her hands were black as antique fire irons.

Every July, Fat Seck presides over the sacrifice of scores of animals (goats and bulls, mostly) to propitiate the various djins with whom she maintains professional relations. Performing these rites had gained her international acclaim; taped to the wall above her double bed was a color feature, clipped from Air Africa's in-flight magazine, describing Madame Seck and her dark talents.

After much debate with Malang—a transparent formality that ended when I agreed to make an extortionate "donation"—Seck led us into her "secret place." This was a backyard cluttered with clay pots, each of which was filled with sticks or bits of bark soaking in water. The solutions, used for dousing the faithful, were guaranteed to ward off evil and bring good fortune. ("They are also useful," Malang added, "when you are out of your mentality.") The oracle's explanation of how it all worked was a bit gnarly, but it seemed to us that Fat Seck was clearly a spiritual mercenary, capable of either lifting spells or inflicting them for an appropriate fee.

Seck's gifts to us were short, stout twigs made of porous wood. Sally and I were instructed to make wishes, then suck small mouthfuls of water through our sticks from out of a plastic tumbler.

Sally sipped first, wishing for peace and goodwill on Earth. I followed, soliciting good health, runaway literary success and a rapid reversal of my black tongue condition.

Fat Seck took my stick from me, sucked an impressive amount of water into her mouth and, without warning, spat it all over my face. As I sputtered and blinked, resisting the urge to wipe off the slobbery kiss, she performed the same messy rite upon Sally and Malang.

"You are now under my protection," she announced. *"Adieu!"*

o   o   o

Our final stop was Joal-Fadiout, a village along the Petite Coast, where we visited the spartan apartment shared by Malang and his family. We stayed for half an hour, looking through Malang's photo albums and helping his eldest son—a buck-naked six-year-old with disturbingly wise eyes—master his new bike. As Sally and I were preparing to leave, Malang disappeared into the bedroom and returned with two narrow leather juju belts. Each was inlaid with three small white cowrie shells, and closed around the waist with two eyelets and buttons.

"These belts are for removing obstacles that may lie in your path." He dangled them in front of us like dead garden snakes. "You wear them beneath your clothing. They will allow you to pass effortlessly across borders and will be especially useful in places where people would harass or injure you." He handed one to each of us.

"You wear them like this?" Sally had buttoned both loops.

Malang reached over and undid the top loop. "Normally you fasten the belt with only one button. Only if you are coming to a very difficult place, a place of special danger, must you close both."

It had been a big day for blessings. We'd need them; the next morning we would depart for St.-Louis, on Senegal's northern coast. From there we'd enter Mauritania and attempt the overland journey into Morocco—if we could find a vehicle that just happened to be crossing the twenty-six kilometers of minefields.

Our driver, whose name sounded like a mouthful of high-fiber breakfast cereal, drove us back to Dakar. Sally slept most of the way. I stared out the window at the dry fields full of bare baobab trees. Their gigantic trunks, I knew, store vast quantities of water; pollination of their flowers is accomplished by bats. But all I could think of was an illustration from *The Little Prince,* in which the hero's home asteroid—B612—is completely knuckleballed by three enormous baobabs.

I dozed off next to Sally, contemplating how simple my own life would be if I had a planet that small.

• 15 •

African Edges

The mango-yellow train left Dakar's art deco central station thirty minutes late, St.-Louis bound. We chugged east and then north, the carriage vibrating like a Harlem boom box beneath our seats.

Leaving Dakar, we again entered the "real" Africa: grain storage huts leaning in dry fields like clumsily woven baskets; women with plates of bread and fish balanced on their heads, their breasts swinging loosely beneath their boubous. Red and white radio towers rose into the parchment sky like swizzle sticks.

I was feeling, in the words of Malang, out of my mentality. Before leaving Dakar I'd stopped at a doctor's office, exhibiting my tongue. The medic had pored through a thick medical tome and slapped the covers shut with satisfaction. *"Voila,"* he'd exclaimed. "You are suffering from *langue noire."*

"Langue noire?"

"Black tongue."

I'd paid a small fortune for this diagnosis and left with a prescription for an arsenal of drugs—antifungals, antibiotics and antiworm medicines—which I'd bought at a pharmacy the morning of our departure. Whether it was my malady or the drugs themselves that were making me woozy I did not know, but the sensation wasn't entirely unpleasant.

To the west, not very far away, the ocean drew a noncommittal line along the horizon. Children on nearby hills waved for the sake of waving. Mule carts waited at the crossroads, their animals staring unblinking at the train. Everywhere, like a species of prolific and immortal tumbleweed, blue plastic bags fluttered amid the scrub.

The town of St.-Louis was the first French settlement in Africa. It was founded in 1659, one year before Dutch Boers settled in the continent's south. Until 1958, when Senegal and Mauritania separated, it was the capital of French West Africa. The "quaint and colorful" section of St.-Louis lies upon a narrow island joined to the mainland by the Pont Faidherbe, a five-hundred-meter-long bridge originally built to span the Danube.

We arrived after dark. Except for a few square blocks near the bridge, where crimson Coca-Cola signs tilted above overlit sandwich shops, the island appeared deserted. Three stray goats—the only living creatures in sight—rounded the corner where the St.-Louis Youth Hostel presented closed blue shutters to the town square. The scene reminded me power-fully of *Invasion of the Body Snatchers.*

It was an awful night. The bed seemed to be made of clay, and the poisonous medicines made me anxious yet dizzily tired. I awoke in a panic at seven, not knowing where on Earth I was. My heart sank when I remembered. Much as I'd longed to get going, to begin the journey to-ward Morocco, the process suddenly seemed interminable.

My spirits improved somewhat when I went into the bathroom to brush my teeth—my tongue had regained its former pink luster.

o   o   o

St.-Louis in the morning was the polar opposite of St.-Louis by night. Thousands of uniformed students poured over the bridge to school, and the roads were packed with horse-drawn carts and taxis. We bought warm pastries and walked toward the ocean, finding ourselves in a melee of boats and fishmongers. Fish heads lay piled on the sand in huge silver mounds. All along the beach, as far as the eye could see, brightly painted skiffs faced the waves. It took a lot of manpower to move these heavy boats into the waves, but they inevitably returned overflowing with fish. St.-Louis—and the entire African coast between northern Senegal and the border of Western Sahara—has one of the highest fish densities in the world, and it shows. The waterfront was a frantic piscine brokerage where the squirming produce was harvested, sold and spirited off to market on creaking carts.

I sat in a skiff and wrote postcards, surrounded by a feral children. Shortly before ten we regrouped at our hotel and packed up our bags.

"Are you wearing your ju-ju belt?" Sally tapped her waist. "No point in just one of us being protected . . ."

"Oops." I unlocked my backpack and fished around inside. "Thanks for reminding me."

o   o   o

By noon we were packed into an old Peugeot station wagon like pret-zel sticks and bound for Rosso, the crossover point on the Senegal-Mauritania border. Our vehicle—a bush taxi, in local lingo—reminded me of those crotchety elder statesmen you see on TV: It's impossible to imagine they were ever young.

Rosso has nothing to recommend it. It's an ugly, unfriendly bardo where cunning and persistent Moors hover like vultures, competing for the privilege of supplying Mauritanian currency. We converted $80 U.S.

in cash and all our remaining West African francs into *ouguiyas* and waited for the boat that would carry us across the Senegal River into Mauritania.

"Can you hold this?" Sally handed me a wad of tired bills. "I don't have any pockets."

A while later, as we squatted on the planks of the packed ferry, a Senegalese businessman told us the score: We'd been had. It is illegal to bring unofficially changed money into Mauritania. Our ouguiyas would be confiscated at the Mauritanian checkpoint. The money changers and customs officials were clearly in cahoots.

"What if we say we didn't change anything?" I asked.

The businessman shrugged. "They won't believe you."

Just so; no sooner had we crossed the Senegal River and filled out our currency declaration forms (lying, of course) than Sally was taken off to a small wooden shed by a plump female *douanière* to be strip-searched.

She called out to me as she was led away, "Button up!"

I waited my turn, dripping with sweat and wondering what the hell she'd meant. Not a moment too soon I understood. My juju belt! I hiked up my shirt and, fingers trembling, fastened the second loop. An instant later Sally emerged from her flossing.

The customs woman walked up, gave me the once-over and waved us through. Just that simple: We were free to go.

Mauritania quickly betrayed itself as a place where problems come fast and cheap, and a white face guarantees a steady supply. Minutes after the ouguiya fiasco, the donkey-cart driver who'd hauled us the hundred meters from the customs dock to the taxi stand tried to extort $20 for his services. I gave him two bucks. He tossed the money at me in a rage, seized my pack and began wrestling it back onto his cart. I grabbed his arm, he brandished his fist, and for a glorious moment it seemed we would come to blows. At that instant a lean, tight-chinned black man who had been hovering by the cold-drinks stand came to our rescue.

Djiallo Abdul Karim spoke fluent, sarcastic English. Dressed in black jeans and a Bob Marley T-shirt, he'd spent the entire day trying to find half a dozen other people who—despising, like himself, the public bus—would share a taxi to Nouakchott, the capital. His quest had by now become frantic, since it was already four o'clock and his night shift at the Regal Nouakchott Hotel began at eight. Djiallo saw in us, accurately, the answer to his prayers, and adopted the role of protector deity. He quickly silenced the donkey boy, and within fifteen minutes he, Sally and I—along with our person-size backpacks and four other paying passengers—had jammed into a rattletrap Peugeot station wagon and set off on the four-hour ride north.

Paradise of the Bas

The landscape changed abruptly as we entered Mauritania. Gone were Senegal's wishy-washy scrub growth and ambitious radio towers; gone the Air Afrique billboards and Jackie Gleason–shaped baobab trees. Instantly we were among dunes. On either side of the roadway the southwestern Sahara swelled up around us, white and caramel and rust, reaching toward the road with long fingers. A fine layer of salmon-colored sand danced upon the asphalt roadway like thin, raving clouds. Oddly close to the highway, bleached canvas nomads' tents stood poled upon the sandscape like peaks of white meringue, their sides opened to the wind. The few villages we saw looked awkward and out of place, their buildings so blandly rectangular that the settlements resembled trailer parks. Sand piled against their sides like snowdrifts.

Just after dark we slowed to a stop. The headlights of oncoming traffic illuminated two gigantic dromedaries, silhouetted on the highway like misplaced myths.

o o o

Zeno would have loved Mauritania. As one approaches one's destination—in our case, the capital city—the delay seems precisely engineered to illustrate his most famous paradox. Halfway from Rosso to Nouakchott there is a police post where everyone piles out of the car for an identity check. Halfway yet again, a customs inspection. Halfway again, another checkpost. Halfway again, another *douane*. During the last fifteen miles of the 120-mile road, checkpoints appear exponentially, and it seems that one will never arrive, will never be permitted to reach Nouakchott itself.

When one finally does arrive in Nouakchott one has the feeling that there is something uncannily odd, something indefinably strange about the city. Indeed there is, though it took me about ten minutes to put my finger on it.

There are no incandescent lights. None at all. Nouakchott was a city lit entirely by bars of candy-colored fluorescence: red, yellow, white, pink and green, all pulsing at fifty cycles per second, strobing against our retinas as the taxi whizzed by.

o o o

Djiallo invited us to return to his compound with him. "There's plenty of room," he insisted. "You can stay as long as you like."

I was dubious, convinced that we were being set up in a long-standing rip-off scheme. Sally, however, trusted Djiallo implicitly. What we shared was a dread of searching for accommodation in Nouakchott; Mauritania was shockingly expensive after Senegal and Mali, and even a fleabag hotel would be at least $60 a night. Dared we pass up the opportunity to be the esteemed guests of a local family, despite the remote possibility that we would end up being robbed, killed and dumped in a distant sand dune?

Dead tired, voraciously hungry and vaguely suspicious, we stumbled through a low door into Djiallo's walled compound. Once inside, we looked at each other in surprise. The open central area was filled with trees and flowering jasmine. Rayon print dresses hung on a line. Lights glowed in the surrounding rooms, and we heard the unmistakable refrain of a Bonnie Raitt song. Djiallo darted off through one of the side doors and returned with two of his family members: Yusef and Claire Ba. Yusef, a Senegal-born filmmaker, was tall to the point of being willowy, and black as the Batmobile. Claire, twenty-seven, was big-boned, baby-faced and lily-white.

Within ten minutes we were installed on giant cushions in a cozy living room, drinking bittersweet mint tea from tiny glass tulip cups and listening to their story.

Claire was from Maryland. She'd completed her two-year tour in the Peace Corps, married Yusef and moved into the large, shady compound in Nouakchott's Socim Quartier with his extended family, all within the past two weeks.

"Congratulations," Sally said. "I'd imagine it's pretty unusual for an American to marry a Senegalese. How'd your mum and dad react?"

"They don't know," Claire replied. Yusef laughed nervously. "My brothers don't even know. We're waiting for Yusef's visa to clear before making arrangements to fly home."

"You're going to show up without telling anyone?"

Claire looked at her husband and nodded. Neither was smiling. "I keep playing the scenario out in my head," she said. "What it's going to be like at the airport, when Yusef and I come walking out of the gate . . ."

Her family would be less than thrilled. Claire particularly feared the wrath of her grandfather, a heroic figure in her life but an incorrigible racist as well.

"He can't stand blacks," Claire said. "The one time I tried to debate the issue with him I ended up in tears."

Claire and Sally left for the kitchen, where the women of the compound were preparing a late dinner of mutton in peanut sauce. I sat with Yusef on the living room floor. He'd made some student films that got into festivals in Burkina Faso, but his career in that country ended when some soldiers burst into his room one night and bayoneted him in the shoulder. He had no idea why. At present he was producing so-called "aid industrials" about family planning. It paid the bills but wasn't satisfying work.

"What I really want is to act and direct." He turned his hands over a coal brazier; it was a cool night for Africa. "I'm hoping my fortunes will take a turn in the U.S.A."

"There's more opportunity there," I agreed. "But have you given any thought as to how you'll deal with Claire's family?"

"It's funny," Yusef replied. "Claire is so worried about them. But my own sense of intuition is very, very strong, and I have a very different vision of how things will be."

"How so?"

"I know that her grandfather and I are going to end up being great friends," he said. "The very best of friends. I just *know* it."

Going Up?

The next morning we accompanied Claire to the market, where we ran into a couple of German travelers. They had just come down from Morocco; the journey had taken them twelve days.

"But this is no difference for you," the one who spoke English informed us. "Going down, yes, you can make like this; but it is not permitted to go up. More than one month ago, during the Paris-Dakar relay, they are giving some permits. Very expensive, too. But now it is completely finished. They don't allow it. There are too many mines. . . ."

His friend said something to him in German; a brief discussion ensued. The English-speaker turned back to us.

"There was some British in town some days ago. They have a bus, and are also searching a permit to go this way. I ask him where they stay, and he says he don't know, maybe they already left. But if they are still here they must be camping at the beach. It is ten kilometers north of here. . . ."

o   o   o

We drove toward the beach in Yusef's Citroën, passing through a desert punctuated by enormous garbage mounds.

"How come you can come down but not go up?" Sally asked peevishly. "It doesn't make sense."

"There's a reason," Claire said. "The Moroccans have a fort right near the border of Western Sahara, on this side of the minefields. If you hook up with them in Morocco, they'll take you right to the Mauritanian border post. But the Mauritanians won't let anyone cross from this side because they don't provide escorts and can't risk an accident. They're terrified that the bad publicity would hurt tourism."

"But there isn't any tourism here."

"Not yet. But they are trying to develop it. Having a couple of tourists blown up on the border could nip things in the bud."

The situation along the West African coast was nasty and complex. Since 1976, when Western (formerly Spanish) Sahara was abandoned by Spain and divided between Mauritania and Morocco, the Algeria-based Polisario Front had fought a bitter guerrilla war for Saharan self-determination. Mauritania, which could ill afford the conflict, withdrew all claims to the territory in 1979. Morocco occupied the gap, and skirmishes with the indigenous rebels had continued unabated.

As we approached the campsite we knew we were in luck. A white and orange expedition vehicle was parked in the lot, its front door open. Claire pulled up alongside.

The bus belonged to Dragoman, an overland expedition company based in England. There were two drivers: a copper-haired, impish Australian named Greg and his dark, full-bearded British copilot, David. Greg and David had spent the past four months carrying five paying passengers on an arduous circuit through Africa. The final leg of the trip was meant to be Mauritania-Morocco, but the route was blocked by a dense hedge of red tape. At the moment the drivers were on their way into town to receive a phone call from Ali, a local entrepreneur who had guaranteed them, for the bargain price of £500, a water-tight border permit.

We drove Greg and David into Nouakchott. Recognizing the impossibility of our plight—Sally and I could never hope to get across the border on our own—they consented to help. If their permit came through, and if we could meet them in time, we were welcome to join the bus on its Saharan crossing.

"When do you suppose the permit will come through?" I asked.

"Dunno, mate." Greg shrugged. "Tomorrow, we hope. But guess what? *This is Africa.*"

By the time we dropped them off at a telephone center, we had hammered out an ambitious plan. Sally and I would leave Nouakchott the next day and head for Atar, a rugged and dramatic region slightly east of central Mauritania. We'd spend a few days there and meet the Dragoman bus at the Hotel Maghreb in Nouadhibou—the center of Mauritania's huge fishing industry—on Monday night or Tuesday.

"Sounds fine," Greg said. "Figure two more days here, and it'll take us another two days to drive up to Nouadhibou along the coast. There's no road, but we've got a spot-on guide. So Tuesday morning, yeah, sounds good. But I don't reckon we can 'ang around too much longer than that; once we've picked up the permit we'd best be on our way. You understand . . ."

"Thanks a million," Sally said. "You saved our bums."

"We don't 'ave the permit yet, love."

"Something will work out," Sally pronounced confidently. "See you next week."

David grinned. "Don't be late."

Starry Bardo

The taxi to Atar pulled off the road at a tiny, anonymous oasis. The surrounding desert was orange and flat, speared with narrow and anemic trees. Camels wandered by.

It was dusk. We had stopped for evening prayers. The men knelt on the bare orange sand, muttering invocations to Allah; a young mother sat on a woolen blanket, drinking milk from a cardboard container while nursing her infant daughter. A few meters away the resident soldier spread a prayer mat on the ground; his pistol was wrapped in a plastic bag.

I looked at the evening sky, disappointingly devoid of anything unusual. How come people like this were never kidnapped by flying saucers?

After prayers—followed by the traditional three cups of potent mint tea—we prepared to leave. I assumed my position in the middle bench seat of our stuffed Peugeot 504, my left arm draped around the shoulder of a diminutive gendarme, my right squeezed tightly against my side. The three female passengers—Sally and two Moorish women—sat behind.

We were two hours into what was reportedly an eight-hour drive to Atar. So far we'd made good time, following a nearly empty highway that, apart from the occasional pothole (and the more than occasional police check post), was surprisingly well maintained. So when our Moorish driver inexplicably spun the steering wheel hard to the left, bouncing us off the paved road and directly into the barren desert, Sally and I cast each other looks of ironic bemusement.

The Peugeot shuddered along at perilous speed for about five minutes, then dropped without warning into a soft, deep ditch. The tires whined helplessly. All six men piled out of the car to push. It took a dozen tries, sand blasting into our faces, but we finally freed the thing. Instead of continuing on, however, our driver returned to the oasis. The reason was soon apparent. A thin, whistling sound escaped from the right rear wheel; we had bent a rim.

There was a healthy spare on the rooftop rack, but this fact was mysteriously overlooked. Instead, the driver and two black conscripts, culled from the shanty oasis village, undertook to disassemble the wheel. The steady clang of hammers on steel rang through the night as Sally and I moved into a small hut where a number of bodies lay curled. We dozed a while—maybe forty-five minutes—before the driver was upon us, prodding my foot.

We clambered back into the car as Orion raised hell in the heavens above us. The driver took his place, started the engine, and off we went—smack into the desert again. There were no landmarks in sight, nor any moon to guide us. After ten minutes of blind driving the arguing in the front seat had gotten so loud that the driver stopped the car, killed the lights and leapt from the vehicle. The tiny gendarme, myself and the three other men jumped out as well.

The men stood in the open desert, pointing at the heavens and bickering about the stars. A minute or two later we piled back in the car and drove for another ten minutes. We stopped again. This time everyone spilled from the station wagon, furiously debating which constellation was which. Finally—the ultimate bad sign—they turned to me.

I was eager to help, but recognized none of the Arabic names they fed me. The only thing I could do was find the Big Dipper and Ursa Major, and scoot down the pointer stars to Polaris.

"That's north," I announced confidently. "And there's south, east and west. *Oui? Nord, sud, est, ouest. Bon?* North, south, east, west."

The Moors turned away from me and continued to argue, their blue djellabas fluttering in the wind. At last they took their long faces back into the car.

We drove for exactly eight more minutes, crossing numerous tire tracks in the hard-packed sand, and emerged onto a broad, dry plain that seemed to stretch infinitely in all directions. The driver zigzagged haphazardly across it, harangued in the local language by his peers and in English by myself.

When we stopped the third time, no one looked at the sky. The gendarme took my arm and quietly led me off a few meters from the other disembarking passengers.

"Is there a problem?" I whispered.

"No," he replied softly.

"Are we lost?" I asked.

"Yes, we are lost," he said.

"That is a problem," I said.

"We are lost, but there is no problem," he said.

"This is the Sahara," I said. "We are lost in the Sahara. That is a problem."

"We are lost, and this is the Sahara, but there is no problem," he said.

I looked around at the empty landscape, the abused Peugeot, the useless driver. The passengers were unloading bruised suitcases and Chinese-made blankets from the luggage rack and trunk.

"We will sleep here?" I asked.

"We will sleep here," he said.

It was an otherwise lovely night. We inflated our mattresses and laid them down over our shawls, creating a windbreak with our packs. Within ten minutes we were gratefully on our backs, staring at the unfiltered stars. Twenty meters away, near the Peugeot, an old man muttered rhythmically while the driver clanged about. Sound carried amazingly well; we could hear the sweep of the occasional car as it passed by on the paved road, however distant it might be.

The wind died down, and we slept.

The waxing moon was low in the western sky when a foot nudged me awake.

"*On y va.*"

I roused Sally, who was weak with stomach cramps, and we packed up our things.

It was five-thirty in the morning. My only hope was that last night's road sounds—coming from the northwest—had reached our driver. With any luck he'd find the highway quickly, and stick with it from that point on.

We never did find the road. The driver continued on through the desert. By dawn, when we stopped for the morning prayer, we were on a sketchy tire track weaving spastically through the deep desert. Once in a while we saw signs of habitation—nomad tents gripping the harsh landscape like white fungi, or camels nodding among the bushes—but mostly it was empty. Empty, empty, empty.

"I propose," Sally said, "that we gather together every single negative aspect of our personalities, and leave them right here in this bardo. Agreed?"

I laughed merrily, but stopped as I entertained a fearsome thought: *My birthday was the day after tomorrow. I would turn forty in this godforsaken desert.*

• 16 •

How I Spent My Fortieth Birthday

I woke up on the moon.

To my huge credit, the first words I uttered to myself on the morning of March 6 were not "I'm too old for this"—although I was. Everyone is. Mauritania is an extraordinary hell-realm, a land of unimaginable inefficiency and bullheadedness, and how we ended up in the lunar wastes of Mare Imbrium on that long-awaited day is a story almost too painful to recall.

We'd arrived in Atar at noon, nineteen hours after leaving Nouakchott, and immediately encountered two French men named Giles and Henri. They suggested that we join them on a brief expedition to Chinguetti, a lush, medieval oasis full of camels, nomads and ancient sandstone mosques. It sounded absolutely perfect. Back when I was sixteen and working as an usher in the now-defunct Plainview Theater, I had watched *Lawrence of Arabia* forty-seven times; I never got tired of it, and the musical vistas of rolling dunes and Technicolor sunsets had served as my original inspiration for a life of travel.

Chinguetti was only a two-hour drive—albeit on rough desert roads—but the Frenchmen had been in Atar all day and had not found a single vehicle.

"We wanted to go to Chinguetti yesterday evening," Giles said. "Everyone said, 'No problem.' But there were not enough people for the taxi. So they said, 'You come tomorrow morning, no problem.' But there is no car this morning also. Now they say to try again at four. So we wait. What to do? It is always 'No problem, no problem.' But there are no taxis."

o   o   o

The Land-Rover left for Chinguetti at 6:00 P.M. It seemed a blessing and a miracle to have found a vehicle at all, and though Sal and I had our doubts about the condition of the car, we decided to go for it. Wasn't that, after all, what this journey was all about? Risk! Taking chances!

During the first third of the trip we climbed through a brutal iron landscape of massive flat-topped mountains, grinding at slow walking speed up a boulder-strewn grade. We passed among gigantic looming buttes the color of mahogany, dust-covered furniture under a powder sky. Loose overhangs leaned above us; the evidence of recent avalanches covered the road. The sun was not strong, but it was strong enough to illuminate the buttes in a dull amber light, as if seen through ten feet of honey.

We stopped at the crest of a pass where a development project of some sort had its local base. Broken, rusted machinery languished in a huge yard; another yard, penned, was full of goats. Our driver and two other passengers spread out mats for their evening prayers.

When we set off again it was dark. The road was covered with those inexplicable undulating ripple marks that happen in the sand. The driver took them at speed, and we were thrown around in the rear of the Rover like guinea fowl at a sumo wrestling match. I was shifting around on the backpacks and jerry cans and cardboard, trying to get comfortable and not succeeding very well, when there was a terrifying explosion, followed by an angry hissing sound. The right rear tire had blown.

It was not your basic puncture. The entire inner tube was split for a length of fifteen inches, a razor-sharp cut completely beyond the dreamiest ambitions of the tiny bicycle tire repair kit that the driver had thought to pack along. There was no choice but to fix it, however; we carried no spare.

For the next two hours the driver, his two young wards, Giles, Henri, Sally and I dedicated every ounce of equipment and ingenuity we had to fixing the flat. A thick strand of green nylon was unraveled from a shopping bag and threaded through a large needle, and the split was sewn up. Giles cut a large rubber patch from the tire liner and painstakingly sanded it to a rough tooth, along with the entire section around the crudely stitched wound. Finally, every last drop of cement from the bicycle tire repair kit was squeezed onto the two pieces of rubber. After a five-minute wait for the adhesive to set they were joined. The driver pounded the patch into place with a crude steel mallet.

This was the moment of truth. The tube was loaded back into the tire, and the tire returned to the rim by a kid using his bare feet and two rusted tire irons. A hand pump was excavated from beneath the driver's seat.

With the first plunge, the pump fell to pieces.

Another hour was spent fixing the pump. By this time it was 11:00 P.M. Finally, incredibly, the pump was repaired, the tire inflated and installed, and our baggage reloaded. We climbed on, gripping the narrow steel roll bars. The engine engaged; we were off.

Thirty seconds or twenty meters later—I can't remember which came first—the tire burst again. This seemed like the final word. Sally, Giles and I took our gear out, cleared a spot in the nearby desert and prepared camp.

A word about the desert. I'd always imagined the deep Sahara as sand dunes and camels, mirages, the occasional oasis. This is sometimes true, but I suspect that most of the Sahara is just as we found it along the Atar-Chinguetti road: harsh, ancient and rocky ground, baked to the consistency of burnt pizza. There were no soft dunes upon which to lay our bags, only plains of sharp-edged stones separated by mangy shrubs. But our air mattresses earned their keep, and I fell into a welcome sleep.

Fifteen minutes or so later we woke to the wheeze of the pump and suspected the worst. Indeed, a representative from our friendly neighborhood transportation company was soon at our feet, coaxing us into action. We packed up our gear—no easy task for Sally or me, carrying miniature Motel 6's on our backs—and groggily, reluctantly, boarded the Rover again.

Again, the tire blew. I lost my temper.

"*C'est permité, nous coucher ici?*" I snapped in clumsy French. The driver nodded that it was. Unfortunately, our new acre of desert—not a quarter kilometer from the last—was even less inviting. It took me forever to fall asleep, and minutes after I did, I was awakened again, by a cold, aggressive wind that flew down from the north and filled my ears and mouth with fine sand.

Occasionally I would look up at the stars and marvel at how perfect everything would be if I had *planned* to be in this situation. How delightful it would be to camp out in the Sahara, secure in the knowledge that the owners of our vehicle, accustomed to plying one of the most remote and undeveloped roads on Earth, had invested in a spare tire. Instead, the grim reality of our situation emerged: We would probably not be able to move in the morning, and the fact that there was a big Ramadan celebration under way in Chinguetti nixed the hope that any other vehicles would take this route. We could be marooned for days, missing both my intended birthday celebration in Chinguetti and our overland bus connection in Nouadhibou.

Dawn arrived eventually. My neck felt like a twisted clothespin, and a cold, sandy wind was whipping down the back of my bag.

There was some activity around the Rover; I heard the familiar clink of tire irons. Fools. I peered off to the left: plain, flat desert. To the right: plain, flat desert. Everything in my entire life, I understood, had conspired to bring me to this precise moment: stranded in the Sahara on my fortieth birthday, surrounded by sand, stones and an utterly useless vehicle. I moaned deeply and rolled over onto my stomach.

My bleary eye met Sally's, crusted with sleep and sand beneath matted chestnut hair.

"You can sleep in if you want to," she said brightly. "It's your birthday."

o   o   o

At ten-thirty in the morning the pit crew signaled us to leave again. They had moved the bad wheel to the right front position, figuring we could drive on it if we maintained a creeping speed. We made a few kilometers, hobbling, before the tire slithered off its rim. For the fourth time the boy removed the wheel from its hub. This time he tried a brilliant new tactic. He unloaded three sheets of corrugated cardboard from the truck bed, rolled them up as tightly as he could and stuffed them into the Michelin. Thus, with paper instead of air inflating our tire, we began to move again. We proceeded, limping through the desert, for another ten minutes.

During our fifth stop in the seventeenth hour of our two-hour voyage to Chinguetti, a vehicle approached from the east. I flagged it down. It was a white Toyota pickup with two sacks of onions in the bed. After explaining our plight with frantic hand gestures, we were signaled to throw our baggage in. We did so with haste as Giles spoke with the Toyota driver.

"We will try to go on," Giles explained. "This man says it is easy to get back from Chinguetti. There are taxis to Atar at six in the morning. He says it is no problem. . . ."

We'd heard that line before. Sally and I looked at each other, jumped into the pickup truck and sped back to Atar, leaving the Frenchmen behind.

o   o   o

Over lunch in Atar I whined and moaned, cursing the fates that had compelled us to spend my fortieth birthday in a flyblown restaurant. Rather than wandering among sand dunes, performing a tribute to T. E. Lawrence, we had been crushed, defeated, abandoned by the powers that be.

"Be that hard on yourself if it satisfies you," Sally snapped in annoyance, "but don't include me in your equation."

As ever, she saw things differently. The event, she insisted, was hardly a personal vendetta on the part of God or karma. It was simply as it was, and that was exactly how it was meant to be.

But even she had to admit that the guardian angels who usually guided our footsteps seemed to be on sabbatical. Mauritania felt empty, unprotected, lacking any redeeming spiritual value. It wasn't a big surprise. What business did we have in a country where—despite a law passed in July 1980 outlawing the practice—people still kept slaves?

o   o   o

There was, at last, a gift. Crossing the desert from Atar to Choum in a Peugeot wagon with a sacrificial ram crowded into the back, we crested a high pass and descended into a fantastic landscape that stretched below us as far as the eye could see, umber and orange, rust and sienna, all the holy earth colors cracking beneath a crimson volcanic sky. For a single priceless moment—one eye-blink confluence of scenery as our taxi churned past—the sky turned fluorescent pink above the mountainous copper land, and the yawning foreground was scattered with blue granite boulders that diffracted the vivid dusk like diamonds.

That was my moment. That was my birthday gift from God.

o   o   o

Choum was a desolate outpost bisected by silver tracks that disappeared on one side toward the enormous buttes in the east and on the other toward a distant coast that faced, impossibly, Miami. It was exactly the kind of scenery one would expect to see in a film about an ill-fated garrison of the French Foreign Legion.

Sally checked us into the only "hotel" in town: an open shelter with a rag-and-web roof and one stuffy, semiprivate room in back. The Berber woman who managed the inn lounged on the floor mats while her slaves played a cribbagelike game on a board made from sand. Sally and I drank bitter tea, followed by big plates of couscous. We made effortful but lively conversation with Sahimed, a Moorish trader and slave owner who had arrived with us in the taxi from Atar. His eyes were all over Sally, who could not resist the scandalous temptation to run her hand over his soft-stubbled scalp.

We slept well in our small, hot room and rose early for a look around. I could make out a line of orange dunes in the distance and immediately wanted to visit them—the better to play out my unrequited *Lawrence* fantasy—so we set off in their general direction. As we passed through town we were approached by villagers, who invited us into their shops for tea. We finally succumbed, entering a small dry goods shop full of mothers and children and flies, amazed by how tragically beautiful the little girls were. One, eleven or twelve, looked like an olive-skinned Mariel Hemingway, and it depressed us terribly to realize that this poor beauty, already sexually mutilated, would probably spend her entire life in this stultifying place.

Any hope we still nursed of visiting the dunes evaporated when we met Mohammed, a medic stationed at the military encampment on the outskirts of town. We ran into him in a carcass-strewn field that lay between the village and the barracks—the place, he explained, where animals were butchered. It was a testimony to the ugliness of Choum that the town had neither bathrooms nor butcheries. The entire south end of the village was a vast open-air toilet, while the north side was this desiccated boneyard.

The dunes, Mohammed told us, were more than ten miles away. "Better not to go there," he advised. "The whole region beyond Choum is heavily mined."

He invited us to visit his clinic instead. We agreed, following him toward a building surrounded by small heaps of sand. As we approached the entrance we saw that the mounds were actually toxic waste dumps of a sort. Each one bristled with used syringes, their bright steel needles poking haphazardly toward the sky. Spent vials from cholera and typhoid vaccines littered the area, glinting between the occasional flag of a bloodstained bandage. The clinic itself consisted of three dark, dingy rooms: one containing a desk, another a folded-up army cot and grime-encrusted sink, the third a locked metal ammunition trunk full of expired pharmaceuticals. We sat patiently by the desk as Mohammed pulled out an inflatable arm collar and took our blood pressure. Mine was a bit high; he advised I eat more meat and try to get a little exercise.

Some places you just click with; there's something about the people, the culture, that sweeps you in and invites you to stay, shift gears, try on another life. Everything about our experience in Mauritania was exactly the opposite. We left the barren clinic, returned to our "hotel" for a simple lunch of macaroni with sliced beets and lay on our backs with scarves covering our faces to wait four hours for the train to Nouadhibou.

Despite the filth and sadness of Choum, there was something about our inn that we liked. It seemed authentic, and the proprietress was friendly. As we lay down to rest through the hot afternoon I watched one of her slaves iron the laundry. A powerfully built black man with bare, callused feet, he filled his mouth with water from the spout of an aluminum teapot and blew it onto the broad white djellabas with the high-pressure hiss of a steam iron.

The sight amazed me. It was staggering to witness, first hand, that there were still people on this planet who would never experience a fraction of the freedom and self-determination that Sally and I so blithely accepted as our due. More than two centuries ago, I realized, men like Jefferson, Madison, Adams and Franklin—some of them slaveholders themselves—had created a framework for political change, a constitution so advanced that its tenets came to serve as the basis for nearly every democracy on Earth. My admiration for America—that brave, crazy experiment with all its polarities, hypocrisies and loopholes—was as broad as the boundless sea.

After our nap I walked to the tiny station and reserved two seats on the train to the coast. At quarter to five we slipped on our backpacks and prepared to pay our host for lunch and say farewell.

She demanded 1,000 ouguiyas—$10 each—for the macaroni lunch.

We refused to pay. The previous night's dinner, a full plate of couscous and vegetables, had cost a quarter of that amount. Aware that we were being fleeced, I agreed to shell out an extra hundred for the beets. The innkeeper shook her head, a handful of the local men rose to their feet, and our backstroke through the limpid pool of conviviality became a frantic dog paddle through a piranha tank.

We argued loudly with the woman and her goons until a tall Berber in a blinding white djellaba faced me down. The man bore a striking resemblance to Arsenio Hall, minus the shit-eating grin.

He spoke in French, addressing me in the sour, commanding tone we had heard so often in this greedy country.

"This is Mauritania," he announced.

"You're kidding," I replied. "The sign on the bus said Aspen. . . ."

"*Ecoutez.* You will pay whatever she asks. Even if she asks for a thousand ouguiyas, a million ouguiyas, you will pay. Or else you will speak directly with our police. In Mauritania you ask the price before you buy—or you pay the price we ask."

Lacking an automatic weapon, I reached for my wallet. Arsenio stepped aside. I handed the woman the money and thanked her graciously. We turned and walked away, sad to have left Choum on such an ugly note. Sad to be in a place where we ourselves became such ugly people.

o   o   o

The train was a mile long. Four engines and 250 freight cars passed the platform before the enormous millipede ground to a halt.

A single passenger car was attached to the rear of the train, right before the caboose. We climbed the steep metal stairs and pulled ourselves aboard.

Up until 1976 the passenger car had led a very different life, as a first-class coach on the French railway system. A map of Bordeaux was still tacked up, miraculously undestroyed, outside the festering loo.

The map was all that remained of the car's former glory. The seats had been torn out, the overhead lights smashed, and every single fixture, including the baggage racks, looted. The broad windows, which once admitted views of Paris and Provence, had been sealed with sheet metal. Bars of light passed in through tiny rectangular portholes, illuminating a human zoo: Dozens of Mauritanians lounged on the bare floor, surrounded by canister stoves and piles of luggage. The air was thick with smoke and the stench of urine. At one end of the car, a cramped kitchen served as a breeding ground for flies, while at the other a locked door isolated the single *couchette* from the masses.

Every square inch of floor space was covered. There was no room for us to sit, let alone lie down through the long night ahead. We stood there in confusion and horror with our packs on our backs, waiting for something to happen. Nothing did. I left the car and approached the station master.

"I was told at the ticket office," I said, "that there are four beds on this car."

He eyed me suspiciously. "Your ticket," he demanded. I handed it over. He looked at it, then back at me. "A thousand ouguiyas more," he announced. "Per person, per bed." I paid without hesitation. He made a note on my ticket. "Wait."

We waited, squeezed into the narrow corridor separating the main compartment from the reeking toilet, until the station master appeared with a key. He slid it into the door of the sleeping compartment and threw the bolt.

The beds were arranged in two double bunks. Another passenger was already in the compartment; he stood up to greet us.

"We can share, no problem!" He laughed loudly, clapping me on the shoulder.

He was a lean and well-dressed Berber, attired in a sports jacket and narrow blue tie. Something about him looked oddly familiar.

"Jeff," Sally whispered, "isn't that the same guy who . . ."

"No, no, no. That guy was wearing a djellaba, and anyway, he couldn't have gotten into the train without our seeing him . . ."

But the longer I surveyed him, the less doubt remained in my mind. Finally I looked him in the eye. "Pardon me," I said, "but aren't you the man we just argued with at the inn?"

He lifted his eyebrows in a perfect Arsenio Hall parody, nodded, threw back his head and roared. Then he raised his right hand high and slapped me five.

"Come in, come in!" He tugged at my sleeve. I didn't budge, but he pulled harder. "Come in! No problem! I am Ibrahim. Would you care for some tea?"

o   o   o

The train left Choum and rolled into the loveliest desert we'd ever seen: Round iron domes a hundred feet high bulged out of the naked ground, and golden *bachat* dunes—named for their resemblance to horns—leaned into the wind. I pressed through the foot-square window of the sleeping compartment with my camera focused on infinity, snapping pictures haphazardly, trying to capture some memory of the fleeting landscape as the sun dropped like a high fly ball into the Earth's seasoned mitt.

We drank mint tea with the man I was ready to murder only an hour before.

Ibrahim was a marabout, but what kind of marabout he was I never figured out. Marabouts teach the Koran and prepare blessings; Ibrahim did magic tricks. They were straight sleight of hand, but in the candlelit train compartment, rattling through the open desert, they had a miraculous, paranormal feel. Ouguiyas disappeared from his palm, materializing in Sally's brassiere; freshly baked baguettes emerged from between his palms; bank notes appeared under my arm; handfuls of vegetables dropped from thin air into our hands.

Where he learned these tricks he didn't say. His grandfather, he claimed, was also a marabout and had instructed him. I personally suspected that this grandfather had served in some capacity with the French Foreign Legion and had somehow won the friendship of an experienced conjurer. Our bunkmate was good; good enough to have Sally giggling wildly, and good enough to convince me that people, at least in Mauritania, are as unpredictable as the desert wind.

Ibrahim sang to us in the small compartment—Arabic ballads full of languor and emotion, delivered to a slow beat he kept on his knee. When he insisted that Sally follow him she quickly deferred.

"I'm tone-deaf," she explained. "And 'Tie Me Kangaroo Down, Sport' doesn't seem appropriate to the occasion . . . Come on, Jeff, you must know something." But the few devotional songs I did know—by Leonard Cohen, mostly—were far too monotonous to be interesting.

So I sang "Havah Nagila." I sang it unabashed, starting soft and slow but working up to a bellowing finish. Ibrahim loved it and, gifted as he was, had learned the words from a single listen. He joined in for the second round, wailing with me through the verses, sustaining with his powerful voice the glorious final measure:

"Ouru a heem! Ouru a heeem!
B'ves ha maaaaaaaaayyyyyyyyyach!!"

He flew out of his seat with joy, pumping my hand, slapping my back, pouring out our third cup of cloyingly sweet mint tea and fishing desperately in his shirt pocket for another Gauloise.

Ibrahim's only drawback was that, God help us, he did not sleep. When he wasn't propped up on his bunk—humming to himself and sucking Gauloise blondes—he was in the main compartment of the car, thrilling the passengers with magic and leading them in song.

"I am the most famous marabout in Mauritania," he'd informed us over tea. Though I'd refused on general principles to take a word he said seriously, I realized, at about 4:00 A.M., that he might have been telling the truth. Everyone was visibly delighted to have him aboard. He was a true celebrity: master of ceremonies, religious leader and camp counselor rolled into one.

The transformation was complete. Ibrahim, formerly the most insufferable asshole we'd encountered in Mauritania, had become the most fascinating man we'd met in Africa.

• 17 •

Road to Nowhere

We checked into the Hotel Maghreb on Tuesday, gladly sacrificing two days' budget for a double room with a cold shower.

The Dragoman expedition, bound for Morocco, was supposed to have arrived at the hotel the preceding day. We looked everywhere, asked everyone, but couldn't find the bus. No one had seen a thing.

It was inconceivable that Greg and David had come and left without even leaving a note. More likely, we decided, they hadn't arrived at all. More likely they were stuck in the vast, duney desert between Nouakchott and Nouadhibou, wrestling some bureaucratic or geomorphological nightmare. And if this were true, who knew when they might arrive? It could be today; tomorrow; next week; never.

The most sensible plan, Sally and I decided, was to take a taxi down to the docks and ask about possible passages to the Canary Islands—a port from which we might find ships leaving for Morocco, Portugal or Spain.

o   o   o

Nouadhibou's fishing industry makes it one of Africa's richest ports, but the fact was well hidden. The town had the spirit of an incredibly wealthy miser who amasses a fortune while his house falls to ruin and newspapers mold in the corners. Dogs huddled in the shelter of crumbling adobe walls, and strangers avoided our eyes.

On our way to the waterfront we stopped into the Clair de Lune Café for coffee and pastries. There, to our great good fortune, we met two Frenchmen. Strapping longshoreman types, father and son had arrived less than an hour before from Grand Canary Island aboard the *Volcan Thisayana*. They offered to introduce us to their Captain, who'd be returning to Las Palmas the next morning.

Captain Jorge Armando was a round, bearded cherub of a man who spoke excellent English and served us a gourmet lunch. He was sympathetic with our plight, having been in the same boat, so to speak, himself. In 1991, BMW had sponsored him to drive a 1000 cc Paris/Dakar Edition motorcycle all the way from Spain to Singapore. Armando had taken off that January, hitting a wall when the Gulf War struck. Immobilized on the fringes of Arabia, he'd had to adandon the effort a month into his trip.

But his own failure did not prevent him from being enthusiastic about our effort. Armando instructed us to be on board for sailing at 9 A.M. the next morning. Our passage would be free; we'd pay just $10 a day for food. It seemed a miraculous turn of events. We shook hands all around and left the *Volcan Thisayana* with lightened, though still strangely heavy, hearts.

"This is fabulous," I said to Sally. "So why am I so depressed?"

"Isn't it obvious?" She wrapped her scarf around her face. "I think the truth is that we really, *really* wanted to cross the desert in that big, clumsy expedition bus, instead of sailing to a resort for rich Germans. And if we do find a ship onward to Spain it will mean missing Morocco altogether. . . ."

We debated the situation up and down, but there was only one logical course. Unless we heard from David or Greg that evening, we would board the *Volcan* at eight-thirty the next day.

We were hand washing our underwear in the laundry room of the Maghreb at five-thirty that evening when the Malian receptionist found us.

"*Vous avez deux visiteurs d'Angleterre,*" he announced.

o   o   o

David and Greg sat in the lobby of the hotel, looking as ragged as Bowery bums. Early that morning their bus had sunk into the shallow quicksand along the beach, and the five clients and two crewmen had spent the day mired—literally—in the process of digging it out.

Now they were awaiting a phone call from Ali, their point man back in Nouakchott. He was the one who, for a total of $1,000 in bribes, had guaranteed the permits that would ensure smooth sailing into Western Sahara and onward to Morocco. David had spoken with him the day before, and everything was in order. One formality remained: the stamp of approval from the Moroccan consulate. Ali would fly up to meet David and Greg with the completed documents tomorrow, arriving on the twelve-thirty flight from Nouakchott.

Ali had promised to telephone with a progress report at noon. And telephone he had, though no one had been on hand to accept his call. But he'd told the receptionist he would try again at six, and both David and Greg had returned to town in anticipation of the event.

When six-thirty passed and Ali still hadn't phoned, nobody panicked. Greg put in a call to Ali's contact in the capital and said he'd try back later. The drivers returned to the bus.

Sally and I left the Maghreb to find Hamady Ba, Yusef Ba's brother, who worked for Naftal, the local hydroelectric company. Yusef and Claire had suggested we might stay with Hamady and his family—a tempting alternative to paying $40 a night for a cold-water room with sprung mattresses and no toilet seat.

A taxi brought us to a walled living compound where two dozen cement houses faced small dirt yards. After making a few inquiries we found Hamady Ba. He was a serious-looking man with large eyes and a long face that brought to mind an African Modigliani. He greeted us warmly, introducing us to his beautiful wife, Binta, and their three children. We asked if we might stay a night or two.

"Just one night?" Hamady raised his eyebrows in surprise and disappointment. "Stay a month, two months, no problem!" He clasped my hand while Binta, laughing, passed a wide-eyed baby girl to Sally and glided into the kitchen to brew mint tea. "You are now our family. Stay!"

"We've already paid for our hotel tonight," I said ruefully. "But we'll see you first thing tomorrow morning."

When we returned to the Maghreb there was a message from David and Greg:

The bus is out!!
Meet us at the Cap Blanc for dinner

We found the restaurant easily. Greg, David and the five clients on Dragoman's six-month pan-African tour sat around a long table discussing their uncertain future. Ali had not called back, and all efforts to reach him had failed. It was starting to seem possible, if not likely, that they'd been had, and that the expedition's dream of crossing from Mauritania to Morocco would remain just that.

Which left Sally and myself in a difficult position.

It was damned improbable that things would work out with Ali. The deal got shadier the closer one looked, and it had looked shady even from a distance. If his scheme did work out, of course, we'd be the first independent travelers since 1978 to enter Western Sahara on the south-to-north route. The more likely scenario, however, was that Ali would prove a snake—and that putting our faith in him would mean forfeiting our only reliable ticket out of Nouadhibou, a hellhole in which we were loath to linger a split second longer than necessary.

"We'll stick it out," I announced impulsively.

"Excellent." Greg raised his glass; David and the others followed. But Sally stared at me with daggers in her eyes, furious that I'd made the decision without her.

She was absolutely right. But we had been through the same impossible debate over and over again. It was a genuine dilemma, and I saw no solution save to spit out a decision and pray that we hadn't—that *I* hadn't—made a grievous blunder. One thing, at least, was unambiguous; if things went to hell in a handbasket, I would know exactly who to blame.

o   o   o

Sally was sick through the night, vomiting copiously from food poisoning. She slept in while I returned to the harbor and passed my regrets to Jorge Armando. The skipper of the *Volcan Thisayana* supported my decision and wished us well.

There was still no word from Ali by Wednesday noon. David taxied to the airport nonetheless, hoping beyond hope that the entrepreneur had simply flown in with the permits as promised.

We checked out of the Maghreb. Once Sally was comfortably installed in Hamady and Binta's guest room, I set off for the harbor again to inquire about other boats. The news was not good. There would be no other freighters arriving from the Canary Islands for eleven days, and the ship due then—the *Caribbée*—rarely took passengers.

I got back into town and stopped in at the Clair de Lune, where I ran into Greg. David had returned from the airport. No sign of Ali.

"We're dead in the water," he said.

Moonstruck

You don't see a lot of I ♥ NOUADHIBOU bumper stickers.

It isn't surprising. The desert wind tears across the peninsula like spite, carrying sheets of blinding, abrasive sand. There is nothing to do but hide. On the final days of Ramadan, Nouadhibou felt like the Twilight Zone: an alien realm of tiny green taxis and tall, squinting Berbers shuffling through the streets in their flowing djellabas like dust-bunny druids.

Friday evening, after dinner, we relaxed over mint tea with Hamady and Binta. The baby was asleep, and their two other children—Hammam and Astou—stared at the television. The image was mostly snow, with an occasional marabout materializing behind a field of microphones.

Hamady and I discussed slavery in Africa. I was fascinated to learn that his own tribal group, the Fulani—arguably one of the ten lost tribes of Israel—had never been slaves. The Fulani were, and are, warriors and nomadic herders, and had never been subdued by the Arabian or African slave traders.

"If you try to capture us, we will kill you," Hamady explained, unsmiling. "And if you do catch us, we kill ourselves. By any means necessary. Before we become a slave, we prefer to die."

Hamady listed the castes of local African society. The Fulani and the Tuareg, their religious arm, were at the top. Below them followed the merchants, musicians, tailors, shoemakers, fishermen, blacksmiths and, finally, slaves. Here was an odd thing: Africans who were captured as slaves but remained in Africa—rather than being shipped off to the Americas—were still considered slaves. Hamady pointed to the house kitty-corner from his.

"Those people are slaves," he indicated.

"But don't they work for Naftal?"

"Yes; but they are slaves. Even if you are a slave, you can still find work. Once you have become a Muslim, your masters must give you your freedom. Still, you are always considered to be a slave."

"What about the African Americans?" I asked. "Are they still considered slaves as well?"

"No. If they are catched and taken out of Africa, it is something different. We do not consider those people of the slave caste."

The television blared away in the background. Hamady and Binta were waiting for the answer to everybody's question: Would tomorrow, Saturday, be Elvitr, the final day of the Ramadan fast?

Elvitr is similar in spirit to Easter, but instead of the risen Christ, Muslims celebrate Mohammed's victorious return from his month-long desert pilgrimage. There is a certain charm to the holiday even in Nouadhibou. Children run around the streets in beautiful clean clothes, unafraid, for once, to laugh and play. The men are elegant in their embroidered *grands boubous*; and the women wear resplendent gowns.

Ramadan begins and ends with the new moon. The fast starts with the first sighting of the moon's thin sliver and concludes one month later, when the hairline crescent is spied again. The first crescent after a new moon appears low in the western sky and sets about an hour after the sun. These days, though, there are two ways to "see" that crescent: visually and astronomically. If it is cloudy, for example, and the moon is invisible—even though it's known to be up there—some Muslims prolong their fast.

The Islamic community is split between these two interpretations. In Mauritania, the determination is made by eye. A special moon-sighting bureau had been set up, and any male citizen could telephone the moment he spied the first sliver.

At nine o'clock the television declared that, since the moon had not been spotted in either Senegal or Saudi Arabia, both those countries would celebrate Elvitr on Sunday. Hamady guessed that Mauritania would follow suit and that Saturday would see business as usual. This was good news, for we had high hopes that Saturday would be a workday.

o   o   o

For the past three days Sally, I and the Dragoman drivers had been schlepping around Nouadhibou in a desperate attempt to gain passage up the twenty-six kilometers of pole-marked sand leading to the Moroccan fort.

The fiasco had begun on Wednesday when, giving up on Ali, Greg and David were told to speak with the commissioner of police. Only he, their sources said, could provide the laissez-passer that would enable the Dragoman bus to cross into Western Sahara. The drivers met with the commissioner, who instructed them to see the army commander. After a day and a half of waiting outside his gate, the drivers ultimately won an audience with the official, who blithely informed them that he could do nothing. Only the secretary of the interior, in Nouakchott, could provide the proper documents, which the governor in Nouadhibou would then have to sign.

It was the classic Afro-Arabian runaround, a hellish hamster wheel that would run them ragged before launching them toward certain defeat. Their only hope was to intrude upon the governor himself and beg him to bend the rules. There was just one problem: Neither Greg nor David had made any headway in securing an audience with the gentleman.

On Friday afternoon Sally and I took over, confident that our collective charm could melt the iciest bureaucratic heart. We marched to the governor's home and stood outside the gate until a soldier with bad teeth emerged and told us to go away. We held our ground and stated our case. At last the guard relented and bade us return at seven. At seven, however, the governor was indisposed.

We waited outside the gate for thirty more minutes, plying the governor's young daughters with trinkets and balloons. The guard, a compassionate man, took pity on us. "The governor is in bed," he said. "Come back Saturday."

"But Saturday will be a holiday. It is Elvitr . . ."

The guard shook his head. "This is not certain. If tomorrow is not the fete, go directly to the governor's office." He pointed to a tall white official-looking building located a quarter mile away on a hill. "If tomorrow is the fete, come back here at ten o'clock in the morning. You can see the governor then."

It seemed impossible that the governor could do anything for us at his home. He would need the official stamps, and those would be in his office. Our only hope was for Saturday to be a workday.

And so we were extremely encouraged when Hamady informed us that because of low-lying clouds, the first sliver of the moon had not been sighted anywhere between Dakar and Gibraltar.

Binta put her children to bed. I drank another cup of tea with Hamady, set our alarm for eight and fell into a comalike sleep.

o   o   o

As we prepared to leave the Bas' house on Saturday morning, Hamady emerged from the living room to greet us.

"Where are you going?"

"Off to the Clair de Lune for coffee," I said. "Then to the governor's at ten."

Hamady nodded seriously. "The Clair de Lune must be closed," he said, "for the fete."

"Fete? But the fete is tomorrow, not today. You said so last night."

"No . . ." Hamady shook his head slowly. "At one o'clock in the morning, they announced it on television. One Mauritanian man has seen the moon. In all other Muslim countries the fete is tomorrow—but in Mauritania, today. Better, I think, you have coffee here. . . ."

We left the compound anyway and walked glumly onto the street.

The café was locked up tight, as Hamady had predicted. An hour later we took our shiny shoes down to the governor's estate, where we were turned away quicker than canned hams.

Hell on Wheels

The Dragoman bus was parked in an open lot outside the police station, across the street from the Clair de Lune. Greg sat inside the café, alone at a table, smoking a Drum cigarette. He looked like a knackered leprechaun, but listened sympathetically as I found a map and articulated our remaining options.

"There are five. No, six." I decided to begin with the most absurd of them.

"First. Sally and I can return to Dakar, find a ship back to the United States, and start all over again. Next September. With a different boat. To Europe, this time. Or Australia, for that matter."

Sally looked at me as if I were out of my mind.

"Okay, that's out. The next possibility is to return to Dakar, head south and cut through Guinea, Ivory Coast, Ghana, Togo, Benin, Nigeria, Cameroon, Central African Republic, Zaire, Uganda, Kenya and Ethiopia to Djibouti."

"Is that feasible?" Sally asked.

Greg shrugged, offering us day-old cookies that tasted like an artful blend of coconut and sawdust. "Yes. I mean no, not really. It took us roughly three months, in a custom-built overland vehicle."

"Choice three, then. We can wait for the next ship to the Canary Islands."

"Minimum eight days," said Sally. "And that's just to find out if the *Caribbée* will take us. If it does, we could be in the Canaries in two weeks. If not . . ."

". . . we're stuck here another month. I vote no," I said. "I'd rather head back to the States in poverty and disgrace than spend the spring of my fortieth year marooned in Nouadhibou."

"Allright, then. What's the fourth choice?"

"The donkey cart." The previous afternoon, we had met a man—lean, shifty-eyed and angular—who claimed he could smuggle us over the border in a cart, at midnight, backpacks and all. I was seriously considering the possibility.

"Yeah, you might try that." Greg nodded. " 'Cept, once you're over the border, what then? You'll be in the middle of the Sahara, fifty-five kilometers from the nearest settlement. No guide. Mines up the arse. And, as we well know, there's not much traffic heading north. . . ."

"Good point. So. That leaves us with two alternatives. Either we get the permit to cross over the border into Morocco—or we've got no choice. We fly from here to the nearest airport, and carry on from there. Shit. Shit. *Shit*."

I couldn't believe it. We were barely out of New York and already it had come to airplanes. "There's *got* to be some way north!" I flat-fisted the table. "There has to be!"

Greg shook his head. His fox-pelt hair, unwashed for three days, fell in front of his eyes.

"There's not. If we can't get the permit," he said wearily, "you can honestly write in your book there was nothing to do from 'ere 'cept fly. The entire bloody Sahara is closed. The route through Algeria is suicide; they're killing foreigners right and left. The illegal road from Nouadhibou into Morocco through Western Sahara is a minefield. You should've seen the pictures of the last expedition truck that tried to get through that way—it hit a mine right on the marked track. The spades stowed in the undercarriage were blown through the roof. If the woman in the front seat 'adn't 'ad her legs tucked up beneath her, they'd've been blown right off.

"As far as Chad goes, forget it. Totally closed. You'd end up in Libya, anyway; not the best place for an American. So what does that leave? Shit, a few months ago you could've gone up through Sudan, but that's out, since the Sudan-Egypt border is closed again. Muslim fundamentalists are shooting up tourists in Egypt now; it's wrecking the tourist industry completely." He leaned back, hands folded on his crotch.

"Basically, you're buggered. You either wait 'ere for a ship, or fly. Unless we get the permit, of course." He laughed cynically.

One hour later the other Dragoman stragglers returned from the public bath. They had formulated a desperate plan. We would pack our bags, clean up the truck and drive to the border, eighteen kilometers north. Today of all days it might be possible to do what no one had succeeded in doing before: *talking* one's way out of Mauritania. And why not? Today was Elvitr, a grand celebration. Today a man might hope to bend the rules, to gamble on the goodwill of his fellow man. Today of all days the border guards—caught in the spirit of the holiday and recalling the Prophet's directive to help and respect all travelers— might agree to cough into their hands and look the other way just long enough for an overland vehicle to roll past them and out of sight.

At two o'clock sharp, we set off for the border.

o   o   o

It was not a pleasant drive. Nouadhibou is one of those unlucky cities that seem to be composed entirely of outskirts. A quarter mile beyond the sandblasted stretch of the center lies an endless expanse of tin shacks, baking on the beige landscape like salt crystals in a bowl of dry couscous. Beyond the shacks there is nothing: a pocked, desiccated world resembling the inside of a dirty oven on the self-cleaning cycle. And beyond this nothing lies a lonely police check post consisting of a tiny customs room and a sandbagged lean-to that serves as the officers' accommodation.

Nouadhibou is located on a peninsula; one passes the same checkpoint coming from the north or south. When we arrived, there were eight other vehicles parked around the post. A dozen westerners lay upon their roofs and baggage racks, soaking up deadly ultraviolet rays. Their languor was a bad omen, indicating that nothing was happening fast. Or perhaps nothing was happening at all. This was, after all, Elvitr, and if the guards were not in the cheery, generous mood we had anticipated, the likely alternative was that they were being incorrigible bastards.

David and Greg left to conduct the negotiations, which seemed to consist mainly of nodding and drawing their toes through the sand. It was a scene we'd witnessed countless times before: petty officials of impoverished countries who commanded no power whatsoever on this Earth, save the power to make people wait. More than one A-type personality has imploded in such company; the very sight of them made me lapse into an autistic fugue state, counting the ridges on my thumb.

After half an hour our drivers returned. They were not contented men.

"It's out of the question." Greg let out a long sigh. "They said we're lucky they didn't arrest us for coming this far without a permit." He tore a chunk of bread from a baguette and planted himself behind the wheel. "Let's go."

I looked back at the checkpoint. Two men, a few dry boards with nails sticking out and forty kilometers of sand were all that separated us from Morocco. If we'd gotten past this point we would have reached Marrakesh in three days. Instead we were driving back to Nouadhibou, our private acre of hell on earth.

Neither Sally nor I could speak. We felt utterly defeated. We'd set off on our pilgrimage with two goals: to perform a global kora, and, by doing so without airplanes, to rediscover the size of the world. Within twenty-four hours, it seemed, we'd be forced to break our overland route.

It was agonizing and infuriating, but we'd made a rather cogent realization. There is no place bigger than a border you can't cross. There is no distance greater than the distance from A to B when someone is standing in between with a loaded weapon.

Morocco was only forty kilometers away, but it might as well have been on the far side of the moon.

o   o   o

As we approached Nouadhibou, a little black boy ran into the street a dozen meters ahead of our bus. An oncoming taxi swerved to avoid him but failed. The boy was hit, swept beneath the Peugeot's wheels and dragged like a rag doll across the roadway. Greg slammed on the brakes, and we leapt from our seats to see if we could help.

The boy was still conscious. The taxi driver, a Berber, stepped out of his cab, glanced from side to side, and walked quickly over to the victim. He dragged him roughly into sitting position and jostled his limbs to see if anything was broken. Satisfied that there wasn't (by no means my own medical opinion), he tried to stand the child on his feet. The boy balanced upright for a moment, then toppled over. The driver picked him up and tried again.

There were many witnesses, but no one seemed the least bit concerned. It was equally clear that the driver had no interest in the situation beyond the fear of personal liability. The moment he had succeeded in arranging the broken child into a seminormal posture, he rushed back to his taxi and drove away unimpeded.

One hundred percent of the human beings I know would have shown more compassion after hitting a squirrel. I turned to Sally, who had watched the scene with her mouth agape.

"We're out of here tomorrow," I stated. *"By any means necessary."*

o   o   o

There are only three places you can fly to from Nouadhibou; two, if you don't count Nouakchott. We didn't.

"So what'll it be?" Sally asked. "Morocco, or Grand Canary Island?"

"If you were a hopeless romantic on a round-the-world trip without airplanes," I said, "and found out that you had to visit one airport—just one airport on Earth—which one would *you* choose?"

· 18 ·

The Bardo of Hope and Fear

The plane to Casablanca disappeared into the indigo sky at nine in the morning, leaving a vapor trail that twisted into nothingness within seconds.

We watched its departure from the ground, cradling our coffee at the Clair de Lune Café. Three of the five Dragoman passengers sat with us, reading old copies of *Marie Claire* and nibbling silently on cinnamon rolls.

There was one more hope, one last possibility of leaving Nouadhibou by land. Bwana—the wizened guide who'd led the Dragoman bus from Nouakchott up to the Nouadhibou peninsula—had called his younger sister, who was intimate with a high official. She had spoken with her lover, who had in turn contacted his military connections.

An elaborate escape route had been contrived. It went like this: Before leaving Nouadhibou we would rendezvous with a car carrying a military attaché. The attaché would board the Dragoman bus with a laissez-passer stating that we were on our way south, back to Nouakchott. We would thus clear the check post—but instead of going south we would turn north, toward the frontier. There, at the final Mauritanian garrison, the attaché would see us into Western Sahara. When this was accomplished—no sooner—we would hand our escort a sealed envelope, which he would deliver to his commanding officer. The envelope would contain roughly $2,000, in American and British currency.

We were to receive the laissez-passer early Monday morning, dispense with customs, and be on the road by ten.

By twelve-thirty Monday afternoon, however, neither Greg nor David had emerged from the customs house. The blue Renault carrying the attaché drove up and down the Boulevard de l'Hopital, looking increasingly suspicious.

I nursed my coffee, remembering the poignant words that Mr. Strauss, my behavioral psychology professor, once used to describe an experiment: "Hope springs eternal," he had reflected, "in white rats . . . and humans."

Our pellet fell fifteen minutes later, when Jill—a shrill British passenger whose cartoonish features bore an uncanny resemblance to the Nigerian fertility mask someone had tacked up in the bus—poked her ovoid head into the back room of the café.

"We're going," she declared.

o   o   o

Jill's call to arms came at one, but two more hours would pass before we quit the cat-litter box of Nouadhibou and set off for the dreaded check post from which we'd been turned back two days earlier. The reason for the delay was typical: The Mauritanians had changed the plan again. We now had to pay the bribe *before* leaving town, rather than after clearing the border. Greg's main argument against paying in advance—beside the obvious fact that it would be an unforgivably stupid way to lose $2,000—was that he needed the hard cash to balance the books. All foreigners entering Mauritania must declare their currency and traveler's checks, and the bank receipts for all money changed while in the country must tally exactly with one's remaining cash when one leaves.

Unfortunately, the mysterious official who was greasing the wheels for us had a ready solution to this problem.

As we waited on the edge of town, a Mercedes-Benz with curtained windows materialized. Inside was the vice president of the national bank. After two hours she had drawn up ersatz paperwork accounting for every cent of the $2,000 that Greg was compelled to place, under extreme duress, in the high official's hand.

"There's no turning back now," he said as he reboarded the bus. "If we don't get through, we're finished."

At precisely three-thirty the Renault sedan pulled up alongside the parked bus, and a soldier in fatigues stepped out of the backseat. He boarded the Dragoman bus and moved unobtrusively to the back. Five minutes later we left the town of Nouadhibou, entered the desert and drove the eighteen kilometers to the police check post. This time there were no other vehicles. Three policemen in khaki uniforms approached the driver's door.

"We are going back to Nouakchott," Greg informed the chief, handing over our laissez-passer.

The officer shook his head and wagged a metronomic finger in Greg's face. "You are lying. You are trying to go to Morocco. We know this. This border is closed. You cannot pass."

There was silence throughout the bus.

"We are going to Nouakchott," Greg repeated coolly. "We could not get a border pass, and we have made arrangements to ship the truck back to England from the capital. Just as it says on the permit."

At that precise moment a Land-Rover drove in from the north, carrying no less than two dozen Mauritanian army troops. The policemen turned their attention from us and exchanged formalities with their dust-covered comrades. There were extended greetings, many hand-shakes and a general air of bonhomie to which we were not party. The police chief returned to the Dragoman bus with an army officer in tow.

"This soldier is also going to Nouakchott," the border guard slyly announced. "You will take him with you."

This was a worry. But now it was David, David of the perpetual Cheshire cat grin, who leaned over toward Greg's window and smiled.

"Can't do it, mate. Insurance. Can't carry anyone 'cept our passengers and a guide or we lose our bloody coverage. We're terribly sorry, but listen—there's another truck following just behind us. I'm sure they'll lend you a hand. . . ."

Our military attaché, silent until now, sauntered over to the window and vouched for David's declaration. The guard nodded reluctantly and within five minutes we were out of there, gone, beyond the pile of spiked lumber and into the no-man's-land separating Mauritania from occupied Western Sahara. The white knuckles on the bus turned pink again.

o   o   o

We arrived at the Mauritanian border just after sunset. A brilliant sliver of moon hung in the sky like torn foil. Greg and the attaché jumped from the bus and consulted with the border guard. Our military escort shook hands all around, secured our permission to pass, and left the bus with a wave. Greg turned around in the driver's seat to face us.

"I reckon we've got two choices," he said. "We can go on, and try to reach the Moroccan fort. But it's lousy with mines out there. The guard I spoke with said we can sleep 'ere. He'll come tomorrow morning with a map showing us the road through the minefields. The way I figure," he grinned, lifting the right side of his mouth more than the left, "it defeats the purpose of our expedition to get blown up. I vote we stay."

It was unanimous. We ate a large dinner, set up our tents and slept, waking before first light.

o   o   o

Since World War II, technology has given maps, like parachutes, an awesome degree of reliability. Most of us have come to take their accuracy for granted. As we leap out into the world, huddled against the head wind of possibilities, we trust them absolutely.

But the scrap of paper brought to our bus by the Moroccan border guard was enough to challenge a lifetime of blind faith. The road indicated on his scrawled sketch was invisible, buried under drifting sand that swallowed our tires whole. Every time this happened Greg would lean out the window, peer at the right rear wheel and give the appropriate command. "Shovels," he'd say, and we'd leap from the bus and dig like mad, sand blasting in our faces, before clamoring back on board and muscling our way out.

Nine times out of ten, though, shovels did not suffice. On these occasions Greg would squint at the mired wheels and mutter, "Mats . . . sand mats this time. . . ." This was our cue to disembark, unload the ten heavy steel sand mats from their undercarriage racks, dig away the sand piled in front of all six wheels, wedge the two-meter-long mats under the tires and step back as the truck sprinted forward another ten meters or so before digging itself, whining, into another rut. It usually took half a dozen sand-matting sessions before the bus reached another patch of solid ground—and even then it was only a matter of minutes before we had to leap back off the vehicle and start the process all over again.

Our spirits were heightened by the edgy, unreal awareness that mines lay all around us. Even though most were antitank weapons and wouldn't necessarily be triggered by the weight of a human, there was always the chance of seeing one's companion—or oneself—blown to smithereens.

"Keep in the tire tracks," Greg warned, snarling at Jill when she giggled nervously. We did our best, but there were many moments, awful and exhilarating, when we found our feet in virgin sand.

It was hard work, and miserable in the whipping wind, but the desert was raw and beautiful, a place of surreal shapes and tumbled boulders and tiny black bits of rubber and metal and plastic, empty cigarette packets erased by the sand, bleached white seashells from the age when the whole region lay beneath the sea. We saw few dunes, but I found the area breathtaking in a classic desert way. There was a quiet, serene mystery to the landscape, and an atmosphere of all-pervading patience. It seemed to me to be the patience of God.

Where The Wild Things Are

The Dragoman bus arrived at the Moroccan fort at ten in the morning. We were directed into a vacant lot and instructed to set up our tents. Nothing could be done before the border guards received official word authorizing us to continue north, toward the Dakhla peninsula. Permission to do so would have to come from Dakhla itself, by radio.

The process could take two days or more. Meanwhile, we were waylaid in another purgatorial desert backwater.

The afternoon wind beat hysterically against the sides of the Dragoman bus. In the vehicle's lee, our big blue cook tent heaved like the
chest of a drowning man. There was nothing around us but a
windswept lot, bordered on one side by the paved road leading north,
and on the other by swollen humps of rock-strewn sand and festering
garbage mounds. Goats nosed through the trash, gorging themselves
on torn clothing, used toilet paper, and the potato peelings from our
lunch. Up the road, the Moroccan border post was a huge square compound with low walls the exact color of the desert. A radio aerial and
TV antenna needled up from within the fort's confines, eerily steady in
the gusts. The bus was full of bold and indestructible flies that no
amount of wind would drive away.

We had gone from the frying pan through the fire, and seemed to
have ended up in an ashtray.

Aside from reading, washing my socks and writing, there wasn't
much to do. To make matters worse, a few letters on my keyboard were
sticking; especially the overused *I,* which was something of a private
embarrassment. I spent the better part of that afternoon on the bus,
teaching David how to play *Minesweeper* on the OmniBook.

David, dressed in a trenchcoat and tie-dyed purple T-shirt, seemed
like a chap who had never worried about anything. With his handsome
beard and long brown hair he resembled the young Eric Clapton, or
Jesus Christ. Twenty-eight years old, a high school dropout, he'd spent
five years as a British bobby in Gatwick and Sussex before buying a
Kawasaki 750 and pointing it due south. It took him eight months to
drive from England to Cape Town and back: a distance of twenty-one
thousand miles. After returning to England he'd worked four months
as a motorcycle courier, then took his current gig with Dragoman Expeditions. He'd been codriving, with Greg and others, for a year and a
half but would soon head his own expedition into East Africa.

After we'd blown ourselves up several dozen times, David showed
me around the bus. She was a customized 1981 Mercedes-Benz 1617:
sixteen tons, 170 horsepower. Dragoman had bought the cab and chas-
sis, then designed and built the entire superstructure—installing everything from the spade storage bins to the overhead net racks and the
comfortable coach seats in between. Thirteen such buses, each slightly
different, made up the Dragoman fleet.

Late in the afternoon there was a huge commotion in the lot. A
Spanish TV crew, one week into a fully sponsored, eighteen-month-
long voyage along the perimeter of the entire African continent, had arrived from Morocco. Their convoy consisted of five astronomically
expensive vehicles. These included a Land-Rover *Discovery* with a cad-

mium-blue gyrocopter harnessed to its roof, followed by a Pegasso overland expedition truck towing a fully equipped motorboat and a top-of-the-line off-road motorcycle. The Rover, Pegasso and boat all had the expedition's coat of arms emblazoned on their flanks, with maps of Africa displaying the *"Ruta UAP de los Exploradores"* etched below.

Gerard, leader of the Spanish expedition, was convivial fellow, and took appropriate pity on our low-budget enterprise. After a few minutes of conversation he extracted a suitcase satellite system from his locker and offered to let me beam a column back to Allen Noren through my computer's fax/modem. I wrote a piece on my laptop and spent the next hour trying, without success, to flog it off. It was incredibly frustrating; one never knew exactly where the glitch lay. Was it in my computer? The satellite? My story? There was no telling.

I was called away from my maddening machinations by Sally. Dinner was served. The Dragoman crew had prepared a fabulous meal of chicken curry with freshly baked chapatis and rice. There was even dessert—something the Brits called truffle. This turned out to be a gooey roux of loose custard and Jell-O, with a dollop of Cool Whip on top. It was the sort of dish that would sit untouched at any Berkeley potluck; but in Goatbreath, Morocco, it was pure ambrosia.

Night fell, landing on our campsite like a case of bad Merlot. When I boarded the bus to fetch my sleeping bag, I found the boys—Greg, David and two clients named Pete and Hunter—loading tumblers with single malt whiskey. I grabbed a mug from the mess tent and joined them.

Greg held court, telling tales of his life as a Dragoman driver. He spoke a lot about Africa—Zaire, mostly, which he claimed was the only truly wild place left on Earth.

"People show up and make millions in fly-by-night gold- and diamond-mining operations," he said. "There must be billions of dollars of untapped wealth in precious metals and stones. People would regularly walk up to me in the street selling one-kilo gold ingots for five hundred dollars U.S."

"Why didn't you buy some?" Hunter, a Southern Californian surfer and contractor who suffered from congenital near deafness, had turned up his hearing aid for the occasion.

"Didn't 'ave the five 'undred, mate."

Greg recalled the bureaucratic nightmares he'd endured as a driver in Africa and made good sport of the snafus awaiting the Spanish TV crew at every border and check post. I mentioned that Gerard had shown me an amazing machine that turned out rubber stamps; you could make any kind of seal you wanted, from a laissez-passer to a visa extension.

"They'll make good use of it." Greg nodded sagely. "All the Africans need to see is a stamp. Doesn't matter what it says. You got a stamp? All right, you're official. Often it's as simple as that." He went on to tell a story about a recent Dragoman expedition through Nigeria. One of the passengers was refused entry into the country because he didn't have a cholera vaccination stamped on his health certificate. Greg had gamely returned to the bus and filled out the card, listing the place and date of the injections, but the passenger was still turned away.

"Problem was, we didn't 'ave a medical seal to make it look official. Finally, though, this guy came up with a brilliant idea. 'E grabbed 'is Swiss Army knife, took the Dragoman rubber stamp and 'is vaccination record and disappeared with the lot for a few minutes.

"About one hour later we breezed through the check post without a 'itch. The officials at the border didn't even question 'is certificate. It was properly signed, all right, and emblazoned with the stamp of the attending physician: **Dr goman**."

Deconstructionist Diversion II

The next morning I wandered far from the bus, beyond the place where everybody peed, and sat alone in the desert. The sand was fine and soft. To the east, the Sahara stretched on for a thousand miles.

I was feeling headachy and depressed, estranged from Sally and obsessive about the time that seemed to be slipping away—away from Turkey, away from Nepal, away from my now dubious rendezvous with Mount Kailas. Time felt precious and limited; a commodity that, like the chocolate and tangerines on the bus, could be recklessly and permanently depleted.

I took a few deep breaths and tried to settle my mind. There was no point worrying about time. There was no point rushing toward Turkey, Nepal or anyplace else. My only real responsibility was to let the journey unfold naturally, with all the frustrations and delays recognized as unavoidable, and possibly instructive, parts of the process. Whether I floated or struggled, sank or swam through these obstacles was up to me. The entire problem seemed to be my attachment to getting to Kathmandu by early May, and my conviction that I had to get back to California by July in order to meet my deadline. Neither of these conditions was objectively necessary, though I felt strangely wedded to them.

Sitting in the sand, listening to the wind, I thought about where I'd rather be. Oakland? I felt a strong nostalgia for that life—but when I examined my feelings more carefully I saw that my longing was groundless. I recalled endless evenings in front of the VCR, browsing aimlessly through bins at the used-CD store or making phone call after phone call in a futile attempt to avoid another night in my own company. In the desert, at least, there was no choice. There was no confusion, and no alternative. We could move neither forward nor backward. Waiting *was*; and beyond the waiting there would be motion, adventure, April in Byzantium, tea in Kathmandu.

Feeling no better, I wandered deeper into the desert. Something was gnawing at me.

The landscape was beautiful. It was morning and still reasonably cool. Reaching a high point—a small, stony mountain overlooking the dry, barren plain—the Semitic atmosphere inspired me. Feeling like a pilgrim on some biblical plain, I began to sing:

> *"If it be your will*
> *that I speak no more,*
> *and my voice be still as it was before;*
> *I will speak no more,*
> *I shall abide until*
> *I am spoken for, if it be your will."*

Something about that particular Leonard Cohen song was a little too much for me, and I found my voice faltering.

> *"If it be your will*
> *that a voice be true,*
> *from this broken hill I will sing to you.*
> *From this broken hill*
> *all your praises they shall ring,*
> *if it be your will*
> *to let me sing."*

The lyrics recalled my brother, and his long struggle with depression, so powerfully that I sat on a rock and began sobbing. My tears fell onto the warm sandstone, evaporating instantly. It was mid-March, the fourth anniversary of Jordan's suicide, but I felt the anguish of his death as acutely as if it had happened that very morning.

"I miss you so much," I choked. "I miss you so much, little brother." The wind blew in my ears and dried the tears on my cheeks. When I looked up again I saw only the world; not a soul was in sight.

What is this place? What is this strange, dry place, where the quality of my suffering seems magnified as if by a lens? What is this eerie, empty place, this desert, this grave?

I blotted my eyes with my bandanna and returned along the rocky track. Earlier I had picked up a stone—something to bring home and place on my brother's grave—but I tossed it back. There would be other places to choose mementos from; places that did not fill me with pain.

North by Northeast

An hour or two after my return a pair of soldiers descended from the fort and walked, with no special haste, toward the cook tent, where Greg, Sally and the other Dragoman campers were coating their faces with Noxzema. Seconds later I heard the words "*On y va,*" uttered casually by one of the soldiers and echoed with fanatical enthusiasm by the others.

The cook tent came down and we hit the road, Neil Young blasting through the open windows. The desert was a wrinkled sheet, broken by the occasional boulder or bachat dune. To the west, sometimes only meters away, sand cliffs flaked away to reveal the ocean.

We crossed the Tropic of Cancer. And I wondered: What would it have been like to grow up in the Western Sahara? What would it feel like to look at a map of the African continent and recognize your country as a sliver of beige, pressed against the sea? The elegant, elongated block of the United States—with the appendix of Florida, the port-wine stain of the Great Lakes and the towering erection of New England— had always pleased me. It was fun to draw, uncomplicated by the drooping hook of Mexico or the amorphous mess of Canada. The Manifest Destiny: bullshit maybe, propaganda certainly, but it sure looks good on paper. People died for it. They would die for it still. Can the shape of your country, I wondered—even its potential shape—determine the shape of your nationalism? All the blood and guts, all that genocide and fervor, for a goal that was selfish and paranoid yet weirdly aesthetic. . . .

Greg stopped for the night in Dakhla, a military town in the occupied Western Sahara. We discharged our escort. The bus drove off to find a campsite, while Sally and I elected to splurge on a hotel. It was worth every penny; we showered until we looked like prunes, and dropped into bed like marmots.

After Nouadhibou, Dakhla seemed like heaven. We gorged ourselves on fresh fruit, green olives, chocolate milk, black olives, yoghurt, garlic olives, almonds, chili olives, fried fish and olives, olives, olives. People were so nice to us that we became shyly self-conscious, unaccustomed to feeling welcome.

The decision was made to drive directly to Marrakesh, some fourteen hundred kilometers north. It would take us a day and a night to get there, depending on the road condition and number of checkpoints. We cleared customs at three and began our exodus an hour later, loaded down with oranges and soft drinks and two huge sacks of olives.

I napped for a while and woke to the sight of fog, red stones, plains of green grass rising up the insteps of coffee-colored foothills. The long nightmare was over. We were back in a place where gasoline stations had little snack bars attached to them.

The bus climbed the foothills of the Atlas Mountains, passing through geology so convoluted that it was impossible to tell which layer of stone had been deposited first. Blood-red poppies and yellow flowers bloomed by the roadside; acacias of some sort appeared among silver-leafed olive trees. The ground became very rich, very red. Ahead of us on the winding mountain road, an old Ford truck churned slowy uphill, spewing diesel smoke. A Berber family stood in back, waving and smiling. We passed their caravan and descended into a broad valley full of pink towns.

I spent many of those long bus hours reading Paul Bowles: *The Sheltering Sky*, *The Delicate Prey* and *A Thousand Days for Mokhtar*. His short stories were like brief, intense musical compositions, each of which produced a distinct shade of mood that colored the landscape we drove through. They were grave, but not the least bit sentimental. They seemed, in fact, to be about people who had left sentimentality behind—or were never even capable of the emotion.

I was suddenly gripped by a strong pull toward Tangier, and a rendezvous with Paul Bowles. The desire was purely intuitive, and part of its strength lay in its mystery. I had nothing particular to ask Bowles, and—short of his blessing as a fellow writer—entertained no notion of what he might offer me. Nonetheless, it seemed crucially important that I seek him out.

o   o   o

We approached Marrakesh along a highway bordered by acres of mustard and ecstasies of scarlet poppies. Men stood alongside the road behind small folding tables, selling honey.

· 19 ·

The Paradise of Oranges

"You know you're in a wealthy city," Sally observed, "when the orange trees still have fruit on them."

But the word *fruit* was inadequate to convey the richness of Marrakesh's urban arbors. It wasn't a question of a few stray globes hanging over the clean sidewalks. Banquets of oranges weighted the limbs of the trees lining Avenue Mohammed V, fluorescent against red clay walls, ripening against an animated backdrop of buses, taxis and horse-drawn cabs.

No place on Earth could have presented a greater contrast to the awful boredom of the Mauritanian desert than that wild glitzy bazaar, that miracle of mopeds and metalwork and men in hooded burnouses walking beneath flowering orange trees.

Sally and I settled our accounts with Greg and David, paying a nominal amount for our food and a whopping $200 each toward the collective border bribe. We bade farewell to the five other passengers, slapped the bus for good luck and moved our bags into the Hotel Ali.

Marrakesh is a phenomenon unto itself. The city is to shopping what Louis XIV was to interior decorating, what Edison was to electricity, what Miami is to blue hair. The town medina, with its labyrinthine souks, claims to be the largest open-air shopping arcade in the world, and I could not imagine that a more impressive display of on-sale commodities exists, or needs to exist, anywhere. For the career shopper Marrakesh has always been a kind of mecca, a place of once-in-a-lifetime pilgrimage where the divine excesses of the discipline are preserved and practiced in their purest, most sanctified form. It makes the soulless, philistine shopping malls of America look like vending machines.

You can buy giant snapping turtles that wander purposefully out of their cages and onto the pavement, saved at the last minute by some attentive passerby as they are about to saunter beneath the wheels of an approaching truck. You can run your hands through bins of rainbow potpourri, necklaces made of cloves, stones that produce aphrodisiac incense when they're burned. You can examine silver daggers in inlaid alabaster sheaths and chess sets of sharply scented Moroccan cedar. You can try on supple leather slippers with colored rhinestones glittering on their toes, silk burnouses with intricate embroidery racing around their collars and cuffs, and Chicago Bulls baseball caps. You can juggle gigantic pottery vases that look just like the one the Zork lives in in *One Fish, Two Fish, Red Fish, Blue Fish* and balance gigantic serving trays made of brilliant chased brass on your head. You can find Brazilian coffee, French pastries, Chinese umbrellas, Korean ginseng, Spanish omelettes, Indian incense, Swiss watches, Japanese cameras, Belgian chocolate, Malian pendants, South African diamonds, English cricket bats, German facial creams, ice cream bars from the Canary Islands, pharmaceuticals from Saudi Arabia and American cigarettes. You can buy forty-seven varieties of olives.

We encountered an old Arab man selling socks. They were decorated with Halloween motifs: jack-o'-lanterns interspersed with grinning white skulls. We instantly awarded him the prize for Most Culturally Dissonant Commodity.

"Excuse me," Sally said, approaching him with a smile. "Do you know what those decorations are?"

The merchant studied the socks and turned back to her confidently. "That is the world," he said, pointing to a pumpkin, "and here is the head of a slave."

Though the medina was spectacular, it was not where I worshipped. Just to the west of the Jamaa el Fna—the inscrutably named "Place of Nothing" where the clowns and dentists and storytellers perform—the city's orange sellers ply their trade. There are dozens of them, positioned behind broad wooden tables sagging under the weight of their cargo. Millions of huge, sweet oranges, the pride of Morocco, rise in four-sided pyramids toward the sky, half obscuring the red-cheeked, thick-wristed men who split and pump them dry in tough chrome squeezers. For 2 dirhams—18 cents—one is handed a tall clean glass filled to the brim with fresh, cold orange juice so perfect and honest and sweet that you burst into tears drinking it. Here, at last, is the Platonic ideal, and everything you've had before—everything else called orange juice—has been but a lame attempt to imitate it. *Thank God for oranges*, you cry, downing your first glass. *Thank God for Morocco, and the planet Earth!* After two glasses you are deliriously happy; after six glasses you're whirling like a dervish, spinning wildly through the Jamaa el Fna, spinning in a beatific citrus ecstasy while blind Moroccan beggars toss coins into the empty glass still clutched in your hand . . .

o   o   o

We visited many places covered with beautiful tiles. We toured the Saddien Tombs, where pigeons zoom expertly as bats between the marble columns and elegant Koranic script wriggles along the garden walls; we visited the empty palaces called Badi and Bahia, where harem girls once sat in their high private rooms gazing down on the court musicians, rubbing their thighs and buttocks with pumice stones, waiting to be chosen.

But there is no need to seek out the palaces, with their parking lots full of tour coaches and knife sellers. Walking slowly down the narrow streets is enough. A glimpse through a half-open door into the clean, tiled hallway of a Moroccan home; a crooked dentist's sign hanging at the end of a pink alleyway; a cart full of mint, radiating fragrance. The smell of a hidden bakery. A glimpse of Lyle Lovett on MTV, viewed through the stenciled window of a street café.

I ducked into a tiny souk in the *mellah,* the old Jewish quarter, where half a dozen women waited to order cases of round local matzoh for the upcoming Passover holiday. The man behind the counter handed me two of the flat flourless cakes.

"When is the first Passover seder?" I asked in French.

"*Prochain samedi soir,*" replied a woman with red hair and a gap between her teeth. "Next Saturday night. Are you staying the week in Marrakesh?"

We would be leaving for Fès on the morning train. I shook my head sadly.

"Where will you be, then?"

"Next Saturday? I'll be in, uh, Tangier," I replied uncertainly. "Is there a synagogue there?"

"Of course! Many synagogues. You just go there," she advised me, "and ask around for a seder. I think you will find one."

Sweetness

The electric train from Marrakesh to Fès passed through lush rolling meadows and fields of wild poppies, countryside so breathtaking that I swore I would return to Morocco—possibly as soon as the following spring.

Sally and I had checked into separate rooms at the Hotel Central, electing to spend the next few days more or less apart. My quarters in the Ville Nouvelle district reminded me so nostalgically of Paris that I found myself suffused with an unrequited appetite for romance. This was the sort of room in which one wanted to spend a morning making love and drinking orange juice and champagne; it was a room where one lay in bed humming "Chelsea Hotel" and fantasizing about getting head from a husky-voiced blues singer.

Now a strong morning wind slammed at the shutters, and my tiled balcony freckled with rain. It was the first precipitation I had seen since New York. After so long, rain seemed an almost unearthly phenomenon, and I leapt up from my battered desk and ran to the windows to convince myself it was real.

o   o   o

"This place is civilized," Sally noted over breakfast. A civilized place, by her definition, was any place where the worship of sugar had reached the level of idolatry. One could walk through the Ville Nouvelle and pass, within the space of a single block, half a dozen patisseries selling the most gorgeous tarts, cakes, muffins, Napoleons, mille feuilles and pastries imaginable. Between the patisseries lay candy stores, milk shake parlors, *glaciers*, date shops, juice bars, sugared-nut stalls, nougat makers and cafés of every ilk. Fès was Willy Wonka land. All was sweetness.

o   o   o

Confusion, for more than a moment, is not possible in Fès. People instantly materialize to assist you—whether out of altruism or for profit, one doesn't always know for sure. In a place like the medina all offers are suspect; elsewhere the motivation is sometimes completely pure.

The man found me inside the gate of the Jewish Cemetery, a tilting acre of whitewashed geometrical tombs attached to the southeastern fringe of the Fès mellah. I had come to light a memorial candle for my brother, who had taken his life four years ago to the day.

There was no point pretending I didn't need help. I was seen wandering around in befuddlement, looking for something that might be a synagogue.

"*Cherchez vous quelque chose?*"

He was not one of those ageless Moroccans. White hair ebbed back from his forehead in two pronounced Us, and a short white mustache formed a hedge beneath his nose. It was a nose with real personality; the sort of nose that had probably brought him grief as a child but had matured into a distinguished asset. I couldn't see his eyes through his sunglasses.

"Is there a synagogue here?"

"No, no . . ." He removed his glasses to polish them with a handkerchief, and I put him at fifty. "There is no synagogue here. In the Ville Nouvelle." He gestured with his chin, back toward the bridge I'd crossed to get where I was. "There are not many Jews in the mellah anymore. When the French built the New City many moved there. Or to Palestine. There are many Jews in Rabat. And Casablanca."

"Is there anyplace," I asked, "where I might light a memorial candle? I wish to recite the Kaddish for my brother."

He nodded quickly—"Wait a moment"—and walked off to speak with an elderly black caretaker. They returned together. "Give this man some money, and he can bring you what you need: candles, matches, and a yarmulke to cover your head."

"How much?"

"Five dirhams."

The black man took the coin, and left through the cemetery gate.

"If there's no synagogue," I asked my companion, "where do I light the candle?"

He put a hand on my shoulder and pointed. Most of the tombs in the cemetery were similar: low, whitewashed half-cylinders rising from the ground. There were two, though, that stood higher than the rest. One was a loaf-shaped shrine (like a big baguette with the ends cut off) covered in shiny black tile. A pipe rose from one end. It looked like a cartoon locomotive, and at first I actually thought it was the custom-built tomb of a Jew who had spent a lifetime on the railroad. The second shrine was simpler. White and symmetrical, it had an opening in one side and a tall, blackened chimney.

It was those two structures that my friend indicated. "There, and there," he said. "Light your candles inside, away from the wind."

"Why are there two?"

He shrugged. "We call them the Father and the Mother."

The caretaker returned with a rose-patterned skullcap, a box of wooden matches and a paper package containing six kosher candles. He handed me my change.

The white-haired man led me toward the black-tiled shrine, which I assumed was the "Father." Along the way he pointed out memorial placards: Jews who had died during the Second World War; the graves of children; the oldest tombs, inscribed exclusively in Hebrew, with no French translation. We stopped for a moment before a memorial to a seventeen-year-old girl, killed by the Arabs when she refused to convert to Islam.

When we reached the high black tomb with its open candle well in the center, the man stood beside me with his hands folded. I lit three candles and uttered what little I could remember of the Kaddish. When my yarmulke blew off in a strong breeze, the man chased after it and returned it to me. I put it quickly to my lips. Once I was convinced the candles were secure from the wind we walked over to the white "Mother" shrine; I lit my remaining candles there.

Afterward we rested on a gray marble bench beneath an orange tree. Fallen fruit filled the shallow square well protecting the trunk. On an impulse—and because I trusted him somehow—I told the man of the circumstances of Jordan's death. He confided that his own brother had also died four years before, at the age of forty. He himself was forty-seven.

"How large is the Jewish community here in Fès?" I asked.

The man shrugged. "Most are in the Ville Nouvelle, where the synagogue is. It's difficult to say."

"How many do you think? Twenty families? Fifty? One hundred?"

"More than one hundred."

"And what about marriage? Do Jews often intermarry with Muslims?"

He held out his flattened palm and tilted it from side to side. "They do."

"That's unusual," I said.

"Not really. In Morocco there is a long history of compatibility between Jews and Muslims. We live together without racism, without prejudice. Jews and Muslims grow up in the same neighborhoods; often our families live so close together that we are like cousins. Jews will have many Arab friends, and Arabs will have many Jewish friends. And once every year—this coming weekend, in fact—the Arabs will visit the Jewish homes and buy bread from them."

"Buy bread?"

"*Bien sûr.* It is the time of year when bread is forbidden in the Jewish homes."

"Of course. I'm sorry. Passover."

"Exactly."

I took a picture of the man sitting on the bench, the gravestones of the Jewish cemetery arrayed behind him, the mosques of Djemma el Bali rising in the distance. He had a pleasant, reserved smile and seemed perfectly content to while away the afternoon in the cemetery.

I asked, "Will your Muslim friends visit your home this Saturday?" He looked confused. "To buy bread." He continued to regard me blankly. "As you mentioned. Do you keep the Passover?"

"Ahh!" His face lit up, and as he smiled I saw that there were still black hairs in his mustache. "No, no. . . ."

"You'll go to a seder elsewhere, then?"

He shook his head and reached out to shake my hand—Morocco's universal gesture of agreement, amity and amusement. "Not this year," he said.

I held his hand and returned his smile. "Why not?"

"Because I am Muslim," he replied, "and we do not celebrate the Passover."

Labyrinth Fatigue

It was difficult to write in Fès. In fact, it was barely possible. Despite infinite impressions and scores of chance encounters, despite countless snapshot glimpses of lavishly tiled mosques and hours spent shopping for fezzes in the manure-strewn maze of the medina, I could not sit down and collect my thoughts.

This sort of thing happens, of course. But on a voyage like ours, traveling incessantly, the necessity of keeping an up-to-date journal chased me through the fallopian byways of West Africa like a rolling juggernaut in an Indiana Jones movie. Even Nouadhibou, which I despised, received far more attention than Fès, the most marvelous bazaar on Earth. As a lifelong shopper I was completely overwhelmed. No place, not even wonderful Marrakesh, prepared me for the sensory overload of the Fès souks.

Part of the problem was Fès itself. Fès is a place where everything is negotiable. It is a city where one learns how to shut oneself off, to turn one's back to all demands. After three days of dodging leechlike guides, shaking off street urchins and repulsing fanatical carpet dealers—after dealing, in short, with a full spectrum of career hustlers—putting off writing for a day (or three) didn't require much effort. My weary self-manipulations seemed embarrassingly flimsy, compared to a kilim seller's spiel.

That wasn't all. One gets tired in Fès. Shopping is exhausting. Nearly all of the sights worth seeing are scattered throughout the medina, lost between the spice and soup and lemonade souks. It is part of my makeup, my blood, that I find tiny shops selling ceramic drums and parrots, Bartholomew Tucker slippers and sinuous brass hookahs infinitely more compelling than a tiled column or dry fountain. The past is dead; shopping is Here and Now. While in Fès I shopped, and after a full day of haranguing and being harangued, of allowing myself to be overstimulated by goods, of bringing myself to the brink of orgasmic purchases and backing down again, the last thing I had the energy to do was sit down and describe the kebab sandwich I ate for lunch.

But let it go on record that I loved Fès, as one can sometimes love a musty labyrinth of infinite turns and distractions. Navigating the souks of the Fès medina was like tripping on mushrooms, like rafting through the canals of my own mind. The diversions were endless. I wandered for hours through the ancient and narrow corridors, wandered until my feet couldn't stand it anymore, wandered in good moods, in foul moods, hungry, bloated, inspired, impatient, buying a sack of olives here, a few wedges of chocolate there, some fried fish here, a plate of hummus there. I bought little else, realizing that nothing I could take away from Fès would be powerful enough to recall the city and its medina with any accuracy. Though there were many items that Sally and I fell in love with, we left Fès empty-handed—and too soon.

Edge City

We stopped to change trains at Sidi Slimane. The air was cool and damp, and the smell of orange blossoms was dizzying. The benches along the platform were painted banana-yellow, tile-red, and olive-green. There was music in the air: an orchestral version of "Black Magic Woman" issued, with impressive fidelity, from speakers perched in the lamp poles.

The tracks were covered with oranges, hundreds of them, and as the express train to Tangier pulled into the station, freshly squeezed orange juice flowed between the ties.

o   o   o

Forty kilometers south of Tangier the African continent, at its most northeasterly edge, drops sharply away and into the sea. Shepherds sit on the cliffs, staring out at the surf as their flocks graze alongside the railroad tracks. Campsites with names like Sahara and Atlantis line the coast, and even the filling stations have outdoor cafés with folding umbrellas.

We passed rolling hills neon-yellow with mustard, a million purple and red and orange flowers heaped together in every possible combination, begging once again the question posed by Doug Coupland in *Generation X:* "Can colors in nature clash?"

I spotted the chalk mark of a muezzin's tower against the indeterminate sky. Out the other window, an array of satellite dishes rose like mushrooms beyond a broad, silty estuary.

The southern outskirts of Tangier—brick-red, chalk-white and Crayola-beige—climbed trampled green hillsides. We spied a row of antique brass cannon pointing toward the sea. I traced their line of fire, but could not make out Spain.

· 20 ·

Three Fingers This Time

The feeling in Tangier is that anything is possible. Not as it was in the 1950s, perhaps, but possible nonetheless. In some ways the city feels like the northern edge of San Francisco: white buildings and long stairways clustering down steep hills that terminate at the docks and the sea. Tangier was the original Barbary Coast, and though time has tamed its deadlier appetites there remains the growl of unrequited hunger and a taste for the indecent. The music in the restaurants is loud, and the drinks are strong. Women sway down Boulevard Pasteur showing their legs, the vulvalike hoods of their striped djellabas lying open on their backs. And Tangier, like San Francisco, is a city of action. Vehicles—ships, trains, taxis and ferries—are continually on the move. The streets are thick with pedestrians. Fish fry hurriedly in narrow outdoor cafés. Boys with acne-scarred faces cast their nets from doorways, peddling sex and hashish.

To a traveler arriving from Europe, the hustle of Tangier is ugly and off-putting; but Sally and I had cut our teeth in Marrakesh and Fès, not to mention Mauritania, and fell in love with the ocean breezes and hot french fries.

o   o   o

The Morocco Tourist Office was a long shot, but it seemed like the most obvious place to start.

The tiled floor led me toward a broad wooden desk covered with travel brochures. A very pretty young woman sat behind the desk, while a middle-aged Moroccan guide with a narrow, deeply lined face leaned against it. He was wearing a heavy cotton burnous and a tall maroon fez. He smiled as I approached, revealing werewolf incisors.

I introduced myself to the woman, requesting two maps of Tangier. When she had circled the central synagogue and a few other sights, I mentioned the real reason for my visit. At this she glanced hurriedly to the side, and the silent Moroccan stepped forward.

"I am Ahamed," he announced, offering his hand. "I know Paul Bowles."

It was three in the afternoon. I returned to our hotel to change my shoes. Forty-five minutes later the guide was hailing a cab on the Boulevard Pasteur, squinting with annoyance as a seemingly endless succession of vehicles passed us by.

Ahamed, a native of Tangier, had been a guide for almost thirty years. He'd been to Bowles's flat a few dozen times, usually bringing foreign journalists, Beat groupies or other curiosity seekers. His most recent visit had occurred about a year and a half before. Since that time, Ahamed warned me, Bowles's health had deteriorated; he could get me to the writer's apartment but offered no guarantee of an audience.

Paul Bowles's flat is located on Tanger Socco, a 7-dirham taxi ride from the center of Tangier. It's in a gray, institutional building bristling with antennas. A small variety store plastered with Coca-Cola signs occupies the ground floor. We entered the building from the back and stepped into a tiny elevator. Though ugly from the outside, the building was pleasant within. Late-afternoon light filtered in through an architectural trellis, illuminating wooden doorways and broad steps cut of white marble.

Ahamed pushed the button marked 4. We emerged into a cold and nearly featureless hallway; to our left was a heavy door distinguished by a small brass plaque: BOWLES. A man selling lilies sat on the nearby stairs, looking like a refugee from a Diego Rivera painting.

Ahamed rang the bell. A leathery, bald caretaker with copper skin opened it. He exchanged a few friendly words with Ahamed, took my card and closed the door. A moment later the door opened again, and the man muttered something to Ahamed. I needed no Arabic to realize we were being offered his regrets.

"Please tell him," I said, "that I wish only to pay my respects. If Mr. Bowles is feeling ill I can return tomorrow."

Ahamed persisted, in that irresistible good-natured Moroccan manner, and after a few minutes of conversation turned back to me with a translation. "He says that Mr. Bowles is resting. But you can see him for five minutes, ten minutes at the most." I nodded. "I'll hold the taxi," Ahamed promised. "We'll leave when you're finished."

o   o   o

Bowles's apartment consisted of four rooms. I entered through the front door, passing a small kitchen on my right, and traversed a living room—the largest room in the house—with dark curtains drawn. Half a dozen kilims covered the floor, and there was a low sofa. A coffee table sat in the center of the room, covered with art books. Against the left wall stood a bookshelf filled with editions and translations of works by both Paul and his wife, Jane Bowles, who died of cancer in 1973. In the corner, beside the bookshelf, was a compact stereo with stacks of CDs piled on the floor around it.

The far-right corner of the living room ended in a square nook with three doors. The door on the left opened into Bowles' study. I couldn't resist peering inside. It was a veritable shrine to the printed word, with three walls hidden by sagging bookshelves. The fourth wall held a huge picture window which, facing east, admitted a broad panorama of the hills and illuminated buildings beyond his neighborhood.

The central door led into the boudoir, lit by an incandescent table lamp. Every inch of the small bedroom was spoken for. Clothes were heaped on the bureau. Two portable stereos and a collection of recordings sat below the shuttered window. Books littered the floor, sat in sliding piles beneath the dresser, edged off the table, infiltrated the chaos of the bureau, congregated under the bed.

The author of *The Sheltering Sky* lay between black paisley sheets, propped on a pillow, wrapped in a pale brown felt robe. A bed table bridged his lap; upon this rested his tea, a few gelatin capsules, a lighter and a hand-painted antique cigarette case filled with *kif* cigarettes.

A circular table in the center of the room was loaded with balms and medicines—an arsenal against the eighty-three-year-old writer's plethora of ailments. Bowles lay in his bed, his physical frailty belied by his sharp gaze and immediate wit. I shook his hand.

"I'm Paul Bowles," he informed me, so that there would be no confusion.

My chair was on the other side of the table. Bowles, his books and myself formed a constellation in the close atmosphere of the room. I placed the lily I had bought on the table. A moment later, flustered, I stood up to shake his hand again.

"You don't remember," he laughed, "because I gave you only one finger last time. This time I'll give you three."

Bowles's face looked long in the photographs I'd seen, but framed between the pillows and the folds of his nightshirt it appeared compact, even gnomic. Deep furrows ran alongside his nose. His eyes were large, blue and very focused. He may have been in pain—he'd recently had surgery to remove a tumor from behind his right ear, and his legs were giving him trouble—but if so it did not register in his face. He appeared completely at ease, immediately engaging and marginally flattered to be a site of pilgrimage on my round-the-world journey.

"I certainly hope you didn't come," he said suspiciously, "to meet the grandfather of the Beat writers."

"Well, that would probably be Burroughs," I said. "Anyway, you're not a Beat writer."

"You're right." He nodded approvingly, as if I'd passed a test. "I never was. But people get that confused. All those pictures of Ginsberg and so forth in Tangier. But I never was a Beat writer, no. I love the English language too much. I was always too . . . I don't want to say *literate* . . . I was always too *literary*."

Bowles, born in 1910, grew up in New York City. During the 1930s he lived for a time in Paris, meeting Alexander Calder and rooming briefly with Gertrude Stein (who, claiming that all Americans stank, forced him to take cold baths). Though he's best known as a novelist and short story writer, Bowles first achieved notoriety as a composer. He studied music with Aaron Copland and as a young man made a good living writing music for Broadway shows. He also served as music critic for the now-defunct *Herald-Tribune*—an experience that led directly, he claimed, to his ability to tackle the challenge of writing a novel.

"I liked doing all that," he said, lighting a kif cigarette. "It was fun. But in order to do it I had to live in New York. And I was getting fed up with the life in New York. I was getting fed up with New York itself, it was changing. It began to change at the time of the New Deal, under Roosevelt. People were looking for food in garbage cans and things were getting very bad. Not for me, no, but for society in general it was not a good era. There were muggings, which had been unheard of before. And because I had already lived for years in Paris, and in Europe, it was an incentive to get out of America."

Bowles moved to North Africa in the late 1940s. He was immediately fascinated by Morocco— a place that seemed to break all the rules—and still recalled the first time he tried to mail a letter home.

"I went into the post office and asked for a dozen airmail stamps, and the clerk told me how much they cost, and I said, 'Really? That much?' And he said, 'Okay, how much you pay?' It was the first place I'd been where you had to bargain for postage stamps."

His first novel, *The Sheltering Sky,* was published to critical acclaim in 1949—one year before his fortieth birthday. He'd celebrated by buying a Jaguar convertible; not a bad vehicle for cruising the mountains of Morocco.

We spoke about Bertolucci's treatment of the book. Bowles was bitter that he hadn't received any additional money for the film (he had sold the movie rights in 1964) and was even more irritated by the Italian director's insistence that the female character in the book (played by Debra Winger) was based on Jane Bowles.

"That was absolute nonsense." He practically spat the words. "Jane had never even set foot on the African continent at that time."

Bowles was especially peeved by the gratuitous lovemaking scene that had been stuck into the screenplay.

"There was no sex in the book," he insisted. "None."

"I'm surprised to hear you talk this way," I said. "In all the interviews I've read about the film you've been very gracious."

"I was gracious," he confirmed wryly. "But not grateful."

The circumstances endured by Bowles's characters can seem dream-like and unreal—often terrifyingly so. *The Sheltering Sky* is a case in point. I wondered aloud how much of his fiction was taken from real-life situations.

"Almost everything I've written is fact. *From* fact," he amended.

"Really? Even *A Distant Episode?*" I referred to his most graphic and disturbing short story, in which a scholarly linguist is captured by a re-mote desert tribe. His tongue is cut out, his clothing is burned and he is forced to perform like a dancing bear for visiting nomads.

"*A Distant Episode* also." Bowles laughed at my incredulity. "What happened, really, was that a young German had gotten all across the Sahara—I don't know what he was doing—and he wanted to get back to Europe. This took place in the 1930s, I think. And as he went on and on from one place to another he would try to find some natives who would help him find a caravan or something. What he discovered was that *they would only help him if he masturbated in front of them.* They thought that was so wonderful! It was something they couldn't even conceive of!" Bowles relit his cigarette, his shoulders shaking with mirth. "But he did, and he had to do it, and that got him across the desert—back up to the Territoire du Sud and to Algiers.

"That impressed me very much. I thought it was so funny. And that was the basis of my story. Of course, it seemed right that my own char-acter should be a linguist, and lose his tongue. There's another story by Camus that came out; it's called *The Renegade.* In it there's a European, I suppose French, who had been living with natives down in—it didn't say. And they removed his tongue so he couldn't talk. I think that was a fairly common occurrence. Common . . ." He rolled the word around. "Well, not very. Perhaps once or twice a year. Anyway, it wasn't *all* invented. . . ."

o   o   o

I told Bowles about my own book and, finding an atlas, showed him how I planned to get to India: via Europe, Turkey and Iran.

"I've no desire," he bristled, "to visit that fascist country."

"From your description, Morocco is pretty fascistic as well."

"Ha!" He shifted beneath the sheets. "It's not *even* fascist; it's *feudal.* In Iran, at least, you can talk about going back to a golden age; Morocco never had a golden age," he snorted. "Or it's still in it. The king has power of life and death over everybody. Literally. If he goes out and sees a house he likes, he takes it. Whatever he wants he takes. He owns practically the whole country."

"Have you met the king?"

"No! I don't know *royalty*." He pronounced the word with irony but became circumspect. "Since I live here, I can't talk against the king. I can't. Even in the cafés, you really get in trouble if you say anything. A Moroccan friend of mine—a well-respected writer—said in the Café de Paris one day, 'There's nobody over me but God.' He spent six months in jail for that. And six months is nothing! Some people spend twenty years. Or forever."

"Have you ever spent time in prison here? You wouldn't be here now if you had, I guess."

"No . . . There aren't very many foreigners in Moroccan jails. They're not worried about foreigners; it's their own people they're concerned with. There are members of the secret police everywhere: disguised as beggars, as high school students . . ."

I told Bowles what had happened to me the previous evening. I'd been sitting in Les Ambassadeurs at midnight, typing on my Omni-Book, when two men pulled up chairs beside me. They pushed my hands off the keyboard and tried to see what I was writing. I refused to show them and turned the computer off. A few minutes later I left the bar. The men followed me outside, grabbed me by the arms and threw me—despite my shouts for help, which brought the entire neighborhood running into the street to watch—into the back of an unmarked sedan. Next thing I knew I was in police custody.

"My God." Bowles looked more amused than shocked. "What did they accuse you of?"

"Espionage. They said the place was a hangout for spies, and that I fit the general description. I guess they decided I was legitimate, because they let me go. The two goons who had grabbed me walked me back to my hotel, apologizing profusely and shaking my hand. 'Welcome to Morocco,' they said. 'You are most welcome here.'"

"You're lucky," Bowles said. "Some people disappear entirely."

Fifty years is a long time to live anywhere. I asked Bowles about the changes he'd witnessed in Morocco, expecting to hear the usual complaints about traffic, population and prices. What he said, though, surprised me. His deepest regret—or his most immediate one—was the lack of good honey in the souks.

"It used to be you could get the most beautiful honey, made from local wildflowers. So thick, and a very deep gold, almost amber, in color." His eyes cleared. "Nowadays you just don't find it anymore. Only the watery commercial stuff, more syrup than honey. It's really a shame . . . ."

We spoke for hours. When I rose to leave it was 9:00 P.M.

"Come back tomorrow," Bowles suggested, handing me his bed tray to carry into the kitchen. "At four o'clock. For tea."

I walked through the living room and let myself out of his apartment. Large was my astonishment when I bumped into Ahamed in the hall. He'd been waiting for five hours—and so had the taxi.

The Four Questions

How many more times will you remember a certain afternoon of your childhood, some afternoon that's so deeply a part of your being that you can't even conceive of your life without it? Perhaps four or five times more. Perhaps not even that. How many more times will you watch the full moon rise? Perhaps twenty. And yet it all seems limitless.

—The Sheltering Sky

Every spring, for as long as I can remember—on the full moon of the Jewish month of Nisan—I have observed Passover, celebrating the liberation of the Israelites with my Jewish and Gentile friends. Though Sally and I had turned down an invitation to a seder in Fès, I was confident we'd find an opportunity to attend one in Tangier. Saturday morning I haunted the Orthodox synagogue on Rue Louis Pasteur, waiting abashedly in the temple lobby while, inside, the men offered their prayers and the women peered down from the balcony.

My attempts to secure an invitation for a seder were somewhat awkward. No one in the congregation spoke English, and I hobbled along in clumsy French. Finally I was told to return at six-thirty in the evening, after the Sabbath services had concluded. The rabbi himself, I was assured, would certainly invite us to join his family for the first seder. Members of the congregation would speak with him about it that afternoon.

To my eternal guilt and damnation, I stood the rabbi up. I spent the entire evening of the full moon on Tanger Socco, planted at the foot of Bowles's bed. He offered me a cigarette; I refused, but accepted a cup of unsweetened tea.

"Yesterday," I said, "you said that words were your ammunition, your 'bullets.' I was surprised to hear you use that allegory."

Bowles shrugged, his open robe hitching on his shoulders. "Well, in defensive terms, sure. Words can be seen as bullets. I've always seen them that way. What do you defend yourself with, if you're a sedentary type? You've got nothing to shoot at people except words."

"Why defend yourself at all? Anyway, that's a rather *offensive* kind of approach."

He lifted his owlish eyebrows. "Is it?"

"I think so. I've never thought of words in terms of weaponry. During our conversation yesterday you just seemed so fed up with that whole aspect of humanity. The aggression, the violence . . ."

"Well, of course. But it seems to me that you do have to defend yourself, you know?"

"Against what?"

"Against the world. The world which is inevitably attacking you. That may be paranoia, but I feel that any creative artist is an enemy of society. I think you have to . . . Well, I don't know that I consider that the entire world is against me now, but people are so likely to misunderstand everything. I mean in your writing. In *my* writing. And then they accuse me of the strangest things. I think most people resent being accused, without knowing of what. If you're a writer, you have nothing at your disposal except words. And that determines your attitude toward words; toward what one does with words. One uses them, hopefully, to express ideas. It's not always easy to put ideas into words. But if you try hard enough you can do it, of course. That's what I mean by ammunition."

Bowles began complaining of an ache in his right foot. I offered to massage it, but he asked me to just pull the sock off instead. I removed the argyle sock and studied his foot—pale and venous—thinking about the fragile corporeal container that serves, for a short time, to schlep our brains around.

"I hope I'm not overstepping my bounds," I said, "but I'd like to ask you—do you think much about death?"

He nodded, more in response to his willingness to answer than as an affirmative. "It doesn't worry me. What worries me is pain. All I want is a quiet death, without writhing around. But you never know what you're going to get. Maybe I'll get hit by a truck and die in . . . what's it called? Jane was in it for about eighteen months. . . ."

"Traction?"

"Traction. With one leg way up there. That's it. I couldn't get it." He appeared worried. "Maybe I do have Alzheimer's disease. . . ."

"You're more lucid," I said, "than most forty-year-olds I know."

"Really? Wow!" His eyes lit up, then narrowed. "How about eighty-year-olds?"

"Well, my grandmother doesn't have your attention span. I don't know many eighty-year-olds, really. Maybe three or four—"

"Actually, death . . ." Bowles cut me off. "There's no such thing. It doesn't exist. One ceases to function, but the existence of death can't possibly be perceived. Therefore it doesn't exist."

"So you see something beyond death?"

"No." He shook his head emphatically.

"You don't believe in life after death, or reincarnation?"

"Why should I? How could I?" He tilted his head and regarded me quizzically. "No. I don't go in for mysticism. I don't like it. It's a kind of superstition."

There was a brief silence. I asked, "Do you expect anything more from yourself creatively?"

He looked at me with bald incomprehension. "I never had expected anything."

"That's useful to hear." I nodded. "I expect a lot of myself, and it's a constant source of guilt and disappointment when I don't deliver."

"That is something I have never felt."

"What motivates you, then? What drives you on?"

"An idea. A possible situation. It's a *game*, writing." He adjusted his legs beneath the blankets, wincing. "You play it with yourself, of course. You set yourself certain goals and try to make the result what you imagined it. You can do it with words; you can't do it with anything else. And if you're a thinker—someone who can deal with abstraction, comfortably, which I cannot—you can decide beforehand what you're going to do. But I've never been able to do that. Neither in a given work, or in my life in general. I don't like plans," Bowles said. "I never knew why people have them."

"I suppose that's true," I said. "You mentioned yesterday that you were always willing to change, to do what seemed right at the time. You had invested a tremendous amount in your identity as a composer. And yet you allowed that identity to shift, to change, without clinging to a concept of yourself as a person whose whole life was music."

Bowles lit a kif cigarette before replying.

"Smells like a pretty fragrant mixture you're smoking there..."

"That's not a mixture," Bowles replied testily. "It's pure kif. Marijuana. I can't smoke tobacco. That's why my leg is bad; if you smoke a lot, which I used to do, your arteries and veins can become restricted.

"But back to your question. No, I never thought that way. I never thought my life was *anything*. In fact I didn't think about my life. I lived. I tried to live; to eat and so on, though I never had any money. Sometimes I had an inheritance, a small sum, which helped a lot, especially if you're living abroad, where the dollar is good and local currency isn't. But I didn't have any concept about having a *life*; or a career, or whatever that is, no. I thought I must do what I'm supposed to do, that's it. What I *think* I'm supposed to do. And I knew that I had to eat for the energy to be able to do it."

The mention of his avatar as a composer put me in the mood for some music, and I asked if I might hear some recordings from his New York days. When Sally arrived, at six, Bowles and I were listening to a recording of his Concerto for Two Pianos, Winds and Percussion (1947) on an Aiwa boom box. After brief introductions Sally peered around the room, trying to imagine how it had looked when Bowles had been married.

"You lived here with Jane, isn't that right?"

Bowles looked her up and down. "No, she had the flat right under me. On the third floor."

"So you didn't share this room?"

"I have never," Bowles revealed, "been able to sleep in the same room with another person. Never. I've never been able to. And I never hope to start trying; it would be absurd. I'm sure, if you like traditional sex, you want to be next to a person, whatever sex they are. You want to be physically close. I assume that's what sex is. But it's something I could never do, never in my whole life." His eyes brightened. "It kept me out of the army."

o   o   o

We drank tea and listened to a few more of his compositions. Presently Bowles slept. Before we left I wandered into his study and watched the paschal moon rise over the hills of Jebala.

Wandering Jew Redux

Our final morning in Tangier I stepped gingerly into the synagogue to apologize for our absence the night before. I was absolved of my guilt, handed several packets of round matzohs and reminded that the second seder would take place that evening. We were tempted to stay, but the pull toward Algeciras was stronger. It was time to bend ourselves in an easterly direction, where lay the remainder of the world's circumference.

We booked tickets on the four-o'clock ferry and returned to our hotel to pack. Once my Endless Journey was loaded I turned to Sally. "I'll be back in an hour or two," I said, and fled the room.

I made my way to the souks, combing the narrow lanes and avoiding the touts who tried to slip black balls of hashish into my pockets. Finally, between a perfumery and a shop selling ceremonial circumcision gowns (male), I found what I was looking for.

At noon—God only knew what Bowles would be doing at noon—I hopped compulsively into a taxi and found my way back to his ever

more familiar apartment building. The elevator was broken; I climbed
the steps silently, as if fearful of being caught.

Walking through the living room, I heard the television. By the time
I reached the doorway into the bedroom Bowles had ejected the documentary he'd been watching on his VCR. The set was alive with snow
and loud static. While he fumbled with the remote I leaned over and
manually turned the volume down. Then I sat at the foot of his bed.

He appeared neither unhappy nor annoyed to see me. Surprised,
perhaps, but not as surprised as I was to be there again. Still, I knew immediately that my spontaneous visit had not been a mistake. I had
acted impulsively—a motivation that Paul Bowles was uniquely prepared to understand.

It was a wonderful afternoon. There was no tape recorder this time,
and no other guests. He began by asking me to define two words he'd
just read in a new book about the human fascination with the death
penalty: *sleazy* and *ditzy*. I did my best, and introduced him to *gnarly*,
gross, and *radical* as well. We segued from there into a discussion about
the universal fascination with death and suffering. Bowles claimed he
didn't understand it—but I suggested that that same morbidity also attracted people to his own works. He took umbrage with this, insisting
that his work was widely misunderstood.

"I don't write about the dark side of humanity," he said, "but about
people driven by compulsion."

"But we all know," I said, "where compulsion has led humanity."

He spoke about stopping, and moving on; about how one can travel
the world, yet never leave oneself behind. He spoke about how so much
of the pleasure of travel is simply being in between places, in transit,
rather than in any place in particular.

"And when you traveled," I asked, "how big was the world?"

"Ahhh." His pale blue eyes were limpid as koi. "It seemed absolutely
immense."

For Bowles, the great motivating force in life had always been travel,
though it was no longer physically possible for him.

"My one regret," he said—probably in a somewhat different context—"is this." He gestured down at his body. "Getting old."

"Would you rather have died young?"

"In some ways it would have been better," he admitted, shifting.
"There's not much point going on like this."

"There's a Yiddish proverb," I offered. *"One should live if only to satisfy
one's curiosity."*

"Ha! Well, I suppose I completely agree."

"I have something for you," I said, and reached into my daypack.

Bowles took the half-liter jar of thick wildflower honey in his narrow, wizened hands.

"Where on Earth did you find this?"

"In a little souk, down in the medina. The jar was extra."

We broke the matzohs together and spread them with the honey.

"To liberation," I said, raising my piece.

"Oh?" Bowles lifted his eyebrows. "Do you think it's possible?"

Presently he rose slowly from the bed, put on his slippers and moved toward the living room to take his soup before the fire.

I took his hand. "I feel surprisingly sentimental about you for having known you only three days."

"I like that," he said, smiling. And added, thoughtfully, "It's too bad you're not staying in town a while longer."

"Thank you," I said, helping him walk, "for your friendship."

"It was *easy*," he replied.

I settled him into his chair and stoked the fire.

"You have my blessing," Bowles said. "I wish you all the luck in the world."

I felt real love for the man and deeply regretted that I could not remain in Tangier.

"Perhaps I'll see you next spring," I said, narrowing my eyes. "You'll be here, won't you?"

Paul Bowles looked at me and smiled— an amused, open smile—and I understood that he had no plans, one way or the other.

· 21 ·

Fast Forward

We left Tangier the twenty-seventh of March, on the afternoon of a beautiful spring day. As the ferry began the short journey toward Algeciras I stood at the stern in second class, holding a cigarette (sometimes you just need to hold a cigarette), and folded my arms over the rail.

In front of me, due south, was all of Africa, still unimaginably huge and foreboding. To the west lay the Atlantic, choppy and black, curving like olive brine toward the horizon. Eastward rose the southern of the Pillars of Hercules (or the Knees of Aphrodite, an image that more closely befit my sense of consummation) and, beyond that giant outcropping of stone, the vast Mediterranean Sea.

To the north, Spain and the European continent welled up like a gigantic green fungus, frighteningly civilized, full of high-speed trains and racy ads for the United Colors of Benetton.

The ferry turned into a long, narrow bay. To starboard, the Rock of Gibraltar—Aphrodite's right knee—bent toward the sky. *A rite of passage,* I thought to myself; but the monolithic landmark, bristling with smokestacks and radio antennas, seemed less a tribute to our long perseverance than a monument to Britannic voodoo.

We docked in Algeciras half an hour late. The train to Madrid left in fifteen minutes. Everything depended on our clearing customs immediately and getting to the station as fast as humanly possible.

But there was a hitch. When we presented our papers at immigration the Spanish officer confiscated Sally's Australian passport and tossed it without ceremony into his tiny vestibule.

"*No puedes pasar,*" he declared without looking up. "You cannot enter Spain. Return to Tangier."

This was a surprise; the French consul in Tangier had assured Sally that her French visa was also valid for entry into Spain. A small detail, unfortunately, had slipped his mind: The diplomatic concession among France, Australia and Spain had expired five months earlier.

Sally begged and pleaded, but in vain. The agent wouldn't even look at us. Once every fifteen seconds he'd just shake his head and repeat: "Return to Tangier." I felt like we'd landed on a talking Monopoly board.

"Okay, here's what we'll do," she said. "You go on to Barcelona . . ."

"Forget it. There's no way I'm leaving you here. I'll go back too."

"*No.* You go on to Barcelona. Take a day or two to write. Leave a note at American Express, and I'll meet you as soon as I arrive."

"I can't let you do that."

"Why not?"

"Because . . . because . . . well, it's *Tangier,* for God's sake." The truth was, I couldn't think of any reason that wasn't patronizing, sexist or both.

"Go," she insisted. "Don't miss your train."

"Look." I motioned over to the main immigration office, where two uniformed men were smoking black tobacco. "Ask them. They're in charge; this guy's just a badge."

Sally nodded and walked across the now-empty customs room. The officers lowered their cigarettes. I watched her back as she charmed them. A minute later the agent who had taken Sally's passport was summoned; a minute after that she came skipping back, clutching her passport and waving both thumbs in the air.

We grabbed our packs and raced for the taxi stand. A driver named an extortionate price. Without bothering to bargain we tossed in our gear and sped off for the station, arriving on the dot of nine-fifteen. The place was utterly empty, save for a single train. An attendant materialized, and I grabbed his arm.

"Madrid?"

"*Si* . . . Madrid."

We leapt aboard as the train started moving. Seconds later we were pulling out of the station into the Spanish omelette sunset, leaving Algeciras, Africa and the Straits of Gibraltar behind.

Deconstructionist Diversion III

Europe was a known quantity, and an expensive one; we had no desire to tarry long there. We blew through Spain and Italy with the windy invisibility of a Pope's plea for peace, mindful of Sally's dwindling finances and my own obsessive compulsion to reach Turkey and make my way to Asia—hopefully through Iran, despite its initial refusal— before the Kailas expedition became a complete impossibility.

We could not, however, zip across Europe without paying homage to two cities, for there were sights in both Barcelona and Florence that I felt magnetically drawn to see.

o   o   o

Barcelona is a place where everything is straining at the edges. The city swells with intoxicating energy, bursting the seams of its thick Spanish wineskin. It's a city infectious with art, a fabulous city where the devil-may-care Catalonian spirit has exploded into full bloom. Nowhere else has a specific geographical resonance inspired so many artists—Miró, Picasso and Dalí among them—to throw caution so fearlessly to the winds. Even the chocolate galleries are a revelation, their artfully sculpted birds, mammals and dinosaurs peering over the huge fitted cobblestones of the Gothic Quarter. We passed one shop that sold paprika in eight savory shades; another that offered only handmade candles; a third specializing in gold-nibbed fountain pens. Every artisan in the city seems consumed by the obsession to create a masterpiece. And scattered amid the storefronts and galleries stand the startlingly inventive cathedrals, *casas* and fountains of Antonio Gaudí, the wildly prolific and conceptually outrageous Catalan architect whose confectionery buildings rise and wriggle in fantastic shapes that we recognize, instantly and intuitively, from our dreams.

We spent hours in the Picasso Museum. It was a revelation to see his famous pigeon drawings, executed in 1890; for though it's quite common to look at what Picasso drew at fifty and quip, "My eight-year-old could do that," it's far more difficult to find the fifty-year-old who can draw as well as Picasso could at eight. It is said that Pablo's father, an accomplished painter in his own right, was so impressed by his son's early sketches that he handed his own palette and brushes over to the boy. "I will never paint again," José Ruiz Blasco declared in 1894. "I now dedicate my career to yours." Picasso was then thirteen. The relationship remained powerful, for many of Picasso's early works are studies of José Ruiz. The portraits convey dignity, strength and an enormous capacity for commitment; traits Blasco must have bequeathed to his son, who pursued the same career with unflagging passion for eighty-five years.

Picasso's mastery of line and color grew like a cinder cone. Hot new powers sprang from his hand with each passing month. By eighteen he had completed *First Communion*, an oil painting that compares favorably to the best work of Vermeer. The most impressive thing about him, though, is that he seems to have lived forever. He was a geological force, shaping the epoch of modern art.

Viewing Picasso's work always has a profound effect on me, calling up an almost unbearable nostalgia for the years when, before dedicating myself to writing, I concentrated on the visual arts. Looking at his bold, playful ceramics made me want to tear up my contract, retire the Omni-Book, move into a bright studio (in Barcelona, Oaxaca or anywhere the light is good, the food is cheap and the women have black eyes) and get my priorities straight. For the argument expressed by Picasso is that man lives to make visual art; that nothing we do, short of sex, can be half as vital or a tenth as much fun. (And they are by no means, as he delighted in pointing out, mutually exclusive.)

But my disenchantment with writing had little to do with Picasso. It was symptomatic only of my exhaustion. Unlike the suspiciously prolific Spaniard, I do not sip from a bottomless well of inspirational nectar. During the thirteen weeks of our voyage my relationship with writing had run hot and cold. There had been days when I'd felt completely fluid, and my prose poured forth like oil from a '72 Chevy Nova. Other times I'd been content to sketch out a scene, or a bit of dialogue, and let the day's work go at that.

Since Marrakesh, though, I'd been in a slump. Places were going by fast, and the real-time task of measuring the size of the world seemed beyond me. Sally and I had begun lapsing, not into culture shock exactly, but into fugues of temporal disorientation. We experienced the dizzy incredulity that comes from being whisked from country to country, culture to culture, in a period of time so compressed that there is no opportunity to digest one course before being compelled to devour another. Boarding the train in Algeciras, zooming off to Madrid for a connection to Barcelona, neither Sally nor I was able to comprehend that our journey had already touched the soil of nine countries and stirred the waters of three seas.

"This is not a trip about Being There," I sighed as we left the museum. "It's a trip about *getting* there."

"It's about Being There while getting there," Sally parried.

She was right, of course. But when I turned on my OmniBook to seek that territory I found no There there.

o o o

As we were about to leave Barcelona I stopped at a covered bazaar to shop for fruit, olives and cheese. Sally waited outside, guarding our gear on the crowded sidewalk. She glanced up for a split second to locate me and her daypack was instantly stolen. Inside were her toiletries, spiritual books and private journal.

After a brief display of rage and disbelief, Sally accepted the loss with good grace. "At least it was mine they took," she said. "I've got my passport and traveler's checks in my money belt. Your daypack has everything: your money, your camera . . ."

". . . and my computer."

"Jesus." We stood helplessly by the curb, caught in a strange little eddy of grief and gratitude.

"If you'd gone back to Tangier," I reflected with irony, "this never would have happened."

"That's right." She managed a laugh and took the groceries in her free arm. "The blessings are always there. It's just a question of recognizing them."

Beneath the Giant Penis

After the sealed-up train compartments of Morocco and Spain it was a relief to be in Italy, where the windows opened and Mediterranean sea breezes swept through the cars; where the stations sold wine, huge bottles of *acgua minerale* and prosciutto by the kilogram. Italy is a place to eat up, a country of passionate appetites and the means for their speedy fulfillment.

We sat in velour seats eating fat sandwiches. The train to Florence passed rapidly through a concatenation of tunnels: long, cool semicolons holding their breath between sea and village scapes, harbors swelling with boats, stations named after various noodle shapes. . . .

o   o   o

Walking along the neon-lit Renaissance promenades surrounding the Duomo in Florence, a new phrase entered my vocabulary of self-abuse: *I am feeling my age.*

We'd landed in a Europe chock-full o' kids: backpacking surfer dudes in tie-dyed shorts; doe-eyed Chilean gals with big hair and black jean jackets; green-haired grads taking their big break before college; voracious packs of crimson-lipped sorority sisters on study-abroad programs. Italy had become a theme park for eighteen- to twenty-two-year-olds. Compared to these tourists I was ancient, a gnarled relic who actually remembered the day Kennedy was shot. I looked forty, and I felt it—so self-consciously that when the lavish Italian sun hit my face I hid behind my Ray Ban Wayfarers to conceal the laugh lines around my eyes (what could be more pathetic than trying to hide your laugh lines?) and watched my table companions "spaz out" as I told them how many rings lay beneath my bark.

I had hoped, even assumed, that after meeting Paul Bowles I was past all this. Bowles was an overripe octogenarian; beside him I was a tart green apple. But in Florence, despite the unarguable blessing of my relative youth, I was shuffled back to the unlucky end of the seesaw. Easter Week in Europe, a Bacchanalian chorus line of hips and heels, tits and ass, dipped me like a gelato cone into a salubrious stew of hot fudge pheromones. I melted.

Over a red-wine-intensive dinner of rigatoni with mushrooms, peppers and black olives—there are few things in life more satisfying than eating Italian food in Italy—Sally asked me how it felt to be surrounded by people half my age. The easy answer, partially true, was that it made me feel like shit. But she already knew this; I'd confessed as much on the steps of the Piazza Michelangelo at sunset, nursing a hand-rolled smoke and bemoaning the irretrievable verve and vitality of my youth. Now she wanted more, the Real Goo, and after giving the question some scrutiny I realized that there was indeed a deeper undercurrent at work.

I looked at Sally, sans shades, and grinned. "It makes me feel like I've escaped."

"Is that so? Escaped what?"

"Escaped getting stuck. Escaped doing what was expected of me: the six-figure corporate job, the second wife, the one-point-four kids, the monthly mortgage payments. Escaped being in a position where I could predict my future—the next twenty years, say—with any degree of reliability."

She refilled my glass. "Is that what you want?"

I shrugged. "On the one hand it's fantastic. My life is my own, I don't punch a clock, and the most traumatic decision I'm facing is whether to spend an extra day in Florence or hightail it to Istanbul. All that is true. On other hand. . . ." I stopped talking.

"Go on."

"All right. Beneath everything else there's this weird, itchy sense that I'm *not supposed to be here*. I'm not supposed to be living like this: riding buses and trains from one scene to another, sleeping somewhere else every other night, cavorting amidst the callow youth. What I'm trying to say is that there's a bizarre factor of guilt in the equation." I finished my wine. "And an element of shame."

"*Shame?*" She was dumbfounded. "What on earth have you got to be ashamed of?"

"Sometimes it feels like what I escaped from was growing up."

o   o   o

Michelangelo's *David* is of course in Florence, one of the few works of Renaissance art with panache to equal the *Mona Lisa*. At 10:00 A.M. the line outside the *Accademia* already stretched half a kilometer down the street.

"The imperfect minions," Sally remarked, "lining up for a glimpse of the perfect."

The interest in David—specifically David—fascinated me. The hordes outside the Accademia implied that an enormous number of people, whether they understood their inner motivation or not, harbored a compelling need to view, directly, this particular face of the Hero: this vision of a single adolescent stepping unhesitatingly into the mythos.

I, too, had always been captivated by the story of the Hebrew shepherd boy. No one can say whether David felt destiny brewing within himself during the first years of his life; but when the moment called, he knew there would be no second invitation. And though countless paintings portray the curly-haired youth, sword in hand, preparing to sever the fallen Philistine's head, only Michelangelo realized where the true drama of the scene lay: at the precise instant when a half-naked teenager, armed only with a sling, stepped forward to answer Goliath's challenge.

Judaism has no Holy Grail; but if a single object were to be culled from history to represent the spirit of the Jewish people, it could only be that sling.

And so we made our way slowly to the entrance, jostled by a thousand chattering tourists who felt mysteriously drawn to find the seed—as did I—of that divine recklessness, that potential for epiphanic risk, that sleeps within us all.

The enormous marble statue, like the rest of Florence, was obscured on three sides by obnoxious scaffolding, undergoing some costly renovation in preparation for the terrifying summer boom. Only the front was fully exposed. I found it intriguing that, from a distance, the face of Michelangelo's David appears to be fixed in a cocksure smile; almost a smirk, really. But as you get close—really close, to the point where you're craning your neck and staring up past the oddly uncircumcised sea cucumber of a penis at the enormous head—you realize that the expression is totally devoid of arrogance. David's face is a study in fearless, focused energy. He is looking straight ahead.

I told all this to Sally, who listened with intent amusement.

"Geoffrey Hill makes a good living prescribing movies for people," she reflected. "You might consider starting your own practice, prescribing museums."

o   o   o

Arthur Clarke once suggested that the invention of eyeglasses (an event that occurred around 1350) may have actually launched the Renaissance by doubling the useful productive lifetime of writers, artists and scientists. The next great expansion of humanity's natural vision, he continued, came some 260 years later—when the heretical Galileo turned his first telescope toward the heavens.

Our pilgrimage to Florence ended with a visit to the Museo di Scienza e Storia, where the great astronomer's two prototype telescopes—hand-ground lenses in simple brass pipes—lie in an unpresuming glass case. Florence, the cradle of so many discoveries, was also the point from which humanity first studied the moon, Milky Way and planets with heightened vision—gazing outward in awe and astonishment before looking back to reassess, with a fresh perspective, the size of this world.

Bardo of the April Fools

Our final night in Florence we ate only gelato: fig and eggnog, spinach and hazelnut, chocolate and mandarin orange, all the flavors of the rainbow scooped from fruit-embroidered pillows of lofty whipped mousse that we just wanted to smash our faces into.

Sally, who had been silent about her intentions since Senegal, announced a momentous decision: She would stay with me until Athens, fly to India from there and wire her patrons in Marin for another "loan." Flights from Greece were plentiful and cheap, and she was down to her last few traveler's checks. I made no effort to dissuade her from this course. Europe had been costly, and I was in no position to underwrite her onward journey. I'd find her in India, hopefully in late April. By then she would have padded her reserves, and we could talk about continuing on together to Kathmandu.

We met four other travelers in the gelato parlor. There was Chris Moon, a precocious physics student who kept a journal recording what his innumerable other selves might be up to in alternate quantum realities; a vivacious, round-faced Chilean attorney named Flora; a Texas-born Korean gardener named Jin; and Vanna, a statuesque, hazel-eyed Canadian art teacher who had decided—while gazing at Michelangelo's masterpiece, no less—that she needed to do something rash and adventurous with her life.

"Any ideas?" Her eyes met mine, flinting.

I fed her a spoonful of persimmon gelato, dazzled by the rush of chemistry. "Why don't you come to Istanbul?"

She pulled back and looked at me strangely. "It's amazing you should say that. For years I've had this recurring dream that I'm standing in that huge cathedral they have there—Hagia Sophia, I think it's called—painting the stained glass windows."

"You must know that famous Kurt Vonnegut quote," I said. "'Strange travel suggestions are dancing lessons from God.'"

The line touched a common nerve, and a wave of daredevil thinking engulfed the group. The evening took on an air of conspiratory and slightly hysterical inspiration. Within fifteen minutes everyone at the table—with the exception of Sally—decided to travel together to Turkey. Vanna was ecstatic; we swore we'd spend an entire day drawing at the magnificent cathedral that had haunted her dreams.

o   o   o

The train to Brindisi via Bologna—the one that hooks up with the overnight ferry to Greece—departs Florence at 7:23 A.M. Sally and I slept through the alarm and woke, physically shot but totally panicked, at seven. I swam out of the hotel in a mental murk, still half-immersed in a dream about hunting chocolate velociraptors with Vanna, and raced with Sally down the cold Florentine streets. We leapt into a taxi, blasted to the train station and arrived on the dot of seven-fifteen. Within five minutes the lot of us had assembled, slouching and bloodshot.

Chris, Jin and Flora were toting heavy rucksacks, but Vanna carried only a canvas book bag. My heart sank.

"I can't do it," she confessed. "It's too sudden. You can ask Jin . . ."

Jin rolled her eyes. ". . . I was up all night trying to decide. But when I really looked at the options I realized there are still too many things I have to see in Italy. I'm sure you'll all have a great time . . ."

The train lurched. My four companions grabbed their bags and jumped on board. I looked at Vanna but could think of nothing to say.

"Chill out," Chris advised as I collapsed into the seat beside him. "You're sharing a sleeper with her in a parallel universe."

We left Florence on the morning of April Fools' Day. The train would stop in Bologna at nine, reaching Brindisi that evening: time enough for a leisurely meal before catching the last ferry to Greece.

When nine o'clock passed, followed by nine-thirty, it occurred to me to ask someone what was up. That's when we found out we were on the wrong train. Or, rather, the right train, but the wrong car. The carriages to Brindisi had separated half an hour out of Florence. We were now aboard the nonstop to Milan, scheduled to arrive at 10:30 A.M. *Fuck! Fuck!* I banged my head against the wall.

Arriving in Milan, we found the Brindisi Express. It took every last second we had to spare to exchange our tickets, jump on the train and round up a few empty seats. They wouldn't stay empty long; in 1994, April Fools' was also Good Friday. Every seat on the daylong journey was booked.

The Center of the Earth

Miraculously, we made the ferry. In economic solidarity with my companions I purchased a ticket for Deck Class, a free-for-all accommodation just a notch above Baggage. The ship departed at eleven. By midnight I was encamped on an oasis of carpet behind the slot machines, which spewed jackpots with unpredictable riotous clamor. To my right lay a pod of wine-swilling Italians who barked like hyenas til 3:00 A.M.; to my left, a bawling babe. Shortly before dawn I fell asleep and had just reached a nub of blissful catatonia when a booted foot nudged my ribs. I opened my eyes and looked at my watch: The little hand was on the five. The steward continued his thankless rounds through the carpeted foyer, waking up snoring backpackers, huddled nuclear families and other luckless travelers who'd been too broke, too cheap or too in love with roughing it to pony up the $24 for a legitimate bunk.

Chris bailed at Corfu. He'd met two pale, beefy frat boys on a junket to a knockoff Club Med for horny twenty-year-olds—a possible universe that had struck him, clearly, as irresistible. That narrowed my Turkish entourage to two: Flora and Jin. We breakfasted in silence, as stunned by our sleep deprivation as bumblebees in a cigar divan.

Some hours later I stood on deck with Sally. The sun flashed off the Mediterranean, and pariah gulls hovered in the ferry's wake. We were in Odysseus's waters.

"I hope you'll manage okay," she said. "I know it's been difficult, and I'm confident this separation will be good for us, but some part of me still feels terrible about abandoning you." The wind swept through her hair. She looked like a goddess, if not a Greek goddess. "How do you feel about all this?"

"I don't feel you're abandoning me," I said. "I know how much you've been longing to get back to India. It's where you belong. Any disappointment I feel comes from the bigger picture."

"How do you mean?"

"It's weird, but even after all this traveling it doesn't seem like I'm discovering the size of the world. It's too fragmented; too piecemeal. All these different countries just seem like a bunch of suburban backyards—connected, but not cohesive. The most amazing thing we've discovered is the sheer *inconsistency* of it all. Going from New York to Senegal to Morocco to Greece . . . there's been no real pattern. It's a crazy quilt. The only common threads seem to be human hospitality, human suffering, and a universal attraction to stuffed animals." I picked a downy feather out of her hair. "I need a larger perspective, and I don't know where I'm going to find it."

"What you'll need to do is write an epilogue."

"An epilogue?"

"Sure. Once you get home, buy a ticket on the Concorde and circle the world in twenty-four hours. Maybe that's the only way you'll discover the mystery. This trip has been about crossing borders; maybe when it's all over you should experience a borderless world."

She reached into her shoulder bag and pulled out a small square package, tied with a red ribbon. "Happy birthday," she said. "Don't shake it. . . ."

I took the box from her and slipped off the ribbon. It was still knotted in a loop. Sally took one end, I took the other, and we snapped it like a wishbone. It fluttered out of our hands and vanished into the Mediterranean foam.

The box was surprisingly heavy. I tore off the wrapping and opened it up. Inside was a handsome nautical compass, a silver cylinder with a gleaming brass face. There was also a handwritten note:

Beloved Jeffji — How tacky to be wishing you happy birthday on a page torn from a travel book . . . but our whole journey seems to be about improvisation and spontaneity.

Here is a reminder for one of "Those" moments . . . a reminder that where you always are is HERE, *at the center of your experience, with the clear awareness that it is all happening within; that from* HERE, *you are the empty clarity for the fullness of life's display. Just a reminder to let you know that where you are is exactly where you're meant to Be; and if you don't like it . . .wait a moment!! It'll change! That's the beauty of movement, and the challenge is letting go into it; a courageous act that is a testament to your love of this world, your availability to experience and the curiosity that has brought you to this moment.*

Greatest blessings for the journey until we reunite in India. I hope that our time apart will bring us closer together. I have faith only in the knowledge of a friendship that, although sometimes obscured, will always bring us to a deeper level of understanding.

Love, Sal

"Look," Sally said. "This comes off."
The brass face of the compass unscrewed to reveal a hidden compartment. Inside was a small slip of paper, mint green:

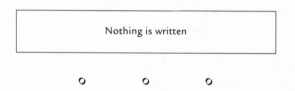

Nothing is written

o   o   o

We arrived in Patras at four-thirty and caught the express to Athens. There, in the train station, we heard about the wildcat strike: Tobacco growers in northern Greece were protesting for higher wages and, to put muscle behind their demands, had abandoned tractor trailers, automobiles and other inconvenient obstacles across railroad tracks and highways. Public transportation to Thessaloníki, hence to Istanbul, was impossible. The strike might be settled the next day, the railway attendant advised. Or next week. Or in a month or two.

We had two choices. The tracks were open as far as Lárisa. We could take the next train there—in twenty minutes—and pray that the strike had ended by the time we arrived at dawn. At the very least, it might be cheaper to take a taxi from a more northerly point. The other option was that we enjoy a leisurely dinner in Athens, catch up on much needed sleep and investigate ferries in the morning.

Both Jin and Flora, surprisingly, were raring to go. And though I was dizzy with exhaustion, the idea of reaching Turkey even one day earlier was more than I could resist. I bought my train ticket and gave Sally a long squeeze.

"We've been together every single day for the past fourteen weeks," she said breathlessly.

"That's right." I laughed. "And there were even a few days when we didn't want to kill each other . . ."

"Were there that many?"

"I love you," I told her, honestly.

"I love you," she said.

She shouldered her lightened load and waddled away, up the metal station stairs, toward overlit Athens.

• 22 •

Lost and Found

Green and silver: I raced through the Macedonian countryside, the sole occupant of a small cabin in a worn blue train, staring out the window at the northeastern anatomy of Greece as it rose and fell, rose and fell, here carpeted with grass, there glazed with snow and ice. Somewhere to my right, the Strymon River squiggled northward toward Yugoslavia. Thessaloníki was behind me. If I left the train and traveled a hundred kilometers south, I'd sink my toes into the uppermost waters of the Aegean Sea. This was where Alexander marched; where Saint Paul preached; where Mark Twain sailed. And I was slouching, wearily but happily, toward Byzantium. . . .

o   o   o

Lárisa had been pitch-black when we'd arrived. Fortunately I'd slept on the train, gotten in a good five hours, in fact, and was able to resume my usual litany of pessimism in the morning. My first premonition—that the tobacco growers' strike was still on—was correct. My second, that the Lárisa station would be abandoned, was not. Half a dozen taxi drivers hawked transport to Thessaloníki at the bargain-basement price of 8,000 drachmas per person. This worked out to $32—too steep for Flora and Jin.

Here the situation waxed awkward. I could pay the price; indeed, I had no choice. Istanbul was etched into my destiny. Jin and Flora, however, operated under no such contractual compulsion. Even if they agreed to pay a small fortune and continue on with me to Istanbul, what if the strike still hadn't ended in a week, when they had to return to Europe? What if they missed their flights? What if they were stuck in Turkey forever, sold into white slavery, forced to work as courtesans in the thick-walled harem of a Muslim sheik?

At the end of the day—which was actually the very beginning, since the sun had not yet risen and the crescent moon still hung like Artemis's crossbow in the sky—my two remaining companions decided to retreat. Even my suggestion that we wait out the day in Lárisa did not move them. There was nothing *in* Lárisa.

"There are twenty youth hostels all over Greece," Jin said, "and not a single one in Lárisa. That must tell you something."

Flora and Jin would return to Athens on the six forty-five and spend the day there. If the strike ended within a day or two, Flora promised, they'd meet me in Istanbul.

At that precise moment, a middle-aged Russian businessman with whom I'd arranged a taxi share to Thessaloníki began waving to us wildly. "*Bus! Bus!*" he shouted frantically. "*Bus! Thessaloníki! Bus!*"

This was something I should have anticipated. If taxicabs could blaze a route through the strike-blocked arteries, why not buses? Clearly they could, and the first such expedition was loading up—onto a rather smart-looking coach, I thought—not three meters from the Lárisa station's front door.

"Flora! Jin!" I cried. "This is it! This is our ride to Istanbul!"

But I knew from the weariness in their eyes that, like women who had leaned too far back on a sofa, their reverse momentum was too great. And I understood, not without a trace of sadness, that I would never see either of them again.

Our farewell was rushed and frantic, our good-bye kisses dry. Next minute I was on the bus, snug in a red velvet reclining chair, amazed to be so suddenly and completely alone. For the first time in three months I had no one to share my fears, hopes or decisions with. For the first time in the entire trip I knew the taste of total freedom. It tasted like an icicle, with pine needles frozen inside of it. I was suddenly a very contented man.

I hit the recline button and felt the hydraulic muscles of the chair provide me with lavish leg room. Out the window, to the east, Earth's nearest star was rising like a Saturn V over the supernaturally green hills of a miniature golf course. Straight ahead stood mountains: gorgeous platinum mountains, naked and streaked with the day's first light. The Russian man, in the seat behind mine, jabbed me in the shoulder.

"Olympus!" he shouted, thrusting the same finger toward the highest mountain, just ahead of us. "Look, look! Mountain Olympus!"

We shook hands. And as the bus climbed toward the snows, over the marble quarries, passing hog trucks and lumber trucks, Easter Sunday cracked its egg over my tired head. A huge gooey yolk of sunlight ran down my cheeks and neck and pooled into my lap.

"*'These are days,'*" I sang softly to myself. "*'These are the days . . .'*"

• 23 •

To: Allen Noren, O'Reilly & Associates
From: Jeff Greenwald, Turkey
Subject: Big World/Istanbul

Received a message from my OmniBook the other day that seemed ominous, even deadly: *"Warning! This Battery Can No Longer Accept a Charge!"*

I knew just how it felt. By the time I arrived in Turkey, after seventy-two straight hours of staring out moving windows, my brain felt like Jimmy Durante's sinus cavities after a triple-cheese pizza. I find myself coming to a point where I simply can't absorb any more stimulation. This continual moving, this endless opera of changing scenery, seems fundamentally at odds with my own hardwired neurology. . . .

o   o   o

The first thing I did in Istanbul was visit the Iranian consulate, a short walk from my hotel near the Sultanahmet tram stop. Despite encouraging words from a travel agent at the Orient Youth Hostel ("It all depends on the mood of the clerk. Charm him," he advised), my encounter with Iranian officialdom was curt and predictable:

"Yes?"

"Hi! Nice beard! I'd like to apply for an Iranian transit visa . . ."

"What is your nationality, please?"

"I'm an American . . ."

"No visa."

"Excuse me, but can I . . ."

"No visa."

"Why . . . ?"

"We give no reasons. No visa. *Good-bye.*"

I waited around, cunningly, until the next clerk came on duty. He dangled the cheese a bit longer before snapping the trap shut. At that point I left. And I had to admit, glancing at the photograph of the Ayatollah snarling at me from the wall, that I was only half-sorry. . . .

With my Iran visa once and for all denied, I find myself faced with three choices.

1. I can leave Istanbul at once and spend the next month threading my way through northeastern Turkey, across the Black Sea, into Georgia, and onward through Turkmenistan and Uzbekistan to Alma Ata, Kazakhstan. This plan has two strikes against it. The first is the civil war in Georgia; passenger trains are being blown up on a weekly basis. The second is the fact that, even if I reach Alma Ata safely, the road linking Kazakhstan with Pakistan will likely be snowed in til June.

2. I can visit agents in the Karaköy district and try to talk my way onto a ship that will carry me down the Mediterranean, through the Suez Canal, and across the Red and Arabian seas to Bombay or Karachi. But you don't really *see* anything on board a cargo ship.

3. I can spend another three weeks in Turkey, then buy (or rent) a magic carpet that will allow me to hop over Iran and reach Karachi by early May: enough time to hustle across India and Nepal to Kathmandu and join the long-anticipated Mount Kailas expedition by May 9.

That magic carpet idea gets more and more appealing. I still owe myself a fortieth birthday present and, luckily, I know where to shop. . . .

Enough on that tragic front. Here, direct from my overloaded wetware, is the latest in this series of scrambled-egg dispatches from the bus, train and taxi junctions of the world. Let's call it:

Marble Baths (and Other Turkish Delights)

"Awe is the salve that will heal our eyes."
—Mevlana Jelaleddin Rumi (1207–73)

My first image of Istanbul, at the end of the seventeen-hour train ride from Thessaloníki, was of a huge tractor trailer squeezing down a narrow ancient lane, filled to the brim with multicolored beach balls.

On the other side of the car, through the windows facing Bosporus Strait, red cargo ships drifted against the city skyline: huge bulbous domes mooning the early morning mist, pinned to the hills with lawn-dart minarets.

"Istanbul," I said to myself; for this is a city, like Marrakesh or Timbuktu, whose name you must roll around in your mouth. It is a geographical mantra, and arriving here after three months of overland travel, I had earned the right to pronounce it.

You cannot imagine how happy I am to be here. Sailing to Byzantium, even now—even by train—is still like arriving at the Navel of the World. This is the place where east meets west and explodes on contact. Stephen Hawking, speaking at the Berkeley Community Center a year or so ago, postulated that if there are such things as black holes ("events" in space where gravity is so extreme that even light cannot escape), there must also be phenomenon he dubbed *white holes:* phenomena from which light and energy gush, but with no apparent source. Black holes exist in our universe, Hawking posited; white holes may exist in an alternate universe, on the other side of black holes.

The point where they meet must be something like Istanbul. How do you approach the spiritual center of the country where Noah beached the Ark, Helen of Troy learned how to walk, Alexander the Great campaigned, Mary (*the* Mary, as in Mother of God) came to die, the Emperor Constantine launched New Rome and Mehmet the Conqueror built Topkapi Palace? How do you get your face around a city that every writer from Saint Paul to Yeats, from Mark Twain to Agatha Christie, has already sunk his teeth into? What do you do with a megalopolis that served, not to put too fine a point on it, as the center of the "civilized" world for two millennia?

The problem, at this point, is finding an angle, a perspective from which to capture it all. And I'm here to tell you that they don't make a lens wide enough. The trick, I think, is to approach the city as you would a Turkish bath: lie back, breathe deeply and let yourself be wrung out clean.

o   o   o

In reality, it's more like being pounded.

I wrote that first bit on Monday. Tuesday night I went to my first *real* Turkish bath. The venue for this obligatory baptism, this watery epiphany, was the Historical (a sign right outside the door says so) Çemberlitas Bath. (Though admittedly ancient, it's by no means Turkey's oldest. Çemberlitas was built by Mimar Sinan, Istanbul's greatest Ottoman architect, in 1584; but there's a bath in Konya—the spiritual home of the Sufi poet Rumi, whose words open this electronic transmission—that's at least a hundred years older.)

After shedding my clothes and wrapping my torso in what looked like a used tablecloth, I followed my masseur through a heavy wooden door into a sort of anteroom—an air lock, if you will—separating the grimy outer world from the realm of steam. In Islam, personal hygiene is religious law; Muslims are required to wash their arms, legs, hands, feet and face before praying, and they're required to pray five times a day. When these guys take a bath, it's not just about getting clean; it's a jihad against dirt.

Walking through the anteroom and into the huge marble bath vault was like falling back in time. Except for a few telltale signs—the bare bulb hanging from the center of the vast central dome, the plastic shampoo bottles and my own digital watch—it might have been the sixteenth century. Dusk light filtered though holes in the central dome, and every sound echoed off acres of damp white marble. In the center of the round chamber was an immense raised table of smooth marble. Men lay strewn across it, sweat pouring from their bodies. Within a minute I was among them, my agonized howls reverberating through the bath as the marble slab baked me like a pizza.

Once I'd sweated out every poison, biohazard and junior high school insult still in my bloodstream, my masseur beckoned me over into a little marble alcove with a marble trough and two brass spigots. He poured bowl after bowl of warm water over my poached form and, using a painfully rough mitt, sanded me down like an old chest of drawers. Forty years of used epidermis molted from my body, leaving me sheathed in a skin I barely recognized.

The scouring was followed by a "massage," conducted by a diapered ogre who was probably expelled from the World Wrestling Championships for throwing his opponent at the judge. He went over me like a rototiller, prying my muscles from my bones and twisting them into funny animal shapes. After that came enough soap to clean the Turkish armada, followed by a scalding rinse cycle.

The best part of the bath, by far, was the end. Staggering from the anteroom, limp as linguine, I was tossed onto a carpeted sofa and swaddled in towels from head to toe. Tea was served. If I'd been able to move my arms, I'm sure I would have enjoyed it.

o　　　　　o　　　　　o

Video clips from Istanbul:

The ancient fluted spires of the Blue Mosque illuminated by spotlights, gulls circling and screaming above the soaring golden finial, stars circling above the gulls . . .

Pilgrims crowding in around the glass case in the Topkapi Palace Museum, muttering prayers before a jewel-encrusted crystal box displaying a single hair from the Prophet Mohammed's beard. . . .

An old shoe-shine man in a knit skullcap sitting on a wooden bench in front of a hammered-brass shoe-shine box, his eyes following my feet as I walk by. . . .

Pages from clipped porn magazines blowing through a Muslim cemetery, past tall granite tombstones etched with Arabic script and crowned by carved turbans, fezzes and feathered hats. . . .

Swirls of multicolored natural dyes, rippling and twisting in a paper-marbling pan. . . .

o   o   o

"When I first discovered the magic of marbling," Hikmet Barutcugil told me as we drove to the university, "there was only one man in Turkey who knew how to do it. And he wouldn't teach me." Hikmet stopped the car to let an old man cross the street—unheard of on the streets of Turkey—and glanced at me with a smile. "But you know, it worked out for the best. If I'd followed his lead, I would be an expert at his method—and would never have discovered my own."

Hikmet Barutcugil grew up in eastern Turkey and moved to Istanbul in 1973. He's forty-two, and his hair and mustache are salted with gray. When they go white, he'll probably marble them. It wouldn't surprise me; he's marbled everything else. Examples of his peculiar genius—marbled lamps, scarves and picture frames, vases, tablecloths and paper canvases—adorn the walls and tables of Barut's Guesthouse, the family-style hostel that Hikmet and his wife, Fusun, own and operate in the Sultanahmet district of Istanbul. If "the aesthetic principle of Islamic art," as Barutcugil claims in one of his many articles, "can be defined as becoming one with God," Barut's Guesthouse is more than a great bed-and-breakfast; it's a shrine to spiritual self-realization.

The art of paper marbling flowered in Central Asia more than eleven hundred years ago, when it was developed as a tool for illuminating religious manuscripts (the earliest existing examples date from the fourteenth century). Twenty years earlier—when Hikmet approached the only living master at the craft—it was in danger of dying out. Barutcugil has almost single-handedly revived the art, and there seems to be general consensus that he is now Turkey's (and probably the world's) finest marbler. A professor at the School of Traditional Arts at Istanbul's prestigious Mimar Sinan University, he's given lectures and demonstrations on paper marbling in Europe and the United States. At a recent exhibition in London, the marbling technique he pioneered was named after him.

Joining Hikmet at class, I watched him work. The technique of the craft is bizarre; you can't help but wonder who on Earth could have discovered it, much less what they were really doing when they did.

Here's how it's done: Brilliant stone-ground colors are mixed with minute amounts of terrifically foul-smelling ox gall, which creates a surface tension that prevents the hues from running together. The colors are then dripped, splattered or flicked onto the limpid surface of a jellylike bath made of water mixed with tarragon sap.

It is there, on the surface of that slimy solution, that the marbler "paints." The colors pool discretely, lying obediently still until coaxed into flowers or swirls. No matter which technique is used, though, each color remains perfectly distinct. If Hikmet drips a drop of yellow into a pool of blue, the result isn't green; the blue forms a distinct doughnut around the yellow.

Adding other colors and swirling them into complex designs, Hikmet creates effects that even his most gifted students can't match. With a few deft flicks of his "brush" (usually the clipped point of a hypodermic needle) Hikmet creates a rose, a leaf, a flame. Once the desired effect is achieved, he drapes a sheet of paper over the colors—laying it down gently, to avoid air bubbles—and taps it flat. When he peels the paper back up, I'm astonished. The colors haven't run; they've been completely absorbed, producing a mirror image of the pattern that had floated on the bath.

o   o   o

Along with the lesson in marbling came a subtle revelation. Watching Hikmet at work, I was convinced that it's in the tarragon bath—not the Turkish—that one will find the most perfect allegory for Istanbul.

"The main goal of art," posits Barutcugil, "is to resolve the puzzles of the chaotic, temporal world of sensory perception."

Viewed with less than an artist's eye, this city embodies chaos. Istanbul (né Constantinople, né Byzantium) is a place of infinite colors; but despite thirty centuries of combing and swirling, nothing actually *blends*. Every hue remains distinct. This is a city liquid in time, never presenting the same aspect twice. More than Barcelona, more than Paris, more than Dakar, New York or Tangier, Istanbul is a place where humanity is continually creating a canvas marbled by genius and greed, inspiration and cruelty, holiness and hunger, thievery and love. It is the biggest city I have ever seen—and the most ambitious canvas hanging on this orbiting gallery of ours.

o   o   o

Before ending this transmission, I must say something about the mosques. There's a cosmic magnificence about them; they look like those lonely domed cities, surrounded by moons and strange gaseous nebulae, that appear on the covers of pulp sci-fi novels. Gazing at the domes, following their perfect curves into the stratosphere, never fails to sweep my mind off its feet. It is well known that Frank Lloyd Wright had a photograph of the Dalai Lama's Potala Palace on his office wall; it was the only edifice he found excellent enough to display. After visiting Istanbul, I can only conclude that his omission of Hagia Sophia—or the equally fabulous Blue Mosque—resulted from ignorance rather than intent. Nowhere have I seen more perfect examples of form following function. For not only do the mosques and cathedrals of Istanbul lift the pilgrim to heaven; they also whisper the blasphemous reminder that we ourselves are God. The Word of Allah—*I Am*—is the subtle subtext of these amazing human creations, these heroic architectural psalms from which the call to prayer is broadcast five times each day.

Ma' shallah! What wonders God has willed!

⚡   ⚡   ⚡

Air Lock of the Ordinary

Barut's Guesthouse, though warm and elegant, was slightly beyond my means. After spending two nights there I moved into a clean but run-down hotel around the corner, paying 175,000 Turkish lire (about $5.75) for a big, cold top-story room with a view of the freighters on the Sea of Marmara and, if I craned my neck, the pink minarets of Hagia Sophia.

At night the beam of the Karaköy lighthouse swept through my bedroom, its periodicity more frequent (but less distracting) than the call to prayer. Turkey was the only Muslim country I'd been to where I awoke to the muezzin with a smile. The melodic Koranic chanting was the polar opposite of what I'd endured years ago in Java, where tone-deaf muezzins blasted the population awake through blown car speakers.

o   o   o

I spent an afternoon in a gold-trimmed room in the Yildiz Palace, listening to the Istanbul Devlet Turk Muzigi Toplulugu, a twelve-member traditional music ensemble, perform. The group boasted an amazing array of instruments: haunting eleven-stringed *ouds;* long-necked *tanburs,* with their four pairs of sympathetic strings; a kind of lap harp called a *kanun; ney,* or Turkish flutes; miniature *kemence,* triple-stringed bowed instruments; and five singers. I sat in a folding chair in their unheated practice room and dozed off into a deep but luckily snoreless sleep as the droning, hypnotic harmonies filled the chilly room.

It was great to hear Turkish music for a change. The stereo in the bar of the Orient Youth Hostel—where I spent a few of my evenings—rattled the windows with Nirvana, Joe Cocker and the Rolling Stones. Though the rock 'n' roll provided a strangely fitting soundtrack to the panorama of cargo ships and storm clouds drifting above the distant Bosporus, I was disturbed by the lack of local tunes. It seemed symptomatic of a subconscious terror; as if the troupes of American and European mosque-hoppers, tipping back imported beers or descending into the fine print of their journals, desperately needed a safety net, an "air lock of the ordinary," to drop into. Getting too involved with an alien culture could be dangerous; it might shift one's attention away from the store windows and into one's soul. Watching Generation X on the hoof, I got the disconcerting feeling that the only reason they traveled was to discover new places to shop.

I burst from the air lock with a Bolivian traveler named Marco, who led me through the labyrinthine alleys behind the Blue Mosque to the Doy Doy shish kebab and *lahmacun* (Turkish pizza) salon. Marco was twenty-three, with dark hair, black eyes and almost effeminate features. He looked a bit like Keanu Reeves. He'd worked as a shepherd in the northwestern Negev for three months, alone most of the time, avoiding the meat-market atmosphere of the Israeli kibbutzes. He had been back in civilization less than a week when I spied him at the Orient, sitting alone at a crowded table with a slim volume of Rumi's *Quatrains*.

Over a dinner of chicken *tavuc* and sheep's-cheese pizza, Marco told me he'd be leaving Istanbul in a day or two for a personal pilgrimage to Rumi's shrine in Konya. When I suggested we make the trip together, he readily agreed.

"There's nothing more I can do in Istanbul." I'd filled him in on my catalog of woes, and picked surgically at my tapioca. "What I need now is a chance to think things out, and decide if I can get away with this whole 'magic carpet' scheme."

"A day or two of divine madness ought to help," he agreed. "At the very least it'll get you away from those *Beavis and Butt-head* reruns in your hotel."

We decided to leave in two days. A ferry would take us across the Sea of Marmara to Yalova, where hourly buses departed to nearby Bursa. From Bursa we could catch an overnight coach to Konya.

o   o   o

American Express in Istanbul was the first mailing address I'd given my friends since Dakar. The next afternoon I made a trip to the office, trembling with anticipation. Sally and I had left Senegal over a month ago, and visions of overflowing mailbags danced in my head.

I presented my passport to the receptionist, who handed me a small box (with a mysterious Manhattan address) and a sheaf of envelopes bound together with a rubber band.

When I opened the package I was surprised to find a card from my New York agent. Jane had actually sent me a gift: a black leather belly pouch with half a dozen zippered compartments. Though I had absolutely no use for it—I carried everything in my ever-present daypack—I was touched by her thoughtfulness.

Within the rubber band were a dozen letters; fewer than I'd expected, but certainly welcome. I tore into them at once.

Eight of them—birthday cards all—were from my mother. There were three others from various friends, and a final missive (I divined with gulping apprehension) from Coriola. Despite a cunning intuition to wait until I could read it in a more sympathetic environment, I couldn't stop my fingers.

Inside was a friendly, almost generic birthday card. As I opened it up, scraps of orange and yellow crêpe—all that remained of the Mexican duck piñata—fell out and onto the toothpaste-white floor.

There was no other message.

o   o   o

That night I dined alone at Vitamin, a cafeteria-style restaurant on Divanyolu, Sultanahmet's main drag. I was in ugly spirits, depressed by my mail and despairing of my overland options out of Turkey. I badly wanted to fly, to snooze in blissful oblivion with a Bloody Mary on my seat tray as the inhospitable and war-torn nations separating me from Karachi passed effortlessly below. Traveling overland made the world, ironically, seem flat. I wanted to see the big horizon, the curve of the Earth as it peeled away beneath me.

As I was digging into my stuffed cabbage, a drunken British social worker slumped into the seat across the table from me. He'd flown in the day before and would be returning to London within the week.

"'Ow 'bout y'self?" he asked. "Ye fly in from the States, Europe, or what?"

After I'd described my route—the whole damned slug trail from Oakland to the Vitamin—he regarded me quizzically.

"So you're on holiday, then?"

"If this is a holiday," I replied, "it's the last vacation I'm taking in my life."

· 24 ·

Liquid Refreshment

April rain is holy rain. During the Sultanate of Rum, when the great Sufi mystic Mevlana Jelaleddin Rumi whirled with his dervishes in the dance halls of Konya, huge urns inlaid with gold and silver were placed outdoors to collect the sacred waters. They were used for ceremonies and ablutions; to be touched by them was a blessing.

Marco and I didn't realize this as we huddled under the overhangs of Bursa, futilely trying to avoid the first real storm I'd seen since Belize. Bitten by cold wind, my legs drenched by a passing taxi, I cursed my fate at having arrived in the old Ottoman capital on the worst day of the year. Little did we know . . . .

It took a while to grow on us, but once it did we were hooked. "Many beautiful girls in Bursa," a Turk named Kanat Erzen had assured us on the boat from Istanbul to Yalova, when the sun was still shining. "And the Ulu Cami, also, is beautiful. It has a pool in the middle; you don't see that everywhere."

"A swimming pool?"

"No no no no. A *pool*, a, a fountain. For washing before prayers. You just visit. You won't believe it. And then later, when I meet you for dinner, we can go to the most famous place in Bursa. You know the famous meat, the sliced *döner* kebab you find all over Turkey and even Greece? We call it *iskender kabab*. It was invented in Bursa. I'll take you to the very place. You'll see; it's the best."

Kanat was the perfect companion. Honest, informed and historically literate, he answered our most pointed questions with passionate objectivity. When Marco asked him about the Kurdish problem, Kanat carefully drew a distinction between the hundreds of thousands of Kurds living peacefully in Turkey and the fringe Marxist-Leninist PKK terrorist group believed responsible for the recent bombings at Hagia Sophia and the Topkapi Palace in Istanbul.

I had a question, too. One of the letters I'd picked up in Istanbul had come from my friend Lisa, an American of Armenian descent. Lisa's grandmother had filled her ears with horror stories of the atrocities inflicted on the Armenians by the Turks in the early part of the century. In her letter, Lisa cautioned me not to send her so much as a postcard from Turkey. "I wouldn't want to be even indirectly responsible," she wrote, "for increasing the wealth of that horrible country by five cents."

Kanat listened in silence as I described the hatred in my friend's letter. The Armenian "relocation" (or Death March, as Lisa and other Armenians called it) was a blot on Turkey's history, he conceded. But he reminded me that the genocide took place eighty years earlier—during the height of World War I, when all of Europe was spoiling to carve up the fallen Ottoman Empire for themselves. The destruction of the Turkish republic was narrowly prevented by the genius and charisma of Kemal Atatürk; but hysteria was running high on all sides, and atrocities were certainly committed.

"Turkey is a different place now," Kanat insisted. "The barbarous acts of the past—committed by Turks, Armenians and Greeks alike—must be put behind us. I wish I could talk to your friend," he said earnestly, "and explain what conditions were like in Turkey at that time. If she understands that, I don't think she can hate us. She may never *like* us, but she may stop hating us so much."

Kanat seemed older than twenty-one, but that was the fact. With his trim beard, wide-framed glasses and droll, low-lidded eyes, he possessed a precocious "been there, done that" demeanor. Part of this was a result of his education; he was studying diplomacy at the University of Istanbul. Now he was returning to Bursa to visit an old friend—a girl he hadn't seen since they were both eleven. Kanat had no idea what to expect, but he sure was excited. Anything could happen.

"Was she just as excited," asked Marco, "to hear from you?"

"I didn't call her," Kanat confessed.

"What? She doesn't even know you're coming? After *ten years*?"

"No." He gave a shrill laugh. "I know, it's crazy. Really crazy. Maybe she's not even *in* Bursa. But I think she is. So I visit. Why not?"

o   o   o

Sightseeing. The word makes my skin crawl. But that's what we did in Bursa, punctuated by bouts of feverish eating. Marco and I stowed our packs in the bus station and bought tickets for the overnight bus to Konya. That left us with a full day to visit mosques, museums and monuments. We did so in a stiff, chill rain, counting the minutes until our döner kebab dinner date with Kanat.

We drank tea in a *çay* shop overlooking the city, as storm clouds rolled in bearing quivers of lightning; we watched a pack of Turkish schoolkids run roughshod through a mosque, dancing in the ablutions fountain and pretending (only because it was too heavy for them to lift) to steal the alms box; we ran in gleeful misery through the wet streets, ducking into every other *baklavanesi* for tiny pillows of pistachio-flavored Turkish delight. Kanat, we discovered, was right: the women of Bursa were indeed beautiful, even in the rain.

The day was not without an episode of transcendence. This occurred at Bursa's Ulu Cami, or Great Mosque, built in the early 1400s—the heyday of the Ottoman Empire. It is Turkey's largest mosque, and though less mind-boggling than the awesome Sultanahmet, or Blue Mosque, in Istanbul, I found it more inspiring.

The mosque is big, all right, but not in the way Mimar Sinan's mosques are big. Ulu is a vast enclosure roofed by myriad domes, as if someone had modeled it after the underbelly of a plastic egg tray. The central dome, which swells above the soothing snore of a marble ablutions fountain, is covered with translucent glass; had it been a sunny day the entire interior of the mosque would have been awash in light.

What made the Ulu Cami absolutely unique, though, was its spectacular calligraphy.

Most mosques, if not all, display panels of gorgeous Islamic calligraphy. Since representational art is forbidden by the Koran, the written word—specifically the words of Mohammed—becomes the primary focus for inspirational imagery. But in Istanbul's opulent mosques, the calligraphy competes with brilliant stained glass, lavish marble work and soaring architecture that makes you lean so far back you fall on your ass.

The Ulu had none of these things. All it had was calligraphy—but what calligraphy! Huge above the doorways, tucked into corners and niches, the words of the Prophet writhed and wriggled in gold on black, black on white, white on black and gold. Some verses had been structured into the shape of leaves; others contrived to form a circle, a spiral, a sword. I could understand none of it but enjoyed the pure fascination that a preliterate three-year-old must feel staring at a poster or sign whose meaning is visually compelling yet completely hidden. Still, it required no knowledge of Arabic to realize that these verses from the Koran, illuminating every one of the Ulu Cami's walls, were the highest expression of written human language that I had ever seen. Perhaps they are the highest expression possible.

We left the Ulu Cami in a state of bliss, and the rain soaked us through...

o   o   o

Marco and I met Kanat at the Heykel, Bursa's central square, at six-thirty. He towed us through the rain to the Kebapçi Iskender, a nationally famous restaurant owned by the grandchildren of the man who first dreamed up the dish. The meal was a real treat: Lamb, vertically grilled, was sliced into paper-thin strips with a broad *iskender* blade and draped over homemade bread stuffed with cheese. The meat was covered with spicy tomato sauce and topped with melted butter so hot it sizzled. A garnish of roasted chili peppers was tossed on, and full-cream yoghurt served alongside. Not exactly California cuisine.

"So how'd it go with your friend?" Marco wanted to know.

Kanat groaned, and laid his head on the table. He'd found her, all right. She was living in a free-love commune and recovering from a near-fatal episode of alcohol shock. When he'd first arrived, at one o'clock, everyone was just waking up; they insisted he stay for "breakfast." When it hadn't been served by three—"My stomach was crying," he said—he left the house to seek sustenance. He returned an hour later to find the household breakfasting, regaling one another with anecdotes about the previous night's drunken revels. Kanat was stunned and picked up his coat—but his friend waylaid him and apologized, begging him not to go. He promised he'd return after dinner—"for a long walk and, hopefully, a very long talk."

After dinner the three of us went out for beers and *raki* at a nearby bar. I sat on a high stool in the smoke-filled room, nursing my ouzo-like raki and listening to Chris Isaak sing "Blue Hotel" as Marco and Kanat exchanged dirty jokes and match tricks.

By the time we left, the rain had stopped. Kanat hailed a cab and rode with us to the bus terminal. I promised to look him up in a week's time, when I returned to Istanbul. Marco and I bid him a warm farewell and collected our gear for the seven-hour ride to Konya.

The Paradise of Dervishes

What is a saint? A saint is someone who has achieved a remote human possibility. I think it has something to do with the energy of love. Contact with this energy results in the exercise of a kind of balance in the chaos of existence. A saint does not dissolve the chaos; if he did the world would have changed long ago. I do not think that a saint dissolves the chaos even for himself, for there is something arrogant and warlike in the notion of a man setting the universe in order. It is a kind of balance that is his glory . . .
—Leonard Cohen, interviewed in the *Shambala Sun*

Mevlana Jelaleddin Rumi was one of the most exquisitely balanced poet-saints in human history. He was born sometime between A.D. 1182 and 1207 in Belkh, which now lies within the borders of Afghanistan. A devout Muslim mystic and philosopher, Rumi transcended the concept of an external God and spent his life composing a body of devotional poetry so beautiful that it seems to radiate off the page.

I would love to kiss you.
The price of kissing is your life.
Now my loving is running toward my life shouting,
What a bargain, let's buy it.

I spent Day 105, the theoretical halfway point of my seven-month journey, at the Mevlana Museum, hoping that a visit to the tomb of this great poet would free my soul for the trials that lay ahead.

*The madmen have seen
the moon in the window;
they are running to the roof
with ladders*

The Mevlana Museum has been called the Mecca of Mystics. It is undoubtedly the greatest shrine ever built to honor a slave of divine love. In the west, the life and work of Rumi are still relatively obscure; I was amazed to find thousands of Muslim pilgrims crowding the museum's plaza and filtering through the doorways, having traveled uncounted miles to spend a moment before the poet's opulent sarcophagus and view with their own eyes the robes and camel hair hat worn by the founder of the whirling dervishes.

*Come, come, come again,
Whoever you may be,
Come again, even though
You may be a pagan or a fire worshiper.
Our Center is not one of despair.
Come again, even if you have
Violated your vows a hundred times
Come again.*

The Sema, or whirling dervish dance, was created by Rumi after the disappearance of Shams of Tabriz, his revered spiritual guide. It represents "the search for the lost Beloved." As practiced by contemporary Sufis, it is an ecstatic ritual of spiritual rebirth. The Sufi *semazens* (who perform the Sema) begin the dance by shedding black cloaks, opening their hearts to Truth. Beneath they wear white cloaks, symbolizing shrouds; their tall camel hair hats are tombstones. Spinning clockwise, one foot always on the ground, their right hands are cupped upward, toward Heaven. Their left hands face downward, blessing the Earth. Holding this gesture, they revolve at astonishing speed, never stum-

bling, mirroring in their trance the divinely animated motion of elec-
trons, planets and stars, and the whirling interdependence of all
things. . . .

> Out beyond ideas of wrongdoing and rightdoing,
> there is a field. I'll meet you there.

> When the soul lies down in that grass,
> the world is too full to talk about.
> Ideas, language, even the phrase each other
> doesn't make any sense.

As I was leaving the grounds of the museum I read a couplet inscribed in gold above the entranceway. It had been written in the fifteenth century by a Sufi disciple named Molla Abdurraman Jami:

> This place is the shrine of divine lovers
> Those who come incomplete are completed here.

I believed it. And perhaps it would come true. But what sort of completion, exactly, was I seeking?

The Sludge Speaks

In the lobby of our *pensiyonu*, half a dozen Turkish men channel-surfed
between a wrap-up of the afternoon soccer game and a brutal Serbian
rocket attack on Bosnia. Head shots of world leaders condemning the
slaughter alternated with images of soccer pros congratulating one another and reliving the highlights of the match. It was a balanced diet:
the best and the worst of the human spirit, played out simultaneously
in two of Chris Moon's parallel universes. *Ma'shallah!*

Marco and I had planned to continue eastward together from
Konya and explore the weird tufa stone formations of the Cappadocia
region. We walked as far as the bus stop, but at the last minute I decided to remain in Konya a few hours longer in hopes of having my coffee grounds read by Ismael, the intense, round-faced night clerk of our
pensiyonu.

Marco himself had inspired me, having mentioned his own reading
the previous night. He, Ismael and Adam—a kid who worked in the carpet shop across the street from the pensiyonu— had been hanging out
together in Adam's shop, drinking Turkish coffee. At one point Ismael,
a twenty-two-year-old mechanical engineering student with the sensu-

ously sleepy expression of a cherub on Valium, let slip that a djin, or genie, sometimes "spoke" through him. Marco had finished his coffee, and after observing certain preparatory rituals, Ismael had read his grounds and made a few predictions about Marco's future. The reading had impressed Marco more than amazed him, but the very idea of it—that our hotel clerk was channeling genies on the sly—was enough to excite me.

I'd mentioned my interest to Ismael around midnight, and he'd consented to do a reading in the morning. But he was still asleep at ten, and Marco wanted to get on the road. We parted ways at a busy corner, and I returned to the pensiyonu to wake Ismael up.

The reading took place in Adam's funky antique and kilim shop in an attic dark with carpets. The windowsills were crammed with metal pitchers and old clocks. Tarnished silver lanterns and bells, covered in a fine patina of dust, hung like mackerel from rusted hooks.

I drank my coffee—self-consciously, to be sure—and was instructed to concentrate and invert the cup onto its saucer. Once this was done we waited a few minutes for the grounds to dry. During this waiting time Ismael frequently pressed his thumb against the cup's bottom, feeling the "power" of the message resonating within. Finally he lifted the cup off the saucer and studied the muddy pattern of sludge on the inside of the rim.

"A terrible loss will befall you," Ismael pronounced at last.

"How do you know? Where do you see that?"

Wincing with the weight of the discovery, he turned the cup toward me. "What's this?"

I shrugged. It looked like a T, or a tree, maybe a cross. . .

"It is head," Ismael said. "Without this." He tugged at his cheek. "Without skin."

"A skull," I said.

"Yes. *Skull*." He sighed. "It will be . . . . it will be . . . I don't know." He pored through a Turkish-English dictionary. "*Confidant*. A confidant. The one you tell all your troubles to. The one in who you . . ."—again the dictionary—"*confide*. Confide everything. Who is this? Who do you think?"

I said nothing. Ismael shook his head. "Maybe your mother. Maybe your sister, or brother. Maybe a very close friend. But it is the one you trust with your deepest secrets."

My brother. "Is this all the future? Or could this be an event from my recent past?"

"This is only the future. I cannot see here the past."

"When do you see this happening?"

Ismael squinted into the cup and shrugged. "After one month. One month to two."

At last it was over. I felt like kicking myself. I'd given up going to Cappadocia with Marco in order to get totally depressed over this fortune-telling nonsense. Why did I persist with these seers? It never ended well for me. I should have stuck to fortune cookies . . .

I had stood up to go when Ismael, who had so far looked only at the cup, peered suddenly at the saucer. His eyes widened.

"You will ride in an airplane!" he practically shouted. "For work. In two or three weeks' time. You will go far away! But with an airplane, you understand . . ."

Enough was enough. I thanked Ismael, paid for our coffees and dragged my bags to the Konya bus terminal.

o   o   o

Attack of the Mole People

The taxi flew over the rolling plains at 120 kilometers per hour, past the turn-offs to Güzelyurt, Guzeimir and Gosterli. Turkish music unwound from the speakers like smoke. It was one of those marvelous moments you sometimes get while traveling; a moment when the outer and inner landscapes converge into a single frame, and you really do feel that the curve of the Earth is letting you roll across its surface as effortlessly as a marble on a beach ball.

I had spent the past two days in Ihlara, hiking through the Peristrema Gorge and exploring the ancient Byzantine churches carved into the high canyon walls. It had taken me several hours to realize that the crumbling frescoes of Jesus and the various saints within the temple-caves hadn't been worn away by time. They'd been deliberately defaced by local Muslims. Most of the destruction—according to "Al Pacino" Mustafa, who managed the Pension Anatolia—had occurred within the past thirty years.

It was a hazy day, and the high round dome of Mount Hassan melted into the white sky. Traces of snow appeared on the low black hills to the south, stark against the billiard green of young wheat fields. *"Gule, gule"* (Welcome, welcome) said the signs as we entered tiny villages, only to leave them a few seconds later. The shadows of the local minarets followed us down the road like spears. I felt fine. For the first time in many weeks, I had escaped the magnetism of cities.

My destination was Derinkuyu, one of Cappadocia's famous underground cities. The soft volcanic tufa that underlies the area is ideal for carving, and as far back as four thousand years ago the mysterious Hittites began their excavations. Later, in the second century A.D., small local Christian communities continued the work, fashioning a refuge from the Roman armies: the first real bomb shelters. They expanded their city eight levels below the ground, deepened the wells and ventilation shafts, and installed ingenious security doors and secret passages.

By the early seventh century the city concealed below the wheat fields of Derinkuyu could house an estimated ten thousand people. The more than two thousand rooms included churches and stables, schools and wineries, communal kitchens and private homes, reaching down to a depth of nearly 150 feet.

I arrived at 9:00 A.M., and seemed to be the first visitor of the day. Fifteen minutes later I was drawn into heated negotiations with Ibrahim Çatal, a twenty-five-year-old archaeology student with a manic laugh and impressive command of English. When he smiled—and he did not smile so much as wear a smile—I knew immediately that he was one of those people who had always been praised for their teeth. He had the innocent, disarming good looks you hate to see in a guide or a carpet salesman, because you know they'll win you over in the end.

I hired Ibrahim on. He immediately proved his worth by launching into an outspoken tirade against organized religion, Islam included. "The hashish of the people," he called it, perhaps paraphrasing Marx, perhaps arriving at the time-honored epithet on his own.

The first place he brought me to was an underground winery, on level 2.

"This place is the winery. Here they stepped on the grapes; there they find the juice. They dropped the grapes in from a hole, there." He pointed to the ceiling. There was a hole, all right, but it was corked with a cylindrical stone.

"Used to be open," Ibrahim said. "Now closed. In 1972 a British tourist up on the ground was taking a picture. He stepped backward, fell into the hole and—snap!—broke his neck."

He led me into an adjoining room. "Another winery. Why so many wineries? What you think? Hmm? Christian city; why drink so much wine? Why?"

I shrugged.

"To forget their problems!" he cried, and began to dance about, laughing hysterically. The outburst was so unexpected that I started giggling myself. "Come on, come on." He pulled at my sleeve. "I take you to meet Mick Jagger."

"What?"

"Just come."

Ibrahim led me down another level, stooping through claustrophobic alleyways and emerging near a yawning ventilation shaft that descended all the way down to the bottom of the eighth level. I stood on the little metal grate and peered up; the sky was a blue coin. We continued downward and stopped in the middle of a narrow tunnel. To our right was a wide niche, from which emerged the edge of a great stone wheel. When the underground city was breached, dozens of such wheels would be rolled out—completely blocking access to the city's deeper levels.

"Like I told you," Ibrahim announced, his voice squeaking with delight. "A rolling stone! Yes? *Rolling stone!* Look!" He slapped the edge of the wheel with his open palm, wheezing with amusement. It was incredible; he must have told the same idiotic joke a thousand times, but it still threw him into paroxysms of contagious hilarity. If this was what two years working in the dim, lightless shafts did to a man, what kind of condition were those early Christians in?

Descending farther still—now we were on the fifth level underground—Ibrahim pointed out the fenced-in lip of a well. "Now, no water," he informed me. "Every year, the water level drops."

"How deep is the well?" I asked.

He shone his flashlight into its depths and shrugged. There was no bottom in sight. "What do you think?"

"I'll drop a coin," I said.

"Yes, yes. Like a wishing well," he said thoughtfully. "Close your eyes, make a wish, throw in a coin . . . *and we'll collect your money at end of season!!*" He brayed like a donkey.

I tossed in a 500-lira coin and waited. After about three seconds there was a dull *thunk*.

"So? How deep?"

I remembered what I could of the gravitational constant. "Uh . . . thirty meters?"

Ibrahim's eyes widened. "It's *exactly* thirty-two meters," he said. And added, admiringly, "You have good biology."

"Physics," I corrected.

"Biology! It's your *brain*, right?! *Eeeeeee!!*" He convulsed with laughter and spun like a dervish, holding his sides. Scant light from a distant bulb reflected off his teeth. I decided I'd had it. He led me back through the spooky catacombs without protest, an occasional ejaculation of laughter shaking his frame.

When we reached the second level the scene had changed dramatically. Six buses full of Turkish tourists had deposited their cargo in the underground city, and the passages were clogged with people. Ibrahim and I stood among them in silence, watching them jockey through the narrow tunnels and crowd down the precarious staircases. Ibrahim turned to me with a look of satisfaction.

"*Reenactment*," he pronounced. "To give you idea of Derinkuyu at its peak. Ten thousand people! All Turks! Look!"

Indeed, the claustrophobic melee of tourists, moving with the stilted deliberation of rush-hour commuters along Fifth Avenue, gave an overpowering and uncomfortable sense that the underground city was alive and thriving. I muttered an expletive.

"Yes!" cried Ibrahim. "Enjoy! I arrange especially for you . . ." With this he collapsed into my arms, a gunnysack o' glee, unable even to walk. I carried him up the stone steps into the light, tipped him profusely and boarded a bus back to Istanbul.

· 25 ·

Forty-Millennia Misunderstanding

The *dolmus* appears on the evolutionary ladder somewhere between the plodding stupidity of Istanbul's city buses and the carnivorous greed of its cabs. In Turkish, dolmus means *when full*, and that's precisely the idea. Dolmi wait at dolmus stands, and once they reach capacity—never more than eight passengers—they set out for their displayed destination without a backward glance.

Some of the limousines are very beautiful creatures. The one I climbed into my first day back in Istanbul was an old but immaculate 1950s Chrysler Windsor, shined like a boot. As we got under way it occurred to me that the car might be exactly as old as I was. I turned to the passenger on my left, a bright-looking man with reddish hair and a Big Dog T-shirt.

"Excuse me, do you speak English?"

"Yes . . . a little . . ."

"Can you tell me, please; how old is this car?"

The man pondered for a few seconds. "Forty thousand years old."

"Really?"

"Of course."

"Can you ask the driver to give me the number of his mechanic?"

The reply was a poignant commentary on the local exchange rate. As of noon that day, one American dollar fetched 33,000 lire. Change $100 and you were a millionaire three times over. It was no wonder that Turks automatically added three zeros to any estimate; a carton of milk ran 10,000 lire, while my bus ticket from Cappadocia back to Istanbul had cost more than half a million.

The most amazing thing was that you could hardly spend the damned stuff. Turkey, even with the recent doubling of many prices, was dirt cheap. The large, clean double room I'd rented in Ihlara, for example—which included a private sink, hot shower, four blankets and a full breakfast consisting of an omelette, cucumbers, olives, tomatoes, bread, butter, honey and tea—had cost $2.60 a night. The private taxi that had chauffeured me from Ihlara to Derinkuyu—a distance of about forty miles, not including the empty return trip—ran $15. And that afternoon in Istanbul's Taksim Square, looking over the pricing schedule for the symphony, I noted that the most expensive tickets—orchestra A-G—cost $2 a seat.

What made it so confusing was that Turkey really was a "developed" country. The intercity buses were huge and spanking clean; the restaurants served their guests on real china; Symphony Hall was trimmed in white marble, with a quotation by Kemal Atatürk emblazoned in solid brass on the wall. I never got a clue as to why the place was so affordable; all I knew was that I started each day with a couple million in hand and, come bedtime, there was still a million and change in my pocket.

Bardo-on-the-Bosporus

April 15 would be a day spent steaming up the Bosporus with a lit stogie in my hand, watching jellyfish drift like Ziploc sandwich bags under the prow. A soulful day, I reckoned. A day to be by myself, with myself, making the tough choices that would shape the future of my expedition. I'd waffled long enough; it was time to chart a course and sail.

o   o   o

I began the morning by getting my walking shoes shined by a shoeshine man with a palace of a shoe-shine stand: a gleaming brass monstrosity decorated with Rubenesque lake scenes and pictures of Lana Turner, Mary Magdalene and Marilyn Monroe. You can trust your shoes to a guy whose shoe stand shines like a million suns. I did, and he did to my FootJoys what the Turkish bath did to my spine.

Ten minutes later I shed my gleaming footwear outside the Yeni Cami mosque and dropped inside for a short meditation; a spiritual preparation for the long and introspective boat ride ahead. For some reason, though, I found it difficult to concentrate. The atmosphere was certainly pious, and the setting couldn't have been more restful. The high domed sanctuaries with their gorgeous Koranic calligraphy, lush carpets and jewel-like windows were nothing but inspirational; yet I lurked among the believers in fidgety lotus posture, unable to dissolve into the divine.

I left the mosque after ten minutes and stepped back into the brilliant sunshine to discover that my worst nightmare had come true: My shoes were gone.

I stood dumbly in my socks, the marble of the mosque steps cool under my feet. In the nearby square, policemen with Czech-made Scorpion rifles patrolled against Kurdish terrorists. I was just about to run down and summon their help when a thought stopped me cold: *I had no shoes.* Going anywhere, even into the square, would be a commitment to that fact. It was a commitment I was not prepared to make.

I scanned the area darkly, looking at feet, as if the criminal who had taken my shoes would simply *wear* them. What I saw discouraged me. Many, many people were wearing shoes, and most of them were black. All seemed well polished.

It seemed to me that of all crimes, stealing someone's shoes from outside a mosque must rank among the very lowest, right down with stealing pencils from the blind and tattooing children in their sleep. The thief must have had his eye on my shoes from the moment I approached the shoe-shine stand. Perhaps it was the shiner himself; we had, after all, haggled over the price . . . .

At that moment a hoarse, insane croak summoned me from behind. A wild-eyed mute hunchback was standing at the heavy curtain leading into Yeni Cami, flagging his hand at me. I followed him in, and within seconds my obsidian shoes were placed in my trembling hands. Through a series of spastic pantomimes, the mute informed me that he had taken the shoes inside to protect them. Grunting like Quasimodo, he histrionically grabbed an imaginary shoe and pretended to scurry away. I nodded, unsure whether to thank him or cane him, but ultimately reached out to take his hand. He snatched it away, and fled.

o   o   o

I boarded the Bosporus cruise ferry aware that I'd been served an omen, and knowing all too well what it meant.

The past few days had been, to paraphrase Douglas Adams, my Long Dark Teatime of the Sole. My shoes—i.e., my ability to continue traipsing around the globe—were in mortal danger. I had hit a snag even more discombobulating than the one Sally and I had faced in Nouadhibou, and though Turkey was an infinitely better place to be stuck in, stuck is stuck.

Ever since I'd learned that my visa application to visit Iran had been turned down I'd been vaguely terrified about how I'd get into Asia from Turkey. Throughout Africa and Europe I'd held on to some vague faith that something would come through. The truth is, I expected a miracle.

But no such miracle had occurred. Without permission to cross through Iran into Pakistan, I found myself faced with having to choose one of three possible routes. Each was a financial, temporal or existential nightmare.

The first entailed biding my time until May 4—nearly two weeks away—and catching a cargo ship to Karachi; a two-week ride. After two full days of knocking on doors I'd been offered this ride through an Istanbul shipping agent, who assured me that there was nothing leaving even a day earlier. The huge chunk of dead time would mean giving up my planned visits to India and Nepal and, quite possibly, Tibet as well. I was willing to spend the requisite days at sea—but was it worth sacrificing the pilgrimage to Mount Kailas?

The second option involved backtracking some one thousand miles northeast to Moscow, then taking a train another two thousand miles southeast to Alma Ata, the capital of Kazakhstan. This would be wildly expensive—the visa fees alone would run close to $500—with the end result that I'd be stuck in Alma Ata until the highway leading to Islamabad reopened for summer.

The third solution was to get as close as I could to the Iranian border, buy a "magic carpet" and hop over Iran to Pakistan. It would be cheap and fast and even understandable, given the realities of the geopolitical world. Thinking about it, however, made me physically ill. The whole point of my book, of my kora-under-contract, had been to go from Oakland, California, to Oakland, California, without leaving the ground. Sure, I *could* fly over Iran; but could I forgive myself afterward?

The cruise from Istanbul to the mouth of the Black Sea took two hours. The spring sun was brilliant, and narrow bridges arced above the Bosporus like tightropes. It was appropriate that I should ponder my fate on this hairline strait separating Europe and Asia. Twenty miles long, a mile wide in places, the waterway served for at least twenty-five centuries as a natural moat that blocked European armies marching east and Asian troops driving west. Byzas, the Megarian founder of Byzantium, had mapped the Bosporus while the Buddha was still teething; Odysseus himself probably sailed through the channel.

Now it was my turn. Potato chips and mineral water in hand, I stood at the railing and watched the mosques and palaces drift past while the options stuttered in my head like a jammed CD.

The ferry's final stop, on the Asian shore, was at a town called Anadolu Kavagi. The boat would wait an hour and a half before returning southward.

High above the village, surrounded by picnicking soldiers and high school lovers, I perched on the battlements of a crumbling Genoese castle and stared at the Black Sea. Russia, daunting and enormous, filled the northern horizon. I could almost smell it—boiled beets and snow, molding ledgers, Mongolian leather.

At that moment, seduced by the intimacy of scent, I made my decision. I would go overland to Alma Ata and see what transpired from there.

The Crying of Law 163

Kanat walked with me through crowded Taksim Square, munching on a bread ring. It was our first reunion since he, Marco and I had gotten drunk together in Bursa. I'd taken Kanat to see *Annie Hall* at the Istanbul Film Festival; now he was leading me to the Kemal Atatürk Cultural Palace for the opening of a one-man show by Turkey's best-known contemporary artist, Bedri Baykam.

Baykam, nearly forty, had been a child prodigy, exhibiting in Turkey and Europe from the age of six. During the eighties and early nineties his work had focused on issues of sexual freedom and the plight of eastern artists trying to break into the western art world. Lately, though, his paintings had become intensely political—a visual counterpoint to the firebrand column he wrote for a Turkish paper.

As we approached the gallery Kanat gave me a short primer on recent Turkish history.

"Practically no one in the United States knows shit about Turkey," he said. "While I was working on the Aegean coast I met a tourist from Florida. He asked me why there weren't more people walking around with missing hands. 'Missing hands?' I didn't know what he was talking about. 'Sure,' the guy said. 'Don't you cut off people's hands for stealing here?'

"Well, we don't. That's a traditional punishment in Iran, on our eastern border, but we don't do it here. We don't stone women to death for adultery in Turkey, or censor satellite broadcasts. Islamic law is not part of the Turkish constitution. Kemal Atatürk made damned sure of that sixty years ago, when he modeled the Turkish republic after the democracies of the west."

Koranic law—called *shari'a*—is said to be the most direct expression of Allah's divine revelation. Unlike secular law, shari'a is ethical as well as legal: It tells its adherents what they should do as well as what they must do. The struggle between democracy ("Kemalism") and the Islamic fundamentalist lobby had grown desperate during the past four years. Turkey, Kanat explained, was in an explosive situation, with both Iran and Saudi Arabia pumping money into the radical Islamic parties. A host of outspoken artists, teachers and intellectuals like Bedri Baykam had dedicated themselves to fighting the ultraconservative tide. Since 1990 more than forty such people had been assassinated for expressing these views.

"The last one was Ugur Mumcu," Kanat said. "He was the best-known writer and investigative journalist in Turkey. He knew they'd try to kill him, so he carried a gun at all times. It didn't help; he was murdered by a car bomb in August of 1993."

After Mumcu's death, fifteen buses were hired to take mourners from Istanbul to Ankara for the funeral. Kanat himself was among the pilgrims. While they were burying Mumcu, though, an even more horrible incident occurred. A group of Turkish writers, singers, artists and political figures, participating in an annual festival in the Anatolian town of Sivas, were trapped in their hotel by Muslim fundamentalists. Chanting "Kill the devil!" and *"Allah hu'ekber!"*—Allah lives!—the rioters set fire to the hotel. Thirty-seven people died in the blaze.

o   o   o

The huge exhibition room in the Atatürk Cultural Palace was packed. Kanat and I circulated through the room, admiring Baykam's gigantic canvases—there were about thirty—and discussing the symbolism behind the images. The most amazing thing to me, as an American, was how propagandistic they appeared. Nearly all contained heroic images of Atatürk, and some even included quotations from the leader's speeches.

"Baykam is a fanatic Kemalist," Kanat admitted. "But what you have to remember is that Atatürk is to us what men like Lincoln or Jefferson are to you. He's our symbol of freedom; our founding father. Without him, this country would have been carved to pieces after World War I. We'd probably be under shari'a right now."

Bedri Baykam stood by the entranceway, near a table loaded with his art books, portfolios and manifestos. A notorious ladies' man, he was surrounded by journalists and society women. He had dark, curly hair and a prominent Semitic nose; I was struck by his resemblance to the late Abbie Hoffman.

"I've met him at a number of political meetings," Kanat whispered. "He used to be a tennis pro, but I think he's gotten a bit paunchy...."

"Can I meet him?"

"I can introduce you. Come."

We infiltrated the circle of people surrounding the artist. Kanat waited until Baykam turned toward him, and reintroduced himself. He pulled me forward.

"Mr. Baykam, this is a friend of mine, a writer from the United States..."

"No kidding? Where in the States?"

I was taken aback by his casual command of English. "I live in Oakland, California, very close to San Fran—"

"Oh, shit, you're *kidding* me!" Baykam slapped his hands together. "Great place. *Great* place."

"What? You know Oakland?"

"*Do I know Oakland?* Listen, man, I lived there seven years. Nineteen eighty to 'eighty-seven. Went to school at the California College of Arts and Crafts, right up Broadway. Taught tennis, hung out at the Café Roma, picked up girls.... great girls there... Listen, you busy tonight? I'll take you to my studio after the show."

Kanat, unfortunately, had previous plans to have dinner with his uncle and couldn't join us. We exchanged addresses, saddened by the suddenness of our farewell. After he left I milled around the exhibition until it closed. Baykam wrapped up an interview with a local critic, took my arm and led me down the stairs, keen for gossip about the East Bay.

His banana-yellow Celica coupe was parked in a nearby alley. As I squeezed into the car Baykam reached under his arm, extracted a Smith and Wesson and placed it in the well between us. He slid the key into the ignition, took a deep breath and faced me.

"This is always the worst part," he said. "Whenever I start the engine I'm thinking, *This could be it, I could be blown to bits in two seconds.* They got my pal Mumcu that way. So I give you the choice: You want to get out now, it's okay. I won't disrespect you."

I pulled down my seat belt. "In for a penny, in for a pound."

Bedri turned the key, and we roared off toward his studio.

o   o   o

The place stank of cat shit. A meter-long Hohner harmonica and a huge box of Rosebud matches—both from Think Big in Manhattan—hung from the ceiling, dangling above hundreds of stacked canvases.

"Your show," I began, "seems like a kind of ultimate response—but I'm not exactly sure to what."

Baykam found a half-full bottle of Jack Daniel's and poured two long shots. "What it is," he said, "is a reaction to the people who criticize Atatürk. I'll give it to you straight. We have two kinds of imbeciles in this country: the fundamentalists, who want Islamic law in Turkey; and the politicians who aren't fundamentalists themselves but who think we should be nice to the fundamentalists—even if they want to overturn Kemalism."

I sat on a threadbare couch and nursed my whiskey. "By Kemalism, do you just mean democracy?"

"No. I mean equality between men and women. I mean belief in science and technology and art as opposed to belief in only religion. I mean the right to grow, to read what you want, to be equal. The right to make no distinctions of race, color, gender or religion between anybody alive. I mean a policy of peace at home and peace abroad. And above all I mean a country under a democratic, parliamentary system. This is what Kemal Atatürk stood for.

"Listen. In shari'a countries, like Iran, the government spends all its energy deciding how people are going to pray. It's a religion that wants to control your life from A to Z—from how a man washes his penis after he's had intercourse to how a woman should be killed if she commits adultery. At every point in life, shari'a intervenes."

He threw back his drink and poured himself another. "When I came back from California and saw the danger this country was in, I had no choice but to do what I'm doing. I've been telling about this danger for seven years now—in articles, at conferences and in my shows. A lot of people have been doing this. Many of them have been killed. Many of them were my friends, and they have been killed." He drained his glass. "You wouldn't believe the power the fundamentalists are getting. It's sickening. It's gotten to the point where defending what the government stands for is practically an underground position."

Baykam's biggest fear—that what had happened in neighboring Iran in 1979 would happen in Turkey—had recently grown teeth. In 1989, Iran- and Saudi-backed fundamentalist groups within Turkey had demanded the right to campaign, as an opposition party, for Koranic law. Since Atatürk, all such activities had been strictly forbidden under a controversial regulation known as Law 163. The movement to overturn this law had been vehemently opposed by activists and intellectuals like Baykam, who believed that no one seeking to undermine Turkey's hard-won democracy should be permitted to enter politics. But the Islamic lobby had won—and the shari'a proponents had launched an all-out media blitz that, Baykam claimed, was rapidly destabilizing the country.

It was hard to believe. Everything in Turkey seemed so . . . *normal*.

"Do you really think," I asked, "that freedom is in danger here? Freedom of speech, freedom of expression . . . are they genuinely threatened?"

He shook his head rapidly. "No. Freedom of *existence* is under threat in Turkey. Because once you politicize Islam, you take a ticket to ride."

"I find it ironic," I said, "that the Islamic fundamentalists are using democratic means to place themselves in power."

Baykam nodded. "I find it full of humor, and I find it full of drama, and soon I'm going to find it full of blood. Because whenever you have a country like this—with so much inflation and political confusion—it becomes very easy to convince people that the only way out is the law of Allah. And when that happens, there will be no way to avoid civil war."

o   o   o

Bedri drove me back to my hotel at 1:30 A.M. I couldn't sleep. The evening had been a diversion but, alone again, all my indecision returned to haunt me. I lay in bed shaking and sweating, the endless arguments for and against Russia, for and against the ship, for and against flying, percolating through my mind like bad acid. My brain was short-circuited, fried, roasted like a marshmallow on a three-tined pitchfork of indecision.

Because the cold, candid truth was that none of those solutions appealed to me. *I wanted to go overland. I wanted to cross Iran.*

Blue Mosque Blues

The following afternoon I found myself on a park bench, staring across a bed of tulips at the Blue Mosque.

It had been a day from hell. I'd rolled out of bed at 6:00 A.M. to the sun ricocheting off the Sea of Marmara and blasting through my window. I hadn't slept a wink. Every blood corpuscle, every nerve ending in my body was aware of this fact.

Any fantasy I'd had of mastering the situation with a bold stroke of discriminating wisdom was shattered the minute I left my hotel. I was so panicked and exhausted that I literally fell down in the street—twice. My visit to Intourist, the Russian travel agency, was a comic farce. After pacing around the office for half an hour, I reversed my previous position and decided *not* to go through Russia after all. Five minutes later I changed my mind again, paid $115 for my Moscow visa and hotel voucher and filled out a mittful of paperwork. Once this was completed I'd torn up the forms, apologized profusely, reclaimed my money, thanked all present for their patience and left the office for good. But the instant I was back on the street I realized the gravity of my error and raced back to confront the astounded Intourist staff yet again. By now it was too late; their agent had already brought the other passports and completed forms to the Russian embassy. I ran from the building, grabbed a taxi, sped to the embassy, found the agent and applied for my visa all over again.

That was the last word; there was no turning back. In a few hours I would board the overnight bus to Ankara, Turkey's capital, and apply for my Kazakhstan visa. It was a way onward, but it did not seem like the right way. I was not a happy man.

As I wallowed on my bench, an elflike Canadian man who was staying at my hotel approached. He sat down beside me, and after a brief exchange of greetings, I spewed out my sorrows—concluding with an impassioned soliloquy on the injustice of the fact that Americans could not get visas to travel through Iran.

"Nonsense," he replied. "I met an American in Iran two weeks ago."

The news hit me like a blow. "But how . . . .where . . . ?"

"He said he'd gotten a 'transit' visa in Pakistan. No problem at all. It just depends on who you ask, who exactly you speak to. The consulate here won't do shit for you. Everyone knows that, eh? But why don't you try calling the actual Iranian *embassy*, in Ankara? You're going there anyway, aren't you?"

It was ten minutes to four. I raced back to my hotel and telephoned Ankara. The Iranian embassy was just closing; but after much emphatic pleading I was finally put through to one Mr. Sadr, the man in charge of consular affairs. Mustering all the charm I could manage, I explained my situation to him.

Sadr listened patiently to my strange and terrible saga, laughing at all the right places. "When you arrive in Ankara tomorrow," he said, "come and see me. Perhaps there is something I can do. . . ."

· 26 ·

Tie Your Camel

The Iranian embassy in Ankara isn't the sort of place you want to pack a picnic.

A spiked metal fence surrounds the compound, which appears gothic and forbidding. One half expects to see Uncle Fester staring out one of the windows. Outside the barricaded entranceway, a guard in a bulletproof cabin scrutinized my papers and spoke into an intercom. While I waited for Mr. Sadr, two tourists in cycling tights edged up to the booth's window. The guard nodded, unsmiling, and handed them their French passports. The couple examined their visas and began to walk away.

"*Pardon* . . . when did you apply for those?" I asked.

"*Hier.*" Yesterday.

Sadr met me by the gate and brought me into a reception room inside the embassy. He was a balding, watery-eyed man—warm, articulate and genuinely sympathetic. We liked each other immediately. We got on so well, in fact, that he offered, out of pure kindness, to do something he'd never attempted before: fax the authorities in Teheran and ask them, with humility, to reverse their decision on my visa refusal.

There were just two catches. The first was that it would take a week, maybe longer. The second was his gloomy prediction that it wouldn't work.

"I believe in you, and in what you are trying to do," Sadr said ruefully. "The goodwill would benefit Iran as well. But the authorities are very strict. What to do? We must at least try."

There was no good reason to place my hopes in Sadr, but I did. If he prevailed, I could continue my overland pilgrimage through one of the least-visited (by American travelers, anyway) and most fascinating countries in the region. The alternate routes seemed artificial, compromises I'd make only because I was under contract to travel without airplanes.

I returned to my hotel and placed a long-distance call to Allen Noren in Sebastopol. It was good to hear a familiar voice. I told him my prayer that, against all odds, I'd get my miracle after all; that Sadr, a diplomat by trade, would convince the mullahs in Teheran that giving an earnest American a one-week transit visa was okay. On that slim chance—that I'd be able to cross Iran at last, even on a night bus and in a big hurry—I would risk everything. My Russian visa would expire during the weeklong waiting period; if Sadr's scheme fell through, my energy for dealing with the fiasco would be spent, and I would surely fly.

"You know," Allen said, "from what I've heard, some people have had good luck by just getting themselves to the Iranian border and bribing their way across."

"What? Where'd you hear that?"

"I don't remember, but it was pretty recently. . . ."

"You're kidding. From the Turkish or Pakistani side?"

"I'm not sure. Anyway, it's at least worth a try. . . ."

Trust in Allah, the expression goes, *but tie your camel.* This I would do. I decided that while Mr. Sadr awaited a response from Teheran, I would take Allen's advice.

The Sirens

I sat alone at a white metal table on the outdoor terrace of Café Dopi, drinking grapefruit juice. The table nosed out onto Yüksel Caddesia, a tree-shaded pedestrian promenade swarming with Turks of every age and description: guys with slicked-back hair and guitars slung over their backs; women with straight black hair and enormous blue eyes; kids climbing over the statues; old men sitting on the benches, pushing back their hats.

It was a revelation. You reach these places that seem so soulless in the guidebooks—a bunch of museums and mausoleums—and you find that they've got great hearts. Yes, this was Turkey's capital, a congested, polluted place where traffic snarled down the central avenues like the bulls at Pamplona. But as I sat along the arboreal street lined with cafés and fountains, bookshops and ice cream parlors, Ankara felt like one of the most vital cities on Earth. I wanted to preserve it; to possess it; to savor it like a peach.

Not a chance. The bus to Erzurum was leaving in two hours—just enough time to collect my baggage, take a taxi to the bus station and eat a quick dinner.

I paid my bill and walked up the promenade. On a small stage set up on the corner near my hotel, Bulgarian schoolgirls in white costumes rehearsed traditional a cappella songs. A banner arcing above their heads proclaimed International Children's Day, coming up the day after tomorrow.

There was an ice cream vendor nearby. I ordered two scoops of chocolate and stood beside a bronze statue, listening to the music and letting the scene embed itself in my memory. Tomorrow evening I'd be in Dogubayazit, near the Turkish border; with any luck I'd slither into Iran within forty-eight hours. This was my last real Turkish moment, and I would savor it for the life of my ice cream cone.

A hand touched my shoulder. "Excuse me; do you speak English?"

A tall, slender woman with straight black hair and a narrow Cypriot nose stood beside me. She looked as if she had stepped right out of King Schariar's harem.

"I do."

"My friends and I"—she tilted her head toward a nearby café; two other women waved from an outdoor table—" . . . would like to invite you for coffee."

Her name was Fatma. Her friends—Jalé and Servin—were equally gorgeous. All three women were nineteen, studying literature at the local university. Their espressos and a plate of picked-at desserts sat beside volumes of Sappho and Isabel Allende. They spoke English fluently, worshiped Jim Morrison and loved Woody Allen movies.

I sipped my cappuccino, a bit stunned. "This is wonderful," I said. "Most of the women I've met in Turkey wouldn't dream of inviting an American to their table. . . ."

"We thought you were Italian!" Jalé laughed, lighting up like the aurora borealis. I fell head over heels in love. "Anyway, you're obviously meeting the wrong kinds of girls. From very conservative families."

We spent half an hour in passionate wacky banter, talking about books and my pilgrimage-in-progress. When I glanced at my watch I broke into a sweat.

"Omigod. Listen, this has been great, really great, but I have to go . . . I mean, *immediately*."

"You're crazy," Servin declared. She was the quietest of the three, with aquamarine eyes and lips like velour cushions. "They're shooting people in eastern Turkey . . . did you know that? Sometimes you can step right off the bus and bang, they shoot you. The PKK terrorists like to shoot tourists. It's much too dangerous."

"Much too dangerous," Jalé nodded. "I forbid you to go."

Fatma peered thoughtfully into her demitasse cup. "Listen, everybody. I have a *genius* idea." She turned to me. "My boyfriend, Erkan, is a caterer; he's staying all week in a big hotel, preparing meals for a foreign film crew. His apartment is empty. We can buy some vodka and go there, maybe go out to some nightclubs later. And you can forget your crazy idea of going to Erzurum."

I hesitated. The offer was irresistible: an evening with three beautiful Turkish women, leading to . . . who could guess? On another level, though, I recognized a test: Would I forge ahead with my valiant plan or—lassoed by my hormones—fall into the web of these femmes fatales? True, the thought of a night with Jalé almost made me swoon, but a higher intuition told me I'd had enough of Turkey. Mount Kailas beck-

oned . . . Sally waited in India . . . it was time to start waking up someplace else.

"I'll get the bill," I said.

o   o   o

I threw my bags together and raced to the bus station in a frenzy, ob-
sessing on what might have been. Still, I couldn't convince myself that
I'd made a mistake. Motion was my elixir; no matter what I was going
through inside, the feeling of the Earth's surface slipping by beneath
me seemed to justify my existence.

The Ankara bus terminal was a miniature hell-realm of fluorescent
signs, unintelligible announcements and cigarette smoke. Five minutes
before my bus was to leave—and buses leave right on time in Turkey—I
wrestled my pack down the cafeteria stairs and to the gate. A boy
loaded it into an open luggage bay.

I was stepping onto the bus when a familiar voice called my name.
Jalé stood at the terminal door, untangling an earring from her hair.

"Fatma and Servin are holding the taxi," she said. "We decided to
give you one last chance to change your mind."

The bus driver took his seat; his confederate loaded a final bag and
prepared to slam the luggage bay shut. I stood frozen, like a deer in the
headlights of a Porsche.

Strange travel suggestions, I remembered, *are dancing lessons from God.*

The driver blew the horn. I tore up my ticket, grabbed my pack and
followed the Sirens home.

Another, Very Brief, Deconstructionist Diversion

Reader. . . . If I could improve on your imagination here, I would. Instead, I invite you to let your fantasies run wild, sparing no vision of
passion or eight-armed, four-tongued ecstasy. "Reality," John Updike
has written, "is the running impoverishment of possibility." I have no
intention of souring those infinite possibilities for you.

Suffice it to say that I woke before dawn in Erkan's bare apartment,
outrageously hungover and utterly alone. When Fatma unlocked the
door at eight, summoning me to breakfast and a day of touring metropolitan Ankara, I was bent over the kitchen sink—sucking water from
the tap and measuring, with a very large caliper, the folly of my expedition. . . .

The Sirens, cont'd.

The main event of that day—which hovers in my memory within a sort of unrequited romantic fog—was our visit to Anitkabir, the mausoleum and museum of Kemal Atatürk.

Americans don't learn much about Atatürk in history classes. If anything, he's cast as a bit of a rogue. Indeed he was, for he single-handedly saved Turkey, with no little bloodshed, from the postwar designs of imperialist Europe. Born in Thessaloníka in 1881, Mustafa Kemal was thirty-eight years old when, in 1919, he launched Turkey's struggle for independence. Without his extraordinary charisma and leadership, the collapsed Ottoman Empire would have fallen beneath the blade of the British, French, Italian and Greek powers. After four years of bitter struggle, the present-day republic was declared—under a series of social and legal reforms so advanced that activists like Bedri Baykam are willing to die for them still. That same year, 1923, President Mustafa Kemal was given the title Atatürk: the Father of Turkey.

I'd heard endless stories about the man and seen universal evidence of his profound impact on the personality of his country and its people, but nothing brought it home like visiting his tomb with Fatma, Servin and Jalé. My three teenage companions fell silent as we entered the enormous marble compound, which would dwarf any of the memorials in Washington, D.C.

There is no parallel in modern America for the devotion that Turks feel for Mustafa Kemal. It explains, among other things, why Turkey's present leaders bear the brunt of so much derision and contempt. Atatürk is an impossible act to follow. He was father, leader and lover, rolled into one.

"Our blond-haired, blue-eyed hero," Jalé whispered as we approached the museum.

"A real smoker, and a real drinker," added Servin, whose daypack, containing half a liter of Smirnoff's, had been temporarily confiscated by the soldiers at the entrance gate.

"And a real—how do you say it?—Casanova," Fatma laughed.

In short, a real Turk.

The Atatürk Museum was stuffed with the great leader's memorabilia: signed photographs, personal letters, his birth certificate and passport, monogrammed stationery and his rock-crystal vanity set. I boggled at the fabulous gifts presented to Atatürk by foreign caliphs and presidents, Turkish corporations, sultans and kings. There were diamond-studded swords and brilliant crystal tea-services, ornate walking sticks and a solid-gold sugar bowl containing (one would guess from their jaundiced appearance) the very sugar cubes poised for use in Mustafa Kemal's morning tea when he passed away at precisely 9:05 A.M. on November 10, 1938. I counted more than a dozen silver, gold and jewel-encrusted cigarette cases, some still containing Atatürk's personalized multicolored cigarettes. There were fine French snifters and an endless array of bejeweled watches and clocks. Every timepiece in the place was set to 9:05.

I found Jalé in the room containing Atatürk's personal effects. She was standing in rapture, fondling the handgrips of Mustafa's rowing machine. Servin, on the other side of the room, stood gazing deeply into the piercing blue eyes of the leader's convincing wax statue. He looked a lot, I thought, like Anthony Hopkins.

"You know," I remarked to Jalé, "it's quite interesting to compare the way leaders are remembered. Last year, in India, I visited the house where Mahatma Gandhi stayed before he was assassinated. His entire inventory of personal wealth consisted of a robe, a walking stick, his sandals and a hand loom."

She shrugged impatiently, as if my gratuitous observation contained a hidden insult, and squatted down to admire a pair of blindingly polished spats. Atatürk and I had at least two things in common: narrow feet and a wandering left eye.

"You can't compare Gandhi with Atatürk," she said.

"But you can, in a way. Both were enormously influential leaders who commanded the devotion of millions. Both shepherded their countries through periods of tremendous danger. Both became almost religious symbols—not after their deaths, but during their own lifetimes. I just think it's interesting how differently they chose to present themselves."

But Jalé had a point; no two men could be more different. Gandhi had been virtually celibate and touched neither alcohol nor meat. Atatürk was a snazzy dresser, a career womanizer and a chain-smoking alcoholic who burned out his liver at fifty-seven.

"You're right," Jalé said. She stood up and waved across the room to Fatma, who was leaning in a doorway watching the changing of the guard. "But you have to remember something: Those two men came from completely different traditions. Gandhi's heritage was Hindu; he was a religious man, and a yogi. Mustafa Kemal came from an Ottoman background. It was a tradition full of gold and jewels and gigantic palaces. When you visited Topkapi, did you see the whole room full of silk robes? And the biggest diamond in the world? This is what I mean when I say you can't compare them. Mustafa Kemal was, in his way, our last sultan. He was a man in love with life. He was in love with the physical things, and the pleasures of this world. *And so are we.*"

The women had brought flowers, and, before we left, we entered the cavernous Hall of Honor to place them on Atatürk's grave. As we stood by the forty-ton sarcophagus, birds squeaking from the distant ceiling, I saw tears running down Servin's face.

"Why are you weeping, Servin?"

"Because we need him," she sobbed. "We need him *now*."

o   o   o

We climbed the Eastern Tower of the ancient Hisar fortress, towering above all of Ankara, and watched kites dipping in the sky above our heads. We returned to our café, bought a lottery ticket and won back the price of my bus fare. We ate Turkish ravioli and *ashure*—a custardy dessert of walnuts, raisins, and peas, which, Jalé explained, was the official food of Noah's Ark. Finally we arrived back at Erkan's empty apartment and drank screwdrivers until it was time for me to go.

Fatma and Servin had night classes. Jalé accompanied me alone to the station and saw me to my bus. We embraced, and I felt my eyes filling with tears.

"'A town becomes a world'," I told her, quoting Durrell, "'when you love one of its inhabitants.'"

After she had disappeared from sight I spontaneously buried my face into the thickly sweatered shoulder of an old Turkish Gypsy woman who, sitting on a bench, had witnessed our farewell. She stroked my head and embraced me, muttering a song that I couldn't understand.

Praying for Rain

There was an excruciating moment during the thirteen-hour overnight bus ride from Ankara to Erzurum—trying to get myself comfortable in the too-narrow reclining seat and reading Joseph Conrad's *Youth* by the anemic glow of the overhead lamp as the steward came staggering down the aisle handing out plastic bags of drinking water and dousing everyone with lemon cologne—when I let the paperback slide onto my grease-stained lap and exclaimed to myself: *Holy shit. This is exactly like being on an airplane* . . . The only difference was that every single person on the bus was smoking like a catfish, there was no loo and it was going to take me as long to reach Erzurum from Ankara as it once had to reach Sydney from San Francisco. The sheer imbecility of my self-inflicted labors pulsed into my tired brain as clearly as an image of Jesus in tree moss.

And I said to myself: *Jeffrey, my friend! My dear, dear friend! What kind of pilgrimage are you on, man? What is your point, old fellow? You're sitting here in a packed bus with a wet handkerchief tied over your face to keep yourself from asphyxiation, spending millions of Turkish lire on a gamble that the government that sentenced Salman Rushdie to death will look the other way when a New York Jew shows up at its door without so much as a visa! What are you on, man? Think! Think! Think!*

But by that time I'd worn myself out thinking and, popping a sexy sea-green Temazepam, fell into a fitful sleep.

When I awoke it was 8:00 A.M. We had arrived in Erzurum. The bus to Dogubayazit, which would put me just twenty-one miles from the Iranian border, was leaving in 20 minutes. There was no time to reconsider; I had barely enough time to find a toilet before heaving my Endless Journey into the baggage well and collapsing into yet another reclining seat emblazoned with vertical stripes. The name of this bus was the Meteor, and it did, I had to admit, resemble a tail of stellar debris.

Now that it was daytime, I could see; and what I saw alarmed me.

It looked as if the Earth itself were teething. Raw volcanic rocks broke aggressively out of the undulating ground, the color and texture of bronze slag. Between them grayish-green hills pulsed like swollen gums. Northward, a chain of high mountains stood crowded together like impacted molars, their battlements foaming with snow.

To the south, beyond a furrowed field, a grove of slender white birches flared into spring like copper sparklers. The green of their new leaves was shockingly vivid, almost pornographic. Huge crows circled above them, and the flimsy-looking limbs supported dozens of dark nests.

The landscape was not empty. In every direction I saw tanks, barracks and heavy artillery, poised against enemy action—not from Iran, but from the PKK, the Marxist-Leninist Kurdish liberation army. Far from reassuring me, the armored vehicles and khaki uniforms seemed an invitation to violence. At any moment, the painful-looking scenery could explode into flame, taking the bus with it. As we were pulled over for another identity check—the first of four—I thought of Jalé, Fatma and Servin, reading Sappho to one another a thousand kilometers due west. They'd warned me about this world, and they were right. It was not a welcoming place.

It was such a rude and masculine landscape that I was surprised to see women on the streets. But as we pulled into Dogubayazit I saw that there were children as well. They were out on the streets in force, singing and parading along the main drag with bright red Turkish flags. Of course: It was April 23, International Children's Day. Back in Ankara the streets would be overflowing with kids, music, carnivals, displays. Even here, in a place where neighbors despised one another, the children had their day.

The sky was hazy, but as I looked to the north I could suddenly re-solve the enormous outline of Agri Dagi: Mount Ararat. Above the rut-ted road, above the chain of barracks and barbed wire, above the snapping flags and floral wreaths circling the statues of Mustafa Kemal Atatürk, Ararat towered toward heaven. I touched my hand to my heart. Here was the place where, for my people, recorded history had begun. Here were the slopes down which pairs of birds and bears, kangaroos and mice had scurried, running off in all directions. And here were the stones that Noah and his family had descended, spared from the Flood.

There was no rainbow over the horizon as I fetched my luggage from the belly of the Meteor and loaded it, with the help of an Iranian man I'd met along the way, into a taxi bound for the border. Dark clouds rolled in from the south, and a convoy of armed jeeps set off for maneuvers among the jagged peaks of the Ishak Pasha range.

I looked at the clouds, realizing that it was going to rain—but proba-bly not enough.

o   o   o

I had imagined a border scene similar to Nouadhibou: tired guards leaning on their rifles outside a run-down shack, playing cards and eat-ing moldy goat cheese. Not quite. As we approached the crossing—a compound of featureless cement buildings ringed by barbed wire—the Iranian sitting beside me watched me slip a crisp $100 bill between the pages of my passport.

"Put that away," he warned, "or they will throw you in prison with-out a second thought."

Entering immigration, I saw what he meant. Iranian officials sat be-hind sophisticated computer terminals, verifying visas with Mullah Central in Teheran. Video cameras, their on-the-air lights glowing, watched every transaction from nooks in the ceiling.

My reception in that no-man's-land can be summed up in three words: *Not a hope.* Five minutes after entering the compound I was ex-pelled like a hairball, Endless Journey and all, into the dust of the taxi park.

o   o   o

There was a moment, on the bus back to Ankara, when I sensed I would never get out of Turkey. One thing or another would succeed in miring me there forever. It might be the hope of a ship, faith in Mr. Sadr, or the fantasy of a smoky night with Jalé, but it would be something. The whole scenario was starting to look painfully like *Groundhog Day*.

As we sped through Central Anatolia, I tasted a sour irony. By driving all the way to the Iranian border and back again, I'd backtracked just as far as I would have by following my original plan and going all the way up to Moscow.

· 27 ·

Oh! Mama! Can this really be the end? To be stuck inside of Turkey with the Shi'ite Blues again . . . ?

"So there is no hope?" I asked plaintively.

"No; no hope."

"We can try nothing more?"

"Nothing more."

"Surely there is something we can do. . . ."

"I'm so terribly sorry. There is nothing."

"There is nothing, then."

"Nothing. I'm terribly sorry."

"Can we try again later?"

"Yes. They said that after one or two years you may try again."

"One or two *years*?"

"Yes."

"So there is nothing we can do for now?"

"No; nothing."

"Then there is no hope?"

"No; no hope."

The empathetic anguish in Mr. Sadr's voice was palpable, but he was at wit's end. Iran was out. Period. I'd had to convince myself of this before hanging up, knowing I'd never be able to forgive myself if I left even a single pebble unturned.

Still, the phone call drew me into a black hole. True, true, before running off to the Iranian border I'd told myself that if Sadr failed I would take a plane. But now, faced with the prospect of imminent surrender, I was sick with doubt.

Because, after all, I could do it. If I had the balls. I could get on with my trip, overland. There was still the ship, leaving from Mersin May 4. The downside, of course, was abandoning all hope of joining the Mount Kailas expedition. But my book was supposed to be about going around the world without airplanes, not about circling a mountain in Tibet. The fact was, I *could* wait.

And what about Russia? A bus to Trabzon; the ferry to Sochi; an overnight train to Moscow; three days and nights to Alma Ata. The new Karakoram Highway linked Kazakhstan with Pakistan, passing over the second-highest mountain range in the world. It would be a rough trip, and it would take a while, but I *could* do it.

Yet something else, a little voice inside, told me I was being ridiculous. Diverging from my overland route wouldn't be the end of the world; it wasn't like Moses refusing to lead the Jews out of Egypt. I had written this libretto, not God. I'd tried to engineer a fun, adventurous pilgrimage to remind myself how big the world was, and to celebrate my fortieth birthday. Instead I was marooned in Ankara, gnawing my nails to the armpit while a Woody Allen quote gerbiled incessantly through my brain: "Mankind faces a crossroads. One path leads to despair and utter hopelessness, the other to total extinction. Let us pray that we have the wisdom to choose correctly."

It was a Piscean's worst nightmare, and I was waking up to it every day.

o   o   o

I telephoned Fatma, who again set me up in her boyfriend's apartment. Jalé was out of town with her family, while Servin was studying for an exam. I was more or less on my own, locked into a dizzy downward spiral, working full-time to convince myself that the time had come, after sixteen weeks, to throw in the towel. The secret, I knew, would be finding a way to rationalize the decision; to create an alibi that made the airplane option not only acceptable, but irresistible.

Sitting alone in the outdoor café where I'd first met the Sirens, I compiled a list.

Ten Best Reasons to Take an Airplane over Iran Instead of Spending a Month at Sea or $1,000 Getting Through Russia

· *Only from the air can you really tell that the earth is big.*
· *Listening to "Like a Virgin" on the in-flight entertainment system while, eight miles below, women are being stoned to death for adultery.*

· *To find out once and for all how much my backpack really weighs.*
· *If I made the trip entirely without airplanes it would be perfect . . . and only Allah is perfect.*
· *Airplane food.*
· *The opportunity to see* The Fugitive *in Turkish.*
· *It was inevitable; the coffee grounds had spoken.*
· *Big fun lying about buying a magic carpet.*
· *The satisfaction of taking a piss over Teheran.*
· *If I ever needed something to feel horrible about for the rest of my life, this could be it.*

But I still wasn't convinced. Over the next two days I telephoned half a dozen people—friends, my publisher, even my agent—in a sorry attempt to solicit "permission" to fly. I never actually said it, but the subtext of my ostensibly objective solicitations was an old Yiddish proverb: *Advise me well, but don't advise me against it.* The consensus was unanimous: Fly if you must, but not if you can help it. My agent went one step further, turning up the heat with a savvy declaration delivered in high-volume New Yawk-ese: "There's *absolutely* no problem if you fly," Jane chortled. "But you have to make up your own mind. In fact, I think it's *wonderful* that you're going through this crisis."

"How do you mean?"

"I'll tell you. This is supposed to be a coming-of-age book, right? And I know that, whatever you decide, you'll end up learning something very, *very* important about yourself."

Aaaarghhh!

Only Elliot, my dear, wise friend Elliot, heard the plea concealed in my tone and made a definitive statement.

"Get your ass on a plane, my man!" He pronounced the words with the confidence of Jesus among the money changers. "You're clinging to some vague purity; some notion that your trip isn't valid—that *you* aren't valid—unless you can do the whole thing without airplanes. But that's nonsense. You want to go to Mount Kailas, and I think it's important for you to be there. So get there. And remember: Whatever you do, it's what you *say* about it that will make or break the book."

"Maybe you're right," I eagerly admitted. "Maybe it's time to decide if this is a pilgrimage, or a dick thing."

"See that?" His familiar laugh was a tonic. "I knew you'd find a way to make a virtue of it."

Elliot's call settled my mind—for about ten minutes. Then the hot flashes started again. An hour later, pacing Erkan's apartment like a caged leopard while Fatma prepared soup, I made up my mind.

I'd take the ship. I'd spend a week touring western Turkey, then return to Mersin with a stack of books and sail to Karachi. It was the only solution I could live with.

Heart racing, I called the shipping agent in Istanbul and told him I wanted on. A wave of relief flooded through my mind like Canada Dry ginger ale.

"So I must be in Mersin by May 3? Or can I get there right on the fourth?"

"Oh, no, no, no," he said. "No need to be there so early."

"Early? Isn't the ship leaving May fourth?"

"Ah! May 4th! No; no; there has been a change in schedule. It will now leave around about fifteenth of May. Maybe some days later. . . ."

I hung up the phone, distraught.

Russia, then. I'd go through Russia. Intourist in Istanbul had given me the number of the Russian Travel Service in Ankara; they could give me the departure times for the train from Sochi to Moscow, and Moscow to Alma Ata. Fatma phoned them—they spoke no English—and I waited restlessly while she jotted down the information. When she was off the phone she read it out to me.

"Okay. Bus service every day from Ankara to Trabzon: fourteen hours."

"Good."

"And there is a ferry every day from Trabzon to Sochi: sixteen hours."

"Good, good."

"Every day, train service from Sochi to Moscow: three days and three nights."

"What?"

"Yes. And from Moscow to Alma Ata, four to five days and nights. They do not know for sure; sometimes, no train."

The intelligence fell upon me like a cartoon anvil.

"More than one week on the train? Eight days and nights?"

Fatma peered at me, shaking her lovely Cypriot head. "It's too long," she said simply. And I knew she was right.

The doorbell rang. It was Erkan; he'd come to join us for lunch. Short and balding, with a hairy neck, beaked nose and Sergeant Pepper eyeglasses, he was one of those people whom you suspect have never betrayed a trust. He and Fatma fell into a passionate embrace on the foldout bed, crushing my map. When they sat up again Fatma brought him up to date on my dilemma. They spoke a minute in Turkish. And then I watched, startled, as Erkan's finger moved across the map in a way I hadn't seen before; in a way I hadn't *wanted* to see.

"You can do it this way." Erkan lowered his glasses and raised his eyebrows. "No?"

o   o   o

One of the strange and wonderful revelations bequeathed to me on my journey—bequeathed, no less, on the bus ride back to Ankara from Dogubayazit—was that my tolerance as a world traveler, and as a human being, had limits. This had not necessarily been true when I was twenty-five, but it was true now. There was a limit to how much absurd discomfort I would subject myself to for appearances' sake.

I was not willing, for example, to tie up the next five weeks of my life getting to Pakistan on a cargo ship. Nor was I willing to spend eight consecutive days and nights on a Russian train, backtracking to Moscow in order to roll across the wilderness to Alma Ata and discover that the Karakoram Highway, with its 17,000-foot passes, was snowed in til late June.

I had set out to discover the size of the world, not my capacity for suffering. But the planet, I had already learned, was not only big; it was made even bigger by unfriendly borders, religious fanaticism, bad weather, floods and wars. There was no need to draw a crazy Etch A Sketch line around the globe in order to prove this.

But the fact was that I had set out to do something (something extraordinary, I thought), and if it was possible to do it within the bounds of my health and sanity I should—*must*—follow through. The line that Erkan traced across my tattered map was terrifying, because there was no way I could argue with it. All I could do was nod slowly and look at my hands.

I folded the map, slid it into my daypack and walked to Santur Travels to cancel my airplane reservation. Muazzez Shen—the angelic travel agent who had been listening to my woes for days, canceling and reconfirming airline tickets as my mood shifted like sand—looked at my map and nodded.

"Maybe you can do this," she said. "Let me make a few calls."

o   o   o

That afternoon and the next passed in a frenzy: getting affidavit letters from the American embassy, visiting foreign embassies and poring over details with Muazzez. She had lived for four years in Saudi Arabia and knew enough to warn me that, in ten days, the entire country would seal its borders for the annual hajj, or pilgrimage to Mecca. We had to work fast.

I would be crossing Arabia against the pilgrim tide—bound for the Persian Gulf. My route would begin in Iskenderun, on Turkey's southern border. I'd drop through Syria into Jordan, cross the border into Saudi Arabia and make my way eastward to Riyadh. From there I could easily reach one of the Gulf ports—from which, according to Muazzez, I would have no trouble finding a ship for the three-day sail to Karachi. The entire trip, as I envisioned it, would be nonstop; for if my connections jibed like clockwork, I could still make it to Kathmandu by the morning of May 8, one day before the Wilderness expedition departed for Mount Kailas.

The only potential obstacle—and it was a thorny one—was the Saudis. I had no trouble getting permits for Jordan and Syria (though I had fudged on one question, listing Buddhism as my religion), but a Saudi Arabian transit visa is as difficult to obtain as a visa for Iran.

The marker had moved up a few squares, but the game was far from over. As I was buzzed into the foyer of the Saudi Arabian embassy—a monolithic fortress bristling with listening devices—I realized that my fate would be decided within the next few moments. Everything depended, once again, on a single visa.

But their answer, after keeping me waiting the entire afternoon, was neither yes or no. It was yes . . . *if*. Yes, they would give me a transit visa, but only if I could show them a visa from one of the other Gulf nations first. Until I could prove that I could get *out* of their country, they wouldn't let me in.

For the next two days I lived on coffee, Mars bars and bread rolls, zooming across Ankara in a blur of taxis and dishing out lire like confetti. Halfway through the first afternoon I ran out of passport-size photos; the new batch, processed at lightning speed and extortionate cost, portrayed a man with wild hair and the radiant inner calm of Franz Kafka.

White Rat Redux

At three o'clock Friday afternoon, I returned to the Saudi Arabian embassy with visas to Kuwait and the United Arab Emirates in hand. The vice consul met me in the reception room, a no-frills air lock with whitewashed walls, metal folding chairs and a portrait of King Fahd on the wall. Aside from a sour male receptionist, one other man sat in the room: a fat Turk, breathing heavily, whose opulent hindquarters overflowed onto the two adjoining seats.

The officer leafed through my passport and sighed. "All right, then," he said. "I gave you my word, and I shall keep it. You may have a three-day transit visa. It will permit you to land in Riyadh, stay overnight and take the next flight to Kuwait."

My blood turned to ice. "Wait a minute," I said. "I told you that I was traveling *overland*. I plan to take the bus to Riyadh, and continue immediately by bus to Dubai."

He laughed, closing my passport. "No, no, that is impossible. Illegal. In a week there is the hajj; even Arabs cannot enter without special permission during that time."

"But I'll be out of Saudi Arabia before the hajj even begins."

The vice consul shook his head. "I can give you a visa to fly. In and out. That's the best I can do."

For a moment I said nothing. Then, "I can't fly."

"Why can't you fly?" The official was losing his patience. "Is there something wrong with you, that you cannot fly? Everyone flies. You, also, must fly."

I hesitated. An explanation of my actual assignment—any mention at all that I was a writer or journalist—would doom me completely.

"I cannot fly," I repeated. "Nor can I tell you why. All my life I have had a terrible fear of flying. It is a phobia; like a fear of darkness, or heights. The very sight of an airplane fills me with dread. Still, despite this crippling fear, I have committed myself to the goal of circling the world. My friends said I could not do it, that it is impossible to make such a voyage without airplanes. But no sir! I swore I would succeed. I would not let my fear stop me. Never!"

The Saudi laughed with real appreciation. "I'm sorry. As I told you already: impossible, and illegal." He handed me back my passport. "If you change your mind, you may return. I will give you a visa to fly." He turned and left the room.

I stood there, rooted to the spot, unsure whether to laugh or scream.

There was a heavy creaking sound as the fat Turkish man, who had watched my exchange with the official in silence, rose to his feet. He walked toward me, wheezing, and placed his hand on my shoulder.

"I know exactly how you feel," he said.

"You do?"

"Yes. What you were saying to the vice consul. About your fear of airplanes. I, too, suffer from the type of fear you described. Since I was a young boy, I have had a terrible fear of pigeons. I have no idea why this is. Who knows? Perhaps pigeons attacked me when I was a baby, in the stroller. One can never say. But if there are pigeons on the street, or on the overhead wires, I must find a different route. Sometimes this takes me far off course. One afternoon, as I was returning from a café, there were pigeons in all directions, on all the roads. I had to pay a small boy to walk fifty meters in front of me and chase them off so I could continue home. It was terrible."

"Do you work here?"

"Yes. I'm a lawyer, the legal counsel for the Saudi Arabian embassy." A coughing fit interrupted him, but the moment he recovered he reached into his pocket for a cigarette. "Wait a few minutes," he said, "while I go upstairs and speak with the consul personally. I cannot make any promises, but I will do my best."

He labored out the back door and disappeared. I sat down and stared straight ahead, not daring even to think.

Twenty minutes later the intercom buzzed. The grinch-faced clerk punched a button. He listened in silence to a deluge of Arabic and signed off, allowing a good ten seconds to elapse before speaking.

"Immigration," he muttered to his desk. "Next building. Bring your passport."

✗

Deconstructionist Diversion V

It looks so simple on my outline: *crossing Arabia to Dubai.* Four words. Twenty-one letters. Nothing to it, really; a paint-by-numbers romp through a series of nearly featureless sandscapes, working with a roller from trays of burnt umber, gray and beige. Beige, beige, beige. The Beige Room.

No chapter number here. The mileposts, once we quit Syria, are covered in sand. No distinction between day and night, morning or noon, lunch or dinner. Think chicken. Think Coca-Cola, in cans so cold they burn your hand. Think about air that hits you like dragon's breath every time you step out of the climate-controlled Mercedes bus to buy another half-dozen liters of water. Think about the way your hair looks after five days of filtering sand. Think about days and nights on a bus, drifting off to *The Fugitive* or being jarred awake at one and five in the morning to stagger through stadium-lit border posts. *They know, don't they? They know who I am. A secret Jew, on the wrong side of Israel.*

Syria, Jordan, Saudi Arabia—geographically, at least, they're as cozy as commuters on the 5:14. We'll dispense with these countries quickly. Not because there was nothing to see; there was, and plenty. I missed it, is all. After a stupefying bardo of relentless stress, I suddenly found myself with no need to do anything except stare out a tempered glass window as it faded from light to dark, light to dark. After four weeks of feeling like a ship in a bottle, I was sailing again. Sailing at last, with a stack of novels and a pocketful of Chiclets. Sailing toward Asia—and I dared not stop.

Arabia: One Dash

Lightning and thunder as we rolled into Syria. Granite boulders; steep hills bristling with pines. A border I never thought I'd cross.

Chain Palaces and Hotels
A Commitment to Tradition:
The Only Chain Covering Syria.

Olive trees and vast acres of cultivated fields lined the highway. Boys strolled by carrying red pails, or rode small white horses through grapevines. I was astonished by how lovely the landscape was. Even the bus, smelling vaguely of bologna in the sudden hail, was not a fiercely unpleasant environment.

Syria: 71,467 square miles. Slightly larger than Washington State. Capital: Damascus. "You've got to stop in Damascus," everybody had told me. "Oldest inhabited metropolis on earth . . . great bazaar in the Old City . . . lovely mosques . . . magic carpets . . . swords . . . Stop in Damascus, fool, or you'll be sorry."

We arrived in Damascus at midnight. Green and red and purple neon lit the thronging avenues, making the polished hoods of disco-bound cars gleam like Christmas tree ornaments. It was nothing like I'd remembered from *Lawrence of Arabia*. The bus pulled over to the curb and the luggage bay hissed open. The driver turned around to look at me. Damascus: yes, or no?

I shook my head. We blew right through. And I am sorry. But what to do? I'd only been on the bus five hours. It was incredible to be moving again. It was gorgeous. For the first time in weeks, I decided to take the path of least resistance.

Besides, my heart was still wrapped up in Asia. If there was even a remote chance of making it to Kathmandu in time for the Mount Kailas expedition, I intended to do it. My uncertainty about the enterprise—as uncertainty will sometimes do—had turned into an obsession, a dangling carrot of desire that would dictate my dash across Arabia.

In four dark hours we sliced through the northern panhandle of Jordan and confronted the vast lunar wasteland of Saudi Arabia. Buses filled with Mecca-bound pilgrims slouched motionless along the high-way, idling with a quiet patience that indicated they'd been so disposed for hours. A thousand feet away, at the border post, jackal-eyed guards sipped tea and betrayed, by way of universal body language, that we, too, would wait; that we could all wait forever, as far as they were concerned.

The bus driver unloaded my gear and urged me to walk ahead through the post. With any luck, he said, I'd clear customs immediately and be able to hitch a ride to At Turayf, ten miles into Saudi Arabia. I could wait there for the bus, which would probably make it through by mid-afternoon.

His subtext was clear. I was the only non-Muslim on the bus. If I was going to have any problems clearing immigration he wanted them to happen now, to me alone, rather than later, when my futile protests and righteous indignation would further delay his passage. He knew my Saudi visa was valid—every single passenger on our bus had scruti-nized it—but long experience had taught him that, indelible ink and of-ficial signatures be damned, Nothing was written.

I shouldered my pack and approached the checkpoint. All eyes were upon me. But the suspicion of the other pilgrims, I deduced, would work in my favor; the officials would hasten me through just to spite them.

Indeed; the immigration officers regarded me with private amuse-ment, looking me up and down before asking, with deceptive non-chalance, whether I thought Michael Jackson was Negro or Caucasian.

It was the riddle of the Sphinx; I thought long and hard before replying.

"He was born a Negro," I replied, "but will die a white man."

They stamped my passport. I was ushered into a bare cement room behind the immigration office and instructed to lay my two pieces of luggage—the Endless Journey and its companion daypack—on a wooden table. Above the table was a sign: a friendly reminder that im-porting illegal drugs into Saudi Arabia was punishable by beheading.

My baggage had been inspected many times, in many ports, but the guy at the Saudi Arabian border was an artist. It was a privilege to watch him work. His hands flew, flinging underwear and socks into the cobwebs while his eyes raked every nook and cranny of the pack. Before I could say "vitreous humor" he was displaying, with the poker-faced confidence of the professional conjurer, the $500 in crisp American currency that I had hidden, with consummate cleverness, I'd thought, in a sealed sterilized packet which, containing one Johnson & Johnson adhesive eye patch, had been buried in the deepest recesses of a zip-pered interior pocket within my personal toiletry kit. Seeing my concealed $100 bills brought so immediately and ignominiously to light, I could only pray (to Allah, out of cultural courtesy) that this mustachioed magician would not similarly dissect the little plastic container of Mack's "pillow soft" Earplugs® . . . for if he did he would be sure to discover, forgotten (up until that moment) in the folds of the product's shrill instruction leaflet (DO NOT INSERT IN EAR CANAL! COVER ONLY!), three harmlessly geriatric, though eternally illicit, tabs of LSD. . . .

I pictured my head on a stake, displayed outside the main Riyadh mosque with a boldly lettered sign beneath it:

BEHOLD THE DRUG SMUGGLING AMERICAN JEW
WHO TRIED TO ENTER SAUDI ARABIA DURING THE HAJJ!

Ignominious! But fate had a slower demise in store for me, and the nimble-fingered guard dismissed me with a nod.

o   o   o

By four in the afternoon the bus had retrieved me from the At Turayf supermarket. We were moving again, plowing through the run-on sentence of the Arabian desert. Once upon a time this had been thick Jurassic forest, shadowed by pterodactyls and enormous dripping ferns. Those eons and acres of thriving vegetation now lay deep beneath the sand, gooey and black, waiting for the opportunity to power my mother's Camry to Walbaum's.

It was like driving through hell. Nothing but sand (much of which was in the air), visibility limited to twenty feet, heat radiating in through the windows despite the continual gasp of the air-conditioning. Any Apollo-era fantasy I'd entertained of visiting the moon was grimly and finally fulfilled. We were crossing a landscape totally pulverized, absolutely forbidding, lethal as the gas chamber. And connected, by a twined line of Earth molecules, to the morning glories outside my back window in Oakland. . . .

Dusk fell, the cuticle-white sky pressing against the beige horizon as plainly and impersonally as planes of color in a Mark Rothko painting. I stared out the window, astonished by the paranoia surrounding this monochrome landscape. What are they hiding it from? I wondered. Why are so many of the world's forbidden places so forbidding? I recalled some lines by Camus:

> Our reason has driven all away. Alone at last,
> we end up ruling over a desert.

We hummed on, hammering at the hot empty night. No moon, no stars. Not only was the Earth flat; we had fallen off its edge.

Dammam Unveiled

Except for the fact that it was a million degrees outside and that they chop off people's heads in the courtyard outside the mosque on alternate Fridays, Dammam could've been anywhere: Ohio, maybe, or one of those awful anonymous strip malls south of Fresno. Banks, fast-food joints and traffic lights dominated the landscape, clustered beneath billboards bearing familiar names ("Coca-Cola—The Official Soft Drink of the Saudi Arabian World Cup Soccer Team"). Huge public sculptures squatted on traffic islands like enlarged aquarium trinkets, ignored by the silent pedestrians who crossed between cut-rate carpet and computer stores. Everything was utterly, painfully normal.

It was profoundly disappointing. I had entered the forbidden kingdom, and it was Bakersfield.

Arun, a young Pakistani man I'd met on the bus—he was visiting his brother, who worked in a frozen chicken factory—offered to let me use the packing plant's communal shower. After freshening up I decided to make an expedition to Dammam's air-conditioned enclosed shopping mall. It would have to be short; I had to return to Arun's dormitory by the afternoon call for prayer, during which no foreigners were permitted on the streets.

The mall, like the bus terminal, was ultramodern but icily eerie. Almost no one was shopping. A Saudi woman, tented from head to toe (save for a narrow eye slit) in a black *hijab*, peered through the glass show windows of a glitzy fashion outlet; another walked out of the Body Shop toting a green shopping bag emblazoned with the words *Against Animal Testing*. On the ground floor, by a dry fountain, a few round tables and plastic chairs had been partitioned off around a coffee bar. The café, too, was empty; a sign near the entrance indicated why:

Women Not Allowed

I'd seen places that were unclear on the concept, but this was ridiculous.

There was a variety store on the mezzanine, and I wandered inside in search of a notebook. I'd been there not two minutes when a note of cognitive dissonance alerted me. It was the kind of feeling you get when you glance at a hand with six fingers, or spy a four-leafed clover. Within seconds I pinpointed the source of my perceptual unease: It was a display, in the hobby section, of postage-stamp-collecting kits.

(top)Day of departure: Dwayne, Sally, Jeff and the infamous Pathfinder on layover in Santa Barbara.

(bottom)Capt. Elmar Wohlgemuth: "I always go direct; only direct."

Coiffure sign in Senegal.

(bottom)Sally and the Ba's: Hamady in the rear, Binta up front.

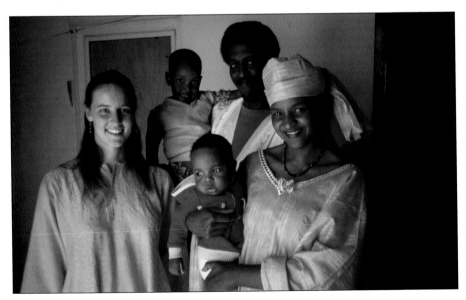

The last thing you want to see in the middle of the Sahara Desert: Off-the-cuff engine repair, by committee.

View, from a nearby escarpment, over the Dogon village of Songo.

How I spent my 40th birthday. (Photograph by Sally Knight)

David (left) and Greg, the unflappable drivers of the Dragoman bus.

Paul Bowles at home in Tangier, Morocco.

Postcards of Kemal Atutürk, the hard-living national hero of Turkey.

A soldier on leave poses for a snapshot in Konya, Turkey.

*(opposite)Marilyn and Mother Mary, together at last on a
shoeshine stand outside the Yeni Camii in Istanbul.*

You can get anything you want in the Cappadochia restaurants...

(opposite)Still life with cook: The aptly-named "mess" of the Fateh El Khair.

(top) Huge painted Buddha statues at Swayambhunath temple, Kathmandu, Nepal.

(bottom) The Great Stupa at Bodhanath, illuminated by thousands of butter-lamps for the 2,477th birthday celebration of Lord Buddha.

(top)View of the Potala, home and monastery of the exiled Dalai Lama, in Lhasa, occupied Tibet.

(bottom)A view of the Tsurphu Valley, with signature mustard and yaks.

Two young monks display photographs of the Dalai Lama and Potala Palace in their dormitory room at Sera Monastery.

(opposite)A Chinese opera star applies make-up shortly before his appearance in a production staged in Chengdu, China.

(top)A little mah jongg before the second act: Chengdu, P.R. China.

Wellcome You to
Shoot a gun in this
Beautiful Place
射擊場
RAKE
It makes you
are in madness
happy

(bottom)A sign in Yangshuo, China

(opposite)
(top)Devotees at the Hungry Ghost Festival in the courtyard of Wang Tai Sin Temple, Hong Kong.

(bottom)Masks in store window behind red cellophane: Yokohama, Japan.

Jurgen Netz, Master of the CTS Bremen Express.

Coming in under the Oakland Bay Bridge.

The big O.

The centerpiece of the display was an enlargement of Winter Olympics commemoratives, featuring the figure skating event. But someone, somewhere, had violently blacked out the bare legs and arms of the women. The male skaters had been left intact, but of the women only torsos—balanced on black columns above neat white skates—remained.

Three aisles down, in home appliances, I encountered the same phenomenon: The distributor (or merchant) had been compelled to eradicate, with Magic Marker, the legs, arms and comely smiling faces of the milk 'n' cookies models posing with the Panasonic blow-dryers, Braun citrus juicers and Black & Decker irons. The result—certainly not what the shari'a authorities had intended—was the illusion that every product was personally endorsed by Al Jolson.

Working on a hunch, I moved into the stationery department and found the cartographic display. Unfolding a Bartholomew world map, my intuition was confirmed: *Israel did not exist.* The cities were there— Haifa, Tel Aviv, Jerusalem—but there was no indication that a republic of any name had been established around them. John C. Bartholomew and Son Ltd., bowing to shameful self-censorship, had achieved with their printing press what the Arabian nations had failed to do with their armies: They had driven Israel into the sea.

o   o   o

Later that afternoon, waiting at the station for the overnight bus that would take me to the United Arab Emirates, I picked up the English-language *Khaleej Times* and read, on page 6, a column entitled "Mark of Dignity for Women" by Syed Khalid Husain:

> There is a misconceived notion among many non-Muslims and some Muslims that hijab, or Islamic veil, is designed to keep women in bondage. "Seclusion" and "segregation" are some of the terms used in the context of the veil that serves to screen Muslim women from the sight of male strangers. . . .
>
> To put the record straight, Islam has not kept woman in male bondage; rather, it has emancipated her. . . . As for terms such as "seclusion" and "segregation," these are false suggestions made with the ulterior motive of misrepresenting Islam. The Islamic concept of the unity of all mankind makes no allowances for differences of gender, race or caste. If that is the case, then wherefore the need for the system of hijab?
>
> Islam has laid down certain norms of dress and social behavior for both men and women. It has given woman a really honorable place in society—as mother, wife, sister and daughter. The woman who enjoys

such a noble status has to be chaste. According to Islam, a virtuous wife is the best commodity of a man. To protect her virtue and to safeguard her chastity, Islam has provided for hijab, which establishes the norms for modesty in dress, social mingling, participation in reform movements, and emergence from the homestead in the hour of need.

I wondered if the same reasoning lay behind the fact that the world maps had expunged Israel's "face" as well. "Out of sight, out of mind." Always a sign of respect, and a mark of the highest honor.

A Good Man, and a Good Muslim

The United Arab Emirates is one of those countries that Americans don't think about very much. The federation of oil-rich states actually includes seven separate emirates, the largest of which—covering 80 percent of the UAE's Maine-size landmass—is Abu Dhabi.

Americans might not think about the UAE, but Russians do. Russians and Pakistanis. Pakistanis, because they make up a work force that outnumbers the indigenous Sunni Muslims; Russians, because the relatively liberated emirs have turned the Emirate of Dubai into a modern, manic duty-free megalopolis where everything is for sale, and bleached blond hookers in miniskirts make small fortunes working the blow-job-and-burgers shift.

I arrived in Dubai at seven in the morning, with the single goal of leaving the Emirates as quickly as possible. But after I'd spent the entire morning visiting travel agencies and phoning embassies, seeking any clue to where I might find a Pakistan-bound ship, my prospects looked bleak. Airplanes, needless to say, were readily available; they zoom between Dubai and Karachi on a daily basis. Who on earth, then, would be crazy enough to travel by sea? Why, drug smugglers, of course, or anyone else on the run from the law. The single lead I found—kited by an eighteen-year-old Indian barber who messily shaved me—was with a friend of a friend of his elder brother, a shady entrepreneur willing to run his unregistered fishing boat across the Gulf, on demand, for the flat sum of two thousand American dollars.

At four in the afternoon, having removed all the bits of bloodstained tissue from my neck, I sat beneath an oscillating fan inside the Liyari Pakistan Restaurant, gnawing on a tandoori drumstick. Within minutes the eatery, like all businesses in Dubai, would close for the midday call to prayer. I picked up my check and walked to the register. The Pakistani manager—Shahid, according to his name tag—made light conversation as he counted my change.

"Not so many Americans here," Shahid noted. "You are on what business?"

"My job," I explained—my God, it felt like a job—"is to go around the world without taking any airplanes. But from the look of things I will be setting up permanent residence here in Dubai."

He nodded sympathetically. "Dubai, good place. But Pakistan is better. You don't go to Karachi?"

"I'd love to go to Karachi," I said. "But the freighters won't take passengers, and the small boats will charge me thousands of dollars."

"Ahh." Shahid handed me a wrapped mint toothpick. "You must go to the canal, then. At night. I think you will find."

"Find what?"

"So many boats going to Karachi! They anchor along the canal at night. You can ask to the captains. Maybe one will agree for you. A thousand dollars?" He shook his head. "I don't think so. Maybe less. Tonight, you go." The metal roller door on the north side of the restaurant rolled down with a crash.

"These captains . . . do they speak English?"

Shahid laughed. "No, no English. I don't think so. Only Urdu. Mostly they are not very educated. But good on the sea. Tonight, you go. After nine o'clock."

"Shahid . . ." I peeled a tip twice the size of my lunch bill off my quickly diminishing bankroll and placed it on the counter. "I don't speak Urdu. I need your help. Will you go with me?"

Shahid picked up the bills, folded them in half and handed them back to me. "I will go for your friendship," he said. "Not for your money. Meet me here, at ten."

o   o   o

The generically named Canal slices into the heart of metropolitan Dubai, jiggling the lights of five-star hotels and churning the sodium street lamps into golden tea. Sony and Pepsi signs toss jazzy neon from nearby buildings, lending strolling lovers a Venusian glow. A broad green park separates the channel from the downtown noise and bustle, but the smells of frying fish and Russian perfume carry.

The heat of the day had receded, and the air was still and warm. Spilled popcorn lay strewn on the paved pedestrian corniche. Shahid and I walked slowly, enjoying the oasis of calm. Along the edge of the canal, worn wooden ships bobbed against the dock with soft crunching sounds. Crewmen's laundry hung limply on the rails; from inside the boats came the glow of battery-powered televisions, or the crackle of radio static. Late dinners sizzled on a few of the decks, the sharp smells of cumin and coriander—those eccentric cousins of the carrot—commingling with drifts of shit and diesel.

Shahid knew the boats well; well enough, at least, to deduce which of them might be bound for Karachi. Every third or fourth seemed a likely candidate, and I would bide my time on a bench while he climbed aboard and negotiated with the sailors. After an hour of this he'd found a possibility; a fishing boat leaving for Pakistan in about five days. I was grateful, but my enthusiasm was tempered by the knowledge that those five days would finally extinguish my dim, but still tenacious, Mount Kailas hopes.

We were hungry and tired, but I urged Shahid to try one more time. After bypassing half a dozen ramshackle ferries—"No good for Karachi," he explained—we came to the last one in line. Beyond it the canal widened, disappearing into the oil-slicked waters of the Persian Gulf.

I popped open a Coke while my companion climbed on board. Fifteen minutes later he reappeared, clutching a slip of paper.

"They will not go to Karachi," Shahid announced. "But a friend of this captain, he must be going."

"When?"

"Tonight. Unless he has already left . . ."

A burst of adrenaline zapped my spine. "Already left? Oh no . . . Which boat? Where?"

"Not here." Shahid squinted at the paper. "The boat is the *Fateh Al Khair*. Captain Hussain. It is docked across the city, at the Jabah Ali port. We must take a car . . ."

We jogged toward Nassar Square. A ferret-faced oil company executive and his "date"—a Slavic call girl with industrial-size breasts—fell back in astonishment as I shot between them and into their waiting cab, pulling the gleeful Shahid with me.

"American way!" he chortled as we roared off. "Indiana Jones! I like it very much."

o   o   o

The *Fateh Al Khair* had not yet left. Shahid found Captain Hussain—a roly-poly sea dog in a soiled yellow caftan — wolfing down french fries in the dockside greasy spoon and watching, with childlike fascination, a rock video of Henry Rollins performing "I'm a Liar" on MTV. The captain, as advertised, spoke no English, but with the help of Shahid and a world map I made my intentions clear. There followed a short dialogue between the two Pakistanis.

"He will help you," Shahid announced. "The crossing will take three days, if good weather." He glanced at his watch. "They will leave at four o'clock. In four hours. You must meet the captain here, and he will tell the police to stamp your passport. If you are late, even one minute late, they will go without you. You agree?"

I nodded. "How much will I pay for my passage?"

"You will give as you wish," Shahid relayed. "But there is no need to give anything. He will help you because he is a good man. A good man, and a good Muslim." Shahid and the captain clasped hands. "Four in the morning. The captain says if you need anything for the trip, you must buy it now."

We got back to town at 1:00 A.M. After buying Shahid dinner (Dubai never sleeps) and thanking him profusely I shopped like mad, purchasing everything I might need for three days on an open deck: sunscreen, lip balm, a straw hat, a towel, sandalwood soap, mosquito repellent, breath mints, two cartons of State Express 555 cigarettes (for the crew), a dozen AA batteries (for the OmniBook) and a case of root beer soda (for me). Repacking my Endless Journey, which lay gutted on my untouched bed at the Salalah Hotel, I made an awful discovery; ten minutes later I was standing in a musty alley, knocking frantically on the shuttered door of the luckless washerwoman who had consented to have my clothes cleaned and dried by next day noon. I brought the dripping load back to the Salalah, stuffed it in my pack and, at 3:00 A.M. sharp, hailed a cab for the ride back to Jabah Ali.

o o o

Captain Hussain was as good as his word. He signed me through emigration and, using the hand gestures that would be our sole means of communication for the entire crossing, directed me to his boat.

The wooden ferries anchored along the Jabah Ali dock lay four deep. The *Fateh Al Khair*, trimmed to sail, was on the outermost edge. It was an athletic effort to wrestle my pack and provisions across the railings, over the cargo and between the sleeping crewmen of the three intermediate boats; a task made no easier by the pitch-darkness or the dozens of cat-size rats and rat-size roaches that scurried underfoot. I boarded awash in sweat, gasping for breath and filthy as a junkyard dog.

It was difficult to get a good look at the barge, but its funkiness was beyond dispute. On the wooden deck, some fifty feet long by twenty feet wide, a dozen used cars and two new HiAce Super Custom vans were lashed down for transport to Pakistan. Above the aft deck loomed a one-room wheelhouse, reached by a wooden ladder. The toilet consisted of two naked planks, separated by a narrow gap, jutting from the stern. Hussain's nine-man crew lay strewn like casualties across the deck and in the wheelhouse, snoring on rough blankets.

The deck was crawling with cockroaches, but the real problem—the only problem—was that there was no room for me to lie down. In a last gasp of lateral thinking I opened the sliding side door of the nearest van and crawled gratefully inside. There, on cushions of cunningly whipped petroleum, I slept.

· 29 ·

Unplugged

It was unimaginable that, beyond the tiny stage of our boat, somewhere over the gunmetal-gray waters of the Persian Gulf (or, by Day 2, the Gulf of Oman), the world was still happening. Israel and the PLO were signing a peace pact; Nelson Mandela was about to be sworn in as president of South Africa; graffiti artist Michael Fay was getting his ass whipped in Singapore. By night, as I lay curled in my dormant vehicular nest, Girl Scouts sold cookies in Wisconsin; Mexicans celebrated Cinco de Mayo; Winona Ryder put on her lipstick. Planet Earth rolled through space, circling its sun at sixty-seven thousand miles per hour, and it was jam-packed with creatures doing funny, mysterious things.

I spent my mornings and afternoons—all the daylight hours, in fact—propped on cushions in the wheelhouse, reading books or typing on my miraculous battery-powered OmniBook as Captain Hussain (whose rank, paradoxically, seemed to release him from any shred of responsibility) hibernated noisily upon his bunk. As I finished each of the novels I'd brought (Pynchon, Asimov, Maugham, le Carré) I would throw it ceremoniously off the stern, watching it bob briefly before sinking into the loam of the Gulf. Pynchon, I thought, would particularly appreciate this burial at sea; there was something poetic about *Vineland* dissolving into the notorious waterway, which I can nevermore think of as anything but alphabet soup.

It was upon the *Fateh Al Khair* that I first experienced the infinite delight of the bucket bath, taken in my tattered red Calvin Kleins behind the leering yellow shade of a secondhand Caterpillar bulldozer. The broad plastic splash bowls of tepid water were a holy baptism, rinsing off my Arabian week of accumulated sweat, atomized sand, factor 15 sunscreen, 100 percent DEET insect spray, primal fear, belly-button lint, fish oil, machine grease, powdered rust, spilled pineapple juice, mosquito hoofprints, chapati flour, toe jam, melted chocolate and loose gray hairs. I took these baths in the heat of the day, making myself scarce as the more devout members of the all-Muslim crew rolled out their woven straw mats for their own call to prayer. Hidden behind my bulldozer, self-consciously semi-naked, I watched their elaborate choreography of devotion. Each fifteen-minute meditation included a ritual of standing, bowing, cupping the hands behind the ears, extending the palms to receive an invisible liquid sacrament and, finally, washing the blessed ether over their dark, pious faces.

There was no mess. The meals, cooked in a wind-screened corner of the deck and served "buffet-style," were hideous, but I ate them with good appetite, chasing away the boldest roaches and swallowing prophylactic doses of Pepto-Bismol afterward. I took up smoking, limiting my intake to three cigarettes a day: one at ten, one at two, and one just after sunset. And I shat in terror, once every morning at seven, clinging with both hands to the thick but fraying rope that, dangling damply from the ferry's stern, was all that kept me from following my books into the Gulf.

o   o   o

The language barrier precluded intimacy with the crew, but a quiet cordiality prevailed. I was treated with unflagging courtesy. By our third day at sea I knew most of the sailors by name. There was Salim Mohammed, the navigator, who looked like a Pakistani version of Neil Young and wandered the decks in black nylon socks; Bahadin Kera Ibrahim, a tall, unsmiling black man who reminded me of a character from a Conrad story; and Ali Abdul Shaktar, second mate, whose teeth were stained crimson from years of chewing *pan*. First Mate Yaakov could always be recognized by his signature blue cap, while Ahmed Allah Rakha, the bosun, chain-smoked and had the laconic round eyes of a frog. The only one who seemed to resent my presence on board was Muhammed Ali, the cook, who found himself with an additional mouth to feed. On the afternoon of our fourth day at sea, when we ran out of food entirely, this ceased to be a problem.

o   o   o

And it was during the fourth evening of that long, exquisitely dull cruise, sitting on the bridge in the moonless sloshing dark, that I realized, with a start: *We had no radio.*

No radio! No flare! No way to signal for help, to alert even the nearest passerby if—as has been known to happen on large bodies of water—
our luck went savagely awry. If something were to go wrong on the
Fateh there would be no hope at all of calling upon the forces that be
for a safe, speedy rescue. No radio! And, tied to the roof of the wheelhouse, only a tiny rubber raft, which, when I examined it closely, had
the words "Not To Be Used as a Life Preserver" emblazoned on its blub-
bery side.

In droll anguish I turned to the captain—dozing off to Hindi show
tunes on a leather-encased transistor radio—and inquired, with a flurry
of sign language, what we would do if there was a problem. Hussain
smiled—a beatific, submissive Islamic smile—and simply waved his
hands, right over left, horizontally, like cards being shuffled and returned to the deck. Right then and there I realized that, for the very
first time on my entire global pilgrimage, I was truly and utterly Un-
wired. There was no stream of radio waves, no electromagnetic impulse,
no vibrating string or even a smoke signal to link us with the World At
Large.

Thus I found myself, after fifteen years of travel, finally able to answer a question that had stumped me eight months earlier at the Third
Annual Book Passage Travel Writers' Conference. This, right here, was
"the single most remote spot" I had ever visited: the blue-trimmed
wheelhouse of the *Fateh Al Khair*, with Mr. Ibrahim at the wheel, morose
Salim the navigator sitting at the foot of his usurped (by me) sleeping
platform and the rotund Captain Hussain lounging in one of those
vaguely yogic subcontinental postures with a Rothman's filter king dangling between his fingers and a pinch of snuff tucked beneath his lip.

There was nothing around us but water, comic-book blue, unbroken save for the very occasional flying fish or the smokelike silhou-
ette of a distant tanker. Anything could happen; and if it did we would
die, finally and anonymously, having for all intents and purposes (as
my friend Pico Iyer might say) "fallen off the map."

o   o   o

By the late morning of Day 5 I knew we were in trouble. We'd left
Dubai with enough fuel to last about 100 hours; come noon, we would
have been at sea for 104. Land was nowhere in sight.

Ali Abdul Shaktar spied a fishing boat, and we changed course to in-
tercept. It took us more than an hour to reach it, but choppy seas forbid an exchange of personnel. Any confidence I still maintained in
Salim evaporated as I heard him—and one needed no Urdu for this—

bellowing for directions to Karachi. The half-naked seamen on the fishing skiff pointed in three separate directions, arguing amongst themselves. Bahadin Kera Ibrahim, usually cool as a cucumber, broke into a sweat. The captain, acting on executive authority, lay down with his arm over his eyes. Salim and the skiff's captain yelled back and forth, establishing something or other, and we hung a left.

Four hours later we accosted another trawler and, hearkening their unanimous counsel, hove 60 degrees to the right. It was five in the afternoon. We had by now run out of drinking water, and I was rationing root beer to the crew. Captain Hussain snored soundly, the stuffed tiger he had bought for his grandson tucked beneath his head.

The sun set. I sat atop my bulldozer, gazing at the evening star and flicking ashes into the sea. At any moment I expected to hear the death rattle of our engine, swallowing its last gulp of diesel and dooming us to slow extinction. What I heard instead was the voice of Ali Abdul Shaktar—old eagle eyes himself—hooting victoriously from the wheel. Strung between the inky sea and indigo sky, Karachi glittered on the horizon.

The *Fateh Al Khair* gagged and sputtered as we entered the harbor, stalling twice before reaching a berth. We had been at sea 112 hours—two days longer than the initial estimate. No sooner had we docked than hundreds of mosquitoes descended upon the boat, eager to graze on our sun-ripened limbs. The cockroaches and rats, sensing our evacuation, reappeared in force, boldly scrambling over the empty food stores and into the dry water barrel. Ibrahim, Salim and the other crewmen bagged their gear and, one by one, abandoned ship for the buses and taxis that would take them back to their families.

I put away my computer, retrieved my backpack and bid a less than fond farewell to the HiAce van that had served as my nest. A generous tip for our narcoleptic captain was folded into my shirt pocket. Every square inch of my skin was itching to get off that boat. Tonight, my first night in Asia, I would go for broke: an air-conditioned taxi, a five-course meal and a first-class hotel with a sauna and spa. Yes! Yes! I grabbed the cook's hands and danced a little jig, unable to believe it was over.

I was about to step over the railing and make my way to shore when the captain, more animated than I'd ever seen him, ran over and grabbed my arm.

"No, no, no!" he said.

"No, no, no!" echoed the remaining crewmen.

I looked at them as if they were crazy. It took twenty minutes of charades before I understood: Immigration was closed for the night. The officers would return at eleven the next morning. Until then I was confined, by letter of law, to the boat.

· 30 ·

To Sir, with Love

Karachi, I hardly knew ya . . . but the lure of motion, of steady, perpetual motion, was in my veins. I felt breathless, adrenalized, giddy with road fever and the insane illusion that I could still reach Kathmandu in the nick of time. What is it about moving? At a certain point the kora, the process of circumambulating the globe, had become a balls-out luge ride, a screaming downhill race, and I never wanted the wind to stop blowing in my face.

Besides, Karachi didn't look very interesting. Except for the local buses, hilariously tinseled and painted to break Ken Kesey's heart, the city was a bardo of blinding industrial smog, a monstrous shimmering grid of immense flat ratlands prostrating at the feet of featureless commercial centers and banks, all lost and groping in a miasma of rabid dog-breath heat. And the traffic! Crossing the street in Karachi was like morphing into a deadly video game, no way out but to leap up and somersault over careening steel projectiles as supercustomized space-invaders sound effects blasted me from every side. All this to buy some bottled water and a few bananas. . . .

It was my sincerest wish to escape the port city immediately and set out for Lahore—the ancient, colorful and ostensibly cooler "City of Gardens" that, situated some seven hundred miles northeast of Karachi, lies a stone's throw from India's northwestern border.

But the crewmen of the *Fateh Al Khair*, employing a well-practiced arsenal of hand signals and head wags, had assured me that it couldn't be done; that I'd be marooned in Karachi for weeks. Id-ul-Adha, the huge Islamic festival commemorating the hajj to Mecca, was only days away, and the entire Muslim world was on the hoof. Every vehicle leaving the sweltering megalopolis was booked solid and would remain so through May. This bit of intelligence was confirmed at the Pakistan Railways reservation office, where a khaki-shirted superintendent splayed his ledger across the desk to demonstrate, once and for all, that every seat and sleeper on the next twenty-one trains had been snapped up months ago.

"If I myself wished to leave Karachi," he moaned, "I could not do so. So what hope, sir, for you?"

What hope, indeed . . . but what hope of leaving Mauritania, for that matter? Or Turkey? An hour later, after shimmying high up the trunk of the national railway's famous bureaucracy, I found myself seated directly across from Ali Khan, the Acting Assistant Vice Superintendent of Everything That Goes Choo-Choo in Pakistan. He was a young man, meticulously groomed from neck to fingernails, and after offering me a cigarette (which I declined, having quit smoking the moment I stepped gratefully onto the Karachi dock), he accepted my passport, leaned back so that the two front legs of his chair were off the ground and inquired of me, with a smile that radiated innocence and longing, "So how does it feel, sir, to live in a completely emancipated society?"

It was the first time I had encountered this syndrome in Pakistan, but it would not be the last. Pakistanis, whatever their private disagreements might be, seem to share the illusion that the United States of America is a sort of ideal world; a place where flower petals and honey rain from the sapphire sky, fertilizing a rich, loamy earth carpeted in dewy dollar bills upon which the lion and lamb romp in conjugal ecstasy.

I spent the next forty minutes disavowing Mr. Khan of this notion while dutifully igniting his Winston Lights and refilling his teacup. At the end of my soliloquy he righted his chair, took my hand and confessed, head lolling, that there might in fact be a free berth on the Tenzan Express, a berth reserved, customarily, for veterinarians or medical doctors but which, if not filled by departure time (two hours hence), could in good conscience be requisitioned for local VIPs or visiting dignitaries; a distinction that he himself could, with discretion, bestow upon his voluble American friend.

So he spoketh, and so it came to pass that, several hours later, I found myself installed in an ice-blue all-male sleeper compartment, sharing my bananas with an eclectic group of Pakistani citizens who found in their American bunkmate a dazed but not unwilling target dummy for their religious convictions and political misconceptions.

Three Brief Conversations on the Tenzan Express to Lahore

I was a curiosity, an oddity, an emissary from Andromeda. I was the famous cousin, *Mon Oncle d' Amérique*, the Giraffe Who Came to School.

Haidar Zaman was the first to engage me. With his immaculately trimmed beard and kind, though piercing, brown eyes, Haidar could have been successfully cast as a supporting actor in a film about a fin de siècle psychoanalyst, perhaps opposite Wallace Shawn as the eccentric Carl Jung. He was well-to-do, an equal partner in his father's large farm, and had earned the honorific title "hajji" by completing the pilgrimage to Mecca ten years before.

He listened attentively to a description of my own round-the-world kora and declared it nonsense. "You have no idea what a pilgrimage is," he stated. "None whatever."

"How can you say that?" I was more intrigued than peeved. "Each person who makes a pilgrimage does so according to his own needs and beliefs. For me—a writer—this trip is the perfect expression of my love for this planet and the God who created it. For you to say otherwise is rather presumptuous."

He shook his head, smiling. "You confuse your needs with Allah's needs. It is you who requires this endless sightseeing, not the Almighty. You have devised a tour of distractions, and as anyone can see you are highly distracted. Isn't it?"

The other passengers were listening to our dialogue with rapt attention. "I'm exhausted," I admitted, "and there are times when I forget the reason I'm on this pilgrimage. But I don't buy this business about my needs being different from Allah's. I'm not even sure"—I was flirting with heresy here—"that Allah *has* needs. Nor do I see any separation between myself and what you call the Almighty."

Haidar raised an eyebrow but took my remarks in stride. "What you believe is up to you," he said. "It changes nothing. But if you wish to commune with the Almighty, you will not succeed in your present course. What you call a pilgrimage will bring you no closer to Him. I tell you this as fact. That's all."

"So what," I asked, "do you recommend?"

"The idea of life is not just to travel, travel, travel. You must stay in one place and pray to God."

It sounded like a fabulous idea. "Maybe next year. . . ."

The man to the right of Haidar had been rocking impatiently from side to side, clearing his throat and refolding his newspaper throughout our conversation. Now he could no longer contain himself.

"May I ask you one question?" He was in his twenties, with prominent buck teeth and a generally ferretlike expression.

"Certainly."

"You are having in your country now, I think, some farmers who use only the natural pesticides? Farmers who will grow the food without the use of chemicals or dangerous sprays?"

"That's right. They're called organic farmers. You can buy their fruits and vegetables in the stores, but it's usually more expensive than the commercial produce."

"Of course, of course. May I ask you something?"

"Please."

"Yes. Why is it that the farmers in your own country will not use these cancer-causing sprays on their own fruits and vegetables, yet they are happy to sell these chemicals to countries such as Pakistan, so we ourselves will get these various diseases?"

"*Oy.* . . . Listen, it's not that simple. The organic farmers in the United States are a small minority; they're not the same people who are selling chemical sprays to Pakistan. Your complaint is with the chemical producers themselves. It works this way: American consumers decide they would rather buy natural, unsprayed fruit. In response, certain farmers begin to provide it. As more people buy organic fruit, the market for chemical sprays declines, so the chemical companies. . . ."

But my inquisitor had made his point, lost interest, and a pudgy, pale-lipped man seated directly across from me leapt in to fill the void.

"Excuse me! Excuse me, please, sir. What is the primary cause of AIDS in your country?"

There was a distinct grinding sound as my brain shifted gears. I ran through the familiar Planned Parenthood pamphlet litany—unprotected sex, infected needles, tainted blood transfusions—while the man leaned forward in his seat, hands folded, belly obscuring his belt line.

"Yes, yes. Of course. All of these things. I know. What I am going to tell you, then, is this: I have set myself the dream, the very goal, of curing the AIDS infection entirely. Of wiping the disease from the planet. This is my destiny. And I will work tirelessly to achieve it."

I was taken aback. "That's marvelous," I said. "I had no idea that advanced AIDS research was being done in Pakistan at all. Is your laboratory in Karachi or Islamabad?"

"No, no! No laboratory."

"No laboratory? You work with AIDS patients personally?"

"No, no! Of course not."

I was swimming through molasses. "I don't understand. Are you a doctor?"

He laughed with delight. "No, no! I am a farmer! Just as this man here." He nodded courteously toward Haidar Zaman.

"A farmer. I see. Can you tell me, then, how you plan to eradicate AIDS?"

He settled back in his seat, hands clasped behind his head. "This, only God can say. Man abides, God decides. Isn't it? Or perhaps it is man who decides while God himself abides. I am simply a farmer, my book knowledge is poor, but my destiny cannot change. Therefore it is I who must abide. Or do you believe that it is for man to create his own destiny? These are interesting questions, and we will discuss them at length should you care to visit in Islamabad. You are most welcome."

Haidar leaned across the cabin toward me, jostling a packet of Dunhills. "Take a smoke?"

I held up both hands. "No thanks."

"What?" He fell back, scandalized. "Why not smoke? All writers are needing to smoke cigarettes."

"Who told you that?"

"It is known worldwide. The great writer with his cigarette and whiskey. Whiskey you cannot find in Pakistan, but, cigarettes, yes, we can provide. Take one, I insist . . ."

My protests were interrupted by two young beggars who entered our cabin. One, eleven or twelve, held an empty shoe-polish container between the thumb and middle finger of his left hand while he drummed upon it, tabla-fashion, with the fingers of his right. He was lightning fast, a ragged virtuoso, and as he coaxed impossible rhythms and tones from the tiny Kiwi tin his partner threw back his head and began to sing. It was a devotional Qawaali song; I recognized it from an album by Nusrat Fateh Ali Khan. The boys sang with power and conviction, achieving a richness of expression rare even on professional recordings. When they finished I was speechless. As I showered the duo with rupees, the lead singer dropped to his knees and clutched my arm.

"*Empty way*," he insisted, shaking my elbow and staring eagerly into my eyes. "Empty way. Please, please, go empty way . . ."

The words dazed me, resonating in my skull. There was a message here, a clue for my ultimate illumination, if only I could grasp it. At a loss, I glanced at Haidar Zaman for counsel.

Haidar smirked, shrugging his shoulders. "This is the dream of every Pakistani musician," my devout friend explained. "He wants you to get him on MTV."

o   o   o

The good Mr. Zaman prepared to disembark at Khanewal. He seemed agitated. It was clear that he wanted to say something, but was not sure how to begin. He retrieved his suitcase from beneath the bench seat and—just before leaving the car—clasped my hand, leaned in toward me and placed his lip inches from my ear.

"Your tongue is black," he whispered.

Anonymous

I spent a full day and night in Lahore, meeting no one. I wandered in awe through the enormous Badshahi Mosque, built by the brilliant but fatally intolerant Mogul emperor Aurangzeb—son of Shah Jahan, who raised the Taj Mahal—late in the seventeenth century. I haunted bookstores, visited the bazaar and religiously gargled Listerine, straight up, in hopes of evicting the recalcitrant organisms that were once again using my tongue as their rug.

Lahore fascinated me, and parts of the city were beautiful. Although I never made it to the famed Shalimir Gardens, the fabulous Lahore Museum—curated, from 1875 to 1893, by Rudyard Kipling's father—swallowed me for an entire afternoon as I roamed its immense viscera surrounded by carpets, miniature paintings and seventeen-hundred-year-old Gandhara sculptures.

These, truthfully, were what I had traveled to Lahore to see. It fascinated me to think that the very first statues of the Buddha (who, like Abraham and Mohammed, had cautioned his disciples never to create or worship graven images) were actually coöpted busts of Apollo, the Greek and Roman god of sunlight and music, executed eight centuries after Buddha's death by artists who had crossed the Khyber Pass.

The specific work I most wanted to see turned out to be the museum's centerpiece. It was an exquisitely rendered sculpture of the ascetic Buddha, a portrait of Siddhartha during the time when, exploring the most extreme paths to enlightenment, he had fasted for forty-nine days and nights on the banks of the Ganges River. Every bone and blood vessel in the wasted body stood out in fragile relief, while the sunken eyes burned with the spark that was to illuminate all of Asia.

I stood a very long time before that famous statue—an anonymous masterpiece that, like Michelangelo's *David*, portrays a single-minded seeker on the brink of entering the mythos. Like all such works—there might be a dozen of them on the Earth—it had much to tell me about the process of pilgrimage.

o   o   o

The taxi ride from Lahore to the Indian border takes exactly as long as the BART ride from Oakland to San Francisco.

I filed this useless bit of information in my already overloaded data bank, cramming it alongside the images that rolled across my retina with the relentless verve of snapshots blinking from an instant photo-processing machine: brick walls painted with Islamic calligraphy; alleys tiled with handprinted patties of buffalo dung; a man and eight children balanced aboard a Honda 100 motorbike. Suburban Lahore was a midway of sugarcane squeezers, driving schools, bagpipe assembly plants, dry ice factories, bamboo scaffolding manufacturers, ice cream vendors and bullock carts. Huge wreaths and banners stretched across the road, proclaiming the festival of Id. A wooden oxcart, rounding a corner with enough mown hay to fill my Oakland flat from floor to ceiling, tipped its load onto a marching band, muting the tubas and exchanging one brand of chaos for another.

My taxi driver—a gray-haired, middle-aged snipe whose sensory organs were bunched together in the very center of his face—wove around these obstacles with one hand on the wheel and the other on my knee, lost in a running monologue about the charms of the roadside maidens.

"Oh! Oh! Did you see that one! Very womanly, very nice. This girl also, on the left. Look, look, she is just going! My God, what breasts! Oooooo! We have a saying here in Pakistan: No rest without chest; no life without wife; no knowledge without college. Isn't it? Is it true in your country also? Are you married? No children? Why not? Never mind, you just come here and I will find you a nice Pakistani girl. . . ."

We reached the border at noon. I leapt from the cab—how many vehicles had I leapt from during the past eighteen weeks?—and exchanged my Pakistani rupees for their Indian equivalent, anxious to complete my formalities before the interminable subcontinental lunch break.

One hour later I left the Islamic world and, after convincing an attentive band of customs officials that my miniature computer was not a sophisticated nuclear device, entered Mother India. A bulbous Ambassador cab, fleet as a senile hippopotamus, conveyed me to the Amritsar railway station. As we crept along the road the clouds turned green. Pink lightning flashed across the sky, thunder cracked against the roof and a fierce hot rain pelted the car. The driver rolled down his window and leaned out to his waist, piloting the wiperless cab against the boiling current of India's youngest river.

The Paradise of Gold and Lightning

Sikhism is a fringe culture to most Americans. The signature beards and turbans worn by devout Sikh men (who also tend to be tall, with intense dark eyes) are exotic and intimidating, a visual throwback to the days of India's opulent Raj.

The Sikhs can indeed be fierce. Centuries of persecution by Muslims, as well as the brutal Sikh Wars (fought against the British in the mid-nineteenth century), established their legendary ferocity. Not long ago, in fact, a tricky question was put before the justices of the U.S. Supreme Court: Should Sikh children be allowed to bring daggers with them to school? It was an issue of major import for American Sikh families, since carrying a "sword" at all times (along with the obligation never to cut one's hair or beard and to wear short pants, a comb in the hair, and the *kara*, a metal bracelet) is the religious duty of all orthodox male Sikhs. The court ruled in favor of the practice, wisely realizing that the more serious threat was to freedom of religious expression.

In truth, Sikhism is one of the most benevolent and tolerant religions in the world. Originating in the Punjab region of northwest India in the late fifteenth century, Sikhism emphasizes beliefs that forbid idolatry and contradict the Hindu caste system. Sikhs believe that a monotheistic deity created all men with equal rights and status. Moreover, they teach that a person acquires dignity and merit through devotion, service and labor—rather than through reflective contemplation (as the Hindus believe) or ritual submission to the will of Allah (as in Islam).

The greatest saint of Sikhism is Guru Nanak, the Sufi-influenced Hindu mystic who created the religion. And Sikhism's greatest shrine is the Golden Temple, set in the center of a huge man-made reservoir on the outskirts of Amritsar. . . .

o   o   o

I huddled in the rear of a motorized rickshaw, peering through a fabric-flapped window slit as we churned through fender-high puddles. The rain was still falling, soaking the robes of pilgrims and running off the corrugated tin roofs of Amritsar in twisting silver ropes. It was three-thirty in the afternoon.

I'd already bought a ticket on the next train to Lucknow, scheduled to leave Amritsar Station at five-fifteen. Every bunk in Second-Class Sleeper, the preferred class of travel on the capillary Indian Railway System, was booked—thanks, again, to Id—and the only available seats were in First Class A/C. During the fourteen years I'd been visiting India every single western traveler I'd met had cautioned me against Indian air-conditioning, but my zeal to press onward was so fanatical that I cast my aversions aside and elected to experience "luxury class" comfort for myself.

My driver skidded to a halt outside the entrance of the Golden Temple, parking amid a flurry of booths selling head scarves and religious trinkets. He would wait one hour, then spirit me back to the station.

The wall leading up to the temple entrance was decorated with hand-painted signs espousing, for ignoramuses such as myself, the basic tenets of the Sikh faith. Entering the compound, I was asked to shed my shoes. A stern guard placed them in a rain-sheltered nook while an earnest teen tied an orange scarf with gold flecks over my hair. I felt like I was about to enter one of the rooms where they assemble the space shuttle.

"You are from where, please?"

I told him.

"And what is your good name?"

I told him this as well.

"Welcome to Golden Temple," he declared. "We are Sikh. You are welcome to stay in our guesthouse. There is no cost to you. Food also, vegetarian, is free. If you wish to make some contribution you are welcome, but we neither ask nor require. Please, please!" He motioned me toward the doorway leading to the enormous open-air reservoir. "Go in! There is singing day and night. Go! Enjoy! Welcome!"

Fresh storm clouds were moving in over Amritsar. Thunder boomed through the vast temple compound, making the structure resonate like a kettledrum. A marble causeway led to the center of the pool, where the Golden Temple itself—a surprisingly small pavilion—sat like an exquisite jewel.

The water in the reservoir rippled in the rain, sloshing over the walkway as an endless procession of barefoot pilgrims filed toward the shrine. As I negotiated the path a gigantic lightning bolt zapped the heavens, exploding with such a clap that the women behind me shrieked with fright. A scene from an old James Bond movie, in which 007 kills a would-be assassin by knocking an electric appliance into the bathtub with him, flashed abruptly into my head. This invited a question: *If lightning struck the pool while the causeway was covered with water, would all of us be electrocuted?* A second blast, bright enough to light the environs like a strobe, made the query seem more than hypothetical. I ran like a cheetah into the shrine.

If certain places on Earth are indistinguishable from Heaven, the Golden Temple of Amritsar must be among them. A spirit of utter peace pervaded the environment; even the thunder booming outside sounded like the roar of a tamed beast. I joined the dozens of other pilgrims sitting cross-legged upon the parquet marble floor and listened, eyes half-closed, to the devotional *bhajans* rising and falling with the rhythms of the tabla and harmonium. Indian rupee notes fluttered across the floor, swirling around the lavish offerings of flowers and incense arrayed beneath a pink silk canopy.

My pants clung to my legs, but all notions of discomfort vanished. It was wonderful to be wet. The desert, once and for all, was behind me.

o   o   o

At this point a strange and terrible thing occurred. Every part of me—brain, heart and gut—told me to stay exactly where I was. I could dine with the pilgrims, spend the night in the guesthouse and wake to the sound of singing in the morning. *There is nothing,* I thought to myself, remembering a Roxy Music song, *More than This.*

Every iota of rational thought still available to me recognized the paramount importance of resting myself, body and soul, before continuing on to meet Sally in Lucknow. Every part of me wanted to stop moving, to stay still, to wait for my tongue to turn pink again. *But I couldn't do it.* A demonic undercurrent, like the electric grid installed in the cage of a laboratory rat, lifted me off the marble floor of the Golden Temple and turned me, a reluctant Pinocchio, toward the door.

You're making a mistake, an angelic voice whispered in my ear. *You're making a b-i-g mistake.*

Oh yeah? the demon answered. *And what about Mount Kailas? Hunh? What about your deadline?*

Forget Kailas. Give it up, Jeffji. And screw the bloody deadline. You're in Paradise. You can afford to spend one day in Paradise.

But the strings tightened, and I felt my limbs jerking inexorably onto the causeway . . . toward my auto-rickshaw . . . into the station . . . onto the train. . . .

o o o

Two hours later my legs and back were adhered to the blue vinyl seat of a hermetically sealed First-Class train car. Meat-locker air-conditioning blasted from a vent behind my neck. Three corpulent Punjabi women occupied the bench seat directly across from me; the instant the train lurched forward they removed their shoes. I sighed deeply, meaning every cubic inch of it, and pressed my face against the grimy, unbudgeable window.

We emerged from Amritsar Station. The storm had passed, the rains had stopped, and the holy golden sun pierced the neon-fringed clouds on the western horizon. An enormous double rainbow arced above the temples and puddles of Paradise, lost.

• 31 •

112°

I remember that the metal handrails of the six-seater tempo were too hot to touch and that thermals rose off the baking riverbed like curtains of cellophane. Hand-painted billboards advertising televisions and computers peeled in the heat, dropping flakes of Devanagari script onto the Lucknow sidewalks like bits of dried orange rind.

"Too much hot," the man seated beside me nodded. Our shoulders were touching, and at the point where they did—at the point where anything touched my body—sweat stains blossomed on my clothing like hot breath on chrome.

It was a forty-five-minute ride from the train station. I remember leaving my backpack and hiking shoes beneath the bronze statue of the elephant-headed Ganesha in the lobby of the Thikana Hotel and walking, dazed, through the streets of Indira Nagar. A small dog yapped frantically from behind a wall. The scorched clouds were hung like thin, worn bandages against the sun.

It was nearly noon. Hari Lal Poonja's morning satsang would be over by now, but his devotees would still be in the air-conditioned assembly hall—drinking fresh lemon sodas, milling around and talking about the day's teachings. Sally would be among them. The thought of seeing her again made my knees weak.

I remember opening the metal gate, stepping onto the shaded cement porch of the satsang house and placing my boots in the familiar shoe rack. Arjun, a wiry Tamil linguist wearing a white Nehru shirt, was the first to recognize me. He clapped his hands around my back and pressed his cheek against mine. His stubble felt like a cat's tongue.

"So wonderful to see you again," he said. "How long has it been? Two years?" He drew away and looked into my eyes. "My God. I'll get you something to drink. You prefer lemonade? Coke? Sprite?"

"Arjun . . ." I hesitated. "What color is my tongue?"

He squinted into my mouth. "Why . . . pink, of course." His eyebrows furrowed. "Are you all right? I think you should drink something . . ."

"Water, please. Just water. Thank you, Arjunji." I racked my brain for Sally's Indian name. "Is Brijbala inside?"

"Ah! Brijbala. She has been waiting for you to come. Right now, maybe, she has gone to the fax center. Anyway, she will return in some minutes. Better, first, you drink something. Wait here, I will bring . . ." He disappeared into the satsang house.

It was the ninth of May. I could still make it to Kathmandu, in time for the Mount Kailas expedition, if I left for Nepal the following morning. The thought caromed around inside my skull like the memory of a recurrent nightmare.

Arjun reappeared with a bottle of purified water, which I drained in a single peristaltic spasm.

We entered the house. The large satsang room was still full of devotees, some standing, some seated on round throw pillows. A man leaned against a wall, tuning a guitar; a child with ebony skin sat still as her hair was braided by a voluptuous woman with a ring in her nose.

Hari Lal Poonja's raised dais, bedecked with flowers, was empty. A black-and-white portrait of his own guru, Ramana Maharshi, hovered above the bright yellow cushions. I peered around, surprised by how familiar everything seemed. There was a lull in the level of conversation, and I heard my name being whispered and repeated.

Arjun led me into an air-conditioned showroom where devotional paraphernalia—books, photographs and meditation cushions—filled tilting wooden shelves. My own contribution to this corner of spiritual materialism, the videotaped interview I'd conducted with Poonja sixteen months earlier, was prominently displayed.

I remember feeling beads of sweat trickle down my back, and the sensation that my arms were covered in goose bumps. I remember hearing a commotion just outside the showroom, seeing the door fly open and watching Sally—radiant, almost saintly in a flowing Punjabi suit—rush into my arms. Her hair smelled like sandalwood, and her breasts pressed lusciously against my chest.

I hugged her as tightly as I could, and collapsed.

The Buddha of Lucknow

It was your basic case of total exhaustion. The rubber-band engine of super-human stamina that had propelled me through Arabia, across the Persian Gulf, out of Pakistan and into the belly of India had finally gone slack. For the next two days I rested in Sally's walk-up flat, bouncing between fever and chills, horizontal and vertical, despair and surrender.

My system had collapsed upon itself like a sinkhole, taking my hopes of reaching Mount Kailas—or at least of reaching Kathmandu in time to join the Wilderness Travel expedition to Tibet—down with it. All the frantic racing, all the anxiety of the past ten days, *of the entire trip*, had been in vain. I'd dashed like a champ, only to choke a meter from the finish line. In the dark ignominy of the moment, a single fact illuminated my spirit: Had I tried to continue onward, I probably would have died.

The good news was that *(a)* I was still alive, and *(b)* my tongue, as mysteriously as it had acquired it, had lost its melanic shine.

The bad news was that Sally, the lovely sweet Salamander, would not be going on to Nepal—nor continuing overland with me at all.

There were two reasons for her change of heart. The first was that she was rooted to Indira Nagar, literally and figuratively, by a cunning commercial inspiration. Dozens of broad, flat growing trays filled the largest room of her modest flat. Each tray bristled with an Astroturf mohawk of sprouting wheatgrass, a plant that, if one bought Sally's spiel, was the healthiest thing to come along since tofu. Every morning she would clip the grass with a pair of scissors, feed it into a hand-cranked juice extractor and grind away. Minutes later she displayed an ounce of deep jade liquor: the ambrosia, she assured me, of immortality.

"There is nothing this stuff won't do. It purges diabetes and cancer, vanquishes gout and mange, flushes the liver, sweetens the spleen, purifies the heart and electrifies the gonads. There are rumors that it reverses the balding process and fine-tunes the body's enlightenment receptors." For the past few weeks Sally had been serving the day's first press to Poonja, who had started displaying the randiness of a young goat. Now she fed the elixir to me, and watched without surprise as my monosyllabic torpor metamorphosed into a frenzy of run-on sentences.

"It's fantastic stuff." She spooned green gook from the grinder into the sink. We had fallen, almost instantly, back into a pattern of bantering friendship. "If I can grow enough of this to sell, say, twenty-five ounces a day—at thirty rupees a shot—I'll eventually save enough to buy a return ticket."

o   o   o

Not that she was eager to leave. Quite the contrary; for aside from launching her own small business, Sally had finally found the center of her own compass: the Here she had been seeking all along.

"Every day is a new revelation, a peeling away of old layers." We sat together at the foot of her bed, immersed in the first real conversation we'd had since the ferryboat to Greece. "The veil of deception continues to fall, but my commitment at this point is unshakable. Surrendering to the perfection of 'What Is' seems to be an endless unfolding—one that must be *total*."

"A total unfolding of what, though?"

"I'll give you an example. Remember all the times I hissed through my teeth, 'Jeff, this is just what's happening in this moment!!'? I was criticizing you for not accepting the situation as it was, when it was *I* who could not accept what was presenting itself—which, of course, *included* your nonacceptance of the situation, as well as my own nonacceptance of your nonacceptance!" She laughed, rolling back onto her pillow. "What a dance I started when I traded in my regular ego for a new, improved one of spiritual vanity, enlightened snobbery and transcendental scorn!"

"You're being unfair to yourself." I held her foot. "I don't think we were fighting because you weren't 'enlightened' enough. We had wildly different hopes and expectations about what the trip should be, and of how to get through it even on a day-to-day basis."

She sat up and folded her legs. "That's true. Even so, I feel that I failed you. First, by not living up to my best assets—the ones that you chose me for—and second, because I wasn't true to my own instincts in the first place. You remember that I was reluctant to go; I wanted to fly ahead to India. You persuaded me not to, but the truth is that I probably should have."

"Maybe I was being manipulative."

"I can hardly blame you; you didn't want to travel alone." We snorted together at the irony. "The most painful thing, though, was that once I *did* commit to going, I wasn't even capable of keeping myself together—especially when I got caught up in my reactions to *your* way of keeping it together. Which, as you know, often comes out being righteous instead of supportive, and arrogant instead of empathetic. Because, for all my appearances of being strong and independent and capable, underneath it's pure illusion. The entire structure is floating on an ocean of insecurity. . . ."

"It was me." I cut her off. "I was an ass. I never took care of you. It never even *occurred* to me. I was so bound up in my separation anxiety, my split-up with Coriola, bullshit deadline issues . . ."

Sally shook her head. "I don't know what started our breakdown. I wish I hadn't felt responsible for changing your attitude when you wanted to complain. I wish I hadn't believed I would have been happier, or in a better position to understand the truths we were being faced with, by being with Papa. I wish I hadn't been so selfishly self-absorbed when you needed a friend. I wish, I wish . . ." She looked up into my eyes. "I can't say I wish we could do it again, and I can't say I wish it hadn't happened. The truth is that we've both gained some insight, and are finally in the postion that we always wanted to be in. You're getting a story worth writing; and I'm living what I feel my true life purpose is."

"So it satisfies you, your role here as a disciple?"

"At this point, absolutely. I can't tell you what a blessing it is to be at the Master's feet. Yet, at the same time, I find myself evolving past the whole duality of 'guru' and 'devotee.' Everything you see here, this whole crazy display, is just emptiness trying to return to emptiness; love falling in love with itself. Being with Papa is being in the presence of Grace. I can't even imagine where I'd rather be."

o   o   o

Truth was, I knew what she meant. H. L. Poonja, or Papaji, as the octo-genarian Master is called by his disciples, may be the feistiest, funniest, most sublime guru in India. A piebald, big-boned Punjabi, Papaji is a retired Indian army colonel, former heavyweight wrestler, onetime re-sistance fighter and notoriously reluctant swami whose age and failing mobility have made him (as his followers wryly admit) a "captive guru." Born in 1910, Poonja had his first religious awakening at the age of eight, when he went into a trance that lasted (to his parents' alarm) for two full days. His thirst for liberation never flagged, and he went on—family, career and army commission notwithstanding—to become a lifelong Krishna devotee and disciple of the great Indian saint Ramana Maharshi. Today he follows the *advaita* tradition; a philosophy that, based on a process of shrewd self-inquiry, holds that our very own Self—pure, awakened consciousness—is the luminous source of all we would seek elsewhere.

My first visit to Lucknow had taken place in January 1993, when, en route to Nepal, I decided to stop in Indira Nagar and visit this guru I'd heard so much about. Articles in *Yoga Journal* and *Inquiring Mind* had piqued my interest, particularly since they were written by friends who, while sharing my cynical point of view, had nonetheless been seduced by Poonja's wisdom and charm. The fact that Sally was also making her first visit to Lucknow at that time—she'd arrived a week before me—was a powerful incentive as well.

I have a factory-installed bullshit meter, but nothing about my first encounters with Poonja made the needle quiver. The guru accepted no money, lived in a modest home on a dusty Indira Nagar corner and wept with emotion reciting the poetry of Kabir. His only vice was big-league cricket, which he watched religiously, having installed a satellite dish on his roof for the purpose. He loved rich food, answered his mail and remembered the names of people he sat next to on trains in 1936. He flirted with, but did not *schtup*, his disciples. He hadn't a single Rolls-Royce to his name.

The satsangs themselves—Papaji's crowded, two- to three-hour-long morning teachings—were extraordinary events. Visitors and devotees would write the Master letters, which were stacked beside his seat on the dais. After a silent meditation period, Poonja would open each let-ter, read it aloud (he spoke fluent English) and call the writer up for a one-on-one reply. The queries ran the gamut, from purely devotional to wholly practical. Some he answered with a direct, piercing glance—for he was a master at *nirdidaksna*, direct transmission through the eyes—which often reduced the questioner to helpless, liberated laughter. Oth-ers he addressed in a more concrete way. When a jittery Australian woman asked the guru how she could conquer her lifelong fear of dogs (a genuine liability in Asia) Poonja brought her a newborn puppy to raise.

All his replies, whatever the question, reflected his absolute conviction that everyone is *already* free, and that the liberation we seek requires nothing more than waking up to that reality. There was no practice to perform; no litany to chant; no dues to pay. Papaji asked for nothing, made neither promises nor threats and finally sent you packing—fortified with the heart, wisdom and courage you already had.

He was, in short, the Wizard of Oz.

o   o   o

You know me, reader; I'm cynical and I'm glib. So I ask that you suspend disbelief for a few paragraphs and bear with me as I describe two brief, mind-altering events that occurred when I first visited "Papaville" in 1993.

Shortly after I first arrived in Indira Nagar, word got out—thanks in large part to Sally—that I was a journalist. It just so happened that a few of Papa's well-to-do devotees had been looking for a person with this specific talent for the purpose of conducting an interview with the Master. The exchange would be recorded on videotape and distributed to Poonja's fans worldwide. To make a long story short, I was asked if I'd like to conduct the interview. Feeling lucky and flattered, I consented.

Television crews from both Lucknow and the local spiritual community were on hand to record the exchange, which took place at a special evening satsang. As the event began I took my seat on the stage, eye to eye with the Master, and humbly presented him with a token gift: a regulation cricket bat, purchased in the local bazaar.

There is no need for me to repeat our intense, convoluted dialogue in these pages. The interview is readily available, both on videotape and in a published collection titled *Papaji*. The moment I wish to recall, however, cannot be found in either of these sources. I will do my best to describe it here.

First, I have to make a somewhat difficult confession. Believe it if you wish, or laugh in my face, but understand that what I am about to say is, for me, an indelible truth: Back in the early 1980s, on an assignment to India's ancient and spectacular Ajanta Caves, *I spontaneously recalled one of my past lives*. The revelation occurred as I was staring at one of the beautiful Ajanta murals and suddenly recognized myself as a character in one of the panels. The insight, which struck like lightning, has colored my worldview ever since.

Imagine my reaction, then, when Poonja responded to one of my innocent interview questions with a specific anecdote, drawn from Asian mythology, which actually included that very character. . . . and my astonishment as he turned away from the microphone, put his lips by my ear and gleefully whispered: "I think you remember! I think you were there!!"

How to describe what transpired at that precise moment? It was as if the entire fabric of time—the whole tapestry of the previous twenty-five centuries—unraveled like a sweater on a thornbush. For a fleeting instant, never to be forgotten, I perceived Time as a single continuum, a continuum throughout which my essential nature—who I was, am and always will be—gleamed with the impenetrable clarity of a diamond. I went into a trance, lost in the ecstasy of the moment; the next thing I remember is Papaji laughing uproariously, shaking my leg and yelling, "Come back! Come back! We have an interview to finish!"

This really happened. I kid you not.

The second event took place shortly afterward. Again, a bit of preliminary explanation is needed. Since my maiden trip to Asia, in 1979, I'd held the unshakable conviction that, at some point in my life, I would find—on the streets of Benares, perhaps, or on the ice of some glacial moraine—a gold ring. The ring would be more than a piece of free jewelry; it would materialize, I knew, at the point in my life where my peripatetic spiritual flounderings "ended," and the path I was to follow lay clearly before me.

After our dialogue concluded, Poonja and I left the assembly hall and walked together toward the waiting press of devotees. The interview had been a success; both of us were exhausted from the heat of the lights and the intensity of our encounter. As we faced the crowd, a man I vaguely recognized stepped forward. He was a German, just about my age, whose name (his real name, believe it or not) was Thomas Joseph Christ.

"You don't know me," he said, "but I know you. I know you very well. You and I, whether you realize this or not, are brothers. We have been brothers many times, in many lives. I knew it the moment I saw you, and I will never, ever forget.

"I don't even know if I will ever see you again," Thomas continued. "But to show you how deeply I believe what I have just told you, I am giving you this."

He removed a gold ring from his finger and placed it in my hand.

I was flabbergasted, and a little bit embarrassed. "I can't accept this," I said, handing the ring back to him. "It's too much. Please, take it back."

"It is already yours," he said, holding up his hands in a gesture of surrender. "If you cannot accept it, throw it out. I will not take it back."

I slid the ring onto my finger, and we embraced. The next afternoon he accompanied me to the train station, where I returned to New Delhi for my air connection to Kathmandu.

The ring, good reader, remains on my hand.

Love and Rockets

Papaville was different the second time around. Despite my long-awaited reunion with Sally, despite the fact that the videotape had made me a minor celebrity in the small spiritual community, the luminous aura of magical self-discovery that defined my initial visit no longer dazzled me.

I saw little of Sally. She would depart for the Master's house at 5:30 A.M., bearing her cup of wheatgrass juice and a change of clothes. An integral part of the guru's household, she would stay with Papa through breakfast, sit beside him at satsang and return to his house to fix lunch and assist with preparations for dinner. By the time she arrived home it was late afternoon, and her trays of thirsty green sprouts demanded what little energy she had left. She was entirely focused on her own spiritual growth, and our encounters were warm but brief.

Even the morning satsangs, while entertaining and occasionally cathartic, seemed oddly off-key, lacking the dynamic chemistry I'd experienced the previous year. Papa, for reasons none dared question, was cultivating a sort of trickster mode, needling his visitors with ribald jokes and shaggy-dog stories. The final hour was given over to starry-eyed songwriters whose earnest devotional ballads, while skillfully performed, I found cloying. Maybe the broiling May heat had something to do with it, or the specific mix of visitors and devotees. Or maybe, after the astounding events of 1993, I expected too much. To expect anything, as Papaji himself was fond of saying, is always a mistake. Only by relinquishing all expectations—by wanting or seeking nothing—can one gain the realization that freedom is not a "thing" to be pursued, or a prize to be won.

"Keep quiet," Papa advised his *sanyassins*. "For one split second, for one finger snap, make no effort. What you seek is all right here, in this moment, *now*. Keep quiet!!"

But my brain just wouldn't shut up. Missing the Kailas trip, the presumed centerpiece of my round-the-world pilgrimage, still weighed on my mind. And Sally's decision to stay on in Lucknow, while not unexpected, had cast me up against the bitter prospect of completing my journey alone.

Those considerations by themselves would have been enough to deflate my spirits, but there was a third factor as well: Late spring meant facing my brother Jordan's birthday, always a melancholy reminder of his suicide.

o   o   o

I was sitting beneath a tree in the yard of the Ashoka Restaurant, making notes on my OmniBook and sipping a banana *lassi*, when I felt a hand squeeze my shoulder.

"May I see you, friend, or are you busy?"

I looked up to meet the familiar eyes of Thomas Christ. He appeared thin—the past year had played havoc with his health—but his face was radiant. He joined me at the small round table and ordered a glass of fruit juice.

Except for a brief trip back to Germany, where he had sold his software consulting business, Thomas had remained in Indira Nagar since our initial meeting. He was living alone now, writing poetry and devoting himself to spiritual study. We talked about his progress for a while, then the conversation turned to me.

"You don't look happy," he said simply. "There's a weight on your heart; I can see it in your eyes. Is it something you can talk about?"

I looked at this man, who had written himself so vividly into my personal mythology, and decided I could tell him everything. For the next half hour I told him all about Jordan—our close relationship, his long depression and the enormous sense of guilt and grief I associated with his suicide.

"Why guilt?" Thomas asked. "Did you cause his death? Or could you have prevented it?"

I shook my head. "Who knows? He shot himself two days after I returned from a long trip to Asia, in March of 1990. Two days. It was a final act of generosity; he'd waited for me to come home so that I could help my mother and sister cope with their grief. But what it means is that I could have called him, the day I got home. There was that one short window of time. What if I had called him? Would it have changed things? I'll never know. But I'm sure it would have bought him more time."

"So this, then, is the legacy left by your brother? Guilt and pain?"

"You don't understand," I said. "There are certain things that happen to a person that mark him indelibly, for life. Losing Jordan was like losing my arm. No matter what happens to me, for the rest of my life, the pain of his death will never go away. I might learn to live with it, to function around it, but I'll never get over it. There will always be this undercurrent of grief. Grief, and guilt."

Thomas moved his chair beside mine.

"If you will allow me, brother"—the word made me raise my head—"I wish to disagree with you. Let me tell you a story."

"Three years ago," he said, "my mother died of bone cancer. It was a protracted illness, and for the final six months she was in terrible pain. Either in pain or completely drugged out. Often I would visit, and she did not recognize me. I would sit next to her bed and hold her hand, watching her die. I could not stop her suffering, and I could not stop her death. I would have given anything to take her pain onto myself. But there was nothing I could do.

"After she died I was crushed. I also felt unbearably guilty. Guilty for the fights we had. Guilty because I never told her how much I really loved her. And guilty, most of all, because I could not ease her pain. For two years I lived this way, torturing myself with regret.

"But during this past year, sitting with Papaji, I realized something: My mother's life was not about her cancer. It was not about her suffering, and it certainly was not about my guilt. My mother's life was about love.

"And I asked myself a question: *If my mother were alive today, how would she want me to feel?* Would she want me to be in pain? Would she want me to feel guilty? My mother loved me—just as your brother Jordan loved you. She would want me to feel this love, to feel it in everything I do.

"My mother is dead," Thomas said. "But her love lives on, inside of me. Once I saw that, it became impossible for me to think of her, or myself, otherwise. Every step I take, it is my mother walking. Everything I see—every bird, or flower, or tree—I see with my mother's eyes. Because this is how she lives. Not through my guilt, not through my pain, but through my love.

"If you loved your brother, love him still. He is still there, inside of you. Don't exchange your love for guilt or for pain—because if you do that, you kill your brother all over again. Let him live through the love you feel, and through everything you see and do. Let this whole trip, your whole pilgrimage, be a way of showing him who you are. Take him with you—not like a scar, not like a phantom limb, but as part of your body and soul, always alive in your heart."

I said nothing. There was no way to convey how profoundly his words had moved me. I felt like a coal miner who, trapped in an underground cave, had just seen a pickax burst through the ceiling, admitting the light of day.

The reason for my visit to Lucknow—unknown to me when I arrived—had been revealed. There was no further need to stay, and the following morning I began making preparations for my onward journey to Kathmandu.

Grace

I still wasn't ready to give up on Kailas; no way. Although I'd missed the Wilderness trip, it seemed likely that other caravans would be making their way to the holy mountain during the sacred month of Buddha's birth. The only way to find this out was to continue north and speak with my friends in Kathmandu.

The day before leaving Indira Nagar I wrote Papaji a letter, seeking his advice and blessing. After dropping it off at his house I took a tempo to the local health club and played water polo with Sally and a dozen other devotees. During the game I met two other visitors—Rob and Lysha—who were as eager as I was to set off for Nepal. We decided to leave together the next morning, just after sunrise.

That evening, Sally dropped by my room to invite me over to Papa's house for supper. "He has something to give you," she told me. "I think it's something for your trip."

Dinner was a casual affair, with myself and half a dozen other guests seated with Poonja around the rectangular table in his small, cluttered dining room. The conversation centered on cricket, a subject about which I knew absolutely nothing. Still, it was a wonderful privilege to be so close to a great Master, and to feel once more the indelible sense of connection that he had hot-wired into my circuits sixteen months before.

After a rich, syrupy dessert—of which the diabetic Papaji, despite protests, had two helpings—the guru rose from the table. Two other guests helped him navigate toward his bedroom. As he passed by me, Papa stopped and placed a massive hand on my arm.

"Brijbala told me about your pilgrimage," he said. "And this morning I was reading your beautiful note." He reached into his pocket and handed me an envelope. "Here is my reply. You have my blessing. You have the blessing of everyone in satsang."

I accepted the envelope and bent down to touch his feet. "Thank you, Papaji," I said, "for inviting me to be here with you again."

"It is you who have called me," he replied, laughing. "I am here by *your* invitation."

Later that evening, before bed, I opened his letter:

Beloved Jeffji,
  The act of pilgrimage is the highest form of motion, for it requires that we move with our heart, not only our feet.
  As a pilgrim, you must move like the wind, neither staying in places that are good nor fleeing from places that are bad. Always remember that

Grace, the supreme power, is working through you. I am speaking of the ultimate power which is the source of all movement. It will guide you as circumstances arise.

External circumstances are no impediment. The impediment is the ego. "I have to do this. I must not do that." The very idea that you are doing something is the impediment. If you act without feeling that you are the doer, there will be no impediments.

You are going to Kailas, the Holy Mountain. By the foot of that mountain there is a lake, Manasarovar. The great swan, Hamsa, sings by the shore of that lake. If you are pure of heart, you may hear that satsang.

With love, Papaji

· 32 ·

A Whiter Shade of Pale

Rob was a stockbroker and career meditator who had spent most of the previous three years in a lay Zen monastery in Los Angeles. He'd report to his office at 6:00 in the morning—9 A.M. EST, when the New York Stock Exchange opened—and return to his zendo at 2:30 P.M. to spend the rest of the day facing a wall. He was athletic in a corporate health-club way, with the deadpan, let's-wait-and-see-what-happens expression common to stand-up comics and living buddhas. Lysha, a spunky, chunky blonde with oversized glasses and chipmunk cheeks, baked enormous pretzels in Vermont.

We met at the satsang house shortly after dawn. I was in a wistful mood, having just said good-bye to Sally for the second time in six weeks—this time for real—and found myself wanting a cigarette. No one, needless to say, smoked. We shouldered our packs as the sun lifted itself with effort above the Indira Nagar skyline and began the tedious process of baking the town to a cinder.

We found a six-seater, loaded up our luggage and made for Lucknow proper. There was a vehicle-for-hire bureau downtown. After a series of surprisingly convivial negotiations we enlisted a sturdy, well-polished Ambassador cab for the trip to the border.

The four-hour drive passed without incident. Without incident, that is, until the border itself, where we hit a loathsome snag: Lysha's six-month India visa had expired two months earlier. She pleaded stupidity, insisting she'd been told that the visa was valid for six months from date of entry. Yet there it was, in plain English: "Good for six months from date of issue." She railed and stomped, but succeeded only in irritating the impeccably groomed border officer, who seemed to relish the option of detaining her—and by association the other two of us—indefinitely.

It looked like we weren't going anywhere, but I was naïve. Calmed by a cup of tea, the officer finally confessed, in that exquisitely convoluted manner that passes in India for subtlety, that he could possibly be moved to make an adjustment, an exception that is, to give our friend special consideration, you see, and that if she herself found it agreeable to furnish in turn some token of gratitude, some small consideration of her own, as it were, he would be most grateful; he was asking for nothing, you understand, adjustments were possible, no fee was to be discussed, the question of a fee, of course, had never even been raised; and the size of the adjustment coming from our side, a gift presented out of pure gratitude and as a gesture of friendship, of goodwill between India and America, the two largest democracies on Earth, would be entirely up to us, according to our means and our feeling of brotherhood for a man, who, after all, was merely a pawn, loyal to his duty and bound by his own personal integrity.

It sounded good to us. Certainly, we had planned to present him with a generous gift in any case.

This established, the officer smiled, stamped Lysha's passport and handed it back to her with a flourish. Lysha glanced at me for a hint; I held up two fingers beneath the desk. She extracted 200 rupees from her purse—about $6—and placed them under a paperweight on the officer's desk.

"That is very kind," he beamed. "Thank you very much; have a pleasant journey. You are always welcome in India."

o   o   o

We breezed into Nepalganj, exacting barely a wave from the customs officers who sat drinking *chia* in their open-air office. It wasn't until four miles later—as we entered the linty navel of Nepalganj itself—that I grokked an extraordinary fact: *We had no visas.* Somehow, no one had stopped us. Nobody had asked for our passports, handed us entry forms or in any way attempted to extract money or information from us.

On the surface, this was a lark; we'd saved forty bucks each. On the other hand, our lack of Nepal visas might return to haunt us. It would be impossible, for example, to change money, obtain trekking permits, or leave the country without enormous hassle. Come to think of it, we might not even reach Kathmandu at all. If there were any checkpoints on the way, we'd be plucked from the bus like rotten apples and tossed right back to India—at best.

And so we found ourselves pulling a U'y between a bike and a bullock cart and—to the chagrin of our driver, who had to get back to Lucknow for his sister's wedding—retreating to the border, where we found the immigration post hidden behind a copse of trees. Despite the fact that we were *already* illegal aliens, we were greeted with supreme nonchalance. Unfortunately, our worries began anew when the authorities requested a passport-size photo for Lysha's visa form. How anyone could travel through Asia without several hundred passport-size photos of herself was beyond me, but Lysha was fresh out. I finessed this obstacle by fishing my Swiss Army knife out of my daypack and snipping her Vermont driver's license into bits. The photo was a bit small, but the officer, charmed by the display of American ingenuity, stamped us through.

We hired three bicycle rickshaws, loaded our gear and raced back toward town in hopes of catching the next express coach to Kathmandu. It was doable—we could easily make the 4:00 P.M. bus—but one look at the battered trash can-on-wheels was enough to make us reconsider. The "good" buses, we learned, were the night coaches, departing Nepalganj at 6:00 and arriving in Kathmandu by 7:30 the following morning. All things considered, this made more sense. We bought our tickets, stashed our gear at the bus station and rickshawed into town in search of sustenance.

o   o   o

My last day in Lucknow I had tried, without success, to send a new installment of *Big World* to Allen Noren in Sebastopol. The failure haunted me; it had been more than three weeks since my previous dispatch, written before my departure from Turkey, had sizzled through the ether. While staying at Sally's I'd put together a breathless summary of all that had occurred in between: racing through Saudi Arabia, crossing the Persian Gulf, visiting Lahore and returning to the spiritual community in Lucknow. I felt an edgy compulsion to put it through, as soon as humanly possible.

India's telecommunications system is notoriously horrible, and my inability to link up from Lucknow hadn't been a surprise. Nepal, on the other hand, a landlocked country that draws the lion's share of its foreign exchange from tourism, has a far more sophisticated infrastructure. While Rob and Lysha lounged in a local restaurant, I walked my Omni-

Book to the Macchapuchare Hotel—managed, I learned to my amazement, by an American woman named Candy, who had lived in Nepal
for twenty-two years—and patched directly into their international
direct-dial phone jack. It took three tries, and cost a small fortune, but
the effort finally paid off. Sending the transmission was an enormous
boost; for the first time in nearly a month I'd touched home base.

Shortly thereafter I rejoined my two companions. We claimed our
baggage and climbed onto the bus's roof to lock our bags and lash
them to the rack. Lysha watched in horror as I stashed my passport,
bus ticket and travelers' checks in the main compartment of my daypack—along with my computer, knife and camera—and slung it over
my shoulder.

"You should really get a neck pouch for that official stuff," she said.
"It's safer to have it on your body."

"I know, I know, I know."

"If nothing else," Rob added, "it's more convenient. They're probably going to be stopping us in the middle of the night for police checks.
Here, I have an extra fannypack you can wear. . . ." He started to unlock
his backpack in order to fish it out for me.

"No, wait, that's okay." I pulled out my own keys and opened the
main compartment of my bag. "I have one too."

My black leather belly-pouch—the birthday present from my agent,
untouched since I'd received it at American Express in Istanbul—was
balled up with my dirty underwear. I pulled it out, put my documents
inside and snapped it around my waist.

"Okay? You guys happy?"

"Never better," Rob said.

"It's you," Lysha agreed.

o   o   o

We left Nepalganj on schedule and started, with a gnashing of gears, on
the long journey north. I can't say much about the ride itself except to
mention that the buses themselves must have been donated to the
Nepali government by an African Pygmy tribe. There was simply no way
to fit into the seats, even two of them, without swallowing my knees—a
feat I became increasingly adept at as the hours passed. Rob and Lysha
were wedged into the seats behind me. I listened to them argue about
the increase of feminist roles in American cinema, and drifted into a
light sleep. The black nylon strap of my daypack, wedged into the rack
above my head, worked its way loose and tickled my ear, waking me.

Around midnight we pulled into Gaura Singh and stopped. A row of small, decrepit restaurants selling *daalbhat*—Nepal's national dish, consisting of rice, boiled greens and lentil stew—leaned around a dirt lot, each illuminated by a single low-wattage bulb.

We spilled off the bus. I had a Coke, shared a packet of arrowroot biscuits and wandered behind one of the food stalls for a piss.

The second half of the ride was hellish. The narrow highway twisted through the Mahabharat Range, one hairpin turn after another. No sooner had I found a more or less comfortable position than the bus would swerve sickeningly around a 270-degree curve, throwing me into the aisle. Empty bottles and loose oranges rolled the length of the coach, bumping into chair legs and metal trunks.

We stopped frequently, taking standing-room passengers for the driver's personal profit. The seat beside me was quickly snatched up. Finally the bus became so crowded that I was effectively nestled into a cozy little nook. Balled up like a fetus, I slept.

o   o   o

Sunlight poured through the windows, hot on my face. I opened my eyes. The short-hop passengers had left, and the aisles were clear. I stretched my arms above my head, feeling every vertebra in my upper back pop back into position. Rob and Lysha, huddled behind me, were awake, staring dully out their dirty window. It was just after 5:30 A.M.; Kathmandu couldn't be more than a couple of hours away.

The bus slowed down and veered off the road, stopping at a funky eatery high above the Trisuli River. The passengers, all Nepalese, filed off the bus in various states of sleepy disarray.

"Breakfast," Rob announced. "Gosh, this reminds me of the zendo."

Early morning light scraped over the foothills and sent long beams down the nearby valley, illuminating the terraced rice fields fluorescent green. Red dirt houses with high grass roofs dotted the landscape, and the river gleamed like a sliver of lathed steel.

"Photo op!" I slid from my seat and stood up, hobbling. My leg was asleep from ankle to groin. "Check out the light, guys. This is your quintessential Nepali morning. It don't get any better than this . . ."

I turned around to grab my camera, and my bowels turned to mush. My daypack was gone.

Dog Balls

Lost, or stolen? Had I set the daypack down when I took a leak, forgetting to pick it up afterward? Or had some vile night crawler absconded with it while I slept? Or had it fallen from the overhead rack onto the headrest of the seat in front of me, hanging there for a tantalizing moment before sliding out the window on a jackknife turn?

Dog balls.

I discussed the situation with the driver, who promised to comb the entire area when he returned to Gaura Singh two nights hence. Two nights! I sweetened the incentive with a $50 reward and resigned myself, miserably, to waiting sixty hours for news.

· 33 ·

To: Allen Noren, O'Reilly & Associates
From: Jeff Greenwald, Nepal
Subject: Big World/Kathmandu

There was a time, not long ago, when I would never have dreamed I could do this: transmit an installment of *Big World* over the Internet itself, directly from Kathmandu.

But so it is. This city, once everyone's definition of the ultimate global backwater, has come of age. No longer a "City on the Edge of the World," Kathmandu is transforming itself into the most user-friendly metropolis in South Asia. Pakistan remains (information-wise) in the Dark Ages, and most of India, for all its hopeful posturing, is still twenty years behind the times; but you can get anything you want in Sri Panch Maharaja Birendra Bir Bikram Shah Dev's (the King of Nepal, FM dance-mix version) Restaurant.

Which explains how I'm able to put this installment together: writing on a borrowed laptop and patching in from Mercantile Office Systems, a state-of-the-art info-boutique just a stone's throw (though no one's really doing that anymore) from the Royal Palace.

My dispatches, until now a more or less biweekly event, will probably become sporadic from Nepal onward. *Big World* relied heavily on my computer, with its built-in fax/modem. The theft of the OmniBook—along with my camera, Swiss Army knife and three weeks' worth of writing—has ominous implications for my column, not to mention my creative process in general.

My friends in Kathmandu, distraught as they are for my sake, feel that there's a lesson in this for me. They insist that the loss of my most valuable possession (and most indispensable tool) is a clever Zen koan—an effort, by the universe, to teach me something. But teach me what? What

I *want* to learn from this is that things come back; that the things we need are returned to us. That would be a wonderful lesson, a lesson I'd never forget. . . .

o   o   o

Wednesday, May 25, was Saga Dawa: the full-moon celebration of the birth, enlightenment and *paranibana* (passing on to nirvana) of Lord Buddha. For the past six months I'd imagined that Sally and I would spend that day together, in southwestern Tibet, breathing the thin cold air surrounding sacred Mount Kailas, the spiritual center of the Hindu and Buddhist cosmologies.

Instead I spent the day at Boudhanath (Boudha for short; nath means temple): the fifteen-hundred-year-old white dome, crowned with the eyes of Buddha, that serves as the spiritual center of Nepal's enormous Tibetan community.

"The Great Stupa," writes Keith Dowman in *Boudhanath,* "providing a powerful focal point of sacred energy, is one of the Kathmandu Valley's great power places and is one of the most important places of pilgrimage for the Tibetan Buddhist peoples of the Himalayas." So, though I was stung by having missed my planned expedition to Kailas, Boudha wasn't a bad second choice.

Tuesday night it had poured, the sky strobing with lightning, thunder booming between the foothills. On Wednesday the weather was fine, sharp lapis skies marked with clouds that looked as if they'd been lifted from a book of Tibetan folktales. I couldn't see the mountains above the valley rim, but that seemed a small cosmic oversight that would surely be corrected before the day was through.

Saga Dawa is one of the four Great Festival Days in the Tibetan calendar, which means that the karmic fruit of all actions—positive or negative—is multiplied by 100,000. But the holiday is also a "Buddha day," so you multiply by another 100. Not only that; since Wednesday's full moon would also see a partial lunar eclipse, the ante was raised astronomically higher: by a factor of 70 *million.* When it was all said and done, the merit gained (or lost) by what one did this Saga Dawa was magnified a whopping 700 *trillion* times. Not the sort of day that you want to say anything mean about your mother, steal an apple or step on an ant. Any act of kindness or generosity, on the other hand, would count just as hugely to one's favor. Making a single devotional kora around the Boudha dome, for example—a distance of maybe one-fifth of a mile—was equivalent to making a pilgrimage, on foot, from Earth to Alpha Centauri.

I arrived at the stupa with Joel Harrare, an old friend and supple American yogi whom I'd met in Kathmandu in the late eighties. We met up in the hot late afternoon under the umbrellas at Mike's Breakfast, ate some dubious cheesecake and shuttled over to the Boudha dome on my rented Yamaha. Once there we performed our first kora together, dispensing coins to the *saddhus,* lamas and cripples who waved aluminum begging bowls from their positions around the ancient monument's circumference, while at the same time shaking off (as benevolently as possible) the professional street waifs who clung, with thespian woe, to our legs.

Halfway around the stupa we ran into a wall. A huge painted elephant was standing outside the old Karmapa *gompa,* surrounded by thousands of gawking Nepalese and Tibetans. The pachyderm was dipping its trunk, making a carnival show of collecting coins from the crowd—an ironic foil to its genuine purpose, which was to carry a statue of the Buddha around the Boudha stupa.

I stopped at the end of our first circuit to light five butter lamp candles: one for my brother and father, both passed away; one for mother, sister, aunts and grandmother; a third for my community of friends; a fourth for Sally; and the final one for myself.

"My computer! My computer! Get me back my OmniBook!!" I hollered it out loud, ringing the huge brass bell suspended above the butter lamps, addressing my pleas directly to the pinnacle of the wish-fulfilling dome. The eyes of Buddha stared back at me, impassive and unimpressed.

I turned to Lysha, who had just completed her own kora and appeared beside me with a packet of incense smoldering in her hand.

"What do you think Buddha would have done," I asked her, "if his OmniBook had been stolen?"

She pondered this for a few seconds. "He would have backed up more often," she replied. I winced with shame.

Festivals at Boudha are always major social events; you run into everyone you know. Or, if you stay in one spot long enough, everyone you know runs into you. Joel and I—joined now by a dozen other expatriate friends—decided to perform an ascending series of devotional koras. And so, after lighting dozens of candles, dispensing many rupees and giving the gigantic prayer wheel at the base of the steps a good spin, we began.

We started at the stupa's lowest level and spiraled our way up the layer-cake stories of the whitewashed, mandala-shaped plinth. At last we found ourselves on the uppermost level, directly beneath the all-seeing eyes of the Buddha, circling alongside the 108 guardian deities set into niches in the stupa wall. And I could not help but feel, happy and confident as I strangely was, that at the end of my circumambulations, at the very moment when I completed the last of my gyrations around the Wish-

Fulfilling Stupa, I would find a figure standing before me, smiling, dressed in monk maroon and holding in outstretched hands my miraculously re-covered computer. . . .

Alas; it was not to be.

By this time the circular avenue leading around the Great Stupa was packed with pilgrims, monks, Indian beggars, balloon sellers, cows, old Tibetan women holding *malla* beads, bickering street urchins, ice cream vendors, incense sellers, nuns, lamas with umbrellas, thick-bodied Man-angi businessmen and mangy pye-dogs. We found a spot with a good overview of the main circuit and watched as the small Buddha statue was loaded onto a palanquin atop the painted elephant. A cavalcade of trum-pets and tubas signaled the beginning of the parade, and the woolless mammoth set off (clockwise, of course) around the shrine. The animal was preceded by a Nepalese wedding band: a dozen men wearing ill-fitting uniforms and organ-grinder monkey caps bleating on trumpets, tor-turing clarinets, coaxing apocalyptic farts from tubas and abusing drums. Behind the elephant came a procession of monks, and behind the monks followed a confetti of ragtag marchers—men, women and children, ca-nines and cattle, all joining the Buddha for his 2,557th birthday celebra-tion. Watching the procession from the second level of the stupa, I suddenly realized why it seemed so familiar. It was exactly like the car-toon parade that used to open *The Rocky and Bullwinkle Show.*

The evening was uncommonly lovely. We sat on the uppermost ter-race of the aptly named Stupa View Restaurant, drinking cold Tuborg and eating steamed vegetable *momos* with chili sauce. Below, saffron-robed monks placed thousands of red, white and yellow candles around the multitiered perimeter of the huge Boudha dome. Slowly, slowly, the gigan-tic orange sun sank behind the shoulder of Nagarjun Hill like God's dozing eye. The sky took on shades of walrus bone, Egyptian glass, Korean porcelain, Bill Evans ivory. Thick black clouds obscured the rising moon; but to the north, above the undulating hills surrounding the Kathmandu Valley, the Langtang and Ganesh Himals exposed tantalizing glimpses of their snow-white flanks in a kind of a geomorphological peep show.

No amount of 70-millimeter film or Hi-8 videotape, no collection of poems, no miraculous dance of globe-trotting megabytes can convey the beauty of Boudhanath on a full-moon festival night. We walked around the ageless dome again and again, relighting candles as they flickered out in the wind and listening to the distant sounds of Tibetan horns and cymbals carry from the old Karmapa monastery. A small group of monks stopped by us and chanted, an anamelodic prayer for the benefit of all sentient be-ings, and it struck me again how miraculous it is that even now, after twenty-five centuries, the essence of Buddha's teaching—wisdom, compassion and the interdependence of all living things—resonates with an undeniable purity.

The dark clouds hovering in the east moved apart, as slowly and ponderously as tectonic plates, and the tusk-yellow moon threw our long shadows across the dome's wax-slicked plinth. Incense and the smell of hot oil filled the air, mosquitoes buzzed around our heads with total immunity and for a brief span of time all was well with the world. My computer was gone, a month's worth of work was lost and I had no idea how I was (or am) going to carry on from here; but for the time being, for *Now,* I was in the right place at the right time, standing at the most beautiful spot on the planet.

Blessed and lucky—as if I ever doubted it.

o   o   o

Unsure where I'll head from here, or how I'll continue my journey. Most likely I'll go north—to Lhasa, Tibet—and continue eastward. Meanwhile I'll stay in Kathmandu, and wait until either *(a)* Hewlett-Packard can find me another OmniBook and courier it out here (please baby please baby please please please) or *(b)* I find a used laptop for sale here.

And so, until we meet again, consider me footloose and at large—somewhere on the pulsing, imaginary grid that covers this Big, moonlit World.

⚡   ⚡   ⚡

The Bardo of Hope and Fear, Revisited

The frightening thing was that I couldn't let go. My days were spent jamming around Kathmandu on a fool's errand, overturning every stone, leaving my phone number at every computer store, placing bigger and bigger ads in the national newspapers offering larger and larger rewards, and trying desperately, employing every strategy I could think of, to skew my path so that it might finally intersect with that of Omniji, my lost computer, my memory, my friend. When was the last time I'd been so attached to a material possession? Never; not even to a dog. More than even Sally, the computer had been my constant companion.

At that point I made a startling discovery—one that actually brought me some comfort. The theft of my computer had to be, without a doubt, the "death" that Ismael had foreseen while poring through my skull-patterned coffee grounds in Konya, Turkey, one long month before.

"It will be your confidant," he had predicted. "The one in who you confide everything. Who is this? Who do you think?"

For the past five months, by land and by sea, the OmniBook had been my chief outlet for self-expression. Every day, or every other day, or twice a day, I'd been able to sit down with my little machine and take stock. When I'd needed to recall conversations, record anecdotes or merely vent my spleen, the OmniBook listened. It was always there, a reminder of my basic purpose. Many times during the trip I'd felt sad, frustrated or alone; but I'd never felt disconnected from my work.

Now I was. I felt paralyzed, unable to imagine the shape my writing would take. For to think about writing was to think about the Omni-Book, and to think about the OmniBook was to remember, with gut-wrenching disbelief, the moment I realized that my daypack was gone.

Seeing the daypack vanish was like watching the *Challenger* explode: It was one of those things that just wasn't supposed to happen.

My final effort, a huge and costly display ad on the back page of the *Kantipur* offering a reward of 10,000 rupees—half a year's salary for the average Nepali—brought no result. The truth, I realized, was that the computer might not even be in Nepal at all. More likely it had been smuggled into India, where it now sat in some cumin merchant's dingy office, hardwired to a jury-rigged adapter. When I tried to think about it, to visualize where it might be, I often felt as if I could reach out and touch it.

The thing had powerful mojo over me, that was for damned sure.

o   o   o

The Wilderness Travel expedition to Mount Kailas had departed Kathmandu as scheduled, ten days before my arrival in Nepal. None of my friends in the valley knew of any other groups going to the holy mountain, but it was safe to assume there would be caravans assembling in Lhasa. Unlike the Wilderness trip, though, which had taken a spectacular trekking route directly through the Himalaya into southwestern Tibet, these informal groups would make the journey the conventional way: a bone-jarring, five-day truck ride west from Lhasa.

More sobering still was the fact that, after Kailas—after that enormous, exhausting effort had been completed—I would still have to go around the rest of the world.

o   o   o

May is usually a horrible month in Kathmandu, dusty and hot and raucous with frustrated traffic oozing irritably through the haze. But the week I'd spent in the city so far—discounting my severe angst—had been lovely. Premature monsoon storms boomed through the valley, lighting up the wisteria trees and clearing the air. The electricity was contagious.

Several things about Kathmandu have always thrilled me. The geography, of course, is wonderful; the valley, still largely agricultural despite the ugly development around the city center, is ringed by beautiful foothills beyond which, on the increasingly rare occasions when the sky is clear, fluted peaks lace the northern horizon like meringue. Hindu, Buddhist and Tantric mythologies have animated the landscape with an all-star cast of deities, and the yearly festival cycle includes some of the noisiest, gaudiest and most colorful celebrations in the world: from the bloody buffalo sacrifices of Dasain to the flickering luminescence of Tihar, goddess Laxmi's Festival of Lights.

My favorite thing about the place, though, is the sense of community, of family, within the city's large expatriate population. I'd spent nearly five of the previous fifteen years living and writing in Kathmandu, and nowhere else on Earth had I encountered a more fascinating group of people. In some ways it was like a remote and beautiful frontier town that had attracted, by virtue of its real or imagined treasures, an extraordinary collection of adventurers, artists and rogues. The early years—when telephones were rare and largely dysfunctional—had created a social protocol that encouraged people to drop in on each other at a whim. It wasn't unusual to see the same friends day after day. There was always something to talk about, always new discoveries or insights to report.

Among my favorite people in the Kathmandu Valley were Thomas Kelly and Carroll Dunham, a husband-and-wife team who'd collaborated on numerous books and films about Himalayan culture, religion and anthropology. Thomas was working on a project in India, but Carroll had returned to town for the change of term at Sojourn Nepal, a study-abroad program she'd cofounded during the 1980s.

I throttled my motorcycle up the brick driveway of their secluded compound and parked it near an algae-covered pool.

Carroll was on the phone when I arrived but gave me a bright wave. I sat on the sofa and leafed through back issues of *Smithsonian* while she concluded an animated conversation in Nepali. Tall and slender, Carroll burned like a Fourth of July sparkler. I'd never met a more energetic woman. At thirty, she had already collaborated on three books, started a successful school and made three documentary films for public television. When the call (pertaining, I correctly guessed, to one of her half-dozen foster children) was over, she approached me with open arms.

"Greetings, *saathi*!" We embraced, then held each other at arm's length. "I heard about your computer," Carroll said. "What a kick in the pants. Last week the power died on me, whammo, and I lost half of the article I was writing, but *three weeks* of work . . . sheesh. You must be tearing your hair out."

We moved to the dining table, where her *didi* was laying out a spread of homemade brownies and *chia*. "I've been better," I admitted. "I've already spent two hundred bucks on ads, but no bites. One way or another, though, I've got to get a replacement; there's no way I can continue my trip without one."

"Well, come on, if worse comes to worst can't you just write longhand?"

"Not me." I shook my head. "I'm left-handed, and I can't write more than twenty minutes without getting a wrist cramp."

"Really? But what did you do when you lived here ten years ago? You wrote *Mr. Raja's Neighborhood* without a computer . . ."

"Yeah; I lugged a seventeen-pound Smith-Corona all over Asia for eighteen months."

We drank our tea. Carroll had spent most of the past month in India, working on an article and documentary film about prostitution and AIDS in the brothels of Bombay. Sojourn Nepal was going well, her six foster kids were great and she was leading two Himalayan treks later in the year. Aside from that—not to mention three magazine assignments, her spiritual practice, work on a parcel of land that she and Thomas had bought and her new business manufacturing therapeutic herbal pillows—nothing much was going on. So what was I up to?

I told her as much as I could, tracing my route with the help of her atlas. When I'd brought her up-to-date she whistled and leaned back against the cushions.

"So where to next?"

The question pulled my plug. I spent the next twenty minutes spouting my misgivings about Kailas and bemoaning the fact that, with my computer gone and the days ticking by, my carefully crafted kora was falling apart at the seams. She listened intently, devouring brownies, until I finished. Then she poured me another cup of tea.

"It sounds to me like everything's going just perfectly."

"How can you say that?"

"Finishing the trips they started, the way they knew they would, is what *tourists* do. Pilgrims get blown around. They set off for one place and end up somewhere else, completely unexpectedly.

"That's the nature of pilgrimage," she said. "It's not about sightseeing, or filling your backpack with trinkets. It's about being stripped of things. It's a ritual shedding of karma, a laboratory for self-examination in which you lose the things most precious to you, and face your most terrifying fears.

"Pilgrimage isn't about cruising around the world in luxury. It's a penance, an effort, a trial by fire. And of all the pilgrimages," she reminded me, "Kailas is the most difficult.

"I can't even tell you how many people I've met who have set out with the idea of going to Kailas and lost *everything* along the way. It's just what happens. When you make up your mind to go to Kailas things start divesting themselves from you, and you're forced to give up all the things you thought were indispensable.

"Now, maybe you will go to Kailas, and maybe you won't. That's up to you—and from the look of things, it might not be a bad idea for you to put that off, at least this trip. But the fact remains that you *are* on pilgrimage, and that the powers that be are going to fuck with your head accordingly. It's not going to be easy, and it won't always be fun. The stuff you're going to lose—not just your computer, but parts of yourself, your own personality, that you probably can't even imagine living without—will literally blow your mind. But if you can roll with it. . . . hang on a second."

Carroll jumped up and skipped over to a shelf, where she extracted a large, square book. She brought it to the couch. "You've seen this. I gave you a copy last fall, right?"

"Yes." The book was *Tibet: reflections from the wheel of life*, with photographs by Thomas and text by Carroll and her close friend, a charismatic adventurer and Tantric scholar named Ian Baker.

She opened the book to page 131, the chapter on pilgrimage. "Look at this," she said, pointing to the right-hand column. "You might find it interesting."

I grabbed the last brownie and leaned over her lap to read.

> *Chatral Rinpoche, a lama from eastern Tibet renowned for his freedom from worldly attachments, was once on pilgrimage with several of his disciples. They stopped at the house of a wealthy trader, who offered Chatral Rinpoche a priceless vase from the Ming dynasty. The vase was carefully wrapped and secured in one of the horse's saddlebags. As they continued on, however, much bickering arose among the disciples over who should look after the porcelain vase. Finally, Chatral Rinpoche took the vase out of the bag, held it aloft, and said, "I'll show you who will take care of it," whereupon he broke it over his knee. The priceless porcelain shattered into shards on the ground. "From this point on," Chatral Rinpoche stated, "our pilgrimage begins."*

The Big Picture

I moved in with Nick Gregory, a close friend I'd first met in 1987 when I was in Nepal writing *Shopping for Buddhas*. One rainy night, we drove his Volkswagen bug up to the Summit Hotel to attend a production of *Tamara*, presented by HAMS, the Himalayan Amateurs.

Tamara is one of those modern, "interactive" plays in which the audience has the option of following a character—or any number of characters—from scene to scene. The theory seems to be that each viewer will gain a unique sense of how the plot unfolded and be able to share this perspective with his or her friends.

By the end of the evening I was hopelessly baffled. I could make no sense of the plot, and had to listen to Nick's virtuoso interpretation—delivered to a large gathering of similarly stupefied patrons—lest I leave the scene in utter confusion. Despite my embarrassment, I appreciated the play's central concept. It reminded me of my own trip; the way an element of chance had orchestrated each of the situations I'd encountered. Is it luck, fate or free will, I wondered, that compels us toward one tableau or another?

But *Tamara*, most of all, was a lesson in synergy. The whole is greater than the sum of its parts. Each scene in the play—no matter how minor or tangential it had seemed—had turned out to be a crucial element in the big picture.

With that in mind, I took a hard look at some scenes from my own unfolding drama. Parting with Sally; losing my computer; missing the Kailas expedition—until that moment I'd viewed them all as isolated incidents, obstructing my progress and spoiling my luck. As Nick and I drove back to town, though, a strangely liberating thought occurred to me: *Maybe those three incidents were related, after all.* Each of those three attachments had conjured an illusion of predictability; each had generated desires that were painful and difficult to renounce. All three had become, ultimately, impediments to my self-sufficiency.

Now the pilgrimage begins. That, I realized, was my challenge: to start anew from this moment, with those lessons, from this place. Here was a chance to target, with the slings and arrows of my presumed misfortunes, an all-embracing metaphor for my strange global kora. Here was my opportunity to shed my karmic skin, and emerge from these trials purified, refreshed and enlarged.

The size of the world, I was discovering, might be impossible to know; but I could perhaps know my own size in it.

· 34 ·

Same As It Never Was

Nick Gregory was a private, cultured Brit with the dry wit and obsessive
will of *Lolita*'s Humbert Humbert. He'd run private schools in Borneo
and Tanzania before relocating to Nepal. It had taken him a while to
find his niche in Kathmandu, but in 1989 he'd hit on the idea of de-
signing clothes and marketing them—along with a full range of Himalayan *tchotchkes*—in Europe and Australia. His fashions met with
success, and the shrewd international businessman I found myself living with was a very different person from the impoverished would-be
journalist to whom I'd loaned 500 rupees seven years earlier.

Nick was renting a handsome brick house in Bishalnagar, an up-
scale neighborhood on the east side of town. We would practice yoga in
the mornings, usually to jazz piano, then I'd put in an hour or two on
his PC clone before he took over the office for accounting. Evenings we
stood on the roof, sipping whiskey as thunder boomed around the base
of the foothills like a bowling ball rolling around the inside of a trash-
can lid. Every evening was the same: the sun eclipsed by a whale of a
cloud, parakeets blossoming in the trees, warm air hitting cool. Then
the rain, slowly at first, knocking the loose purple leaves off the
jacaranda trees, patterning the patio with inkblot drops before the sky
opened up for real. I loved the reliably fickle weather, the easy cohabita-
tion with Nick, the whiskeys on ice. With every passing day it became
more difficult for me to think about leaving. It was a sweet, grateful
sadness. If I ever stopped feeling this way—when I could just up and go
without regret—it would mean I was finally out of love with Nepal.

One Lucky Turtle

I woke up one morning to a seven-page fax from my sister, detailing
with heartbreaking humor the myriad tragedies she'd been dealing with
while I roamed the globe. Her life had been a concatenation of horrors
far more ominous than the theft of my OmniBook. Multiple accidents
in her Firebird, the death of her husband Richie's partner, fiascoes with
their new house and, last but not least, Richie's mysterious and terrifying seizure during a visit to the Bronx Zoo represented a litany of woes
that made my own setback seem ludicrous by comparison.

"Horlicks?" Nick walked into the living with two cups. "Or do you
Yanks run screaming at the mention of the stuff?"

I was standing on my head, completing the Five Rites of Rejuvenation, a twenty-minute yoga ritual that Joel, our mutual friend, had guaranteed would keep us young forever. "What is it, sort of a liquid Marmite?" I lowered myself to the "downward facing dog" position. "Put it on the stereo, I'll sniff at it in a minute."

Nick sat down at his piano, an old Aeolian upright, and picked out a Bach prelude. "You know, I was thinking." He swiveled around on the bench. "Losing your computer might be the best thing that ever happened to you. I'm convinced that the situation will set off a chain of events, or lead to an encounter, that will totally change your life. I just know it's true."

I stood upright and took a deep breath. "No, Nick, I don't think so. That's not how it will happen at all." I retrieved the Horlicks and sipped at the foam. It tasted like rancid Cheerios. "Whenever something like this happens, people always focus on the most dramatic aspect of the incident and assume that's the crucial part of the event. But it never turns out that way. The theft of the OmniBook will turn out to be meaningless, a completely secondary pain in the ass. The loss of my *tweezers*, however—my Swiss Army knife was in that daypack too—that'll be what makes the difference. Wait and see. Five years from now we'll look back and realize that it was the loss of that knife, or my alarm clock, or my flashlight, that changed everything. It just so happened that the computer had the bad luck to be in the daypack as well. Hey . . ." I tilted my head at the phone. "Did you read that fax from my sister?"

"Yes, I did. Sounded pretty awful. Ah, well . . . such is life in *samsara*. This cozy little world of suffering. Speaking of which, are you off to Boudha this morning?"

"Thanks for reminding me." It was Saturday, my favorite day in Kathmandu. At ten-thirty in the morning, Chokyi Nyima Rimpoche—the witty and perspicacious head abbot of the Ka Nying Shedrup Ling Monastery at Boudhanath—would give his weekly Buddhist teaching. The talks were direct and prosaic, touching upon the most basic elements of Buddhism, but it never hurt to be reminded. I took a quick shower, dried off the seat of my Honda Escorts 100 and set off on the fifteen-minute ride to Boudha.

o o o

I arrived just after eleven. There were already plenty of shoes in the monastery's fourth-floor foyer. I lifted the heavy cotton curtain and stepped into the meditation room.

The morning sun filtered through the yellow curtains hanging over the windows, illuminating the broad, rectangular room in a honey light. Two dozen westerners had arranged themselves on the thick Tibetan carpets that covered the floor. A low sofa, also draped with carpets, rested against the wall below the curtains. Against the opposing wall stood a large wooden hutch displaying dozens of deities, all dwarfed by a large golden Buddha with sly, feline eyes. Among the smaller statues I recognized Tara, the goddess of compassion; Guru Rimpoche, the saucer-eyed wizard who had brought Buddhism from India into Tibet; and Manjushri, master of discriminating wisdom, with his flaming sword poised in the air.

Chokyi Nyima sat upon a cushion atop a modestly raised platform. He wore a dark maroon robe that passed over his left shoulder and below his right armpit. A red silk vest and bright yellow undershirt were visible beneath the robe's heavy swoop. On a small table in front of him sat a *dorje*, a Tibetan bell, a silver altar box and a pile of red blessing cords that he knotted as he spoke.

I took a place on the sofa and accepted a cup of tea from an attendant while the Rimpoche continued his talk.

"So what means Buddhism?" I loved the lama's clipped, economical English. "In this world there's many different types of religion. But Buddha dharma is not the same like other religions. Understand?" There were a few interrogative grunts. "What I think—and also true!—is that all religion sits one side; and science, physics, sits another side. *And Buddha dharma is in the middle.* Buddha dharma is a religion; but Buddha dharma is not really a religion. Buddha dharma is a science; but Buddha dharma is not really a science.

"So what is Buddha dharma?" The Rimpoche lowered his voice and spoke slowly. "Buddha dharma is common sense: *Truth.*

"Other religions are also searching truth. Science, also, searching truth. Each has a different way of searching, and each has a different idea of what makes truth. Many religions are based on devotion, faith. Buddha dharma is also; but not on blond . . ." There were titters from the front row. "No? Oh! *Blind.* Blind faith. Better we test for ourselves. So Buddha says: 'All my teachings are true; but don't just believe. First check carefully. If any question, ask. If any doubt, ask. Only like this can you see that the dharma is correct. Because if not correct, what use to believe?'

"Okay? So. What means 'buddha'? Buddha means wisdom. And what means 'sentient being'? Sentient being—like you, me, animal, ant—means samsara. Sentient being has ignorance, suffering. Now, all sentient beings have buddha nature; but sentient beings are not buddha! Why?" His eyes combed the room. "Must be some obstacle, some block. Otherwise, why not all sentient beings be like Buddha?"

He peered around quizzically, but there were no takers.

"Who makes the obstacle? What is the obscuration? Some religions say it's sin. Oh, no! Sin! Some religions say you're too thick; some say too smart. But what is the obscuration to buddha mind?" Silence. "Okay. I tell you. Obscuration to buddha mind is big, negative emotion: like anger, jealousy and fear. Even thinking itself is obscuration of buddha mind! Unless you can give up the very *idea* of self and practice—*the very idea of enlightenment*—you cannot experience buddha mind."

I grinned, noting how similar this Tibetan Buddhist concept was to the philosophy that Papaji taught. This was the paradox, the catch-22 of spiritual seeking: The act of seeking itself, the lust for enlightenment, could be as great an obstacle as any other.

"Okay?" Chokyi Nyima adjusted his robes, ignoring the sudden chirping of his cellular phone. "So. What else? Many sentient beings, all have buddha nature. But only one kind—just one!—can liberate. Just one kind of sentient being can understand, can practice the teaching of Buddha. But which kind? Anyone know?" He surveyed the silent room with an ironic expression. "No one know? Really? Is it dog? Can dog liberate? Hmmmn? Cat? Ant? Yeti? Which?"

The phrase *human being* was muttered throughout the room.

"That's right! Very good! Only human being." He displayed a winning smile. "All here, human being," he observed. "Lucky. Very lucky! So lucky to be human being!

"How lucky? I tell you. Maybe you know this story. Tibetans say, some *turtur* . . . no? One *turtle* swimming in ocean. Swimming, swimming. All alone, ocean so vast. And somewhere, somewhere, floating on the ocean, a kind of . . . *ring*. Floating, floating. So. One time—every hundred years—turtle comes up to surface of ocean. What chance, you think, turtle will come up through ring? What chance? Very small, I think. Very, very small. But to be born as a human being—this is an even *smaller* chance. Much smaller! Better chance of turtle coming up through ring than of sentient being taking a human rebirth. Understand? So what this mean? Hmmmn?

"It means this: Human life is very, very rare. Very, very precious. And if you understand how precious, and how rare, you will never waste. You will never, ever waste this opportunity for study, for practice, for liberation."

o   o   o

When the teaching ended I left the monastery and walked clockwise around the Boudha dome. I spun every one of the hundreds of copper prayer wheels, the first time I'd accomplished that dizzying feat. At the end of my kora I spied a street waif sleeping on the path. His clothes were in tatters, and his face covered with flies. I pushed a folded 50-rupee note into the tattered pocket of his shirt, gleefully imagining how he'd feel when he discovered it: the polar opposite of how I'd felt waking up to a stolen computer.

The Good Doctor

As I was preparing to leave the Boudha environs I ran into David Shlim, the director of Kathmandu's most prestigious western clinic. He invited me to have lunch with him at the Stupa View Restaurant. I gladly accepted.

I'd first met David in 1983, during my first extended visit to the kingdom. Over the years I'd grown to like him enormously. Lonely and insecure when he first moved to Kathmandu, he had been profoundly changed by his relationship with Tibetan Buddhism.

Trained in Oregon, Shlim moved to Asia in 1979. His introduction to Buddhism came in the late eighties, when he set up a free clinic for Boudha's monks. This had required working directly with Chokyi Nyima Rimpoche, and even though David had scant interest in the dharma he found himself irresistibly drawn by the young lama's humor and insight. The Rimpoche, for his part, was fascinated by western medicine and intrigued by the fact that a professional caregiver from the world's wealthiest country could also be, in David's words, "a complete neurotic." The men became friends, and over the course of just a few months, their meetings evolved into real spiritual dialogues.

We found a window table in the Stupa View and ordered fresh lemon sodas and daalbhat. We spoke briefly about his recent work—Shlim had just completed groundbreaking research on a newly discovered intestinal parasite, soon to be published in *Lancet*—and segued into a discussion about Kathmandu itself. It struck us both that Nepal, after all these years, still remained a place where people came to *find* something.

"Why Kathmandu?" Shlim placed his motorcycle helmet on the table and picked a purple thread out of his auburn beard. "Why the Himalaya? Why aren't tens of thousands of people spiritually drawn to the Alps, or the Pamirs, or even the Karakoram Range? For some reason it's the Himalaya that people come to—and they come full of expectations. Expectations and the confidence that, in the shadow of these incredible mountains, their lives will change. They come *wanting* something. And you know the most amazing thing?"

"They get it," I replied.

"That's right." We sat for a moment in silence. Two steaming plates of rice, daal and vegetables—a far cry from the slop I'd encountered at the Gaura Singh truck stop—were placed before us. "When I came to Nepal, I wanted something too; although it would take me years before I could articulate exactly what it was.

"My own vision," he said, "was that I'd climb a steep hill to some Himalayan gompa, and be immediately recognized as one of the 'chosen.' I'd be singled out, and pulled away from the other tourists into a private room. There, beneath the icy flanks of Tham Serku and Ama Dablam, I'd meet the High Lama and be given the secret teachings—and when I left that mountain I'd be an enlightened man.

"That was my dream," he said, grinning. "Ridiculous. Embarrassing, even. But you know what? Last year, as part of my meditation practice, I was visiting Tulku Urgyen Rimpoche, Chokyi Nyima's father. The Rimpoche was on his cushion, reciting sutras behind his little table, and I was sitting with him, meditating. Just the two of us. It was a beautiful day; you could see the mountains, which is pretty unusual from Kathmandu these days. Anyway, I looked out the window, and at that moment I suddenly realized: *Holy shit, it had happened after all.* There I was: alone with one of the highest lamas in Nepal, deeply immersed in the dharma and very much at peace within myself. I had gotten exactly what I came here for. It just took a lot more effort—and time—than I had expected."

But there was a darker side to the force that drew certain people to Nepal. As head of the CIWEC clinic, Shlim was often confronted by strange, sometimes inexplicable deaths. A new disease, known for the moment as sudden trekker death syndrome, had already claimed three lives; all its victims had died in trailside teahouses, and each fatality had occurred between five and six-thirty in the morning. In unrelated incidents, a woman had recently been helicoptered out of the mountains without a single white blood cell in her bloodstream; a yoga teacher had dropped dead from sudden acute leukemia; an otherwise fit tourist had died suddenly, of unknown causes, in his hotel. What seemed like a simple cold had claimed the life of a child. And just days ago a fit, enthusiastic 25-year-old tourist from Brooklyn had been trekking across the Cho La Pass when a huge boulder fell silently from an overhang, killing him instantly.

"It's hard to explain why such things happen here," Shlim said. "The Buddhists say that a 'ripening of karma' can occur, without much preamble, in and around this valley. It may be, in other words, that some people actually come here to die." He called for the check and paid it before I could resist. "Western visitors are often obsessed with the 'why' of their injuries and illnesses," reflected Shlim. "But any doctor who works in Kathmandu quickly realizes how little we really know about cause and effect."

The Nagmani

Long, long ago—in 1979, in fact—there appeared the first neon sign in all of Kathmandu. The single word *Bhajaj* blinked on and off above the traffic and hustle of New Road, hawking Indian-made fans in huge pink letters. The sign, which drew local sightseers from all over the valley, was a harbinger of things to come. Within days the middle 'j' had flickered out, and the New Road urbscape—Kathmandu's most modern business thoroughfare—instantly took on the run-down ambience of industrial Denver.

My, how times had changed. Now there were dozens of multicolored neon displays all over the city, buzzing with ads for everything from airlines to noodles. At the foot of Durbar Marg, the broad avenue spilling south from the Royal Palace, a new Jumbotron billboard pulsed through a seven-minute microchip-controlled loop promoting Compaq laptops, Tibet Tours and San Miguel beer.

The green, orange and yellow lights flickered through the windows of the Gupta Indian Restaurant, dancing in my spoon. I was having a late dinner with Carroll Dunham and Vidhea Shrestha, a dark-eyed, razor-sharp Nepali woman who worked as Tom and Carroll's assistant. We'd waited more than an hour for Ian Baker, but the kitchen was closing and we'd had to order without him.

Carroll and Vidhea filled me in on their recent trip to Bombay. The assignment had taken them through the back alleys of Kamathipura— the infamous red-light district that included Falkland Road—where they'd interviewed dozens of hookers.

"The most incredible people were the *hijras*," Carroll said. "They're these big, tough eunuchs who started out as men but have undergone surgery to remove their testicles and give them artificial vaginas. Before we went down there, everyone warned us about them—I guess they can be pretty nasty if you get on their bad side. But we hung out with them for days, met with them in their rooms and listened to their stories. Most of them were real sweethearts. They became our guardian angels the whole time we were in Bombay."

A tiny waiter in a ludicrous chef's hat gathered our plates. Vidhea lit a cigarette. "The most interesting ones to talk to, at least for me, were the teenage Nepali girls," she said. "I'd heard for years about how little girls are kidnapped from their villages and sold into the flesh trade. What we learned, though, was that that's not always the case. Quite the opposite, in fact. What really happens is that they see their cousins and aunties return to the villages with lots of money and jewelry, and think to themselves, 'My God, that sounds a lot better than spending the rest of my life chopping firewood and killing chickens . . .' So they go to India, to the big city, and some of them are actually quite happy doing what they're doing. The main problem really is health awareness. Each girl services fifteen to twenty guys a day, and safe sex hasn't exactly caught on. I think a high percentage of them must have AIDS."

"That's the scary part," Carroll picked up. "Since most of the clients are harried Indian men who go to the eunuchs and female prostitutes for quick blow jobs—something no decent Indian wife knows how to do—the disease is spreading like crazy."

The waiter returned with tea and a paper bag holding our leftovers. Vidhea reached over to steal an ashtray from a nearby table. "Tell him about our idea."

Carroll hesitated, but only for a second. "Okay. Here it is. Our personal scheme for stopping the spread of AIDS in India. What we decided to do is pitch a development project—to the World Health Organization, of course—employing the prostitutes and madams in an outreach program. We'll send them into the cities and villages, where they'll teach Indian women how to give great head."

"The beauty of the whole thing," Vidhea added, "is that it benefits local agriculture as well. I mean, what will the women practice on? It has to be bananas, right? Bananas, or cucumbers. So we support the local growers, boost nutrition, get the prostitutes on salary and fight the spread of AIDS, all in one fell swoop. . . ."

The restaurant door opened, and Ian Baker rushed in. He looked sheepish and out of breath.

"The reason I'm late," he said, glancing at Vidhea, "is that I've been with the trusteeship. Everything's prepared; we're meeting at three in the morning."

Vidhea shook her head. "Not again."

"Again." His kelp green eyes, which seemed larger since radial keratotomy had cured his myopia, moved to Carroll. "This time they're serious. I'm going to see it this time. I have a feeling. Tonight's the night."

"See what?" I looked from Carroll to Vidhea, but both women were staring fixedly at Ian.

"The *nagmani*," he replied.

o   o   o

Once upon a time, the Kathmandu Valley was a vast inland lake. Within its crystal waters, a tribe of powerful *nagas*—multi-hooded cobra gods—dwelt in harmony, guarding the Earth's underground treasures and directing the seasonal rains. When the great lake drained, the nagas slithered off to nearby ponds and rivers, abandoning their home but giving up none of their powers.

Of all the treasures guarded by the nagas, none is more potent than the nagmani, a mythical "snake jewel" that bestows spiritual power and fulfills every wish. Condensed from the venom of these sacred snakes, the egg-shaped nagmani represents the transformation of the Earth's most deadly poison into its most coveted gem.

There aren't many ways to get your hands on a nagmani; no one even knows how many exist. The route that had led to Ian's involvement was more convoluted than an epileptic cobra, but the long and short of it was that he had been selected, through a shady network of Tantric priests, to become the custodian of a gem currently in the possession of a local guru. The next step, apparently, was for Ian to view the nagmani itself. Since the snake gods were understandably keen on recovering their treasure, the encounter would be conducted in utmost secrecy.

"I checked out the meeting place." Ian helped himself to Carroll's tea. "They've got it completely prepared. My chair is in the center of a giant mandala made of honey, since nagas can't cross honey. All the windows are blacked out, so that when the nagmani is revealed, the radiation won't leak out. It's so intensely bright that we'll have to wear eye protection. I showed the trustees my sunglasses, but they laughed and handed me a welder's mask."

"I don't understand. They're just going to *give* you this thing?"

"Not at all." Ian reached into his jacket and pulled out a sheaf of forms. "I'm supposed to be *buying* it." He showed me the papers. They constituted a formal agreement letter, laying out the terms of the purchase. My eyes bugged out when I saw the price: *six million dollars.*

"This has been going on forever." Vidhea looked over my shoulder as I read the contract. "In the beginning," she said, "I was involved as well. I dressed up in my best sari, posed as a New York art collector and accompanied Ian to some of the meetings. It was good fun, but after a while it started getting risky. I was afraid someone would recognize me. So I dropped out. That was a year ago, but Ian still hasn't seen it. Unless you want to count that one time. . . ."

"No, no. . . ." Baker fidgeted. "A couple of months ago some other people tried to sell me a different nagmani. This one was a bargain, only fifty thousand dollars. But when I examined it closely it turned out to be a pumpkin seed, doused with phosphorescent paint."

"If nothing else, you've got a great story." I folded the papers and returned them to Ian. "Have you thought about writing all this down?"

"As a matter of fact I have. I was going to start this week, but I'm waiting for my new Mac to arrive from Hong Kong. It seemed right that it should be the first story I wrote on my color laptop . . ."

Carroll grabbed Ian's shoulder. "That's right! I totally forgot. It's coming in this week, yes?"

"It should arrive on Tuesday's flight. Why? What's wrong?"

"Nothing. Where's your old one?"

"The PowerBook? It's at home. I was going to put an ad up on the UN bulletin board on Monday. . . ."

"Don't bother." Carroll raised her wineglass and touched it to mine. "I don't know about you," she said to Ian, "but I think our wandering pilgrim here has just found his own nagmani."

· 35 ·

Ice-Blue Eyes

The evening after I bought Ian's PowerBook I bicycled across town to Pashupatinath. The ancient temple, a compound of gold-roofed pagodas and stone cremation ghats set along the banks of the Bagmati River, is dedicated to Lord Shiva: the awesome creator/destroyer of the Hindu pantheon.

Shiva wears many heads. He is known as Nataraja (Lord of the Dance) and as the fierce, multiheaded Bhairava. *Saddhus,* Hindu holy men, worship him as the ultimate ascetic, capable of torturous penances and supreme concentration. In his female form, Shiva becomes Shakti, the divine (and how!) essence of female sexual energy; but as Pashupati, the usually fearsome deity assumes the more benign role of Lord and protector of animals.

It was one of those rare occasions when Pashupatinath completely hypnotized me. I handed a few coins to a begging *pujari*—a female sorcerer with ice-blue eyes—and climbed a grassy hill for an overview of the grounds. Monkeys, the jealous guardians of the compound, played and slept beneath green wooden benches as Shiva bhajans issued from the temple complex below. I lay out on a bench and slept as well, dreaming about snakes as the late sun disappeared behind the dark shoulder of Nagarjun Hill.

I felt a hand shaking my foot, and opened my eyes to face the pujari. She was dressed in a collage of rags and furs, and thick strands of beads rattled around her neck. Her bare feet were wide, callused and flat, as if she'd walked to Kathmandu from . . . where? Her remarkable eyes puzzled me. Afghanistan? Western Tibet?

I stood up. "Where are you from?" I asked her in Nepali; but she laughed and danced away. A moment later she was back, talking a mile a minute, babbling in a language I couldn't understand. Finally she grabbed both my hands and put her face inches from mine. Her eyes were perfectly round and inhumanly blue.

"*Maadat chainchha*," she said in Nepali, shaking my hands rapidly. "Help me. You have to help me."

Help her? How? What did she expect me to do? I reached into my belly-pouch and extracted a 50-rupee note—far more than I usually give such characters—and pressed it into her palm. To my astonishment she flung it away. I retrieved the bill and stood before her, baffled. "What do you want?" I asked her. "How can I help you?"

The pujari stared into my eyes for a full minute. She then retreated, turned around and spun toward me again, her fingers bent as if to claw me. When I backed away she laughed loudly and raced away, down the hill and across the footbridge toward the temple, her ragtag clothing flapping in the wind.

I stood rooted to the spot, trying without success to make sense of the encounter.

The light was failing. I walked down to the river and performed a brief *puja* to Ganesha, the elephant-headed protector of travelers, taking a bit of red powder from the stone pachyderm and touching it to my head as a few onlookers nodded their approval.

o   o   o

The next morning I had breakfast with Rob, the Zen stockbroker who'd accompanied me on the ill-fated voyage from Lucknow to Kathmandu. I hadn't seen much of Rob or Lysha during my weeks in Nepal. Rob had been sick a good deal of the time, down with an intermittent virus. He appeared fairly healthy now, though, and I suggested he consider joining me for the overland trip to Lhasa.

"Where are you going after Tibet?"

"There aren't a lot of options," I admitted. "I'll get across China somehow, then try to work my way into Vietnam through its northern border. Depending on time"—I was already a month behind my original schedule—"I'd like to continue on through Southeast Asia toward

Malaysia and Indonesia, drop into Australia and catch a ship home from Sydney."

Rob poured syrup over his waffle, depositing a few drops in every cell. "I'll tell you what. On top of the mantel at my parents' house, in Seattle, there's a picture of my older sister at Machu Picchu, and one of my little sister in front of the Great Pyramid. Here's the deal: If you would take a shot of me, standing in front of the Potala Palace—well, that would be the ultimate. Sibling victory would be mine."

"You've got it," I said. "What about China?"

"My only limitation is that I've got to be in Thailand for a meditation retreat by the end of July. That's six weeks away. If you think we could make it to Hanoi by then—"

"Easily."

"That's it, then. Sign me up."

Snickers Satori

Two days before my departure I tore myself away from an ever-expanding list of errands and made time for a final pilgrimage. I collected Carroll from her office. She flagged down a taxi, and we set off toward Pharphing.

Pharphing itself is a small Newari village, remarkably rustic despite its close proximity to Nepal's sprawling capital. Just above the town, though, on the flanks of a pointed hillside, is the dark and narrow cave where Guru Rimpoche himself attained enlightenment. Above the cave, on the crest of the stony hill itself, sits one of the most breathtaking places in the entire valley: a grove of murmuring pine trees, festooned with thousands upon thousands of waving, shimmering prayer flags, high above the valley floor.

The hill was our destination. Earlier in the day I'd stopped in at one of the Tibetan shops near the Boudhanath stupa and bought a long string of fifty red, white, blue, yellow and green prayer flags, blessed by Chokyi Nyima with grains of colored rice. Carroll and I would hang the flags, recite prayers for my safe onward travels, and dedicate the merit of our gesture to the benefit of all sentient beings. Once we'd accomplished that act I could depart for Tibet in good conscience, knowing I'd covered my bases as best as I could.

The drive was fraught with delays. Our first taxi made it as far as the Royal Palace before the engine exploded. The second got out past the Ring Road when the front right tire blew. We stood on the shoulder, glancing up at a disturbing new billboard:

Everest Mouthwash:
Destroys Plaque Before It Destroys Your Teeth

"It's just a question," Carroll reflected, "of spitting it out at the exact right moment."

The flat was fixed in five minutes, but no sooner had we started up the winding road toward Pharphing than we came upon a metal sign with a skull and crossbones: BLASTING AHEAD. We got out of the taxi and waited patiently for half an hour as explosions rocked the ground and gigantic boulders sailed through the air.

"It looks like our entire outing," I said, "is going to be defined by things blowing up. I'm trying to see it as a good sign, but . . ."

"It's a great sign!" Carroll, one of the wisest women I knew, was laughing at me.

"You ought to know that by now. This is what pilgrimage is all about. Releasing those pent-up negative energies! Cleansing the karmic slate! What all of these signs are telling you is very simple: *Let go!* Drop your expectations! Abandon your best-laid plans!"

I grunted sullenly.

"Either you make those decisions yourself, or they get made for you." The driver signaled to us, and we made our way back toward the cab. "Isn't it true? You plod ahead, losing everything you thought you needed, facing difficulty after difficulty and getting more and more frazzled and bent out of shape until finally—*hopefully*—something inside of you snaps and you realize: 'Holy cow! Maybe my problems aren't coming from Out There at all, but from the internal conflict between what I expect to happen and the way life actually unfolds!'

"And that, my dear Jeffji, is when you realize that you can't cling to any assumptions about The Way It's Gonna Be—because all our plans, all our hopes and fears about the future are based on nothing but past experience. This, *right now*, is not only what's happening; it's *all* that's happening. And in this moment, this ageless and futureless moment, there is nowhere to be but *Here*, nothing to do but *This*, and no time to do it in but *Now*."

She sifted around in her daypack. "You want half a Snickers bar?"

I accepted the fix, remembering all the times that Sally had told me the very same thing—and recalling the final words I'd said to Papaji in 1993 at the end of our marathon interview.

I thought I had some pretty tricky questions, I'd told him in admiration, *but they all have exactly the same answer.*

o   o   o

Huge, pearlescent clouds drifted above the cultivated landscape, appearing both ominous and benevolent—like the enormous ships of the Overlords in Arthur Clarke's *Childhood's End*. We reached Pharphing just before six, lit candles in the Ganesh/Saraswati temple at the base of the hill and climbed up a narrow dirt track to the summit.

The valley below was a patchwork of light and shadow. In the distance, above the brick pagodas of Kathmandu itself, a rain shower wriggled in the air like a rainbow trout. Flute music filtered up from Pharphing. Somewhere on a lower hillside, someone was chopping wood.

I shimmied up a medium-size tree and tied one end of the prayer flag string to the highest limb. Carroll, below, unraveled the line and attached the other end to a gnarly shrub that seemed rooted to the very omphalos of the sacred hill. This done, we stepped back to admire our work. Few things are more satisfying than watching your newly hung prayer flags whip energetically in a fresh wind, sending blessings across the fertile landscape in an ultra-benevolent crop dusting. Carroll and I grinned at each other, a mutual glance of spiritual complicity, and I realized once again, for the ten thousandth time, why I was so madly in love with Kathmandu. Aside from being my spiritual mainframe, the valley was a community of brilliant, hardworking guys and gals who would shrug off their deadlines, pack a Snickers bar and skip town on a weekday afternoon to hang a string of prayer flags with a friend.

We stopped briefly on our descent, taking a few minutes to sit quietly inside the cave where Guru Rimpoche meditated en route from India to Tibet. Butter candles illuminated severe-looking deities, and mosquitoes whined in damp corners. Just to the left of the cave's womblike entranceway, blackened from centuries of tactile worship, was Guru Rimpoche's hand print: a live outlet of spiritual power. I pressed my palm into the recessed grooves, removed my hand and slapped myself across the face with it.

o   o   o

As we drove back to Kathmandu the sky cracked open, unleashing a sudden downpour. We weren't just caught in the rain; we were virtually underwater, driving door-handle-deep through vast puddle-lakes. Wiping my fogged-up window, I half expected to see Karkot Naga Raja—lord of the sacred snake gods who once inhabited the valley—leaping through the air like a Chinese kite. When the glass fogged up again, I rolled the window down.

"Hey," I asked Carroll, "what ever happened with Ian Baker? Did he finally get a look at the nagmani?"

"Get this. He arrived as planned—at three in the morning—and everyone was waiting for him. There was only one problem. The honey mandala they'd painted around his chair was swarming with ants. He said they were two inches deep in places. The priests decided that a naga could get at Ian by crawling over the ants, so they called the whole thing off. They'll try again next month. . . ."

The rain blew in, dampening my face. It was the long, warm, pre-menstrual rain that would deepen and burst into the monsoon, and with a long breath I let it wash me clean. In the enormous river that swelled past the cab's open window I watched my stolen daypack float by; watched my beloved lost OmniBook sail past like a raft; saw my vanished camera bobbing in the waves. The thousands of rupees I'd spent on futile newspaper ads swirled by in a wind devil, and all the hours I'd wasted combing through computer stores and sleuthing in camera shops dissolved like Alka-Seltzer in the boundless holy stream.

Carroll had found a KitKat bar in her jacket pocket and was nibbling the chocolate off a wafer. Rain hammered the roof. "*Time Is a River Without Banks*," I recited softly. "That's a painting, somewhere. By Chagall . . .?"

She broke off a choco-biscuit and fed it into my mouth. Outside, the bleary eye of a motorcycle swam past us, a luminous fish at great depth.

"I keep waiting to get bored with this place," she sighed. "But it never seems to happen."

The Bardo of Johnny Walker Red

The night before Nick left on a business trip for Saigon—one day before my own departure—we sat up until midnight. I listened to his stories of life in Borneo and Tanzania; to his tales of lions and elephants; to the endless narratives of his sexual exploits; to his delight in his advancing years and his gratitude for a surprising and wonderful life that continued, despite its pains, to be wonderful and surprising. I listened with envy and, when it was my turn to talk, spoke frankly about the demons that had haunted me the past year.

"Oh, I've noticed them," Nick said. "Very definitely so. But I still feel that happiness is within your grasp.

"I'll be completely honest with you." We were on our second whiskey, and I was ready for a lecture. "But first of all, let me praise your good qualities." I shifted on my cushion. "You like people," he said, "and people like you. You're very intelligent, and very, very funny. You're the funniest person I know."

"You should have met my brother," I replied.

"Ah." He nodded, and swirled his ice. "But this is precisely what I'm talking about. Since you've arrived in Nepal, I've noticed a new trait in your personality that has alarmed me. I don't know what to call it except a foreboding, a dark shadow about your future. It's as if you've developed a sort of deep misgiving about what awaits you, what life holds in store. What you need, I think, is to release your self-image as a free-floating, disconnected spirit and go for the 'corny' things in life: love, commitment, stability.

"I think you would be a far, far happier person," he said, "and I mean this very sincerely, having given it much thought—I think you would be a much happier person if you could only learn to trust the future."

"I haven't had much positive reinforcement in trusting the future."

Nick gave me a surprised look. "Haven't you? You're here, right now. You're in the middle of an assignment that, although difficult and certainly exhausting, is infinitely preferable to having an office job in some Los Angeles high-rise; and you're surrounded by friends who truly love and admire you. No; I believe that if you could learn to trust the future, and have some faith in your ability to attain happiness, it would become a kind of self-fulfilling prophecy." He looked at me owlishly, unblinking. "And I also believe that, conversely, your dread of the future is quite capable of becoming a self-fulfilling prophecy as well—and turning into a source of real unhappiness."

I nodded, knowing the truth when I heard it.

"You have an absolutely perfect life," Nick said. "Don't ever doubt it. And never, ever forget it."

The Final Frontier

It was time to leave Kathmandu; something I wasn't very good at doing. Ever since my first visit to the kingdom, at the age of twenty-five—when I sat in the garden of the Kathmandu Guesthouse and wrote the words "Welcome home" in my travel-battered journal—my relationship with the valley had been one of intense magnetic love, a physical addiction that ran through my blood like liquid iron and drew me back again and again, year after year, to my spiritual center. The sawtooth mountains, swollen luminous monsoon clouds, lounging cows and smoke-stained pagodas with their giant brass bells were huge electromagnets, pulling at me from the core of my being, compelling me to return. At first I thought the phenomenon was abstract: a feeling, a desire, an emotional attachment. Now I knew it was a force, as real as gravity. There is something about Nepal, something in the Day-

Glo green mandala of the Kathmandu Valley, that draws certain people in with the power of a whirlpool. We don't know how to gauge it, but when we devise a way of measuring such vibrations I'm convinced that the Kathmandu Valley will burst our instruments to slivers.

No, I could not pretend otherwise. I'd been captured and tamed, for the seventh time in fifteen years. Finding this valley, and finding myself in it, was a fateful blessing—and like the hero of *Lost Horizon*, I'd be thrashing through the wilderness until I found my way back again.

o   o   o

Lightning flashed around the house like a drug bust, and rain battered the broad banana leaves in the garden. The dog next door whined pathetically, ceaselessly, samsara's canine megaphone. I woke at six, carried my recalcitrant erection to the window and searched the northern horizon, seeing only clouds.

By sunrise, miraculously, the weather had cleared. Standing on Nick's roof, I watched the striated faces of the Langtang Himal taking on a peachy glow. The red cylindrical tiles on the nearby rooftops steamed in the sun, and birds ran riot in the trees.

At precisely 7:00 A.M. a purple Nissan beeped outside the gate. I ran down to let it through. Rob got out and stretched, then beat his chest like a gorilla. I loaded my backpack and Macintosh PowerBook into the trunk, turned off the power in the house and slid Nick's key beneath the door.

"Nice morning," Rob said. "Must be clear all the way up to the border."

"To the border—and beyond." I climbed in the back and pulled the door shut. "*Sri driverji?*"

The taxi pilot turned around and grinned. "Yes, *sahib?*"

"*Engage!*"

• 36 •

Hard Rock Bardo

It was a gorgeous drive. The rice paddies sparkled like Colombian emeralds, and early monsoon clouds performed the Dance of the Seven Veils between the foothills and major peaks. We caught brief but delicious glimpses of the mountains, their surreal sno-cones towering above terraced hillsides as vivid and green as electron-microscope images of parakeet feathers. Animals were everywhere: cows lazing on the shoulders, cranes sailing beneath enormous clouds, goats butting each other in the middle of the street, dogs humping beneath jacaranda trees. The Bhote Kosi, a pulsing muddy artery, paralleled the road, which was everything a road could be—silky smooth, hairpin, poxed, pitted, perched along the edge, steep as shit, way too narrow, dead ahead and holy, paved with gravel, bone dry, broken to bits, blocked by boulders, damp with dew. It was an odyssey, a true taxi pilgrimage, and aside from our nagging worries about what would happen at the Chinese border, perfect in every way.

Our anxieties about crossing into Tibet arose from the erratic reports we'd heard in Kathmandu. More than one travel agency had declared, simply, that we wouldn't get in; the Chinese, famous for changing the rules at the drop of a hat, were now allowing only approved group tours into the Tibet Autonomous Region. As individual travelers, Rob and I would be a security risk. There would be no Chinese "guide" on hand to steer us away from potentially embarrassing (to them) encounters, or to keep us from asking pointed political questions of Tibetan monks and peasants who had been under Chinese occupation for more than 40 years. We had visas, of course—arranged by a backdoor tour company at substantial cost—but these promised us nothing. The border guards would instantly realize that Rob and I planned to enter Tibet unescorted. A simple *"mei yo"*—the pat refusal that serves as the anthem of the Chinese bureacracy—would find us back where we'd started by sunset.

Thirteen miles before the border we came upon a landslide that blocked the road completely. We paid off our driver and hiked across the detritus to where the road was clear again. A flatbed truck was waiting. We agreed to pay dearly for transportation to Zhangmu (the first town inside Tibet), assured that we need give nothing until we were safely over the border. Clinging to this dubious guarantee, we received our exit stamps in Kodari, crossed the "Friendship Bridge" and climbed the cattle-track hill toward Zhangmu in first gear.

Half a dozen uniformed border guards stood waiting to examine our documents. They watched us with the viperlike concentration of frontline volleyball sharks, ready to send us careening back over the net.

As we approached the post, I noticed that one of the guards—the one with the most little stars on his hat—had a fairly horrible infection in his right eye. The moment we leapt off the truck I pulled out my first aid kit and approached the official with a small tube of ophthalmic ointment.

"If you hold still," I said, "I can treat that eye . . ."

Five minutes later we breezed through customs without a hitch, waving to the amiable immigration guards while our drivers waited patiently for their payoff. We compensated them as promised, too happy to be in Tibet to worry about a little key money.

Finding transportation from Zhangmu to Lhasa is not a problem. Land-Rovers, Toyota Land Cruisers and Range Rovers routinely ferry tourists from Tibet's capital to the Nepali border, turn around and make the two-day return trip empty. We spied four such vehicles waiting outside the Zhangmu Hotel. While Rob waited I arranged for the best of them—a brand-new, olive-green Range Rover with pictures of Mao and Deng Xiaoping hanging from the rearview mirror like fuzzy dice—to carry us the five hundred miles to Lhasa. The non-negotiable price was $50 each, U.S. currency only.

The driver took our deposit and vanished. We loitered in the car park for about half an hour before learning the score. None of the vehicles was going anywhere fast. The reason for this was simple; there was no longer a road to drive on. The previous night a huge avalanche had swept down a nearby hillside, throwing boulders the size of UPS trucks across the road and rendering the way to Lhasa impassable. We discussed this with the Zhangmu Hotel receptionist—a thin, friendly Tibetan wearing huge gold rings—and were assured that repair crews were at work on the problem even as we spoke. Everything would be fine by morning.

"No problem," he chortled, "unless rain. If big rain, maybe stuck here some time."

We ate a slithery lunch of pan-fried noodles and checked into the hotel. Although our watches said one-thirty—accurate in Kodari, just two miles away— it was 4:00 P.M. in Zhangmu. The Machiavellian arrogance of China's leaders extends across the breadth of their empire as businessmen and nomads alike, from Kashi to Canton, share the dubious privilege of living on Beijing time. But Rob and I were beat, and after carrying our bags into our room we collapsed. When I opened my eyes again it was six-thirty, and pissing down rain.

The roar of a nearby river made it sound louder than it was, but it was definitely raining. I peered out the window, watching flumes of water shoot from the drainpipes and cascade down the nearby valley. It was easy to imagine any remnants of the highway dissolving like sandcastles, and to envision gigantic stones tumbling onto the road and settling there with the stolid immobility of tax increases. As I paced around the room in agitation, Rob sat complacently on his bed and watched me.

"Relax," he breathed. I could see his Zen training was coming in handy. "Tomorrow we might be able to drive as far as the avalanche site, walk over it and pick up a vehicle on the other side of the mess. In the meantime, why not ask yourself: '*Who's* experiencing the frustration? *Who's* experiencing the angst? *Who's* projecting a week in Zhangmu? *Who?*'"

We put on our raincoats and wandered through the sewery streets to a restaurant, where we drank until one in the morning—10:30 P.M., as far as the Earth was concerned—and went to bed praying for clear skies.

o   o   o

I rolled out of bed around eight and, finding no water in the sink, washed my face with tea. Afterward I spread a comforter over the floor and launched into the Five Rites of Rejuvenation. My attitude toward the exercises had changed; they were no longer work. An element of enjoyment was creeping in, a sense of body-wellness that both Nick and Joel had assured me would come.

After yoga I stepped into Rob's half of the suite. He was lying in bed underneath the metallic yellow bedspread, his eyes half-open, regarding me blankly. I asked how he was doing.

"I hate to tell you this," he said, "but it's been another long, dark night of the soul."

During his entire month in Kathmandu, Rob had been complaining of an intermittent malaise: fatigue, occasional fever, a general lack of energy and severe diarrhea. I'd assumed from his descriptions that it was a bacterial infection or flu, both endemic in the Valley around the monsoon. But as he told me about the night's raging fever, skull-shattering headache and bed-soaking sweats—similar to the three-day-long bouts he'd been experiencing all month—I changed my diagnosis.

"You've got malaria," I said. "The only thing for you to do is go back to Kathmandu for treatment."

It wasn't that simple. He'd already been tested for malaria at the CIWEC clinic, and the results had been negative. But such tests, as we both knew, could be wrong.

I sat on his bed and discussed options. We spent some time debating the advantages of continuing on to Lhasa and seeking treatment there, but the long and difficult overland journey made that seem a foolish, and potentially lethal, risk.

It was a nightmare, but it was unambiguous. In the end there was nothing to do but pack his bags, buy the China and Vietnam guidebooks he'd bought in Kathmandu and help him carry his gear back to the border post.

And so, barely twenty-four hours after setting off with my Zen stockbroker companion, I found myself alone again. Alone, and looking at the full breadth of China to cover. Alone, with no guarantee the road to Lhasa would open anytime soon. Alone—and, after about an hour, alone in the rain.

Rain Shadow

The Range Rover I'd hired for transport to Lhasa, being an official China Tourism vehicle, had arrived in Zhangmu with an attractive Tibetan guide named Tashi. She had an expressive mouth and the jet-black braids I'd always associated with Pocahontas. We ate lunch together in a restaurant above the local clinic.

"What I don't understand," I said, "is why our driver won't at least run me up to the landslide. I'm sure I could find a vehicle on the other side."

"The Rover runs on diesel," she explained. "It is very hard to find in this part of Tibet. He has no intention of using up any fuel until he knows for sure that the road is open."

"What's your best guess on when that will happen?"

Tashi shrugged. "I don't know. I'm staying here with some friends . . . if I can find them. You might get out late this afternoon, but I don't think so. Probably tomorrow morning, at the earliest."

Even this seemed optimistic. According to a report from three tourists who'd just arrived in Zhangmu after making the journey from the landslide by foot, repairs would take another two to three days.

Zhangmu was a frontier town and, like its cousins the world over, displayed the worst attributes of the nations between which it sat. Prices were high, and the eateries swarmed with border police. Listless monks and stranded traders shot pool under sagging plastic tarps. Steep, unpaved roads, flooded by the rains, flowed with human and animal excrement. Zhangmu, not to put too fine a point on it, stank, and I had no desire to abide there any longer than necessary. While Tashi set off to look for her friends, I wandered off up the main road to stretch my legs and plot my escape. But I hadn't gone two hundred meters when I spied something of cataclysmic significance. Two unfamiliar Land Cruisers were higher on the hill, *coming down toward me.* As the first one approached I forced the car to a stop.

"Where are you coming from?"

The driver jerked his thumb backward.

"Is the road open?!"

"Yes! Open!"

I charged back down the hill, eager to share this news with the Range Rover crew. But my driver was already outside the hotel, flagging me down with his hand.

"Now going!! More rain . . ." He made an avalanching gesture with his hands. "You come, yes or no?"

I threw my gear into the back of the Range Rover and took the front passenger's seat.

Within minutes we were off, up and out of Zhangmu: Zhangmu with its upward spiraling hillside, its piles of raw ginger outside the door of the Friendship Restaurant, its pool-shark Khampas and bare-ass kids shitting on Main Street. Away from the Zhangmu Hotel, with its gold-dust velvet bedspreads and matching curtains; Zhangmu, where bored Chinese soldiers chased giggling waitresses with fly swatters, and hotel clerks played solitaire to the looping soundtrack of rain on tin. Out of Wild West Zhangmu, and good riddance.

o   o   o

An hour later we had passed through the cleared slide areas and arrived in Nilamo—a one-wok frontier town with a dilapidated dance hall and absolutely no bathrooms—to pick up a few more passengers. We set off with every seat filled, motoring across the shingles of the Roof of the World. The raw, rugged mountains were a palette of every color I knew, every color I'd ever imagined. As we crossed the Himalaya, breakers of mile-high peaks—buckled upward by the relentless butting of plate tectonics—lined the horizon like bleached nomad tents.

Not a single aspect of the world around us seemed futile or weak; nothing was for show. Every crag, every stone and sword-cut valley seemed exactly in place, inhabiting its own eternal kingdom.

Protean clouds pulsed across the sky like dynamos, illuminated from within by flickering electrical storms. Columns of rain danced between the cloud banks, never touching the ground. When sunlight hit the suspended downpours the drops of rain blazed like opals. I rolled down my window, smelling ozone and ice.

In just four hours of slow driving, from the Nepal border to the region just beyond Nilamo, I'd passed into the rain shadow of the Himalaya. I had left the Kathmandu Valley—with its lush mythology, saturated rice terraces and snake gods—and ascended into the spare, luminous wilderness of the Tibetan plateau. Gone were the dairy cows and mangoes; gone the balmy nights and poolside ice cream socials. The relatively approachable gods of the Hindu pantheon had stepped aside, abandoning the stage to the mercurial earth spirits of a far less forgiving terrain. Tibet's landscape is so vast and powerful that you know it's alive; water, air and lightning gods have inhabited these hills for eons, and the arrival of Buddhism did not displace those deities as much as make them reconsider their loyalties.

Yaks grazed along twisting rivers, which, viewed against the sun, unfurled like silver kites. Gutted castles and monasteries dotted the landscape, their ruined towers rising like anthills on the vivid green plains. We climbed and climbed, my head spinning, to the crest of a 16,000-foot pass; then down again, twisting along the switchback highway as the sun sank toward ten-o'clock dusk. Just ahead, beyond the nearest hills, the sky was doing strange things—and as we barreled around a curve I shouted out loud. A hole had opened in the swarming clouds, and a single bolt of brilliant low sunlight shot through the thunderheads onto a rainstorm. The result was a rainbow so intense that it looked like a solid object; it towered into heaven from a spotlit golden hill, rising into a cloud the color of new Levi's.

By the time we reached Tingri the rainbow had faded, but the entire sky was illuminated in an unearthly golden light. The snowfields of the highest Himalayan peaks—Lhotse, Nuptse and supreme Chomolungma, "Goddess Mother of the World"—were reflecting the sunset upward, angling it back into the sky and creating one of those wild panoramic backdrops that we take for granted in Indiana Jones movies but never, ever expect to see in real life.

We pulled into a small encampment. The driver and our three other passengers made their way into a small lodge. I ran, breathless from the altitude, to the top of a small hill. Once the first stars had come out I made my way back, following a couple of whistling yak-herders, to the lodge. There was a fire burning, and a carpeted bench to rest on. Our driver signaled to the *aama*, and she poured me a cup of rich *pö cha*.

The thick, brothlike aroma of black tea and rancid butter rose to the back of my nostrils, and as I put the ceramic cup gratefully to my lips I knew just what it meant. I'd crossed over, once again. This was Tibet.

o   o   o

At ten the next morning we reached the second and highest pass between Kathmandu and Lhasa. It was there, at 17,000 feet, that I hung my last string of Chokyi Nyima-blessed prayer flags. The driver watched in amusement, pissing in the snow, then hustled me out of the wind for the long drop to Lhatse.

Lhatse was a relatively pleasant town of fruit orchards, variety stores and filling stations. We stopped for lunch and continued on through

rough, sparse ranges in alternating rain and hazy sun, passing convoys, bouncing in and out of deep valleys on washboard roads that rattled my eyeballs like dice. I was no longer having fun, a condition accentuated by the fact that, since lunch, I'd been experiencing severe stomach cramps. Sulfur burps, a tight, bloated stomach and a continual need to either belch, fart or do both in two-part harmony made me suspect that most socially awkward of intestinal malaises: giardiasis.

The time-honored phrase "silent but deadly" hardly describes the flatus produced by one's intestinal tract during a bout of giardiasis. It is as if one has just emerged victorious from a thousand-year-old-egg-eating contest with Cool Hand Luke, and one's bowels—at least, the parasites dwelling therein—have become a factory for transforming the ill-advised meal into an aerosol so potent that the smallest quantity of it, delivered in a warhead from some sympathetic Pacific atoll, could easily bring North Korea, and most of mainland China, to their knees. Every hour one produces enough of this noxious gas to inflate the *Hindenburg*. It's gotta go somewhere. Protests that I roll up my window were quickly replaced by the electric whir of my fellow passengers' windows rushing down, and the dust and rain that filled the Rover between Lhatse and Shigatse were greeted without complaint.

The malady seemed to pass after my visit to the Tashilunpo Monastery, where I fended off rabid dogs with my dragon-handled umbrella and lit a butter candle below the giant Buddha. By the time I returned to the waiting Rover I felt a good deal better, and deduced that my malaise had been nothing more than a reaction to the shifts in altitude, undulating roads and ginger chicken with onions, garlic and black fungus that I'd consumed for lunch.

o   o   o

The massive Potala first appears on the skyline about fifteen miles outside of Lhasa. Driving in under a gray sky, I remembered the first time I'd seen the sight, almost seven years before. The infinite loves and diversions, the plans and projects contained in those years evaporated into the ever-present ether of *Now,* and my whole life in between—from thirty-three to forty—seemed but an eye blink in history.

I checked into the Yak Hotel and washed my face over a long cement trough. The two big tents in the parking lot-cum-courtyard were full of travelers—sharing stories, drinking cheap Chinese brandy or writing postcards by candlelight. Two Danish men knelt on the ground with a huge map of China spread out between them. Drivers leaned against the hoods of their Land Cruisers, smoking Marlboros and laughing.

The hotel's housekeepers, six Tibetan women, gambled with raisins and matches in their one-room dormitory.

Famished and exhausted, I used my last ounce of strength getting to Sonam's, a small Tibetan restaurant specializing in pot stickers and pumpkin pie. No sooner had I stepped through the door than I ran into my old friend Holly Wissler, a classical flautist and trek leader who lived in Kathmandu. She was spooning up Sonam's famous dessert with, of all people, Gary McCue—the very man who'd led my narrowly missed expedition to Kailas.

Kathy Butler, Gary's partner, made room for me at their table. I ordered a Tibetan burrito and a large pot of tea.

"So give it to me straight: What'd I miss?"

Gary laughed. "It'll kill you to hear about it."

"No, it won't. Tell me."

He told me. I died.

• 37 •

Wandering Jewels

Holly and I spent our first day in Lhasa exploring the myriad temples in and around the Jokhang—Lhasa's central Buddhist cathedral—with Kathy and Gary. They were ideal companions. Both had spent months exploring the hidden valleys and back alleys of the region, and Gary's recently published *Trekking in Tibet* was the guidebook of choice for any excursion into the countryside.

We began our morning with a visit to the Jokhang itself, a labrynthine temple complex circled by an outdoor bazaar (and a kora in its own right) known as the *barkor*.

The Jokhang was erected over a small lake, located directly above the heart of a fierce underground demoness. Buddhism, the legend goes, could not take root in Lhasa until the demoness was subdued. After much divination, building a temple above her heart seemed to be the solution. The main engineering problem—building on a liquid foundation—was solved by laying a wooden lattice over the water. A single bedraggled goat (working off God knows what kind of karma) hauled in sack after sack of dirt to cover the framework. This explains why the city was originally named Rasa, Place of the Goat. After the Jokhang was completed, however, its name was changed to Lhasa: Abode of the Gods.

Approaching the main entrance to the Jokhang is an exercise in sensory overload. Thick clouds of juniper smoke unfurl from white, womb-shaped censers, and wooden tables sag beneath mammoth piles of *kata* scarves and rainbow-colored prayer flags. The air, 12,000 feet above sea level, tastes of barley and pine. Men, women and children from all over Tibet converge on the temple's western plaza, sliding their robes or rags across stones polished by centuries of similar abrasion. The sound of Tibetans prostrating before the Jokhang is a sound like no other; the continual muttering of mantras, accompanied by the rhythmic swishing and sliding of knee and elbow pads, generates a rolling tide of white noise that inspires inner silence. Shouts, bells and bargaining rise from the surrounding barkor, and two giant copper prayer wheels squeak hypnotically on either side of the enormous doorway.

The inner sanctum of the Jokhang was officially closed, but an authorized tour group was being led inside. We clung to their coattails, and the heavy door was bolted shut behind us.

As we crossed beyond the preliminary passageway and through an open courtyard, I saw a number of *anis* (nuns) throwing handfuls of colored rice and small coins onto bright brass plates.

"Every time they toss the rice and coins onto the surface, it creates a sacred mandala," Kathy explained. "They do this thousands of times a day. . . ."

We were stepping through a beam-and-lintel archway into the maze of inner rooms when Kathy stopped us. She nodded at Holly.

"The point where you're standing," she said, "is the exact geomantic center of the Jokhang. The entire cathedral was built in accordance with strict spiritual formulae; and if you were to draw a series of lines connecting all the holiest shrines and statues in the Jokhang, they would intersect right here."

Holly's eyes lit up. "So what does that mean?"

"If you pray for the benefit of all sentient beings—if you pray for *anything* here—it will absolutely come true."

After a few moments Holly stepped aside, and I took her place on the spiritual keystone. I emptied my mind and tried to feel the energies of the temple coursing through me. The moment I did—when a shiver ran up from the soles of my feet and escaped in a slight tremble from the top of my skull—I made a selfish wish. For I had determined, during my bittersweet stay in Nepal, that nothing I had to offer—no goodness or wisdom for the outside world—could be of any use until I was at peace with myself.

o   o   o

The Jokhang is a series of temples within temples, rooms within rooms. One always circles through clockwise, making a respectful kora. Each gateway and pillar has its own story; every relic and shrine is tied to the whole by some fascinating bit of folklore and local mythology. I'd thought that the Cultural Revolution, China's massive purge in the 1960s, had stripped Tibet's temples bare, but gems are everywhere. There are fist-size turquoises in massive silver mounts, zebra-striped *gzi* stones embedded in the solid-gold headpieces of huge gilt statues, semi-precious stones set into the floor. A fortune in jewels encrusts the crown of Guru Rimpoche, the earrings of Tara, the bracelets of Manjushri.

Nothing, though, compares to the Jowo. The Jokhang's most sacred object, this golden statue of the youthful Buddha—supposedly a life portrait—was part of the wedding dowry brought to Tibet by Princess Wencheng, the mythical "White Tara" who wed Tibet's first king, Srongtsen Gompo, twelve centuries ago.

The Jowo Buddha is barnacled with rubies and diamonds, but there's more than meets the eye. Somewhere *within* the statue, Gary explained, is a magical wandering gem.

"Pilgrims touch their heads to the statue's knee," he said. "If the gem occupies that spot at the same moment . . . *Bam*. Instant enlightenment."

Kathy led us to a stone cistern that protruded from a damp wall. Water trickled in from a small hole inside the basin.

"This little well is fed by the lake beneath the Jokhang," she said. "Long ago, when the lake was above ground, two sacred birds played together on its shore. Tibetans believe that they're still there"—Kathy leaned over, placing her ear near the source—"and say that, if you're pure of heart, you can hear them singing."

I tried, listening very, very closely. I heard something squeak, but it might have been my shoe.

As we spiraled back toward the doorway, Gary drew us into an alcove and pointed to the wall. He showed us an eerie painting, lit by butter lamps, of a flaming sword with gleaming buddha eyes on either side. The characters *Om Om Huun* shimmered below.

"This is a *rongjön*," he said. "A 'self-arising' image. The Jokhang is full of them. The sword, buddha eyes and Tibetan letters you see have materialized here during the past ten years, miraculously manifesting on the wall. No one paints them. They just appear, getting brighter and sharper every day. Everywhere you go in Tibet you'll see such rongjöns. Paintings like this are unusual. Most of the time they seem to be little statues of Tara or Guru Rimpoche, growing from the walls of meditation caves."

I moved around the painting, watching the eyes follow me. They were sharp and spooky and seemed to be illuminated, somehow, from within. Had they gotten there all by themselves? I thought not; but the issue, I understood, was completely beside the point. The rongjön, like nearly everything else in Tibetan Buddhism, is a metaphor, pointing unerringly to a beautiful secret truth. Everything, after all, is self-arising. Where did the four of us come from? What gave birth to the animals, the trees and the rocks? Every last thing on this Earth is a rongjön, self-arising, manifesting itself from wild atoms and amino acids, a miracle of energy and chance. What are humans but the Earth's own eyes, regarding itself? And what is our galaxy but a huge spinning rongjön, a self-arising jewel careening through limitless space?

o   o   o

We left the Jokhang, stepped carefully between prostrating pilgrims and began walking clockwise around the barkor. Merchants lined both sides of the cobblestone kora, selling everything from amulets to saddles. I bought some prayer flags and stopped at a table covered with Buddhas, but Gary pulled me away.

"You can shop later," he said. "If you start now we'll be here forever."

Halfway around the kora from the main Jokhang entrance we turned into a narrow alley. Kathy led us through a wooden archway and turned right. We suddenly found ourselves in the sunny courtyard of a small but obviously important temple. A huge crowd of pilgrims—mostly ancient men and women with long, rootlike teeth—sat in rows on the ground, muttering prayers and spinning dull copper prayer wheels.

"This is Meru Nyingma," Kathy said, "the Lhasa residence of the Nechung Oracle. Everyone you see is deeply immersed in an annual ritual. They'll be here every day, probably for three months, until they've chanted a total of three hundred million mantras."

In the temple's dark, musty interior, a fifty-one-year-old monk sat on a carpeted bench. Gary and Kathy sat on either side of him, conversing in a hodgepodge of Tibetan and English.

"Lobsang's come here from Drepung monastery," Gary explained. "It's about ten miles out of town. Two members of his family, including his father, were killed during the Chinese occupation in 1959."

The monk's bitterest complaint, though, was not the murder of his family. It was the dismantling of Tibet's traditional educational system, and the fact that the Tibetan language was hardly taught in the schools anymore. Almost all instruction, the monk reported, was now in Chinese.

"The main part of Tibetan Buddhism is the educational system," Gary translated, "and its guts have been ripped out. If you're a monk or a nun you really can't go much beyond the fifth grade level. Past that point there just aren't any teachers. That's what you hear so many Tibetans refugees saying in India: that they went there to continue their religious education. It's simply impossible in Tibet."

Kathy shook her head. "It's been bad for years, but this is a particularly awful time. People feel totally helpless. Four weeks ago, when the Clinton administration delinked human rights from trade and granted most-favored-nation status to China again, the Tibetans who heard about it walked around telling each other that 'we've lost our best friend.'

"Just after the vote," she continued, "there was a crackdown. Meetings were called of all the local work groups. That's how things are under Chinese communism: Everyone is part of a work group. Anyway, at these meetings, the Chinese officials told the Tibetans, 'Okay, you've lost your only ally. America's turned its back on you; now you're going to have to do things our way.'"

Her comments became unbearably poignant when, as we stood up to leave, Gary thanked the monk for his gracious company. Lobsang waved him off, embarrassed.

"Don't thank me," he said. "I thank *you*. America is such a great friend of the Dalai Lama."

There was no sarcasm in his voice. Lobsang was completely sincere, wisely cognizant of the vast gap that so often exists between a people's moral sentiment and their government's economic policy.

Two Views of Lhasa

Gary and Kathy would be in Lhasa only a few more days. At the end of the week they'd travel south, toward Everest Base Camp, and celebrate Kathy's fortieth birthday in a secret, sacred cave.

Before they left we took one long day-hike together. Hitching a ride in the back of a truck, we made our way to the northeastern edge of the Lhasa Valley. Up in the foothills was a small nunnery that even Gary, the consummate Tibet trekker, had never visited. On the nunnery's roof, a dozen anis waltzed back and forth with primitive earth pounders, singing with all their hearts as they compacted loose dirt into a dense, waterproof surface. Their tools looked like wheels for the Flintstone-mobile: heavy, discus-shaped stones—about eight inches in diameter—with long wooden poles jammed into crude holes bored in their centers.

Kathy took a long swallow from Holly's water bottle, and pointed her chin at the workers. "What's interesting," she said, "is that, before 1950, there were no wheels used for transportation in Tibet. None whatsoever. The central activity of people's lives was pilgrimage, but this was always carried out either on horse or, more often, on foot. It was that direct contact, that intimacy with the land that created the deep spirituality so prevalent in Tibetans even today; that sense of the holiness, the power of the land."

We left the nunnery and began to climb a long, rocky ridge leading toward the ruins of an old monastery. I'd forgotten how utterly exhausting it is to hike at high altitude. Lhasa itself sits at 12,000 feet; by the time we reached the ruined gompa I was gasping for breath. Gary's altimeter read 14,200.

Lhasa Valley spread out below us, a magical scene. The Dalai Lama's monastic fortress rose from the landscape like a crystalline outcropping, white and purple, and I instantly understood Frank Lloyd Wright's admiration.

But the massive Potala and dramatic crags surrounding the Lhasa Valley weren't all that we saw. Down on the northern outskirts of the city, rows of bright tin roofs marked two of Tibet's most notorious prisons: places where, even as we watched, monks and nuns were being tortured with electric cattle prods, thrust naked into tanks of freezing water, hung by their wrists with their arms tied behind their backs.

"And the most incredible thing," Gary said, "is that some of the worst torturers are Tibetans. Not only that; the most brutal and sadistic ones are Tibetan *women*."

"But how can that be?" I asked. "How can they do it?"

"It's a way of being accepted, of getting in with the Chinese. Like we told you this morning: Subsidized medical care has just been suspended for all native Lhasans, except those considered 'heroes' by the Chinese. Well, there are your heroes: right down there, torturing their fellow Tibetans in the Drapchi Prison."

Himalayan Griffin vultures circled in the air over our ridge, no doubt aware that we had run out of water. The uplifted earth was peppered with purple phlomis and primula, wild roses and asters. Shrikes and hoopoes flipped among the trees, and shape-shifting clouds tumbled through the stratosphere like confetti in God's own kaleidoscope. I unpacked my string of prayer flags, and wondered if I'd ever been in a place more beautiful and grim.

· 38 ·

To: Allen Noren, O'Reilly & Associates
From: Jeff Greenwald, Lhasa, Tibet
Subject: Big World/Live from the Yak Hotel

Sitting on a worn green sofa in the courtyard of Lhasa's famous Yak Hotel, my eyes and nose full of smoke from the wood-burning stove that heats the showers. The sky was thick and gray this morning, threatening rain, but by now, noon, it's broken up into pearlescent cumulus clouds. The sun is foundry-white here at 12,000 feet, and the air is thin, but after a few days you hardly notice it (unless you try to climb even a few feet higher . . . then you're wheezing for breath).

Seven years have passed since my last visit to Tibet. Lhasa, still the spiritual and political center of this high plateau, remains an occupied city, and thanks to an ongoing population transfer the Tibetans are rapidly becoming a minority in their own land. Nonetheless, there is still magic and mystery to be found here, and the spirit of the Tibetan people flows as an indomitable undercurrent—seething below broad avenues lined with Chinese restaurants, beneath the watchful eyes of the omnipresent police and under glitzy billboards portraying, in Tomorrowland graphics, the new, industrialized Lhasa envisioned for the new millennium.

Lhasa is a city of hidden worlds, havens of wisdom and compassion tucked beneath and between the fingers of a merciless Chinese grip. It is a city of musty temples painted in van Gogh blues and yellows, prayer rooms thick with the smell of burning ghee, the eyes of wrathful deities staring down from beneath gilded crowns, lone monks sitting on worn carpets and reciting thousand-page sutras as they bang rhythmically on broad drums with fiddle-fern drumsticks.

But the social and political mood here in this city of 170,000 is glum, following Bill Clinton's decision to separate human rights concerns from the renewal of China's most-favored-nation status. The Tibetan people, under the thumb of the Chinese since 1959, had felt that by conducting their campaign for self-determination with honesty, civility and nonviolence they would win support from the most powerful democracy on Earth. They have learned that they were wrong; that the economic perks to be gained from kowtowing to China outweigh all other concerns.

Chinese response to the White House decision was instant and severe. Less than twenty-four hours after Tibetan Voice of America broadcast the news, Chinese party officials called meetings of local Tibetan work groups and informed the citizenry that the days of leniency were over. Subsidized medical care was suspended, and taxes on Tibetan shopkeepers were doubled. "There's no point in complaining," the officials said. "No one's going to help you anymore." In response the merchants closed their shops and staged a strike, massing in front of the regional tax offices. It was a long and nasty afternoon; seventeen people were beaten, and seven of them were hospitalized. Five of the organizers are now languishing in prison.

"There's no doubt," a well-informed expatriate journalist told me, "that the Chinese were acting very cautiously while the United States kept an eye on them. Incidents of torture had plummeted, and the Tibetans adamantly believed it was thanks to American pressure. Amnesty International and Asia Watch had a hand as well, but they themselves can *do* nothing. What everyone is concerned about now, with the human rights agenda removed from MFN status, is that the incidents of torture are going to go right back up to where they were before. There are already signs that this is the case. Since the announcement, demonstrators are being publicly beaten, stomped and dragged off to prison. We don't know what's going on *inside* the prisons, but we do know this: The police do what they're told. If they're warned not to be unneccesarily rough, they're not. If they're told otherwise, they beat the hell out of everybody.

"China's leaders," he continued, "are very smart. They always say, *No pressure! China will never submit to meddling in its internal affairs!* They maintain a very hard line, and they're experts at bluffing. But if the United States had any sense, any spine, it would have realized that there are infinite shades of gray. You *can* push China. You *must*. You absolutely must prove to China that you are not a nation that will capitulate just because China demands that you capitulate. Once you've done that, you're finished. You are never, ever again considered strong or credible by China again.

"I'll tell you what's happening right now; China is gloating. The very night the announcement came through—all night long and all through the next day—there were meetings on every level, from work groups to party officials, discussing how China had beaten America and deciding how local policy was going to be reformulated in that light. And the very night the MFN decision was announced, the staff of Drapchi Prison—the official penitentiary here, with two hundred sixty prisoners—threw a party! They feasted, they sang, and they made drunken speeches about how America had been defeated by China."

o   o   o

Outside on the streets one sees few signs of tension. Lhasa is a strange, gagged city where every new setback is met, superficially, with equanimity; where Sonam, returning to his restaurant from a meeting in which he learned that his taxes would be doubled, greeted my worried glance with a forced smile. "Good news today, very good news!" There is no sign of trouble despite rumors of recent arrests in the monasteries; no sign of social unrest even though, one week ago, a Tibetan man whose pregnant wife had died on the doorstep of the local hospital—he couldn't raise the 1,000-yuan "deposit" now required for her admission—returned with a pistol, killing two of the hospital staff before shooting himself.

To the unschooled eye, life proceeds unchanged. Tourists are hauled in minibuses up the rear ramp of the Potala—the Dalai Lama's former residence, now converted into a museum—and shown around by Chinese guides. How many realize that their tour of the Potala, conducted *counterclockwise* through the altar rooms, is a snickering insult to the exiled leader? The spectacular monastery, stripped of its treasures, has become a cash cow. Chinese tourists pose on its roof in Tibetan clothes for souvenir photographs. Meanwhile, a few miles west, the Norbu Lingka—the Dalai Lama's Summer Palace—has been converted into, of all things, a zoo.

The ultimate irony, though, is found on the barkor, the circular flea market surrounding the Jokhang. There, browsing among felt hats and mass-produced prayer wheels, naïve foreigners purchase colorful woven wristbands, never suspecting that these coveted emblems of political solidarity with the Tibetans are now manufactured and marketed by the occupying Chinese.

o   o   o

But I haven't spent much time in the city. Most of my visit has involved daylong excursions to the spectacular monasteries and valleys lying several hours, by road, from the capital.

Yesterday's trip to Tsurphu was a case in point. I made the expedition with Holly Wissler (an old friend from Kathmandu) and Bill Thompson, a former *National Geographic* photographer who, having spent years shooting cigarette ads for Marlboro, came to Tibet to reexamine his priorities and spiritual path.

We woke up at five-thirty and hit the road an hour later, the sky still powdered with hanger-on stars, the barely waxed moon beaming so bright that you could pick out the remains of Apollo 11's *Eagle* with the naked eye.

Leaving Lhasa, we motored across a rugged landscape that was once an ocean floor, now uplifted into sharp reefs of stone. Velvet meadows stretched to the bases of gray hills that rose vertically toward the sky. Smoke plumed from distant villages, their salt-white houses festooned with prayer flags. The moon was sinking toward the jagged precipices, appearing fragile as a soap bubble, and we stopped the Montero to view the sphere through binoculars.

Standing on the roadside, watching Earth's moon disappear behind the gem-colored meadows of Central Tibet, I found it impossible to believe that anything so perfect as this planet of ours could actually exist. This tiny marble, this vapor-shrouded ball bearing rolling around a middle-aged star on the barren hip of curved space, seemed so unbearably beautiful that I almost felt unworthy. Who the hell are we, anyway? What are we doing here? What's the motive, the meaning, the cause? Is it all, as the Tibetans maintain, an illusion, a completely subjective manifestation of our five gross senses? If so it is a magnificent one, peerless in imagination, staggering in its variety. There can be no question of our deserving it or not. It is ours completely, and we belong to it absolutely. Our fates are eternally and inextricably interwined.

We turned from the main highway up into the Tsurphu Valley. Now we had entered paradise. Fields of mustard, neon-yellow, covered either side of the rough dirt track, and simple carts pulled by donkeys hove aside to let our Montero lumber past. We were closer to the villages now, and climbing. Yaks grazed in the meadows, and the smells of tea, grass and burning dung commingled with the dust. Anyone who has seen a rice paddy in season, or walked through a Himalayan meadow at 12,000 feet, knows that something completely indescribable can happen to chlorophyll. Under certain conditions, it reacts to sunlight the way a cat reacts to catnip.

Continuing up the valley, we followed a river that churned gray stones and branched out into ingenious irrigation schemes that had filled the landscape with rich crops. Bill forced the vehicle to a stop every five or ten minutes, leaping from the car to take slide after slide of villagers, landscapes, yaks.

"This place is a landscape photographer's dream," he whispered reverently, holding an 18 percent gray card in front of his Olympus lens. "Just incredible."

"You know," I said to him, "you really have got to stop doing those cigarette commercials. The karma's just plain lousy."

"I know it. I *have* quit. That's why I'm here. To decide what comes next. Like I told you, I want to start making children's films."

A few small horses grazed in a nearby field. We somehow got onto the subject of the Marlboro man, whom Bill had photographed several thousand times.

"Any time you open up *Time* or *Newsweek* and see that guy in an ad, chances are almost one hundred percent it's my photograph," he said.

The Marlboro men aren't models, he explained, but handpicked "real cow-boys," completely capable of roping a steer while galloping along at thirty-five miles per hour.

"Did you work with the original guy?" Holly asked.

"Yup. Darryl Winfield. Sure did. Fantastic guy. Everybody thinks he's dead."

"That's true," I said. "He died of lung cancer."

"Complete bullshit," Bill snorted. "He's alive and well and living in Wyoming. He consults with us on every shoot. The guy is a very heavy smoker, but he isn't dead yet. I know; I was playing cards with him when the story came out on the wire. His wife's sister called with condolences, but Darryl's wife didn't know what the hell she was talking about. 'He's right here, playing gin with Bill,' she said. But somehow the rumor got started, and everybody believes it."

Holly, riding in the front seat, glanced back at him. "You smoke?"

"Hell no!" Bill shook his head violently. "I can't stand cigarettes."

o   o   o

Our destination was the home of the seventeenth Karmapa, the ten-year-old reincarnation of the sixteenth Karmapa, who died of cancer in Chicago. I'd seen pictures of this new Karmapa everywhere. He has a round face, flat nose and vastly intelligent black eyes. He had better be in-telligent; the young lama has been chosen (by dubious means, some claim) to head a religious sect worth somewhere between $500 million and $1.2 billion (making him the only kid in the world worth more than Macaulay Culkin).

It was our collective goal to visit the boy and collect blessings from him. For while the Dalai Lama is the political and temporal leader of the Tibetan Buddhist religion, the Karmapa occupies an equally lofty spiritual apex. Far older than the Gelug sect (over which the Dalai Lamas hold sway), the Karma lineage combines ancient teachings and profound mag-ical powers. The Karmapa's most potent spiritual ally is a black hat, made from the hairs of a thousand fairies, which he wears during specific rituals. I was present when the sixteenth Karmapa performed the Black Hat cere-mony in Santa Barbara in 1981, four years before his death. During the entire event he kept his hand firmly planted on the huge hat's crown. When I questioned one of the attendants afterward, he told me why. "His Holiness holds the hat," the monk said, "so it will not fly away."

The monastery where the young Karmapa lived was a sprawling com-plex of chalk-white and maroon buildings, destroyed during the Cultural Revolution but completely rebuilt since 1990. We parked in a broad dirt lot alongside half a dozen other minibuses and jeeps. The Karmapa's daily blessing, we were told, would occur promptly at one; this would give us just enough time to complete the kora, or devotional circuit, along the towering cliffs behind the monastery grounds.

Following the directions in Gary McCue's guidebook we set off to the north, passing high walls covered with intricately carved *mani* stones. Sheep, goat and yak skulls were piled on cairns, engraved with the mantra of Chenrezig: *Om mani padme huun.* By the river, white nomad tents with blue Tibetan motifs billowed in the breeze.

The kora was an arduous walk, climbing steeply to an altitude of over 15,000 feet. Prayer flags fluttered from high crags, delivering blessings to the incessant wind. Caves used by past Karmapas and itinerant saints, cut into the cliff walls centuries ago, were now enshrined within white-washed *lakhangs* (hermitages), and within their protective walls I spied monks and nuns brewing butter tea. Bits of hair and yak wool clung to the branches of wild rosebushes, which perfumed the air with an alpine ambrosia I've come to associate, now and forever, with Tibet. Far below, the monastic complex spread out in a series of interlinked roofs. Scores of pilgrims were already massing in the parking lot.

Holly and I stopped for a water break, eating waxy Chinese chocolate bars and feeling deliriously happy. For an individual who makes his living complaining, I found it a highly threatening situation.

Five minutes later Bill Thompson caught up with us, enraptured by an encounter he'd just had. About five hundred meters down the trail, he had been invited into a small lakhang by a group of monks. They had poured him a cup of butter tea and, reaching over, sprinkled a fine powder into the cup. When Bill looked closely, holding the cup to the light, he saw that the powder was pure gold.

This was obviously a fabulous blessing, and I was keen to have a cup of this auspicious tea myself. I ran back down the kora, searching high and low for the lakhang he had described. Finally I located what might have been the place—but it was inhabited only by a young ani who poured me some watery tea and wanted to charge me half a yuan for it. It wasn't until I'd wasted twenty minutes running up and down the trail like a madman that I realized the truth: This had been a blessing for Bill and Bill alone. Nothing that happens in Tibet—nothing of importance—can ever be duplicated; and not every miracle is for everybody.

o   o   o

At twenty minutes til one, at a signal we failed to recognize, all of the Tibetan pilgrims in the parking area made a beeline for the monastery doors. Bill, Holly and I joined the back of the line, clutching our silk kata scarves. We crept up the stairs, arriving finally in a foyer where the Tibetans were relieved of their knives.

The gesture was not for show. There has been some controversy over this ten-year-old's appointment, and there is reason to fear for his life. Not from the Chinese; the occupying power is pleased to have the new Karmapa in Tibet, where he can be carefully monitored. No, the threat to this black-eyed boy comes from a rival Karma sect in India that claims that it, too, has discovered a new, more legitimate Karmapa. Aside from the giddy assets involved, the future of the Tibetan people may be at stake. The Gelug sect—of which the Dalai Lama is titular head—wrested power from the Karma sect during the Mongol invasions of the fifteenth century, and some people think that the death of the current, fourteenth Dalai Lama might provide a golden opportunity for a reversal of the Karma school's historical fortunes. Deadly intrigue fires the Tibetan sects; one is reminded of the struggle for power within the Christian papacy.

After relinquishing my camera to a poker-faced monk, I entered a very obedient line winding into the sanctum sanctorum of the reincarnate lama.

Having seen so many impressive photographs of his young eminence, I was a touch disappointed. The seventeenth Karmapa sat on his throne with a vaguely bored expression, picking his nose. The kata scarf I'd brought was plucked away by an attendant, who motioned me forward. A cloth amulet, suspended from a hook, hung in front of my face. It was connected to the Karmapa's hand by a string. I was directed to touch my head to the amulet. It was, I deduced, a spiritual version of a tin-can telephone; the boy's blessing would travel through the string (I couldn't help but wonder if string had been discovered to be the best conductor for this purpose) and pass from the amulet into my skull. Waiting to feel something, I tarried too long. An attendant hustled me onward, and a third handed me a piece of red yarn to tie around my neck. This was the official Karmapa blessing, certified evidence of my pilgrimage to Tsurphu.

I tied the yarn in place, recalling the words of a gruff Australian man I met last night. "It can't hurt," he'd said of his own red cord, "and I'm not afraid of it."

o   o   o

Afterward we picnicked on the banks of the river, smearing sunblock on our necks and talking about the future of Tibet.

"Ten years from now," Bill bemoaned, "this whole place might be underwater. The Chinese have plans to dam every valley in Tibet in order to power their development schemes."

He was probably wrong, but I took his point. There is definitely something about visiting remote places these days that feels, somehow, like waiting for the end of the world. During fifteen years of travel writing I've seen places develop so rapidly that I simply can't bear to visit them again. And the most drastic changes, it seems, have occurred within the past decade. The number of globe-hoppers is increasing exponentially, while the information revolution is bringing the tools of communication—and, by association, capitalism—to every corner of the map. There are very few human beings who wouldn't jump at the chance to have a television or telephone in their homes; soon enough, the list will include computer links and Internet access.

One dares not complain about this. It's the most obnoxious brand of reverse cultural imperialism to decry the desire of indigenous peoples to possess the tools of "progress" that we find so indispensable. Unfortunately, the introduction of these new tools—and the power sources they require—is usually followed by a shift away from traditional values and appropriate technology. It's heartbreaking to imagine how the process might affect Tsurphu. The road up the valley will be paved, inviting unbridled sightseeing traffic; countless restaurants and snack stalls will open, creating a major litter and human waste disposal problem; the simple wooden carts that ply the present dirt road will be elbowed aside by tourist buses and Land Cruisers, driving out local farmers and filling the pristine valley with smoke and spilled oil.

We had already seen one such harbinger of Tsurphu's future that morning, on our drive up from Lhasa. A mother was working in the fields, spraying her crops with a new Chinese insecticide. The breeze carried the vapors back toward the woman, wafting them past her head and over the infant tied upon her back.

o   o   o

Late in the afternoon, we walked to the outskirts of Tsurphu and climbed a low hill used for "sky burials": an enlightened Tibetan tradition in which one's physical body, having served its purpose, is offered as a gift to the Earth.

The method is always the same. The bodies, set in fetal position, are carried up the hill in rough burlap sacks. They are laid out flat, facedown, on slabs of stone. The vultures arrive at this point, but at a word from one of the *tomdens*—monk-butchers specially trained in the art of sky burial—they scatter to overlooking crags.

First, the soles of the feet are flayed. The corpses are then split lengthwise, down the back, arms and legs. With practiced motions the tomden slices the flesh away, tossing it onto the ground. When he has removed as much meat as he can, the monk steps away and shouts.

"Shey, shey!!" (Eat!!) The vultures descend in droves, tearing at the corpse until it is reduced to a skeleton. Then, at a word, they scatter off again. Now, using mallets and saws, the tomden smashes the skeleton to pieces. He throws the bones into a pit and, adding *tsampa* flour, grinds the cranium and femurs and teeth, the hips and pelvis and vertebrae, into a fine mash. The vultures are called in again. When they depart, the slab has been picked clean.

The tomdens and birds of prey had, of course, missed a few small pieces here and there. Wandering around the hillside, Holly and I found a lower jaw with four molars intact; the ball joint of a hip socket; scattered ribs and bits of random bone. Empty burlap sacks clung to the bases of stone cairns, and an entire tree was covered with long tresses of white and gray hair. Pieces of clothing, eaten through by the elements, were everywhere.

Standing on that hillside under the naked sun, walking on a landscape littered with human bones, I was reminded of the last place I'd seen such a macabre sight. But I could think of no greater contrast, at least on a spiritual level, than the one between the sky burial site of the Tsurphu Valley—where the bodies of the dead are offered back to the Earth in a spirit of gratitude and generosity—and the heart-wrenching killing fields I'd visited in Cambodia.

o   o   o

The mustard was brilliant in the late evening light, a psychedelic yellow that swept up the valley like a spotlight. A crucible sun illuminated the peaceful villages scattered beneath curls of smoke and oscillating prayer flags. This was It: a Big World of earthly delights, set higher than the crest of Mount Rainier. We knew just how lucky, how blessed and lucky, we were to be there.

My only hope was that the prayers of this occupied nation would finally be answered, so that the people who actually belonged here—the generous, courageous Tibetans—might feel as blessed and lucky themselves.

· 39 ·

Deconstructionist Diversion VI

At this point, savvy reader, you are probably asking yourself a pointed question: *What about Kailas? I thought this guy was trying to get to Kailas....*

He was. I was. At least, I thought I was. And let me tell you, there was no lack of opportunity to get there. Hand-lettered notices, tacked, taped and glued to the swarming bulletin board at the Yak Hotel, announced numerous expeditions to the holy mountain. All were leaving from Lhasa, at a fraction of the cost of the Wilderness trip. One of them, in fact, was being assembled by my friend Joel, the peripatetic yogi who had taught me my morning yoga regimen. Working with a Russian-born New Yorker named Boris and a local travel agency, he'd organized a month-long, two-vehicle trip to western Tibet leaving (for the purposes of this chapter) tomorrow. The expedition could take a total of seven people. Six had already signed on; Joel and Boris invited me to complete the mix.

It was the perfect opportunity to visit Kailas, do it cheaply, and perform the pilgrimage with a group of friends, Buddhists and scholars who had lived in Asia (except for Boris) for years.

I said no.

It was a hard choice, but I had my reasons. A few of them even made sense. Primarily, of course, there was the time factor. It was the first of July; according to my original plan I should have already been in Indonesia or Australia, if not on my way home. The amount of time I had to actually *write* this book was dwindling down to nothing, and the pressure was ringing in my ears.

The next thing to consider was my energy level. I'd been traveling for more than six months; the very prospect of a month in a truck, driving west to Kailas and back again, made my kidneys beat at my lower ribs in protest. I know that travel writers aren't supposed to get tired of traveling, and that every moment of torture translates to pages of side-splitting anecdote, but it seemed I could undergo enough colorful misery by simply continuing my eastward course.

Ultimately, though, it was a question of balance. It seemed to me, quite honestly, that Kailas would no longer *fit* in this book. Kailas is the Center of the Universe; a kora around the sacred mountain is a once-in-a-lifetime event. Suppose I *did* go with Joel and Boris? The entire trip, epiphanic as it might be, could not be given more than two or three chapters. It didn't seem fair. Kailas weighed more; it deserved a book of its own. Someday, maybe even next year, I'd return to Tibet, circle

Kailas, and write that book. For now, though, I'd stick with my original plan: a kora around the planet. It ought to be enough. . . .

o   o   o

But continuing eastward from Lhasa was hardly a stroll in the park. There were only two ways to do it, neither of them easy. What it boiled down to, as usual, was determining which one was possible.

The southerly road from Tibet into China is essentially a military and truck route. Indeed, the word *road* is something of an exaggeration. Wild, serpentine and ill maintained, the track winds around the base of Namche Barwa—one of the highest Himalayan peaks—and splits in two near Bamda. From that point one can continue on a northerly route (toward Sichuan Province) or keep to the south, skirting the Indian and Burmese borders and arriving, one or two weeks later (barring avalanches or breakdowns), in Chengdu.

There are no buses or public transportation—nor do the Chinese issue travel permits for "aliens"—along this route. It would be necessary to hitch rides on trucks, diligently avoiding the checkpoints.

The alternative to that route was the Tibet-Qinghai Highway. Completed by the People's Liberation Army in 1954, the T-Q is the highest road in the world, rarely dipping below 13,000 feet. It runs due north from Lhasa, terminating in the garrison town of Golmud in Qinghai Province. From there, trains carry passengers east to Gansu.

After considerable research, I chose the Golmud route. The thought of hitching didn't particularly worry me, nor was I cowed by the police; my main fear was of being buried alive under a million tons of mud. The Sichuan route, after dropping off the Tibetan Plateau, would enter a mountainous, jungly region at the height of the monsoon. July and August are the mud slide months, and the road beyond Namche Barwa would almost certainly be impassable. I could go for it anyway, but chances were good I'd emerge from my odyssey a few millennia later than scheduled, in the approximate condition of Lindow man.

Besides, the Tibet-Qinghai Highway held a sexy appeal. Not only was it the highest road on Earth, it had the added panache of being exactly as old as I was. It would be interesting to see which of us had held up better.

o   o   o

Joel's expedition left for Mount Kailas the morning of July first. Fighting a cold and plagued by second thoughts, I watched the voyagers load up. It was too late to change my mind—they'd already found a seventh rider, and the trucks were filled to capacity—but that didn't stop me from indulging in pointless regrets. One of the most difficult lessons I faced on my planetary kora was learning to trust, for better or worse, the intuitive process that guided my decisions. If I was not going to Kailas, there must be a reason.

An hour after they left, I discovered what that reason was.

One Day in the Life of Ghang Sik Dondrup

I was standing behind the counter of the Potala Pharmacy, squeezing shots of Buddha brand nasal spray up my snout, when the nomads walked in.

There were two of them, in their late twenties. Both men wore olive-green fatigue jackets, and their long, unwashed faces descended beneath ragged, fur-lined hats. The older of the two carried a cardboard box, riddled with airholes and tied with a leather belt.

They walked up to the counter and set the box down, undoing the strap and waving the pharmacist over for a look. He peered into the box and shook his head rapidly, backing away.

When the pharmacist retreated I took his place. I couldn't quite make out the creature inside. I thought it might be a fox, or a badger, but its head was buried in a corner. The younger brother reached in, placed his hand under its middle and pulled it out of the box.

As he set it on the floor my brain did a backflip. I was looking at one of the world's most beautiful and elusive animals: a baby snow leopard.

The cub was a healthy creature, muscular and plump, creeping across the cement on lunar-lander paws. Its coat was thick silk, a dappled storm-gray that would ultimately turn blizzard-white. The leopard couldn't have been more than a month old; when I held it against my chest it nuzzled into my arm, nursing on the non-colorfast fabric of my short-sleeved shirt.

I looked at it, it looked at me, and a chill ran up my spine; for I recognized, beyond question or doubt, the ice-blue eyes of the pujari at Pashupatinath. I understood at last what the sorceress had been preparing me for—and knew that it was an obligation I could not refuse.

The snow leopard wandered out onto the sidewalk. A small crowd gathered, forming a semicircle around the cub. One of the onlookers—a student, guessing from the plastic pencil box he carried—spoke a bit of English. Through him I was able to learn a little bit about the animal, and the circumstances of its abduction.

The nomads had come from a village in the mountains above Yang-

bajain, six hours by truck from Lhasa. A snow leopard had been deci-
mating their livestock, they claimed, and they had been forced to de-
stroy it. After shooting the cat—an adult female—the nomads
discovered the extra mouth that had compelled her to stalk human settlements in the first place. They bundled up the cub and brought it to
the city in hopes of selling it. The reason for their visit to the pharmacy
was suddenly clear: Snow leopard bones are a prized Chinese tonic, and
the animal could fetch a high price from an interested buyer.

"How much do they want for it?" I asked.

My young interpreter furnished the reply: "Two thousand yuan."
This was exactly $232.56.

I was in a quandary. To begin with, I certainly didn't have 2,000 yuan
on me. But even if I did—even if I were to buy this snow leopard out-
right—what would I do with it? Baby snow leopards are adorable, but
they grow up fast. And while a carnivorous Himalayan beast would undoubtedly be a useful sidekick in Oakland, the logistics of bringing
home a member of the world's most endangered species were beyond me.

I watched in conflicted frustration as the nomads placed the docile
cub back into its box, fixed the leather strap and left.

I followed them. They seemed bewildered by my presence, but as
they spoke no English there was literally nothing they could say. We
crossed Xingfu Donglu, the busy main avenue, and made our way toward the People's Cultural Park.

The woman collecting admission fees exchanged a few words with
the nomads and spoke into an intercom. We were sooned joined by a
dour-faced man in a blue blazer. Whether he was Chinese or Tibetan I
could not tell. He pushed his black bicycle toward a compound of official-looking buildings, and we followed close behind. My presence did
not please the man. He turned around, regarded me with disdain and
waved me back; I could come no farther. I ignored him. A minute or
two later, as we were about to enter the compound itself, he demanded
that I leave. I looked him dead in the eye, and spoke calmly.

"You listen to me, pal. I come with this animal. If you want to call
the police, be my guest. Nothing less than physical force is going to
keep me away from that cub."

My bravado was lost on this non-English-speaker, but he nodded
gamely. He offered no objection as I tailed him into a narrow, whitewashed alleyway, where I was immediately attacked by guard dogs.

There was a rusted cleaver lying on a nearby oil drum. I seized it,
brandishing the blade at the charging hounds. They zipped nimbly by,
renewing their challenge at a safe distance. I kept hold of the weapon as
we were led through the alley and into the man's home.

We entered an open courtyard, a lush terrarium filled with exotic cacti and blooming bushes. A parrot perched on a swing, shitting profusely onto the ground. In a nearby room I could see a wide-screen television with a large clock sitting on top. Gaudy chandeliers and knickknacks were much in evidence, staples of the Han Chinese taste in consumer goods. His wife held the dogs at bay, and all three of us were offered chairs. I set the cleaver down.

The cat was freed from its box. As it began lapping at puddles on the leaf-strewn cement, a loud debate ensued. Though I speak scant Tibetan, I comprehended the exchange. The animal, the man insisted, was not a snow leopard; its color was all wrong. The nomads disagreed, however, as did his wife. She left the courtyard and stepped into an adjoining room, returning a moment later with a rolled carpet beneath her arm. It was the pelt of a full-grown snow leopard, creamy white with prominent black spots, framed in a brocade of red Chinese silk. The nomads nodded, gesturing with their hands. Now the animal was small, they said; when it matured its coat would lighten, taking on the pearlescent hue of the carpet. The wife concurred: "*Chik paray*," she insisted over and over again, nodding first at the animal, then at the rug. "It's the same."

The snow leopard, it seemed, faced two possible fates: It could be ground up into an aphrodisiac, or crafted into a floor covering.

But the blazered official, for reasons I didn't understand, chose to pass. Perhaps he was biding his time; perhaps he was inhibited by my presence. The three of us quit the compound, taking the cardboard box with us.

We returned to the main avenue, where the nomads entered a small restaurant. I assumed they were stopping for lunch but, to my surprise, they ordered only warm milk for the cub. A few scraps of raw meat were also placed in the box, but the leopard seemed blasé. He was too young, I guessed, for a solid-food diet.

A small group of tourists came in. Their guide was Tibetan, a slight young man in a T-shirt and jeans. I explained the situation, and he agreed to interpret while I asked a few more questions.

The Tibetan nomads, I learned, did not want to see the cub harmed—though they apparently had nothing against selling the animal off to a Chinese merchant who had no such qualms.

By now another crowd had gathered, composed mostly of Tibetans. Through the interpreter, I advanced a plan. It was wrong to kill the snow leopard, I agreed. Though I had little cash, I knew other tourists who might. If one of them would buy the leopard, we could donate the animal to the local zoo.

The nomads smiled and slapped me on the back as the young interpreter walked me to the nearest phone.

I felt a slight twinge of panic, wondering what the hell I was getting myself into.

I phoned the Holiday Inn, angling for the wealthiest westerner in Lhasa. But Bill Thompson wasn't in his room.

All was not lost. I had one backup plan. If the nomads would agree to wait at the restaurant, I'd return to the Yak Hotel and speak with someone there. My interpreter put this suggestion forward, and the nomads nodded silently. As I was leaving the older one stepped forward, head down, muttering.

"He wants to come with you," the guide explained.

o   o   o

We caught a minibus to the intersection near Sonam's restaurant and walked to the Yak from there. The nomad was jittery, cowed by the presence of so many affluent foreigners. I took his hand and led him up the stairs, the cardboard box clutched beneath his arm.

During my week in Lhasa I'd had numerous intense conversations with Brock Owen, a soft-spoken Tibetan scholar from Georgia. Brock lived at the Yak almost full-time, poring over obscure manuscripts and cohabiting with Francesca, his beautiful Chilean girlfriend. I found his room, pushed aside the hanging brocade and knocked with my fingertips. Brock opened the door and squinted at me through the slit in the curtain.

"I'm with a Tibetan nomad who speaks no English," I said. "May we come in?"

o   o   o

Brock and Francesca were stunned by the sight of the snow leopard— stunned, and fatally charmed. I told them all I knew, and explained my plan for donating the cub to the zoo.

"But you cannot give it to the zoo!" Francesca cried, hugging the cub to her breasts. "It is a torture place. It is no better than death."

"She's right," Brock said. "The zoo is a joke. We'll have to find some other way to deal with it. But first things first: How much does this guy want?"

"Two thousand yuan."

Brock snorted. "*Jesus.* This is bullshit. Another classic scam. Know what he's doing? He's *ransoming* the animal. I mean, if he's so concerned about the cub, why doesn't he just give it to the zoo himself?"

I shrugged. "Maybe he's trying to recover the value of his lost live-stock. I don't know. And what do you mean, a 'scam'? Is this a common occurence? Have you seen other snow leopard cubs for sale?"

"No. . . ." Brock softened, and took the animal from Francesca. He scratched it between the ears. "You think he'll take a thousand?"

"Might as well offer; all he can say is no."

Brock set the cub back into its box, unlocked a green metal trunk and removed two bundles of 10-yuan notes. He counted out the money and placed the stacks on the carpet in front of the nomad.

"One thousand yuan," he said in Tibetan. "Take it or leave it."

The nomad smiled but shook his head. Brock calmly leaned over, collected the money, placed it back in his trunk and snapped the lock shut. "Good-bye," he said, and turned back to the manuscript he'd been leafing through when we walked in.

There was a beat, and the nomad coughed sharply. "He's changed his mind," Francesca guessed. Indeed he had. Brock silently reopened the trunk, removed the bills and handed them over. The nomad folded them into a thick wad with a huge, innocent grin on his face. He dropped into a crouch, and removed the leather strap from around the cardboard box. When he had recovered his belt he stood up to go.

"Wait a minute." Brock opened a drawer in his dresser and ex-tracted, from a small stack, a picture of the Dalai Lama. This he pre-sented to the nomad, who pressed it to his forehead with a prayer. Brock nodded, piercing our visitor with a stare.

"Just so he knows," he said quietly, "where our motivation comes from."

When the nomad had left, Francesca examined the cub. "He's a boy," she declared.

"A boy, hunh?" Brock sat down beside her. "Well, he obviously needs a name."

My own suggestion—Ralph—was quickly vetoed, as was Francesca's more poetic Spanish inspiration, Nubita.

"He's got to have a local name," Brock insisted. He pulled a Tibetan lexicon from a shelf and leafed through it knowledgeably. "Okay. Here we go. This is perfect: *Ghang Sik Dondrup.*"

"Meaning what?" Francesca was dubious.

"The Snow Lion Whose Every Wish Is Fulfilled."

o   o   o

Brock ran down to the corner to buy some human infant formula and a bottle; Francesca went off to find a larger box. When Brock returned he had a plan of sorts, though how it would be carried out was any-body's guess.

"The zoo is out," he drawled. "Somehow, we've got to get this ani-mal out of China. He has to be smuggled, overland, into Nepal. From there it's a matter of getting him into Darjeeling, India. There's an ex-cellent zoo there, with a special habitat where they breed and take care of snow leopards. That's what has to happen, and it has to happen soon—because this thing is going to grow. In another six weeks he'll be like this"—he spread his arms about three feet apart—"and he'll know how to use those claws."

The problems with smuggling the snow leopard out of Tibet were twofold. First of all, possession of any animal belonging to an endan-gered species was a criminal offense. The second problem was keeping the animal hidden in the interim. If confiscated by the authorities, it could command a very high price: thousands of dollars, Brock guessed.

Getting the snow leopard over the border would be the hard part. Once in Nepal, the situation eased. There were dozens of naturalists and wildlife specialists in Kathmandu, many of whom would know how to handle the animal. International phone calls could be made, faxes could be sent without fear of government snooping and a vast web of official and nonofficial allies could be recruited for help.

"I'll do it," Francesca offered. "I have to go to Nepal in a week. And I'm already smuggling things that are harder to hide than a snow leopard."

I raised my eyebrows. "Like what?"

"Like two hundred bottles of Chanel No. 5 perfume."

o   o   o

That evening I found Bill Thompson and brought him to the Yak. He fell in love with the animal and vowed to do whatever he could. He'd be flying back to the States the next day, and offered to use his network of *National Geographic* contacts to help the cause.

"The person I really need to call," he said, "is George Schaller. You've heard of him, right? He's the guy Peter Matthiessen trekked with in *The Snow Leopard*. I've worked with George; he's the director for science of the Wildlife Conservation Society in New York. He's done loads of stuff with Chinese pandas, and he's the leading expert on snow leopards as well. If anyone can help you, it's him."

This was excellent news. We thanked him profusely, and I took him out for a brandy and cheesecake before saying good-night.

o   o   o

I was awakened at 6:00 A.M. by a steady pounding at my door. It was Bill Thompson, on his way to the Lhasa airport. He was in a state.

"You'll never fucking believe this," he said. "I got back to my hotel last night, and just as I was opening my door the people in the next room came out. Guess who?"

It was a miracle. George Schaller, his wife, Kay, and a grasslands specialist named Dan Miller had checked into the Holiday Inn the night before, back from an assignment in Mongolia. Bill had told the naturalists about the snow leopard, and George had gone ape shit—not with enthusiasm, but with trepidation. Huge penalties awaited us if we were caught in possession of the animal—let alone smuggling him out of Tibet.

"Call Dan Miller this morning," Bill advised. I nodded groggily, freezing in my purple underpants. "Contact him first, and let him discuss the situation with George Schaller." We shook hands, and he left.

After breakfast I returned to my room to find a note from Miller. His advice—and Schaller's as well—was that we turn the cub over to the Tibet Forest Bureau, which would figure out what to do with him. At ten o'clock I called the Holiday Inn and spoke to Schaller personally. He agreed to come by, but only if he could bring a liaison from the bureau with him.

Brock and Francesca were livid.

"The minute any Chinese official knows about this it's finished," Brock said. "Why the hell can't Schaller come over here by himself? Is he too busy and important? Well, I'm sorry. The three of us are risking our necks over this animal, and I'm not willing to hand him over to the Chinese government at the first opportunity. I'd rather see him get to Kathmandu, regardless of the risks, than end up in a little cement box in some Chinese city, enriching a bunch of scumbag officials. These guys rent panda bears out for a million dollars a year to foreign zoos."

I telephoned Schaller again. "Listen," I said. "I've spoken with my friends, and we all agree. We'd like a candid meeting with you before getting any officials involved."

I'd expected an argument, but Schaller was surprisingly receptive. "Okay," he said. "I'll be at the Yak within an hour."

o   o   o

George Schaller was a tall man with a high forehead and the calm, nononsense mien of a Kansas City sheriff. He was capable, I guessed, of being entirely clinical; but as he stroked the cub we watched a lifetime of scientific objectivity melt away.

"In all my years studying snow leopards," he said, "I don't think I've ever seen a juvenile this young. He's. . . . Well, he's beautiful."

Brock and Francesca held hands, beaming like the surrogate parents they had become.

Both Dan Miller and Kay Schaller—a copper-haired woman who looked like she did her crossword puzzles in pen—concurred. The animal must be protected at any cost; the only question was how.

Schaller and Miller had meetings through the afternoon, but the six of us got together that evening for a brainstorming dinner at Sonam's. It was a bittersweet event, as Schaller examined and rejected various strategies for dealing with the cub.

"Forget the idea of taking him to Nepal," he warned. "Even if you can get him there—and that's a huge risk—he probably wouldn't last a week. Snow leopards live at very high altitude, where few microorganisms survive. Not only is Kathmandu eight thousand feet lower than Lhasa, it's the middle of the monsoon. There are dozens of diseases there that the animal has no natural immunity to. Within a couple of days you'll have a sick snow leopard on your hands—and what will you do then?"

"In that case," Francesca said, "why not just take him back into the mountains? At least he can fend for himself."

"Absolutely wrong," Schaller said. "Returning big cats to their natural habitats is extremely difficult. Snow leopards learn to hunt with their mothers; it would take months to wean the cub, and a year or more to train him to hunt in the wild. Even then, he'd probably only be able to take down domesticated animals like goats and sheep—which would eventualy lead him to the same fate as his mother."

"I understand the argument against smuggling him to Nepal," I said, "but can't you use your contacts to at least get him out of China? There must be a zoo that'll take him. Someplace like the Bronx Zoo, where there's a good snow leopard exhibit. . . ."

Schaller shook his head. "There's a problem with that, too. Since snow leopards are an endangered species, no reputable zoo will accept one without paperwork. It would be like a stolen Rembrandt showing up at the door of the Met; there's not a chance they would take it. The same would hold true for Darjeeling, or any other zoo."

Someday, he said—in a year or two, perhaps—it might be possible for Ghang Sik Dondrup to be sold or traded to a high-budget western habitat where he could live out his years in comfort (and, presumably, with company). Until then, there was only one solution. George and Kay would be leaving Lhasa in a week. They would discuss the matter with the Tibetan government, bring the cub to Beijing and use whatever clout they had to assure he was well taken care of. It was less than ideal, but it beat the alternatives.

"I guess the most important thing is that he lives." Francesca stared into her beer, her voice edged with bitterness. "But it's also his quality of life I'm thinking about. From everything I've heard the Beijing Zoo is horrible. They sell kids toy guns so they can pretend to shoot at the animals."

"Not this one." Kay handed Francesca a tissue and gave her husband a long look.

"He'll be all right," George Schaller said. "I'll do my best."

o   o   o

I left for Golmud the next morning. Peach and banana sellers lined the sidewalk near the main bus terminal, and I stocked up on fruit and water. Chinese police in green uniforms were everywhere. The Dalai Lama's birthday, Brock explained, was only four days away.

The Tibet-Qinghai bus looked like a soft-drink can that had been dropped from the top of the Empire State Building. I lashed my Endless Journey to the roof, climbed down and grasped Brock's hand.

"Did you ever stop to consider," he said, "that the entire reason for your trip—everything that went into thinking about it, writing the proposal, and doing it—might have all been a karmic scheme to save the life of that snow leopard?"

"If that's true," I replied, "it was worth every minute."

• 40 •

The Bardo of Phlegm

Riding on the Tibet-Qinghai bus was like watching a twenty-six-hour-long television documentary unreel across the windows in a single, unedited take.

The Kunlun Mountains rose into view, their soft white cones lifted above endless pastures filled with yak, cattle and, by morning, camels. Every few hours the driver stopped to let everyone get out and pee; a shameless line of exposed genitals, male and female, watered the dry ground alongside the bus. Less frequently we stopped to eat, ordering in tiny roadside restaurants that looked all right if you didn't look too closely, selecting ingredients from white enamel bowls containing cakes of firm *dofu*, onions, garlic cloves, dubious-looking mushrooms, tiny cauliflower florettes, potent green chilies and bovine eggplants. The food was tossed by handfuls into oil-slicked, Astrodome-sized woks perched over gas burners that roared like the north wind, an all-pervasive sound I never even noticed until the food was cooked and the flames shut down. I dug out a fresh bottle of Pepto-Bismol (I'd traded an issue of *Wired* for it in Lhasa) and toasted the chef with a pink nightcap.

Less comforting were the hellish condition of the road (I was a *much* younger forty), and the gurgling phlegm-fests of my fellow passengers—particularly the one seated directly behind me, whose marathon chain-smoking was broken only by lengthy operatic fits of retching regurgitation that unfailingly climaxed with a mason jar's worth of snot splattering onto the floor beside me. By night the dusty roads and frigid high-altitude temperature forced us to close the windows, turning the bus and its cargo into a tin of smoked sardines. Every stop—at one, three and five in the morning—admitted a breath of Arctic air that shriveled my balls into walnuts.

o   o   o

Is it fair to think of maps as "perfect" journalism?

Like journalism, cartography seeks to objectify, inform and even influence the course of history. Thanks to their famous precision, however, maps aren't often subject—like their brash and approximate cousin—to the scrutiny of public debate. They're viewed as sacrosanct, products of hard-nosed physical law rather than mere mortal contrivance.

Our reverence for maps has given them considerable power, benign and deadly. During the Middle Ages, for example, etchings portraying the world as a flat disk ringed by monsters effectively stifled exploration. When Columbus at last sailed west, he mistook the Bahamas for India; Native Americans are "Indians" to this day. On the other side of the globe, half a million citizens of India itself (a country whose name, incidentally, was coined by western invaders of the Indus Valley) died in bloody purges after a British cartographer rewrote the map of their country to establish Pakistan.

Those are severe examples. What was nagging at me, as we rolled through an area described by the Lonely Planet guidebook as the "Siberia of China," was something far more subtle.

We had entered a stark, dramatic landscape concealing labor camps, dumping grounds and nuclear-test sites. Until recently the entire area, called Amdo, was an integral part of Tibet. Today, it's not even part of the shrunken Tibet Autonomous Region. Faced with the tangible evidence of that fact—as I traced our route on my "official" map of China—I suddenly understood what was troubling me. Maps, because they *are* so visual and convincing, can be the ultimate tools of propaganda. All Tibetans under forty, I realized, had been indoctrinated with the idea—reinforced on every map they saw—that their nation was indelibly part of China.

o o o

But the land itself was magnificent, unfurling past the windows in a series of Abstract Expressionist brushstrokes. We rounded a snow-capped mountain crowned by a smaller, nipple-shaped peak; a flooded emerald meadow peppered with the black corns of yak herder tents; an enormous uplifted cliff that, riddled with every color of the rainbow, resembled a masterpiece of Turkish marbling.

I say *we*. . . . I was seated beside Karyn Smith, an effervescent, butter-brickle blonde who'd been traveling alone for six months. Back in March, while visiting Dharamsala, India, she'd met a guy who wanted to marry her and, what the heck, she'd said yes. They were traveling separately for now, but would soon reunite in southern China. Our routes would coincide as far as Chengdu.

Karyn carried a stack of *mobs:* fresh, crisp and virtually worthless bank notes. In the morning—after we'd been on the road more than twenty-four hours—she began tossing handfuls of them out the window.

"A Tibetan friend told me he likes to do it," she said. "Those nomad encampments are so poor; it must be fun for them to find a little bit of money." I smiled at her, and yawned; her eyes saucered wide in alarm. *"Oh my God."* Karyn gripped my knee with catastrophic urgency. "Do you know that your tongue is black?"

I could only sigh and sink deeply into my seat. "Not again. . . ."

There must have been moments when Odysseus, years after his return from the Trojan War, relaxed on a sofa with a glass of wine in his hand and muttered to Penelope, "You know, that was actually a pretty sweet trip." That's one of the strange things about traveling. The infinite highs and lows, tumbled around in memory, emerge with a lapidary smoothness. What is wonderful to begin with stays, somehow, wonderful, while even the most hellish agonies ultimately take on the ripe, fulsome aspect of a strong cheese.

And that, good reader, is how the ride to Golmud is immortalized in my memory: like an aged and stinky cheese that I'm proud to have eaten and will never, come hell or high water, eat again.

Lush Organic Nightmares

The train ride from Golmud to Xining, in "soft sleeper," was a lesson in relativity. The stained and soiled tablecloth thrown upon my collapsible tray rest seemed a four-star touch; the battered thermoses of hot water were an astonishing delight; the bean-bag pillows, filled with those tiny stones you always find in Chinese rice, provided no less comfort than a nap against Minerva's bosom. The ride itself was smooth, save for the frequent occasions when the train stopped or started, at which moments one was pitched rudely onto the floor. The only genuine drawback was the toilet. I thought I'd seen the worst this planet had to offer, but China Railways offered a brand-new standard compared with which the foulest *charpis* of Nepal seemed first-class.

The landscape of northern Qinghai rolled past our window for eighteen hours, a newscast of late-breaking geological textures. Just beyond Golmud the hills were Martian-red, poppy-seeded with round black stones. Lakes and rivers trickled into view, widened, and vanished; outcroppings of glittering pink stone ran up to our windows then fled back, like partners at a square dance.

Xining was first truly Chinese city I visited. Downtown was modern and sprawling, filled with municipal buses, kids on the backs of bicycles, pedestrian overpasses, alleyways lined with laundries and bakeries, blinking Chinese neon and gigantic statues of communist workers facing toward the future, united and unafraid.

I walked into a brightly lit pharmacy and displayed my tongue to the resident health care professional. He studied it, nodded brusquely and located a bottle of foul-smelling elixir, instructing me to rinse my mouth with the solution no fewer than eight times a day. But the vile prescription wasn't enough; I wanted answers. I combed through my anemic phrase book, lighting on the simplest query I could find. I pointed to the phrase, to my tongue and to the book again. *What is this?*

The pharmacist picked up a pencil and jotted down a few Chinese characters. They were meaningless to me.

"*Hei she tou,*" he announced imperatively. "*Hei she tou . . .*" When it became clear that no amount of repetition would make me understand, he grunted, disappeared into a back room and rematerialized with a tattered Chinese-English dictionary. After fifteen minutes of intense concentration he was satisfied with his translation, and scrawled the words on a pad: *Black tongue.*

o　　　　o　　　　o

Fifteen miles south of Xining lies the town of Huangzhong, site of one of the great monastic complexes of ancient Tibet. Built on the birthplace of Tsong Khapa—founder of the Gelug sect—Ta'er Monastery was founded in 1577. The present Dalai Lama received his early education there, and I was curious to see how time (not to mention four decades of Chinese occupation) had treated the place.

I arrived in Huangzhong after a long, uphill bus ride past miles of wooden beehives and fields of wild cannabis. The paved central square was filled with horse-drawn carts. Pink banners advertised watches and dentures; display boards covered with gold teeth gleamed in the sun.

The entire Ta'er complex was under construction. There were work crews everywhere, digging trenches, setting stones and mixing cement for new walkways. It took me a few minutes to understand, but I finally got it. The place, like the Potala, was being turned into a theme park.

Picking my way between bulldozers and cement mixers, I was struck by the difference between these eastern temples and the ones I'd seen around Lhasa, in Central Tibet. Ta'er was more classically Chinese. The buildings were decorated with intricate geometric motifs, and frenzied floral designs—lotus fronds, chrysanthemums and stylized dragon heads—writhed over every surface like the lush organic nightmares in John Carpenter's *Thing*. There was much to admire. The high wooden pillars of the Great Meditation Hall, wrapped in thick wool carpets; stone guardian lions covered from mane to paw with embedded silver coins; the heavy wooden flooring by the entrance to the Nine-Roomed Hall, worn into grooves by centuries of prostrating knees and elbows.

But there was no doubt the place was dying, like a prayer plant moved into unsuitable light. The reconstruction was efficient but soulless, a transparent bid to turn the ancient monastery into a durable showpiece. I didn't feel that the ugliness was intentional; I didn't think even that much thought had gone into it. The directive, clearly, had been to finish the job quickly and economically, turning Ta'er into a roadside attraction that would delight tourists while underscoring the notion that Tibetan Buddhism, at least in China, is obsolete. Every one of Ta'er's six major temples was being fixed with a placard that, while heradling the building's history and architecture, nimbly sidestepped its spiritual aspect. One temple had even been converted into a museum, displaying the horns, bells, and elaborate costumes of the oracles and lamas like stuffed giraffes. How must Ta'er's monks feel, I wondered, to see their sacred masks pinned onto walls behind fingerprint-smudged glass?

I was pondering this in the Nine-Roomed Hall when a group of uniformed PLA soldiers walked in. They entered the temple joking, laughing and poking each other in the ribs, but the sight of the enormous golden Buddha image moved them to silence. When they at last filed out I approached the statue and stood before it.

It was the loveliest Buddha I'd ever seen. His face was serene, his posture perfect, and the palms of his hands were emblazoned with subtle, intricate mandalas. Nothing happening around the temple—nothing that had happened in Tibet during the past fifty years—had put the slightest furrow in his brow.

I realized then and there that nothing the Chinese did to trivialize Ta'er—or any part of occupied Tibet—could degrade its spiritual power. The smile of that single Buddha would foil all their attempts, and no amount of cement or asphalt could hide it.

Scenes from a Carriage

I couldn't speak. The bug I'd caught in Lhasa, nursed on the freezing Tibet-Qinghai Highway, had crystallized into a case of laryngitis that permitted little more than a squeak to issue from my throat. Communicating with the Chinese, difficult under the best of circumstances, became a Keatonesque comedy of hand motions, body language and hasty references to a pocket phrase book designed specifically, it seemed, to hamper social intercourse. The book proved especially useless in restaurants, where my fear of indigenous food-storage technology necessitated reliance upon a triad of sentences that ostensibly meant, *"I am a vegetarian. I eat no meat. Please bring me only vegetables."* The request inevitably culminated in the arrival of a huge tureen of clear noodle soup with a boiled leg o'mutton protruding, Flintstones-style, over the rim.

Voice or no voice, I had no plans to tarry. My destination was Chengdu, the lively capital of Sichuan Province. From there I would catch the famous Chengdu-Kunming railway, a spectacular ride that would place me in the heart of Yunnan Province—just two hundred miles from the Vietnamese border. In Kunming, travelers in Lhasa had assured me, I could obtain my Vietnam visa and purchase a ticket on the overnight train to Hanoi.

Chengdu, as the plane flies, is less than five hundred miles from Xining. By land, however, the journey would entail a solid week of bus travel over the most primitive roads imaginable. I plotted my route, which sounded like something out of *On Beyond Zebra*—Xining to Tongren, Tongren to Xiahe, Xiahe to Zoigê, Zoigê to Hezuo, Hezuo to Songpan, Songpan to Chengdu—and set off on the long voyage south.

o   o   o

Sandstone pillars lined the roadside cliffs, their monstrous red profiles looming over us like gargoyles. Far below, as soft and human as the cliffs were forbidding, the Amdo valleys unfurled like down comforters, quilted with yellow mustard and grass.

The road cut through the mountains, winding down a serpentine canyon where a mocha river, swollen from the previous night's storm, raged through the narrow gorge and exploded over gigantic boulders. Here the landscape was terrifying. The canyon walls were alternating layers of sediment and slate, deposited at leisure but uplifted in haste, when unimaginable forces stood the world on its ear. Time had worn away most of the sediment, leaving the slate standing in knife-edged sheets. The effect was like looking at the side of a massive textbook whose millions of pages had been eaten away haphazardly by insects or mold.

The road was littered with rocks. Usually we were able to clear a path, but at one point—finding a bridge completely washed out—we were forced to leave the bus and cross the river by foot as the driver blazed over a precarious detour alone.

As we approached Tongren the wild canyon we were driving through cracked open, revealing a lush grassland. The western hills, streaked with red and yellow clay, looked like petrified fire, and. . . .

Deconstructionist Diversion VII

Reader. . . . enough purple prose. Let me level with you.

It was the two hundredth day of my trip. I was hoarse, my butt hurt and my tongue, though much improved, was still a velvety kiwi-brown. I'd been on buses or trains for fifty of the preceding seventy-two hours, and mile after mile of unforgettable scenery had shorted out my brain. Tongren, hidden in the mountains between Xining and Xiahe, was the right place at the wrong time. Too much happened too fast, and if I try to report it all we'll be here for fifty pages. Nobody wants that.

Someday, if ever we meet, I'll buy you a drink and tell you all about my three days in Tongren. I'll tell you about the labyrinthine alleys of Longwu Monastery, where I fended off rabid dogs and stumbled into temples filled with ten-foot-high statues of deities and dragons, made entirely out of butter. I'll tell you about Danzengjiumeigedan (Dan for short), the sixteen-year-old lama claimed to be the reincarnation of Tsong Khapa himself, and about the old Tibetan nomad sitting on the steps of my guesthouse selling *dongchongxiacao*: the dried, nasty-looking "winter worm, summer grass" that, half-caterpillar and half-fungus, is said to be the most powerful aphrodisiac in China.

By now we'll be on the second round; you're buying. I'll remember Sangyaka, a Tibetan man who told me how, in 'fifty-seven, the Chinese rounded up a group of starving Tibetan families, separated the parents from their children, butchered the adults with bayonets and machetes, then cooked them medium-rare and served them to the kids (I didn't believe it). I'll tell you about the Chinese district, with its brutish revolutionary architecture relieved only by a silly bronze statue of a neutered steed rising from what appeared to be an immense mound of horseshit. And I'll report, sparing no detail, on the Tibetan side of town, where the cackling soundtracks of a dozen ultraviolent videos issued from every storefront, a manic miasma of over-amped music and kung fu blows. Every theater was packed with maroon-robed monks. I'll recall how I strolled down the unlit main street with my hands in my pockets, glancing into the saloons and wondering to myself: *What are all these monks doing here, anyway?* Why are they leaning intently over snooker tables, slurping watermelon wedges and spitting the seeds at one another? Why are legions of adolescent monks crowding the video parlors, and packing the bars like sailors on shore leave? Is no one in control?

A strange place, Tongren. I'll tell you about it someday.

Pilgrims' Progress

Xiahe was a madhouse. It didn't take long to find out why. In two days, Khangtang Rimpoche—the beloved patriarch of the vast Labrang Monastery complex—would publicly deliver the three-day-long Kalachakara teaching. It would be the tenth time the seventy-year-old Rimpoche had presided over this rare religious empowerment, and it would almost certainly be the last.

The parts of China I was now visiting—places that, five decades earlier, had belonged to Tibet—seemed, on the surface, less politically charged than the region around Lhasa. It was only natural that the remote capital, home of the Dalai Lamas, would be more politically volatile than these well-traveled monastic centers on the Chinese frontier. But religious oppression under communist rule was endemic, and the Chinese despots had long forbidden mass religious gatherings.

Only now was this beginning to change. The Kalachakara teaching was being made available to lay Buddhists for the first time in more than fifty years, and Xiahe was flooded with pilgrims. Thousands were arriving every hour, spilling out of buses and off the beds of trucks. They came from Qinghai Province, from all over Gansu, from as far south as Sichuan and as far north as Mongolia. Their tents, ranging from elegant white shelters to threadbare quilts of rags and scrap wool, salted the hills above the Daxia River and carpeted the rolling Sangke grasslands where, a few miles south of Xiahe, the rites would be performed.

Morning, noon and night, the muddy kora circling the walled monastery swarmed with men, women and children. The pilgrims wore their most lavish finery: brocaded silk gowns, flowing purple robes, smart felt caps and shampooed carnivore pelts. The women's hair was meticulously braided, plaited with chunks of turquoise and huge round beads of amber and coral. Gold teeth gleamed, earlobes sagged with silver, and mysterious zebra-striped *gzi* stones—some worth tens of thousands of dollars—hung suspended around thick necks layered with insulating grime.

The faces were extraordinary. I couldn't stop staring at the old people—at their black, intelligent eyes that had taken in so much, seen so much suffering and change. But there were young pilgrims as well. Men in embroidered silk robes swaggered by with copper amulet boxes dangling from their necks. Women with sun-blackened cheeks in pink satin shirts and fur-lined *chubas* pointed at me in hysterics, Tibetan ten-gallon hats riding squarely on their heads. It was the closest I'd ever come to time travel, for the faces and costumes I was seeing on the streets of Xiahe—six years shy of the third millennium—could not be very different from what Marco Polo himself had witnessed more than six centuries before.

o   o   o

It rained the next day, an obnoxious, pissy rain that saturated the ground and shrouded the hillsides in mist. The pilgrims performed their koras imperturbed, wrapped in crude ponchos made of plastic sheeting. Juniper smoke billowed incessantly from within the monastery walls, pleasing the gods but adding to the day's gray pall.

In the midafternoon I bought an admission ticket and explored the Labrang complex. I was amazed at the opulence of the place; it was far more lavish than any Tibetan temple in Lhasa. What made it doubly impressive was that the entire monastery had been destroyed during the Cultural Revolution and authentically restored. The great Prayer Hall, designed to seat four thousand monks, burned to the ground a second time in 1985, but was rebuilt four years later.

Labrang's high walls shelter five different colleges, all affiliated with the Gelug sect. There are two Theology Institutes (Higher and Lower) as well as law, medicine and Tantric Buddhism campuses. I saw little monastic activity; the monks were engaged in preparatons for the Rimpoche's teaching.

I was about to leave the complex when I spied Karyn, back from an organized tour. We spoke briefly, and she told me how much she'd enjoyed her "official" guide. He was a monk, she said, but a real rabble-rouser.

"He kept making references to how much the Chinese had destroyed, and talking about the ways things were 'when Tibet was free.'" At that moment she spotted a tall young man with narrow arms and a small head, leading a small tour group toward the main temple. "There he goes, if you want to catch up with him," Karyn said. "But I'm going into town to get something to eat."

It was a tough call. I was exhausted, wanting nothing more than to sip a Nescafé and watch pro basketball on satellite TV. But I trotted gamely after the group, jockeying for position as they toured the circuit of gompas, meditation halls and vast theological libraries. As he led us through the buildings, the monk decried the costly repainting, rebuilding and restocking necessitated by the Cultural Revolution—most of which had come, and was still coming, out of the pockets of pilgrims.

Fifteen minutes into the tour, the group stopped to take photographs. I caught up with the monk as he strolled briskly ahead.

"Is it still possible," I asked, "to get a real education here?"

He gave me a penetrating look. "Good question. The answer, actually, is no. You can get an education, but it is very, very difficult. As you know, Labrang—before the Cultural Revolution—housed thirty-eight hundred monks. Now there are sixteen hundred; but a government regulation says that only six hundred of us can be educated at one time."

"So what happens to the other monks?"

"It's a big problem. The monastery cannot feed them, so they go into town to eat. They have nothing to do." This, then, explained the truant monks I'd seen in Tongren. "Once every year—during the celebration of Tibetan New Year—they are allowed to come into the Great Meditation Hall and recite sutras with the six hundred chosen monks. But otherwise...." He shrugged, and the stragglers caught up to us.

We continued on together, talking. This summer, he explained, would be his final season as a guide; he had been admitted into the Higher Theology Institute, and would soon begin a program leading to the Tibetan equivalent of a Ph.D.

"Congratulations," I said. "So that's ... what? Four years of study, and another four years of guided practice?"

He laughed, widening his eyes. "No! It must be fifteen years of classes. Then comes a ten-year apprenticeship. So, I'm twenty-five now ... everything okay, I graduate at fifty."

"*Fifty?*"

"Still young! No?"

When the tour ended, we wandered around the complex together. I offered him a mint. He accepted, pointing his chin at the Dalai Lama pin on my zipper pull, and gave me a surreptitious thumbs-up.

"It was His Holiness's birthday four days ago," he remarked.

I was surprised to hear him mention it; I'd seen no evidence of celebrations anywhere. I asked him why this was so.

"This is *China*," he said, smirking. "They celebrate in Dharamsala, in the U.S., maybe even in Lhasa. But here, no one. No one but me. I went up to the mountain, meditated and sent up paper prayer flags. But other people are frightened. If the police see, big trouble." He stopped walking and leaned against me, pretending to fix his sock. *"And I think there are spies in this monastery. Some young monks, but a few of the old ones, too. They report directly to the Chinese."*

We entered the Great Meditation Hall, where five enormous silver *chortens* (small Tibetan stupas created, despite their convincingly antique appearance, since the Great Fire of 1985) hold relics of the monastery's original founder and his four subsequent reincarnations.

Labrang's founder was a great scholar and "living buddha" named E'ang Zhongzhe, who built the original monastery in 1709. Since his death E'ang had returned to Xiahe in five consecutive *tulkus*, or reincarnations. The current tulku, my guide explained, was born in 1946. He lives not at the monastery but in Lanzhou, an administrative center some eighty miles to the northeast.

"He wanted to stay here," the monk said thinly, "but the Chinese wanted him to be a 'Leader of the People.' So he is in Lanzhou."

"Like the Panchen Lama," I suggested, thinking of the great Tibetan spiritual leader who—captured after the Dalai Lama fled into exile—had been taken to Beijing, tortured and pressured to become a propagandist for Chinese-Tibetan "unity."

"Not like the Panchen Lama!" the monk hissed. "The Panchen Lama was a great man. The Chinese tried to get him to say how good it was that Tibet was part of China, but he slapped their face. In 1990 the Chinese made a big meeting of all the religious leaders and told them the Panchen Lama was going to make a speech about the 'New Tibet.' They thought they had brainwashed him. But when the Panchen Lama spoke he called the Chinese criminals and said that Tibet should be free.

"That night, at midnight, he died. The Chinese said it was a heart attack." He tapped his chest. "But we Tibetans think, killed."

"So this fifth incarnation of E'ang is not as brave?"

"No. He helps the Chinese. Some old Tibetan people respect him, but the young monks . . ." He shook his head. "For us, the great leader is Khangtang Rimpoche. He is a very brave man. Very good for the Tibetan people."

We walked out of the Great Meditation Hall and into a large court-yard dignified by a few white chortens.

"In 1980, when I was a little boy like him"—my guide pointed to a ten-year-old nomad clinging to his father's sheepskin coat—"Khang-tang Rimpoche was released from prison. He had been held for twenty-one years. He immediately came to Xiahe, and moved into Labrang. My father was an important man in the Tibetan community, so we were in-vited to come to a secret meeting, at nine o'clock at night, in this court-yard here." He swept his arm in a semicircle.

"Khangtang Rimpoche came into the yard. For the next three hours, he told us what it was like to be in prison. He told about how he was forced to work at hard labor, and the many ways in which Tibetans were tortured. He told us how he saw his own teacher, his root lama, beaten to death. As he was talking, many people in the room—my mother and father, and so, so many old people—began to cry. I was so surprised. Tibetan people, they don't easily do this. So I looked to Khangtang Rimpoche, to see what he thought about it. And then I saw that Rimpoche—even Rimpoche!—he was crying, also.

"I was not crying. I was too young to understand what they were say-ing. But I remember that night. Even now I remember. . . ."

I had been listening to the monk but scanning the courtyard, dis-tracted by the ebb and flow of pilgrims. Now I looked back at him, un-certain what to say; for after fourteen years, he had learned how to weep as well.

• 41 •

Process of Elimination

It was in Xiahe that, after a lifetime of unquestioning usage, I finally fathomed the frontier-era origin of one of the most vulgar idioms in American English.

The revelation struck me during my morning visit to the Labrang Monastery Guesthouse toilet, a foul cesspit on the far side of the inn's muddy courtyard. It was a typical setup: a small concrete room divided into two stalls (for men and women) by a low wall. In the center of each compartment's floor was a hole, bordered by two wooden planks.

There was neither seat nor bowl. One squatted above the chasm, a foot on each plank, and did one's business.

The problem was, half the people had missed the hole. About four inches behind the opening was a mountain of feces deposited by individuals who had failed to determine, prior to defecation, the placement of their assholes.

I contemplated this bit of anatomical idiocy as I assumed the position, feet flat on the raised boards. I'd placed myself well forward, so that my elbows pointed right toward the hole. At that moment—mere seconds before committing the very breach of etiquette that had so appalled me in the first place—I made an astounding discovery. *My elbows were a good six inches forward of the business end of my anatomy.*

I shuffled forward, aiming true. And that's when it hit me; right then and there. I quit the noxious depository secure in the knowledge that I, at least, knew my ass from my elbow.

Woodstock III

Afterward I joined Karyn for breakfast at the Snow Lion Café. We dined on french fries, instant coffee with *quanzhinaifen* (powdered yak milk) and a two-egg omelette smothered in local mushrooms as tender as the back of a cheerleader's knee. On the way out I grabbed an empty foil packet of quanzhinaifen and read the description on the back:

> *This product is made with extra care through scientific process with the milk of yak and high quality sugar. Yak is a special cattle which live in the natural condition: very cold, no oxigen and the frozen time long as half a year. It's emulsion protein more than a times to ordinary milk, and no pollution, it's the best nutrition of sickness, elders and children.*
>
> *On the basis of free radical theory, humen beings decrepit, pathological changes is all cased by the increase of free radical of oxyhydrogen. the plant in plateau contained resistant to free radical ingredient. Always eat the eatable plant in plateau can get more health, resist illness. The milk powder product by the yak milk of always eat plant of plateau, it's nutrition and health protection effect much higher than ordinary milk.*

And I'd thought I was feeling the mushrooms . . .

When we hit the road at ten, Xiahe was nearly a ghost town. The pilgrims had left, making their way by flatbed truck or public bus, tricycle-taxi or bicycle, Land Cruiser or Beijing Jeep, on horse or by foot, to the site of the teachings.

Karyn and I squeezed into a minibus and arrived at the Sangke grasslands twenty minutes later.

The visual gestalt of the Kalachakara intitiation was a confluence of colors that, though rarely seen together in nature, seemed utterly natural in context. The huge main tent beneath which Khangtang Rimpoche sat was emblazoned with deep blue swirls and Tibetan motifs. A golden finial crowned its crest. Sitting before the big top were Labrang's six hundred monks, wrapped in purple robes, covering the flat ground like Day-Glo lichen. Behind the monks, scattered over a thousand acres of grasslands, the pilgrims waited. Though they were all dressed differently, the effect—seen from a nearby hillside—was a pointillist seascape of deep, uniform indigo spiced with red and orange dots. Beyond the pilgrims, between the swollen river and the road, lay a vast expanse of white Tibetan tents.

Good information is hard to come by in China, and during the past few days we'd overheard innumerable theories about what to expect. There would be singing and dancing, we'd been told, and acrobats from all over China. Elephants would dance, tigers would leap through flaming hoops and high lamas would levitate above the crowd. Sixty foreign journalists were being flown in, by helicopter, for the festivities. At least 250,000 pilgrims would be at the event—closely chaperoned by thousands of police and People's Liberation Army troops being bused into Xiahe from as far away as Beijing.

In reality there seemed to be around forty thousand pilgrims: about the number of people you'd find at a Grateful Dead show, but not quite enough to fill a football stadium. Police were indeed in evidence, but no more than you'd see at a western event of the same size. We saw no PLA troops at all. The most visible keepers of the peace were an elite corps of Tibetan horsemen who, armed with juniper switches, whips and electric cattle prods, kept the seething crowd of devotees at bay. What they kept them at bay *from* was not entirely clear. I'd heard that certain regional groups were being prevented from commingling, but that seemed ridiculous—there had been plenty of opportunity for mixing in Xiahe itself. Nonetheless these local Hell's Angels performed their duties with enthusiasm, showing no pity to those who would break ranks or surge forward. No one got hurt; Tibetans are used to rough play. But it was strange to see these Buddhist bouncers brandishing their bullwhips, chasing down women and children as Dalai Lama pendants jangled around their necks.

There were no acrobats, no elephants, no tigers. The Rimpoche, a distant speck in his elaborate shelter, delivered the initiation in a monotonous drone that was broadcast to the devotees through scratchy loudspeakers. Occasionally, on cue, the thousands of pilgrims would rise to their feet, chant a familiar sutra or toss silk kata scarves toward the main tent. Meanwhile—as their parents meditated in silent rapture—babies screamed, kids wrestled in the mud and toothless aamas smoked long bone pipes. The whole scene was powerfully reminiscent of Woodstock: a three-day carnival of holy communal fun, dedicated to saving the world. There were no Porta Potties, no naked hippies dancing in the mud and no free acid—but whatever the event lacked in sex, drugs and rock 'n' roll it made up in mysticism, multiphonic chanting and yak dung.

The Sichuan Route

After a futile attempt to hitchhike south, Karyn and I caught the bus to Hezuo, a quiet town near the border of Sichuan Province. We traveled the forty-five miles in ease, grinding along the Daxia River and winding between hills that seemed to get greener as they got steeper. I sat behind the driver, halfway through Jung Chang's compelling autobiography, *Wild Swans*. It was the section of the book detailing the author's teen years in Chengdu, and I was intrigued to read of the critical role that Sichuan's capital had played in the early days of communist rule. Chengdu was, among other things, the springboard from which Mao launched his Great Leap Forward: a disastrous attempt to divert every one of the nation's resources—from primary schools to farm communes—toward industrial production. The resulting slump in agriculture, complicated by severe floods and droughts, led to mass starvation in the early 1960s.

Pierre Schavey, a Belgian computer scientist and old China hand (notorious throughout Sichuan for his six-inch handlebar mustache), was seated across the aisle. He'd met enough locals on his previous visits to China to understand the human toll of Mao's despotic inspirations. "You can't imagine the suffering these people have seen. Anyone our age—forty or older—has been through a series of wars, purges and famines that would make your hair stand on end. There's a deep misconception in the west that only the Tibetans have suffered under communist rule; that's nonsense. Almost every person in China has been strongly affected by the changes in this country."

Hezuo was clean and peaceful, with an elegant mosque and wide, tree-lined boulevards. Walking with Pierre down the main street, looking at the shopkeepers illuminated by the low sun, I found myself surrounded by the visual tableaux I'd always associated, in my mind's eye, with China. A Muslim Hui bootmaker with a long gray beard and white skullcap held hands with his little boy, watching us pass; a thin rug seller lounged on a pile of carpets; an old woman sat beneath a red awning and smiled at us, showing two long teeth.

We entered a Hui restaurant, looking for lunch. There was no menu; I trooped into the kitchen, indicating what we wanted by lifting up trays of uncooked tofu, raw spinach and leathery black mushrooms. For good measure I pointed into my phrase book: *I am a vegetarian. I eat no meat.* The cook nodded rapidly in agreement, and I returned to our table.

No sooner had I sat down than Pierre and I were set upon by a group of local adolescents. There was no preamble; they simply pulled up chairs, opened a few beers and watched us like television.

"There is no word," Pierre explained, "for *privacy* in Chinese. The concept simply doesn't exist here." One of the teenagers began tugging at the hair on Pierre's arm. "During the three times I've visited China I've been subject to every kind of indignity. I've had the book I was reading snatched away in midsentence; I've seen my daypack grabbed and emptied out for inspection; I've been sitting peacefully when a bunch of guys appear out of nowhere and start pulling my mustache."

"You handle it very well," I said.

"It won't last long," he said. "Watch."

After a minute or so one of the kids started barking questions at him. Pierre answered in Chinese. There was brief, clipped dialogue, during which his tormentors seemed to shrink visibly. Suddenly, without a word, they fled the restaurant. Pierre lit a cigarette.

"You see," he said, "I've developed a way of coping with them. In China, for some reason, one of the very worst insults is to call someone a 'rotten egg.' Anything connected with smelly or bad eggs is considered extremely insulting. So whenever a group of these guys comes up and asks me my name, I just look up and say, 'Why, *Huai Dan.* Rotten Egg is my name.' They withdraw immediately, usually with a look of disgust on their faces. 'How can that be?' they ask. 'Who gave you such a name?' 'The people who found me on the street gave it to me,' I tell them.

"That's usually enough," he grinned. "They leave very quickly, as you can see. And they don't come back."

There was a flurry of motion by the kitchen door. "Our lunch," Pierre guessed. Indeed it was; the smiling cook emerged from the mess, bearing two big bowls of sheep's head stew.

o   o   o

The Sichuan Route from Hezuo to Chengdu is a formidable track requiring days of difficult travel; more if the roads are washed out. Even in good weather it's a full day's journey to Zoigê, another fourteen hours to Songpan and a notoriously horrible final ride—up to thirty-six hours, depending on accidents and landslides—to Chengdu.

Northbound travelers, on their way to Xiahe and Tibet, filled our ears with dire stories of breakdowns and avalanches, wild dogs, pestilence and plague. Pierre, smart cookie, elected to backtrack north to Lanzhou and take the two-day train into Chengdu from there. Karyn and I continued south, gluttons for suffering. I was loath to miss an inch of scenery; she especially wanted to visit Zoigê (pronounced, inexplicably, *raw-guy*), a nomadic settlement famous for its tough, bronco-busting nomads.

The bus's warbled windows contorted the landscape into funhouse-mirror shapes, lava lamps of geology bubbling toward the sky. We panted up a pass, the engine wheezing pitifully, and as we crossed over, the universe popped open like a soap bubble. Yak-dotted rangelands, wet with rain, stretched out so far and wide that the entire sky, clouds and all, was mirrored perfectly on the plain.

Zoigê was a hell-realm. The town was nearly empty. Its cowboy-nomads, Buddhists all, were up at Sangke attending the Kalachakara. The toughest characters we met were the mosquitoes, as big as wasps and as aggressive as Jehovah's Witnesses. Zoigê was an ugly place with no center and a mean-spirited monastery; a town where people passed us on the street, waved cheerily and called out *"Fuck you!"*—as if some ugly American, laughing up his sleeve, had taught them that the insult was a traditional western greeting. *"Hello! Fuck you!"* How do you reply to such civilities?

At the local triplex, Stallone's *Lock Up* shared the bill with two Hong Kong bullet banquets. The showcase in front of the Public Security Bureau displayed photographs, in glorious black-and-white, of a recent public execution. Karyn reached out to pet a chained puppy, and it tried to tear her heart out.

Zoigê: Give it a miss.

o   o   o

Songpan was Zoigê's polar opposite, a Chinese village so funky and picturesque it could easily serve as a set for a Zhang Yimou film. The buildings were wood and brick, their slanting eaves festooned with dragons and phoenixes. Houses leaned over the river, smoke pouring from their chimneys as gnarled trees erupted through their porches. After dinner, walking past teahouses twinkling with party lights, I realized I'd found my own private Shanghai. Water gurgled from unseen sources, the sky bristled with dazed stars and black hills rolled away toward Never-Never Land. Old men sat on the street in front of glowing grills, brandishing skewers of yak meat; women crouched in the market behind baskets of enormous peaches. I wandered in and out of road-side shops selling sesame seed cookies and fox furs, and browsed through pharmacies displaying watermelon-frost cough lozenges, antler powder, twisted ginseng roots and a dozen grades of dong-chongxiacao. It was heaven, and it was China—a combination I never thought I'd see.

Someday—within a few weeks, maybe—Songpan will be one of the great tourist meccas of Asia. The town lies between Jiuzhaigou—China's newest and most spectacular national park—and the Wolong Nature Reserve, a famous panda habitat. Songpan itself is already de rigueur for vagabonds on the Lonely Planet circuit; two- and three-day horse treks depart for the Munigou highlands daily, guided by local entrepreneurs who beat each other bloody competing for the issue of each arriving bus.

Did I ride a horse? You bet I did. I spent two days in the wilds of northern Sichuan, my PowerBook stored safely back in town. I swore beforehand that I wouldn't write a word about the excursion (I was, after all, on "holiday"), but there was one sight I'll never forget.

High above Songpan, in a monastery tucked into the forest, a group of prepubescent monks dragged me into their dormitory to see their most prized possession. It was a poster, in living color, of the Palace of Fine Arts in San Francisco, viewed over the adjoining lagoon. The instant I saw it my eyes got watery, my voice choked up, and I knew, in a flash, that there was something I wanted more than a hot bath; more than a tube of antihistamine; more than an inflatable pillow for my saddle.

I wanted to be sitting on one of the wooden benches next to that stinky urban lagoon, wolfing down a turkey sandwich from the Chestnut Street Deli and gulping a cold mango Snapple.

I wanted to go home.

o   o   o

To: Allen Noren, O'Reilly & Associates
From: Jeff Greenwald, China
Subject: Big World/Chengdu

> *"China, on the loose."*
> —Walter Lippmann on the
> "worst fate that could befall the world"

There's comfort in knowing that, even here, cosmic phenomena exert an irresistible grip on the human imagination. The front page of the *Chengdu*

Daily features an artist's perspective of the planet Jupiter, seen from a comet's-eye view. I reckon that eyes all over the planet are oriented in that direction, as humanity enjoys its third collective sky watching in twenty-five years (the 1969 moon landing and non-event Halley's comet being the first two). No one is immune. Last week, when I was camping in the highlands outside of Songpan, some local horsemen borrowed my binoculars and squinted raptly upward, shouting to each other in the local dialect as they resolved wobbly glimpses of the fifth planet. (Glimpses that, despite the cataclysmic drama rippling Jupiter's methane seas, couldn't compare with their close-up view of our very own moon.)

But let's get down to Earth. At the moment I'm sitting in Room 603 of the "Traffic" Hotel, a fan oscillating noisily in the corner, maids fluffing sheets in the hallway. After two weeks of bumping and thumping across Qinghai and Gansu provinces (occupied eastern Tibet) and finally into Sichuan, I've treated myself to a "real" hotel: a place with twenty-four-hour hot water, electric wall sockets and a bar serving ice-cold Tsingtao beer. The perfect place, really, to prop my saddle-sore butt on a mountain of pillows and write this long-overdue installment, which I shall call:

The Paradise of Kung Pao Chicken

If travel (as an Englishman told me in Songpan) is 10 percent ecstasy and 90 percent pain, I ate a big slice of dues-pie on July 17. Here are a few of the songs you can sing, in involuntary vibrato, during the eighteen hours you're staring out a grimy window while your kidneys are being shaken (not stirred) on the rattletrap bus to Chengdu:

American Pie ("This'll be the day that I die . . .")
America ("I'm empty and achin' . . .")
California ("I'm comin' home . . .")
These Are Days (To forget, as quickly as possible.)

We set off at dawn and hit the (unpaved) road immediately, bouncing past the vivid infernos of lime kilns, eating the dust of lumber trucks laden with virgin forest. After about two hours I became aware of a subtle shift in the spiritual landscape. The high, craggy peaks and green passes were empty. Sheafs of prayer flags no longer fluttered against the sky. At some point, tossing my cookies along that hellish stretch of highway, I had left Tibet.

Boulders the size of large-screen televisions lay scattered across the road. Our driver swerved skillfully, missing them all. Looking up, I could see where they'd come from. Pinnacles rose along the roadway on either side of us, sprouting from the iron ground like mutant thorns. My entire journey through China has been a lesson in the Secret Life of Magma. I never realized the Earth could work itself into so many shapes.

We passed through fields of sunflowers, villages full of the delicious sweet smells of cold pine and warm corn, small towns where dozens of wooden stalls sold sliced watermelons. Lunch was an in-and-out affair; Chinese drivers don't linger over their cappuccino. It's heaps o' meat, a good spit, and on the road again.

America, one quickly realizes, is a miracle of maintenance. The road to Chengdu doesn't have a right to exist; they ought to be helicoptering people south from Songpan. Since the late 1980s, when a Gansu bus company was successfully sued by the parents of a Japanese tourist who died in an accident, the Sichuan government requires foreigners to buy life insurance for the trip to Chengdu. The policy covers only death or obvious injury. It doesn't apply, unfortunately, to generalized agony. Staggering off at Chengdu's Ximen Bus Station at 9:30 P.M., I felt like I'd been rolfed by Robocop.

But oh Mama, the lights of Chengdu. . . .

o   o   o

One thing I've learned on this trip is that I love cities—and Chengdu may be the most vibrant city in China. The place has style, flair, even a kind of grace. It's not just the relative absence of spitting on the streets. The people here are friendly and helpful, and seem glad to be alive—a marked contrast to most of the other Chinese I've met (witness the woman at my hotel in Zoigê, who shut her eyes, pressed her palms over her ears and finally burst into tears when I asked for a second quilt).

But descending from the highlands of Tibet and Gansu nearly did me in. My first morning in Chengdu I woke up so hot and sweaty that I stuck a thermometer in my mouth to see if it wasn't dengue fever. When my number came up normal I got dressed and went out for breakfast, hoping some java would cure me. Wound up sharing a table with Pierre, a Belgian man I'd met a week ago up in Hezuo. Halfway through our conversation a 747—the first one I'd seen in months—roared by. I watched it pass with transparent longing, and Pierre fell silent. As it faded from sight he raised his glass of orange juice.

"To victory over temptation."

After declaring myself fit to face Chengdu's steam-bath humidity, I rented a Flying Pigeon bicycle and set off in search of a Mac-compatible info-boutique. I found one at last in the well-hidden Computer Center of the posh Minshan Hotel and effortlessly printed out a letter. Faxing it, however, was another matter. There's no such thing as corporate responsibility in China; the consumer pays for Mao Bell's mistakes. Three attempts to reach America via China's data pipeline cost me enough to buy twenty-four watermelons—and I get to do it all over again tonight.

Fortunately, every expedition onto the streets is an adventure. The Chengdu roads swarm with Brownian clouds of bicyclists who navigate wide bike lanes and swerve expertly around fruit carts, paper sellers and mammoth city buses driven by beautiful teenage girls wearing white cotton gloves. Traffic lights are timed, the seconds to go counted down on huge LED displays that lend a Le Mans mania to the morning commute. The Jin Jiang River flows like Freon through the southern part of town, passing the poet Du Fu's thousand-year-old cottage and driving a cooling breeze over the tablecloths of the waterside restaurants. Farther south, on "Electronic Brain Street," sandwich boards line the sidewalk hawking hard drives, software and ultraviolent video games.

The city is a riot of images, bite-size vignettes pasted against an ever-changing backdrop of modern high-rises, dilapidated buildings, bamboo groves and smoky doorways. Merchants squat on the pavement gossiping behind baskets heaped with walnuts and chamomile flowers. A wooden trellis loaded with multicolored hats leans against a tree. A petite woman cycles by, a black trombone case strapped like an airplane wing to her bike rack, but my attempt to photograph her is foiled as a businessman blunders by in a bicycle rickshaw, blabbing into a cellular phone.

The focus shifts every nanosecond. As in quantum physics, phenomena occur where you place your attention. Just as often, the attention is on you. An eight-year-old boy approaches as I'm stopped on the sidewalk, bent over my "UP-TO-DATE MAP OF TRAFFIC MEALING LODGING AND TRADING OF CHENGDU":

"Hello! Hello! Hello! Hello!"

Don't bother me kid, I'm busy. . . . But as the slighted waif passes he jabs me right in the kidney: instant sidewalk shiatsu. I yelp, crumple up my map and chase him down the street, but he shimmies up a tree. . . . Let me tell you something. There's nothing like being a forty-year-old in a country of 1.1 billion people to remind you that more than 75 percent of the world's population is under twenty-five. Nowhere has my windy slide down the back of the bell curve felt more reckless than in Chengdu, where the universal conversational gambit—"Are you married?"—has been modified to the rather less subtle "So, how many children do you have?"

Another question nags at me as I drift through this blizzard of humanity. *Why are the people here so happy?* This is, after all, Red China. There's even a gigantic marble statue of Mao smiling down South Renmin Boulevard, his right arm hoisted in the classic (if oxymoronic) gesture of despotic benevolence. "Mao was 70 percent right, and 30 percent wrong," official wisdom declares. But here in Chengdu, the secret of the People's Contentment blooms like a smirk beneath his distant gaze (flanked, as it were, by two huge signs advertising Pabst Blue Ribbon beer). Chengdu's citizens are happy because there's money here, loads of money, and still more money to be made. Free-market enterprise has come to Sichuan, a counterrevolutionary fever expressed in multiple ice cream flavors and Olympic-size public pools, silver Mercedes purring along Hong Xing Road, shops selling Rollei cameras and Lester Young CDs. It's a beautiful sight, but it fills me with apprehension. If this is the shape of China's future, the Big World—as we know it—is about to end.

Look out, Big Apples and Little Tigers: The Great Red Whale is about to blow.

⚡   ⚡   ⚡

So Sorry

I left my bike with a trillion others, paid my 1-moh parking fee and wandered down the alley leading to the Wenshu Monastery. On either side of the street stood dozens of stalls selling joss sticks and incense, huge bankrolls of fake money, firecrackers and paper flowers, porcelain statuettes of the Buddha and Guan Yin, the goddess of compassion. Outside the temple gate cripples slid up to me on sleighs of corrugated cardboard, twitching their ruined limbs and giving me the old thumbs-up. Don't let anyone tell you there's no begging in China; even the Glorious Revolution of the Proletariat has a few holes in its net.

I spent about an hour at the temple, lighting red candles and lunching on textured gluten cleverly disguised as garlic-braised sea slug. On my way back to my hotel, zipping between the infinite cyclists and pedestrians on Renmin Nanlu, a dog ran into the bike lane. I swerved to avoid it, but my pedal caught the spokes of the bike next to me. Both of us went down, sprawling.

The Chinese woman I'd hit picked up her cycle and came toward me, limping.

"*Debuchi.* . . . So sorry. . . . Are you okay?"

"I'm fine, I'm fine," she replied in English. "Let's get off the street."

We got safely to the sidewalk, and I nodded at her leg. "You're limping."

"It's not your fault. But your elbow's bleeding. Come here, I have a tissue . . ."

She was a slight, angelically beautiful woman with jet-black eyes and a page-boy haircut. We wheeled our bicycles to an outdoor café, and I ordered two Cokes.

Her name was Ying Shu. Her limp, she told me, was the result of polio; she'd undergone a dozen operations on her right hip. Despite her disability she moved with lithe grace, and I found myself enthralled.

Ying Shu was eager to practice her English—it was already quite good—and as we sat by the river she told me about her life. Her father, she said, was a lawyer; but since his family had been connected with Chiang Kaishek's Nationalists he was exiled to a remote labor commune in 1962. He met his future wife there, and Ying Shu was born in 1968. Seventeen months later she contracted polio, and was sent back to Chengdu to live with her grandparents.

Ying Shu was waitressing at the Mushroom Cloud, one of the trendy restaurants near the Traffic Hotel. She had to make her afternoon shift, but we arranged to rendezvous when she got off.

o   o   o

It was past sunset when we met again. We walked awhile, stopping on a bridge above the Jin Jiang River. The moon hung like a gas lamp over the black water, an amber bead among the reflections of blinking hotpot neons. All along the bridge, blind fortune-tellers sat on folding stools, waiting silently for customers.

"Are they any good?"

"Depends who you ask." Ying Shu shrugged. "You want to try?"

After some deliberation she selected an old man in shorts and a v-neck T-shirt. He took my left hand in his, squeezing the mounds of my palm. A crowd of Chinese gathered round, nodding quietly as Ying Shu translated my fate into rough but ready English.

"You should marry a woman born in 1962 or 1963," Ying Shu declared, "or, failing that, 1966 or 1967. The next twenty-five years will be lucky for you—and between ages of sixty-six and eighty you might be very, very happy. But it's *very* important you find this girl and marry her." The old man added something. "You have until next November."

"When were you born, Ying Shu?"

"Never mind." She slapped me on the arm. The fortune-teller continued his mutterings without pause. "You are working on something now," she said. "True?"

"Yes, that's so."

"Okay. He say, whatever you do now, big success. But even so, big change coming."

"What kind of change?"

"At age of forty-two, you will change your whole career."

"To what?"

"He doesn't know."

"Anything else?"

"You will live to be eighty-six years old. Thirty yuan, please."

I bargained him down to twenty.

We walked together up Renmin Nanlu, past the billboards glittering above the Jin Jiang Hotel. I noticed the ring on her finger.

"Are you married, Ying Shu?"

She said nothing for a moment, then told me the story. In 1991, she had fallen in love with a Finnish man. He was forty-eight—more than twice her age. At that time she was a model, with a part-time job in computer graphics. Despite bitter protests from her family she married the Finn a year later and, at his insistence, quit her job.

In March, Ying Shu told me, her husband had returned to Finland "on business." She'd heard nothing from him until three days ago, when a letter arrived in the mail: "Please prepare the papers for a divorce." The letter had left her clueless, ashamed and embittered.

"I remember when all my family was warning me and objecting," she said. "He said, 'No, no, no, I'll stand on your side whatever happens.' Now he won't even call me. He wants me to communicate by letter, but I'm tired of writing letters."

"What reason did he give you for wanting a divorce?"

"No reason. He said that we argued, that we disagreed about things. But isn't that always true in a relationship? I thought when you marry someone, even if there are problems, you work things out. But now he wants this divorce." She leaned against a pole, favoring her left hip.

"I never even met his family," she continued. "And when he went back to Finland, he took my whole portfolio. They were professional photographs, very expensive to make. He said he was going to sell them to some Finnish magazine. Maybe he did; who knows. But now I have no pictures. No pictures, no money, no marriage."

We stopped at a sidewalk exhibition of traditional Chinese painting. There were hundreds of scrolls, but the subject matter was strictly Chinatown kitsch. Colorful carp, spirited stallions, rugged rockscapes, prowling tigers and cuddly pandas—thousands of damned pandas, in every imaginable pose—cavorted between scarlet *chop* marks and black calligraphic squiggles.

"So many pandas," Ying Shu reflected sadly. "All the same. . . ." She whirled around and looked at me with brutal intensity. "You're an American," she said. "Can you tell me something? Can you tell me why a western man might decide to do like this, with no warning, no visit, no call?"

But there was nothing I could say to comfort her. The situation Ying Shu found herself in, unheard of in China only twenty years ago, was a single example of the crossed signals and missteps that will define, for another generation at least, the skittish tango called East-meets-West.

· 42 ·

Notes from the Twenty-Four-Hour Train Ride from Chengdu to Kunming

9:40 a.m.—Before boarding the train I bought a chain cable—trying to avoid, at any cost, a repeat of the Nepalganj nightmare. A minute ago it occurred to me to test my new purchase. At the first tug the chain snapped in two. The weak link was merely first among equals. What to make of this, save a joint enterprise between the thieves and locksellers?

1:15:04 p.m.—We enter our first tunnel.

1:15:38—Our second tunnel.

1:15:55—Our third tunnel. There will be 424 more tunnels before Kunming, for a total of 427 tunnels and 991 bridges on this 690-mile stretch of track. That's an average of one tunnel every three minutes; a bridge every ninety seconds.

1:46—I'd love to see this railway line from the air. Four hundred twenty-nine segments of truncated track, twisting between the hillsides like broken ramen noodles.

4:46—Lounging on the bamboo mat covering my sleeper berth, sipping tea from an aluminum cup. Every time we emerge from a tunnel there's a fresh tableau. White water pours down a precarious gorge; ears of corn rise behind a stone wall; vertical cliffs the color of a waterfall drop from unseen heights into the river below.

6:49—After spending most of the day in cool mist we emerge from a long tunnel into brilliant sunshine. Now the rivers run red over red boulders, and green hills are piled up on either side of the valley like gaudy throw pillows. I've passed the last eight hours, I realize, without uttering a single word.

A Bold and Cunning Plan

A thunderstorm elbowed its way over the western hills, three miles distant. The rain-soaked streets of Kunming were alive with bicyclists and pedestrians, lovers huddling under the eaves of the Your Saviour Drugstore, workers leaning over tipped-back bowls of pig-ear stew and pickled vegetable broth. Cyclists plied the bike lanes of Beijing Lu like candied druids, cloaked in a gumdrop array of ponchos. I wove between them in a frenzy, trying to arrange something—anything—that would ease me into Vietnam.

I'd been misinformed. There was no consulate in the city, no place to get a Vietnam visa at all. Plenty of travelers were making their way to Hanoi, all right, catching the overnight train from Kunming, but every one of them had already purchased a special visa in Beijing or Canton. Crossing the border without one was impossible. I met half a dozen people who'd tried and failed, despite lavish bribes. You could get a visa on arrival at Hanoi airport, but that did me no good.

The irony of all this was not lost on me. I'd spent most of high school desperate to avoid, at any cost, a trip to Vietnam; now I was willing to sneak, beg or bribe my way in.

My only alternative—taking a three-day train ride to Canton, waiting two weeks for my visa to come through and then *back-tracking to Kunming all over again*—was ludicrous.

There had to be another way. In a last-ditch effort I tracked down the Kunming office of the China International Tourist Service. The other travelers I'd spoken to had told me such a move would be useless; that the CITS, like Russia's Intourist, specialized in arranging Kafkaesque runarounds at moon-shot fees. But bad information had gotten me into this spot in the first place, and it would cost me nothing to try.

Wouldn't you know . . . I got lucky.

Ms. Yao Yi was brilliant, inventive and energetic, the Chinese equivalent of a high-octane Hollywood agent. I told her of my plight and explained why, unlike other, "normal" tourists, I couldn't simply hop on a plane and get my visa in Hanoi. Within minutes she had devised a bold and cunning plan.

"Okay! Here's idea. You ready? Sure? Okay. First, I telephone Vietnam consulate in Canton. I tell them, 'Wow, big American travel writer here, good for tourism in Vietnam!' Right? Okay? Then, I do this. I photocopy your passport, letter from your newspaper, everything. Fax to Canton. Yes? Good. So. They make visa for you. One week only. Special rush job for Mr. Big VIP. Meantime, you go to Canton. By train. Go slow! See Guilin, Yangshuo, like that. Beautiful scenery, you know? Like Chinese painting. Everybody love this. Okay? So. You get to Canton in one week. No problem! Visa waiting! Right? You take visa, fly back to Kunming. Understand? Then, next morning, train to Vietnam. Direct! No problem! Easy. So. I call Canton now. Vietnam consulate. Right? Okay?"

It was a mind-boggling concept. I could go overland to Canton, then *fly back to where I'd started from*. Very tempting—but was it kosher?

Maybe, just maybe, it was. Since I'd be returning to Kunming, I wouldn't be breaking my overland route . . . and afterward, when I wrote the book, *I could ignore that little side trip entirely*. It seemed like a watertight plan.

"Let's do it," I said.

Yao got to work, shouting simultaneously into three telephones—one red, one white, one blue—while I waited patiently in a patent leather chair. Within an hour everything was arranged. My documents had been faxed to Canton (Yao had even telephoned the consulate to make sure they'd been received) and a one-way airplane ticket, Canton-Kunming, was in my hand.

"Okay, listen," Yao said. "Now you buy train ticket at Kunming Station. Yes? Stop Guilin, Yangshuo. Spend three, four days. From there, bus. Easy. Leave Yangshuo by overnight bus, late Sunday. Arrive Canton Monday morning. Then, you go right away to Garden Hotel. Room 924: Vietnam Airlines. Speak with Mr. Ruan. He will have your visa. Cost fifty dollars. U.S. only, no yuan. Okay? So. Ruan. *R-U-A-N*. Right? You pay him, he give you visa. Then, Monday afternoon, six o'clock, fly back here. Meantime, I make train ticket for you. Kunming-Hanoi. Okay? Understand? No problem? Don't worry! I arrange everything."

I leaned across the desk. "What year were you born, Yao?"

"Year? 1971. Why? How come?"

"Just a thought."

o   o   o

After leaving the CITS I felt so good that I decided to have my ears cleaned and my shoes shined—at the same time.

I walked to the corner of Beijing Lu and Huangcheng Nanlu, where a dozen such professionals stood waiting to serve me. I picked one of each, sat on a wooden stool and placed my foot on a shoe-shine stand. Both service providers set to work at once. The shoe-shine woman began dabbing at my shoes with thick polish while the ear cleaner, using a tool that looked like a coke spoon, poked around in my auditory canal. It tickled unbearably, but I tried to hold still. After half a minute of reaming, the young man withdrew the scoop from my ear, displaying what looked like a small ball of opium. He shook his head, cleaned the tool off with a tiny scrap of cloth and dived in again. He emerged with another bounty, clucked disapprovingly, and called over an older ear cleaner standing nearby.

The shoe-shine woman continued her work unfazed, spreading black polish liberally over my shoes, socks and trouser cuffs.

The older, ostensibly wiser ear cleaner tilted my head to the side, peered appraisingly into my cranium and called for a tool. He prodded so deeply that when he finally pulled out the probe I expected to see my brain on the end of it. But there was only more black goo, which looked suspiciously like what the shoe-shine woman was gumming all over my insteps.

After displaying the result of his excavation, he pulled a plastic compact from his shirt pocket. Inside were at least a dozen lumps of earwax, in a variety of shapes and sizes.

He pointed to the smallest one with his scoop. "This, one yuan! And this"—pointing now to a medium-size, booger-shaped mass—"five yuan! This one"—tapping the largest, a veritable Godzilla of earwax that you could've rolled into a candle—"ten yuan!"

"Very nice," I replied. "But I'm not in the market. If you've got a crock of toe jam, though, or mittens made of belly-button lint. . . ."

"*No! You!*" He leveled his tool at my ear. "Too much wax! Ten yuan! Ten yuan pay!"

"Ahhh," I said slyly. "I get it. You want to charge me according to how waxy my ear is. Rather like charging me more to wash my clothes if they're really dirty, or raising the price of my hotel bed if I'm an especially sound sleeper."

He nodded, smiling.

"Forget it, Junior." The shoe-shine lady started buffing, and my voice vibrated inanely. "W-w-w-one yuan. *One.*" I held up my finger. "*Y-y-y-yi-yuan*, and not a *m-m-m-moh* more, or you can get your unsterilized p-p-p-pickup stick the hell out of my aural cavities. Do you get my d-d-d-drift? Do I make myself clear, you conniving acoustical *qu-qu-quack?*" One of the great pleasures of being in a non-English-speaking country is that you can say anything you like; anything your heart desires. The only rule is that you must remain smiling, and keep your tone completely neutral.

The senior scraper shrugged and stepped aside. My original ear cleaner—an apprentice, I deduced—moved back into position and set to work on my right ear with the one-pointed concentration of a child dredging the depths of a Cracker Jack box for the prize.

When it was all over I felt like a new man. The world was a symphony of long-forgotten nuances and tones, and my blindingly bright FootJoys raised me, in local estimation, a notch or two above the Nike-booted ranks of my fellows. I walked my shiny shoes across town to Green Lake Park and spent the afternoon among the swan boats and musicians, pagodas, flower gardens and bumper cars.

China can be so charming.

Tricky Business

That evening, at the Happy Café, I met a man named Ned Garnett. His narrow face, big eyes and clean-cropped beard gave the impression of keen intelligence and amiable harmlessness.

Garnett had been ten months in China, investigating the impact that China's marriage laws had had on minority groups during the 1950s. His grant was from the National Academy of Sciences, but his academic affiliation was with U.C. Berkeley. We waxed nostalgic about the Oakland jazz clubs, redwood parks and used-CD stores. Both of us felt like scuba divers who'd spent a little too long at great depth. Our air was running out fast, and it was high time to make our way back to the surface.

The waitress at the Happy Café was a beautiful woman with high cheekbones and unusually angular features. She liked Ned so much that she'd stolen his bicycle key, threatening to keep it until he was "nice" to her. While they were flirting I asked him if it would be tasteless to inquire what her ethnic origins were.

"She's Yi," he declared without hesitation.

"How d'you know?"

"Because she's got those, what do you call them, not freckles . . . birthmarks. Here, here, and there." He pointed to her right temple, left temple and the middle of her forehead.

"Give me a break. All the Yis can't have moles in exactly the same places."

"They do! They do! Just like all the Han Chinese have a cleft pinkie toe. Or they did; now they just have a vestigial ridge, or a little bump on the side of their feet."

Something about the woman was enormously attractive. I called her over and ordered a pizza.

"It takes a long time," she said seductively. Then, smiling at Ned, "But it's worth waiting for."

It was the frankest come-on I'd ever heard. I couldn't understand why Ned, who would be in Kunming for two more weeks, hadn't rolled into the café with a bouquet of roses and a box of dongchongxiacao.

He rolled his eyes. "You don't understand. This business with Chinese woman and western men is tricky."

"How so?"

"On the surface, it's easy to guess why they're attracted to western men. They like high noses, they like height and they're intrigued by facial hair. But you never know. Is it *you* they really like, or is it the possibility of getting that green card? They're extremely flirtatious, very shrewd, and totally self-interested. You have to be very, very careful.

"Besides," he said, "her family probably already has somebody lined up. Someone with a future in noodle-shop joint ventures, or the People's Liberation Army."

My pizza arrived. I'd ordered pizzas everywhere from Antigua to Kathmandu, and I'd tasted some pretty lame concoctions, but this one was in a class by itself. What our Yi beauty served me was a greasy potato pancake, stuffed with an unctuous ratatouille of mushrooms, bean sprouts and runny egg. I could barely swallow a forkful.

We finished our beers and paid off the bill. Ned had eaten earlier, but I was still starving. We combed Beijing Lu in search of my dinner. I wanted to find a restaurant offering a wholesome regional specialty called "Over-the-Bridge Noodles," a do-it-yourself meal in a bowl. It works like this: Several dishes of half-cooked ingredients are brought out; the waitress then delivers a cauldron of scalding broth, topped with a layer of sesame oil. One drops the prepared ingredients into the soup, stirs slowly for three minutes and adds the noodles.

Ned finally found a place that served it, across the river from the People's Cultural Palace. It was a typical Chinese dive. The floor was knee-deep in trash, clients spat enthusiastically onto the floor, and a waiter crouched in the entranceway, washing dishes in a pail.

Any dish with a name like Over-the-Bridge Noodles, of course, has a legend behind it. To wit:

> Long ago, in a galaxy far away (in southern Yunnan, actually), there lived a scholar who, bedeviled by the clamor of his village, retreated to the solitude of a small island in the middle of a lake. His wife brought him his meals, crossing the long wooden bridge that connected the island with the shore. The problem—especially in the winter—was keeping the food hot. One winter morning the wife slept in. The previous night she'd stewed a chicken, and found, to her surprise, that the broth was still piping hot. The fat had formed an insulating top layer, preserving the heat. In a flash of insight, she realized that she could prepare all her husband's winter meals by carrying over the "insulated" soup, while the food cooked in the broth.

That is the local version of the story. Here is my own:

> Once upon a time there was an American writer who decided to slake his appetite with a hearty bowl of soup. He crossed a bridge over a small waterway, sat down at a restaurant and ordered the local specialty. The waitress brought his meal: a plate of sliced cold cuts, some raw vegetables, a miniature egg and a big bowl of noodles. She then carried over a huge tureen of very hot broth, insulated by a layer of oil. The writer spooned the ham and chicken into the soup, then the vegetables and the egg. But

when he tilted the bowl of noodles the entire mass o' pasta catapulted into the soup bowl like a cannonball, splashing a liter of scalding broth and hot oil into his lap. The writer leapt to his feet, howling, and ran back over the bridge all the way to his hotel, where he hopped around like a wind-up frog for half an hour.

o   o   o

The next morning Ned accompanied me to the train station and, employing his excellent Chinese, tried to help me arrange a sleeper on that afternoon's Kunming-Guilin Express. We ran into a potential snag, however, when the clerk at the ticket desk scrutinized my counterfeit student card.

"He wants to know exactly what it is you're studying," Ned said.

"Umm . . . Tell him I'm studying Chinese panda painting."

Ned did so as I demonstrated with sweeping pantomimes. The clerk nodded, gave me the thumbs-up and rattled off another question.

"He wants to know who your teachers are."

"Teachers? What? Yes! Of course! My teachers!" I stammered, trying to think of a few Chinese names, but the only ones I came up with were Mao Zedong and Confucius. *Think*, man. *Think* . . .

"Amy Tan," I blurted. "Amy Tan, Erica Jong and . . . Spike Lee."

The clerk grinned, offered another thumbs-up and left the room with my card. Ned pointed his chin in the direction of the man's desk.

"Do you see that book?"

I did. It was a nondescript, average-size paperback with a plain yellow binding and five large Chinese characters on the cover.

"That's the *Collected Works of Deng Xiaoping, Volume III.* Everyone's supposed to study it. You see them everywhere, in every office—but you can tell by looking at the spines that none of them have ever been opened."

"Well," I said, "it's better than seeing his picture on every wall."

"If they had to hang a picture, it would probably be Mao's."

I thought about Mao for a minute. "You've got to admire Mao," I blurted. "Maybe he was wrong about a lot of things, but the things he did right are pretty impressive. He unified China, and turned it from a mess of warring provinces into a credible, and economically viable, nation. . . ."

"Mao bankrupted China," Ned returned dryly. "His schemes, like the Great Leap Forward—not to mention the Cultural Revolution— drove the economy into ruin, and pushed the country into virtual civil war. He was the perfect example of absolute power corrupting absolutely. No; it wasn't Mao. All the reform you see around you here, all the prosperity and up-and-coming capitalism, is Deng Xiaoping's work. What Mao accomplished was purely administrative—and that could all blow away in a stiff breeze."

The clerk returned with my tickets, and I paid in cash. It was settled, then. I'd spend three days in the Guilin area, get to Canton Monday morning, and fly back to Kunming that night. In less than ten days, I'd be in Vietnam.

Three-Banana Bardo

For the first few hours there are whitish boulders everywhere, tossed over the landscape like kosher salt. You have to wonder how they got there. You have read, in Tom Clancy's Sum of All Fears, *that fields can literally "grow" rocks; water seeps deep into the ground and freezes upward, pushing stones toward the surface. It must be so. How else could the Chinese have built the Great Wall and still have any rocks left? You ponder this, eating a banana.*

By afternoon the topsoil has ebbed away, and the infinity of individual boulders is revealed for what it really is: a substratum of undulating bedrock, punching through the ground in long, bony knuckles. As you continue eastward the knuckles flex, and the geomorphic appendages thrust upward like thumbs and fingers of stone. Some are bare, weathered and streaked by the elements; others harbor twisted trees that cling to the cliffs like climbers, their indestructible roots bolted like pitons into vertical cracks.

By sunset you have entered, as advertised, a Chinese landscape painting. Rows of overlapping peaks stagger away toward the horizon, receding in a pale purple wash. In a heavy ground mist they would fool the eye—floating above the clouds like islands, removed from any earthly anchorage.

You eat another banana.

o   o   o

"Yangzhuo!! Yangzhuo!!"

The exit platform of Guilin Station is lousy with touts. A short old woman with an iron grip grabs you by the arm and steams ahead like a tugboat, pulling you toward a fleet of waiting minibuses. Your first inclination, of course, is to break free; anyone so manipulative must be a shyster or a crook. Suddenly, though, there is a shift in your thinking, a road-weary surrender. You "baaah" softly beneath your breath and let yourself be shepherded along. You have been cooped up in a train for a day and a half, surrounded by smokers and spitters and screaming infants, and your body knows the truth. You are helpless, far too exhausted to resist. "Where are you taking me?" you mutter feebly, more for show than any hope of an answer.

You are on a minibus. Slowly it fills up. Tired as you are, you peel a banana

*and glance around the bus park in annoyance, peeved that you're not yet mov-
ing, anxious to see if any of the other minibuses will set off before yours. None do.
Within ten minutes you are on a sort of freeway, skirting the lights and luxury hotels of Guilin, heading south. You mop the sweat from your forehead and wonder
if this place, this next place, will be any good.*

*Outside the window huge dark shadows rise up like smoke signals, occluding
the heavy July clouds. You have come to see the shape of the world here, and you
sense you will not be disappointed. You wonder what the restaurants will be like,
and if you will find a quiet hotel with twenty-four-hour hot showers.*

*You have been traveling seven months, to the day. Something in your head is
swimming and dizzy, as if you've just gotten off a ship and don't have your land
legs back.*

You suspect you will feel this way for years.

Music in Every Room

Traveling consists of two types of events: situations and stories. In
China I encountered innumerable situations, but they didn't always fit
together into stories. Things happened—interesting things in interesting places—but they rarely culminated in the kinds of cultural apotheo-
ses that every writer looks for.

"Some other places were not so good," Hemingway wrote in the introduction to his *First Forty-nine* short stories, "but maybe we were not so
good when we were in them." And so it was with me, in China. Things
happened; I wrote about them. But later, looking over my sketches in
the light of all that had come before, I realized that they were not as
sharp or as compelling as I had imagined at the time. Maybe it was me.
I was in overdrive now, plowing eastward, the smell of the Pacific a
magnetic tang in the back of my snout. China was overwhelming, fascinating and eternal, but it was not my place. The scenery—especially
around Yangshuo, that classical realm of miniature mountains immortalized by poets and painters—was awesome, but oddly unmoving.

Arriving in Yangshuo, I found myself back on the "circuit." Scores of
tourists and travelers from Europe and the Americas—not to mention
China—piled onto the motorboats plying the Lijiang River, tirelessly
photographing the scenery before returning to Yangshuo to feast on ice
cream and bargain for T-shirts.

I spent my mornings biking through the countryside, enjoying the
scenery and climbing Yangshuo's famous overlook, Moon Hill. The
view from Moon Hill is magnificent, like sitting on a shark's tongue
and peering out over the lower teeth. Regiments of sharp peaks recede
toward the horizon, jagged and forboding. Moon Hill is high, but not

high enough. Far below, trucks on the Guilin-Guangzhou highway
blast their air horns as they pass each other in a manic game of cat and
mouse, drowning out any hope of poetic contemplation.

Yangshuo was the Chinese Club Med, a perfect microcosm of free-
market enterprise gone wild. Camera stores, art galleries, discotheques
and bars lined the cobbled streets. Antique shops sold copies of Mao's
Little Red Book alongside used John Grisham novels. I counted four cappuccino machines. Behind Minnie Mao's Café (no relation to Mickey
Mao's, just down the street), a back-room "university" offered classes in
cooking, chop carving and the deceptively simple art of Chinese landscape painting. I bought a set of brushes and tried my hand at it, but
after two humiliating days of producing Rorschach-like canvases I
switched my major to mah-jongg.

Spelunking was another big attraction. Should you ever visit Yangshuo I highly recommend Assembling Dragon Park, a natural wonder
that is to caves what Mr. Eggroll is to Chinese cuisine.

The 20-yuan admission fee is costly, but barely puts a scratch in the
attraction's enormous power bill. I knew I was in trouble right from the
start when, in the very first chamber, a brilliant neon sign flashed an incomprehensible message in Chinese characters. I turned to the ticket
taker.

"What does it say?"

She squinted at the manic idiograms. "It say, '*Welcome to Our Foreign
Guests.*'"

"But your foreign guests cannot read Chinese."

"Yes. . . . Well, you are welcome anyway."

The vast underground cavern, with its plethora of stalagmites and
stalactites—God help me, but after forty years I still don't know which
is which—was illuminated like a bad acid trip. Red, green, blue and yellow fluorescent lights, hidden behind natural upcroppings of lime,
threw a flashback glare onto every slimy spire. Leave it to the Chinese
to turn even a cave into a consummate kitsch-fest. Here, at least, there
was a plot; the odd natural shapes—unconvincingly named Dragon's
Throne and Snow Lotus Blossoming Upside Down—told a story, a tale
drawn from Chinese folklore. Our guide, unfortunately, comprehended
no English. She had memorized the translation by rote, waylaying huge
chunks of it in the process.

She led our group into a subterranean amphitheater lit up like the
bachelor pad of Sonic the Hedgehog, and launched into a droning nar-
ration:

"*Now look see Dragon Throne. Now dragon only tail, you want see dragon
head he hiding now you must come morning. Cave closed morning, what to do.*

There is table. So many fruits: pineapple, grape, peach. Before, monkey came. Now only peaches left on dish of Dragon Queen. But only small peaches, queen take bath, monkey eats the big one. Too big for monkey, he falls on frog. Welcome to old man, still guarding treasure. Head, beard, leg. Gold coin in stomach of frog. Behind is scenery of Li Mountain, so famous, also giant banyan tree. Oh no a cat is in tree. Can anybody find the cat?"

We stood paralyzed with bewilderment. The guide swept her flashlight into a high crevice, tripping a photoelectric switch. Next thing, the sound of mooing—or a very bad recording of a cat—filled the cave.

At long last we were loaded onto a broad raft, stable in the shallow water. As our boatman poled toward the exit, hidden speakers serenaded us with Chinese Muzak. At that moment I recalled the title of John Krich's plaintive transglobal narrative, *Music in Every Room*. It was true. No place was safe; not even the Center of the Earth.

o   o   o

On the evening of my fourth day in Yangshuo I boarded the Special Touristic Air-Conditioned Overnight Luxury Coach to Canton. It was much the same as every other Chinese bus I'd ridden, with one key difference. To maximize the efficiency of the air-conditioning (broken, of course), the windows had been sealed shut.

I spent the night marinating in my own sweat, clinging to my daypack like a lab monkey and dreaming about a peach too big to eat.

The bus dropped me off at an anonymous intersection in metropolitan Canton. It was the end of lunch hour, a time when humans had best be insulated within layers of impact-resistant steel. The driver handed my pack down from the roof, and as I staggered beneath its colossal weight I lit upon a giddy, comforting truth: *At some point on this seemingly endless journey, at some miraculous future point, I would step off an Overnight Luxury Coach for the very last time.*

• 43 •

Garden-Variety Bardo

Canton's Garden Hotel is a five-star monolith that rises like El Capitan above the seething enterprise of Huanshi Donglu Road. I stepped out of the city's malarial heat into meat-locker air-conditioning, shivering uncontrollably as every sweat gland in my body contracted like a sea anemone.

I felt like a character from *Wagon Train* who, opening the wrong soundstage door, suddenly finds himself on the set of *Star Trek: Deep Space Nine*.

The marble floors were credit card clean, and fountains bubbled everywhere. Capsule elevators—white suppositories of glass and polished steel—soared angelically upward, lit like vanity mirrors. There were bakeries and magazine kiosks, beauty salons and snooker parlors, gift shops and bars. A deafening hubbub filled the air as tour groups of well-dressed Americans and Europeans walked their luggage to a mission control-size reception desk. Across the lobby, a quarter mile away, a Chinese woman played "My Way" on a grand piano.

I stood alone in the middle of the gigantic lobby, quaking with culture shock.

What was the cure? Breathing. A few deep breaths, and a long drink of water. I gulped down half the contents of my water bottle, inhaling through my nose as warm rivulets ran down my neck and beneath my shirt.

Culture shock is a strange thing; it only affects me in one direction. Sneak up behind me in my Oakland flat, blindfold me and drop me off in a rank woolen tent among the yak herders of Dolpo—lucky me. But beam me into a Chinese luxury hotel in the middle of the summer rush and watch me fall apart. Maybe culture shock isn't about "culture" at all; maybe it's a form of information sickness, a physical reaction to data overload—like being blasted out of a deep, sweet sleep by the head-slamming jingle of a Denny's ad.

Whatever it was, my hands were shaking as I reached into my belly-pack for the paper bearing Yao Yi's instructions. As I pulled it out I realized that I'd scrawled her directions on the back of something—a folded letter.

I opened it. It was the note that Sally had given me, along with the heavy brass compass, for my birthday. I read the message again:

> . . . *Just a reminder to let you know that where you are is exactly where you're meant to Be; and if you don't like it . . . wait a moment!! It'll change! That's the beauty of movement, and the challenge is letting go into it; a courageous act that is a testament to your love of this world, your availability to experience and the curiosity that has brought you to this moment. . . .*

I replaced the letter, shouldered my pack and headed for the elevator bank.

o   o   o

"Mr. Ruan?"

I stood in the doorway of Room 924. An elderly man wearing bifocals sat behind a cluttered metal desk, surrounded by airline tickets, passports and ledger books. A Vietnam Airlines ashtray held a smoldering fag.

"I am Ruan."

"Good afternoon." I stepped forward. "I'm Jeff Greenwald, the American journalist. Ms. Yao Yi of the China International Tourist Service faxed you my documents last Monday, from Kunming. I was instructed to pick up my Vietnam visa here today."

"Ah." He returned his attention to the pile of forms on his desk. I waited for a moment in silence.

"Mr. Ruan?"

"I am Ruan."

"Uh . . . I'm here for my visa? I'm to pick it up this afternoon. Ms. Yao Yi faxed you the forms from Kunming."

He didn't look up. "No fax come."

"But that's impossible," I said, smiling. "She called you up and confirmed that everything had arrived. Maybe"—I pointed to a high stack of faxes on the corner of the desk—"it's with those other forms."

Ruan reached over and leafed noncommittally through the papers. I spied mine near the bottom, pulled them out and set them before him. They seemed to jog his memory.

"Oh, yes. Everything come. One week ago." He pushed my documents aside. "But you must pay money. No money, no visa."

"Ah, yes, the money. Ms. Yao Yi told me about the money." I reached into my wallet and pulled out a crisp $50 bill. "I've got it right here."

Ruan took the currency out of my hand, examined it and set it down.

"Okay," he said cheerfully. "I give visa. No problem."

"Thanks so much."

Time passed.

"Mr. Ruan?"

"I am Ruan."

"My visa, sir . . .?"

"Visa? No problem. Two weeks, you come back, get visa."

"*Two weeks?*" A thin sweat collected on my brow. "Listen," I said. "I was told I could pick up my visa *today*. I must fly to Kunming tonight. My train to Hanoi leaves tomorrow."

"Who say? How? You fax forms, but no money! No money, no visa. Now, okay." He tapped the $50 bill. "Two weeks, visa. No problem."

"It *is* a problem," I moaned. "A big problem. Why can't you just process it now?"

"Impossible. Necessary send Hanoi for approval. Two weeks only." He peered at me above his glasses. "You go now. Visit Yangshuo. Very nice place. Two weeks, come back here."

I stood there in silence, my head swimming. Amazing, how short a time it had taken for everything to fall apart.

The whole situation was starting to look like a Chinese fire drill. Waiting two weeks in Canton—an open-air sauna—was out of the question, and there was clearly no point in flying back to Kunming.

I taxied through Canton in a daze, looking for the CITS office. I'd explain the situation, get my plane ticket to Kunming refunded—it had cost me a cool $100—and consider my options from there.

The clerk at Canton CITS scrutinized my ticket, and handed it back to me.

"Not possible to refund this here," he said. "You can refund only at place of purchase."

"But that was in Kunming. . . ."

"Correct. You can refund only in Kunming."

"But I just came from Kunming!"

"No problem. You just go back."

I narrowed my eyes. "How the hell am I supposed to get back to Kunming?"

He tilted his head, bewildered. "You have ticket. Why not fly?"

o   o   o

Canton was Bedlam, an oven, a zoo. The traffic was so thick and chaotic it made Karachi look like an Amish farm. I stashed my bags in the Garden Hotel branch of the U.S. Information Service and planted myself in the hotel's vast lobby, drinking ginger ale and waiting for *Now* to go away.

I examined the lay of the land. I could bide my time in China, return to Canton for my visa, fly back to Kunming and continue to Vietnam overland, as planned. By then it would be August; if I raced through Southeast Asia and got on the first ship leaving Malaysia, I could be back in California by Halloween. Workable? No way. Never mind that my deadline was the end of November; there was the cold fact of cash to consider. I took out my wallet and counted my traveler's checks. Eleven hundred bucks. That was it. I'd closed out my savings account from Kathmandu.

I sank into my chair, feeling faint. Vietnam, Thailand, Malaysia, Indonesia, Australia; the route that Sally and I had sketched out back in Oakland, a lifetime ago, it seemed, was burned onto the interior of my cranium like the letters on King Belshazzar's wall. I shook my head like an Etch A Sketch, trying to make the map fade away, but the effort made me so dizzy I had to put my head between my knees.

A tiny slip of green paper had fallen out of my wallet and lay on the floor by my feet. I gazed down at it, reading the message in the quivering auroric light:

> Nothing is written

The Paradise of Remy Martin

The Xingsu ferry steamed down the Pearl River, leaving Canton behind. I stood on the prow, nursing from a bottle of cognac as heat lightning flashed across the night sky. The warm wind smelled of ozone, and the distant banks twinkled with ruby ideograms. The ship's horn blasted once, sending a shock wave down the length of my spine. I drained the bottle and threw it overboard.

I was not going to Hanoi. I was not going to Bangkok, or Bali, or Perth. In Canton, that afternoon, after 216 days on the road, calmly and without self-blame, free from the gnaw of guilt or the clutch of desire, I realized I'd had enough.

I missed Oakland. I missed the Bay Area, with its broken foggy coastline and pachyderm redwood trees. I missed the Italian restaurants, the damp tennis courts, the pumpkin ice cream that would arrive at Double Rainbow a week before Halloween. I missed Yoshi's Nite Spot, long walks around Abbott's Lagoon, quiet evenings cooking Trader Joe's black tiger shrimp at home. I missed Black Oak Bookstore and Red Tail Ale. I missed my friends. I missed my pillows and sheets, and the way Coriola had looked tangled up in them. I missed waking up to Scoop Nisker's manic KFOG newscasts and walking down Piedmont Avenue to buy hot bagels. I missed my own damned coffee, my own damned music and the familiar chime my computer made as I turned it on for a full day of writing. I even missed my answering machine.

There was no need to cart my exhausted brain into Vietnam, Cambodia and Thailand, down the Malay Peninsula, across the Equator, through Sumatra and Java and Bali and down farther still, along the entire infinite coastline of Australia, to look for a ship in Sydney. There

was no need to visit every last country on Earth. The corona of molecules I'd deposited across the planet's surface, in an unbroken chain
from Oakland to Canton—indeed, to the very spot I was standing—
gleamed like a necklace in my inner eye.

I had learned its diameter. I could take myself home.

The Pearl River delta widened, meeting the South China Sea. Lightning flashed and hot, heavy drops pelted the deck. I ran out of the rain
and into the ferry's recreation room, catching the last act of *The Fugitive*
on TV.

At half past eleven I climbed into my bunk. We would arrive in Hong
Kong at dawn. A huge weight—for nothing, as Papaji had said, weighs
more than our expectations—had been lifted from my shoulders.

But I was not, despite my temporary ecstasy of relief, off the hook.
My months of wrangling for visas and sweating on luxury coaches
might have ended, but my pilgrimage was far from over.

I still had an ocean to cross.

· 44 ·

The Bardo of Egg McMuffins

One advantage of being a West Coast travel writer is that one gets to
know people all around the Pacific Rim. A friend in Hong Kong was
leaving for England the morning after I arrived, but gave me the keys to
his flat. And so I moved, in the space of two days, from a ragged bus
knee-deep in spittle to a lavish apartment appointed with two air con-
ditioners, a dehumidifier, a 1-bit CD player, satellite television, chocolate chip cookies in the fridge and—blow me down—a washer-dryer in
the pantry. Lightning cracked outside the balcony, splitting the summer heat like Oakland gunfire, but in my temperature-controlled paradise it was a cool autumn evening and the kettle was on.

It was strange, very strange, to be in Hong Kong, weaving between
skyscrapers of glass and titanium, watching heavy clouds drop their
shadows into the South China Sea. Part of me loved the dizzy, hardwired megalopolis, the candy-colored neon skyline seen from the Star
Ferry, the store windows packed with Nikons and Sonys and video cameras the size of Pop-Tarts, the cylindrical blasts of air that shot through
the tubes of the underground as the MTR trains to Central sailed into
Tsim Tsa Tsui Station. I loved the cold, dry air-conditioning that gusted

from the boutiques, carrying a hint of perfume, and the black-haired girls in clinging dresses waiting for streetcars along Hennessy Road.

I wandered down the whistling cacophony of Bird Street, where Chinese men stared hypnotized into the high-stacked cages as if they were a storefront wall of color TVs. I haunted the Foreign Correspondents' Club, where I could get a bowl of butter almond ice cream, with a cookie and strawberry in it, for $1.75. And I cherished the memory of a morning, not two weeks before, when all I had needed to be in heaven was a tub of hot water, a packet of Nescafé and a hard-boiled egg.

It was amazing and horrific to be back in the path of it again. Back in the path of *Penthouse* and McDonald's, WALK and DON'T WALK, Madonna and cold cuts, the Hard Rock Café.

It had happened so fast.

o   o   o

Scores of ships sail from the world's largest containerport each month, but finding passage on even one of them is virtually impossible. Hong Kong is a city consummately without a sense of humor, a habitat belonging to the no-nonsense school of enterprise. I grew accustomed to the look of blank bewilderment in people's eyes when I described my mission. Go home by ship? *Why?*

The fact that I was now in the air terminus of East Asia made my plight surreal. Day and night, the sky was filled with airplanes. Ferrying between Kowloon and Hong Kong Island, watching an endless procession of jets bank eastward across Victoria Harbor, I felt like a pelican who'd been caught in an oil spill. Every 747 was full of weary travelers heading for Seattle, San Francisco, LA. They'd be snug at home, unpacking their socks, before I ate my next Egg McMuffin.

I spent my afternoons in an air-conditioned cubicle at the Foreign Correspondents' Club, poring through the *Shipping Gazette*, pounding out faxes and calling every single shipping line servicing the West Coast. Hyundai, "K" Line, Maersk, Mexican, Mitsui, NYK, Sea-Land, Hapag-Lloyd; I tried them all. Few of the operations managers said no directly. It was always a matter of calling back after a few days, and a few days more than that, for my paperwork to creep up and down the chain of command. The main obstacle, as ever, was liability, but there were other alibis as well. The new containerships were designed for reduced crews and had no extra beds or life preservers. Sea-Land—leaving for Oakland in a week!—had a dozen extra rooms, but was training a group of seamen from Shanghai. The Japanese and Chinese lines simply didn't want any Yankees on board; the Koreans were afraid I wouldn't like their food. The cruelest blow of all came when American President Lines, based in my own home port, stonewalled me completely.

Big Fun

You want adventure? I'll give you adventure. Adventure is a long Monday night sitting alone on a foldout futon in a Clear Water Bay apartment, eating leftover cucumber salad from a plastic take-out container and listening to Neil Young on the component stereo....

The days went by. I passed my second Tuesday in Hong Kong without speaking to another human being, except for various robotic service personnel.

This put me in a quandary. All day long I'd been looking forward to my Event of the Week: getting home early, switching on the Pearl Network and watching *NYPD Blue*. Then I'd watch half an hour of *Twin Peaks*, read another hundred pages of *Fearless* and spend an hour or two writing. The problem was, I had nothing to write *about*.

But there was something going on in Central, as I guiltily knew. The Fringe, Hong Kong's only alternative theater and performance space, was hosting their bimonthly "Partners in Rhyme" night. The event began at eight, thirty minutes before *NYPD Blue*.

The conflict annoyed me. Was I so desperate for something to do that I'd actually go to a poetry reading . . . in Hong Kong? All right, in New York or Chicago or San Francisco, sure. But poetry in Hong Kong would be like pizza in Kunming. "Partners in Rhyme!" For the first time in my life I was torn between live performance and television. What finally resolved the decision was my hope, albeit slim, that I might meet other writers at the event. My life-in-waiting, a one-act drama set within the fluorescent funk of a seemingly endless low-pressure system, was undermining my usually infectious joie de vivre and addicting me to KitKats.

I rolled into the Fringe at quarter past eight, bought a pint, took a table near the stage and waited. At eight-thirty sharp the MC, a tall blond chap who resembled a goat, took the mike.

"We've got a mercifully short reading this evening," he announced. "We're competing with some great television tonight . . ."

The MC read first. His poetry was so bad it rhymed. He was followed by a Canadian with a misleading resemblance to Eric Bogosian who seemed to believe that high-volume garrulity could compensate for the vapidity of his verse. His poems, hurled at the audience like Greek traffic insults, were incomprehensible, though an undertone of misogyny emerged, skunklike, from the thicket.

The third reader was a Texan named Willis. Despite extreme stage fright he orated well, with a clear, strong voice. His poems narrated concise, honest episodes of devastating romantic failure with adolescent Chinese girls who wore too much eye shadow and had never heard of Camus. He was a soulful kind of guy, one of those perpetual outsiders who sometimes surprise you by having a sense of humor about their plight. I invited him over for a beer, but after ten minutes my attention flagged. I was looking for someone dangerous, or at least surprising. A woman, preferably, with black eyes and a cat and some idea of how to have fun in this empty place.

But finding a soul mate in Hong Kong was like looking for a bagel in Riyadh. I took the long ride home in the bright blue brushed aluminum glare of the MTR, cleaning my nails with my magnetic ticket. A girl was standing next to me, wearing a solid-gold Mickey Mouse ring and clutching a canvas tote bag—clearly of Japanese pedigree—with a large red slogan on the side:

**MR FRIENDLY
YOUR BEST ALLY!
HE ALWAYS STAYS NEAR YOU,
AND STEALS IN YOUR MIND, TO
LEAD YOU INTO A GOOD SITUATION**

Where was this guy when I needed him?

Mr. Friendly

Typhoons rolled up the South China Sea, skirting the Philippines, dumping their accumulated rain along the beleaguered coast of Guangxi. Large jets thundered over the Admiralty arcade, windows illuminated, their full cargo of relaxed and happy passengers drinking Absolut from tiny plastic bottles and watching Meg Ryan on small video screens. I craned my neck to follow them.

Ships continued to arrive and depart, but none of them had a place for me. I rented an apartment in Kowloon and bought a motorcycle. A month later I went to the Humane Society and brought home a dog, a white terrier that symbolized my final divorce from any of the preconceptions about the future that I might have harbored during those first two weeks, those first naïve and hopeful weeks after my arrival in Hong Kong.

It took me months to get used to the idea of going out to bars to meet people, but there wasn't a lot of choice. I joined the Fringe Club and started reading at the "Partners in Rhyme" series, taking chances, my desperate elocutions uncomplicated by any hope of rescue or fame. For the first time since adolescence I began to

write purely for myself, for the rhythm of the words. One Tuesday night in No-
vember I met a Burmese expatriate, a thirty-year-old woman who had escaped
her country's despotic regime and fled to Hong Kong to raise money for a small
band of freedom fighters encamped on the Laotian border. I took her home. She
moved in with me three weeks later, and brought her cat.

    The moment continued to expand, blossoming into space-time like baking
bread, the yeasted miracle of Now growing endlessly out of the pan. I was just an-
other raisin, carried along in the cinnamon loaf of Creation. It was not a bad
thing to be....

o   o   o

The line between reality and fantasy, hope and fear, was blurring. The sense of finality I had enjoyed upon leaving Canton was pure illusion. It could take months, years even, to find my way home. Still, there was no debate about it. I would take a ship, or I'd rent an apartment. No way was I getting on a plane.

    After two weeks of research, every shipping company save one—Hapag-Lloyd, whose chief op was on vacation—had turned me down. I telephoned Allen Noren, aware that it might be our last contact for many moons.

    "I can't believe you called," he said. "I was just about to fax you . . ."

    "No need to rush. I'll be here at least a couple more months. My plan is to sell my passport on the black market, and use the money to buy a sea kayak. If the currents are good I'll be home by next June. . . ."

    "No. Wait." His usually equable voice held a note of urgency. "Call your friend"—I could hear him shuffling papers—"Dwayne. Immediately. You have his number?"

    "Dwayne? You mean Newton? Is everything okay?"

    "You might say that. He called me this morning. Said he may have found you a ship."

    It was incredible, but true. Newton—Mr. Friendly incarnate—had come through again. The *Micronesian Pride*, part of the China Navigation fleet, would leave for Oakland on September 6. Captain Dennis Mitchell, the company's operations manager, was agreeable to signing me on.

    The *Pride*, a small and oddly designed container vessel (the superstructure was close to the prow, improving visibility but guaranteeing a rough ride), would take twenty-five days to get to Oakland, stopping at Saipan, Guam and Hawaii. There was just one catch—it would leave from Manila.

    The passage to Manila takes two to three days, depending on weather and currents. I went back to the *Gazette*, phoning the half-dozen companies ferrying cargo between Hong Kong and the Philippines. After a few days of back-and-forth negotiations, I'd landed myself a ship. The *Infinity*, a Fleet Trans vessel commanded by Captain Ricardo Janeo, made the round-trip once a week.

But it was too late to qualify for the next departure, leaving that afternoon. I'd have to stay in Hong Kong one more week.

The Bardo of Hungry Ghosts

Hong Kong's Festival of the Hungry Ghosts takes place during the seventh lunar month. The event is remarkably similar to Mexico's Día de los Muertos, during which the spirits of the dead visit their progeny for a nostalgic feast.

I got off the MTR stop at Wang Tai Sin and followed the signs up to the Taoist temple. There were a dozen old ladies outside the gate, begging for coins with paper McDonald's cups. Kiosks sold incense, gaudy good-luck ornaments and bright foil pinwheels that stood motionless, like silver lures in a still summer pond.

The temple was a new building, erected in 1973 in the traditional dragons-by-the-dozen style. There was a turtle solarium, an obsessively neat "Good Wish Garden" and a row of aluminum drinking fountains offering Hygienically Filtered Water. The Wang Tai Sin housing complex towered above the complex, a forest of bleak gray monoliths covered with an acne of dull balconies. Drying clothes fluttered from their high railings like battle-worn flags.

There were hundreds of people at the temple, laying out baskets of suckling pig, barbecued duck, ripe fruits and fat red candles. The air was thick with smoke. Scores of devotees kneeled before the main prayer room, igniting small bonfires of rectangle-shaped origami and putting the match to flat folded constructions that resembled terminally overstarched shirts. I'd seen these paper inventions for sale by the gate, and couldn't figure out what they were. Equally puzzling were the thick-wristed bankrolls of "Hell Bank" notes, always in astronomical denominations.

The refuse bins at every corner of the temple courtyard overflowed with sheaves of brilliantly colored papers, emblazoned with bold Chinese characters and faux gold and silver leaf. My friend Paula, an Oakland collage artist, would relish these découpageable scraps. I had scavenged an impressive stash when a middle-aged Chinese man wearing Ray Bans and a point-and-shoot Canon stopped me. I glanced at him guiltily, wondering if it was some sort of sin to steal religious garbage.

But the man was grinning. "Do you know what those are?"

I sheepishly admitted that I didn't.

"Look." He took a sheet from my pile and, with a few deft folds, transformed it into a lightweight replica of a gold ingot. "You burn these," he explained, "and they become like real. We do this for our dead families." He gestured at the ground. "Down there."

"Down there? You mean in Hell?"

"Of course. The spirits of our ancestors stay there, but one time in a year—starting today, for two weeks—the gateway between Hell and Earth is open. Then the ghosts can come visit—but they must have money to spend. So we burn this paper money, and it goes to them. We also offer the food. The ghosts don't eat it, they just enjoy the smell. We bring it home and eat it ourselves."

"Why," I asked, "do you assume that your dead relatives are in Hell? I mean, couldn't they be in Heaven?"

"Ha, ha, ha! I don't know." He became suddenly serious. "I think, maybe, Hell."

I found this Chinese perspective an intriguing reversal of original sin. We're not necessarily *born* evil, but by the time we die. . . .

The man gestured to the starched shirt patterns in my hand. "Sometimes," he said, "some ghosts, they haven't got anyone to offer them food or money. They have nothing, not even clothes. What to do? So some generous people, they burn these. That way, even the hungry ghosts without family will have something to wear."

o   o   o

Taoism, as practiced in Hong Kong, contained many elements familiar to me from Nepali and Tibetan Buddhism. On the Wheel of Life the Hungry Ghost Realm is one of the six realms of existence, a dry piece of spiritual real estate situated between Hell and the Animal Realm. While not subject to the torments of true Hell, beings trapped in the Hungry Ghost Realm suffer terribly. They are afflicted with a continual, gnawing hunger, and although mountains of food surround them, their mouths are the size of pinheads. They can never assuage their hunger, can barely slake their thirst. Greedy consumption is the whole of their existence.

All of the six realms (even the Human one, real as it seems to us) are illusory states, way stations visited by consciousness on its long, slow climb toward nirvana. Each has its own specific quality. Anger scalds the Hell realm, while greed torments the Hungry Ghosts. The Animals suffer from ignorance, the Demigods are afflicted by jealousy and the

Gods themselves are crippled by pride. Chokyi Nyima Rimpoche once pointed out that the unenlightened mind visits all of these realms each day, spinning haphazardly from ignorance to pride, from jealousy to anger. The attribute defining the Human Realm, the lama informed me, is desire. But desire is a sword that cuts two ways—for it is the desire for liberation that leads, ultimately, to freedom.

And what, I wondered, was the buzzword of my own pilgrimage? Not anger, certainly, although I'd experienced my share. Not ignorance, despite the fact that the main thing I had learned, in nearly eight months of travel, was how little I knew about the world. It was not jealousy, certainly, even though the sight of roaring jets made my heart itch; and there had been too many balks and fouls for me to feel overwhelmed by pride.

Desire, of course—the desire to honor my vocation and my planet—had motivated my global kora from the start. But if anything had interfered with those best of intentions, it could only be greed. Greed for experience, sensation and exotic visas.

This was nothing new. Growing up on Long Island, I was afflicted at an early age with "map fever." This was more than a compulsion to cover my walls; it was a need to *possess* the places those maps represented, to accumulate destinations. In the tribal rituals of the ancients, a boy was hiked into manhood by vision quests or by bagging a difficult pelt. My American initiation, a coming-of-age in the land of consumerism, had combined aspects of both. I wanted not only to experience mysterious new places, but to collect them as well. Nothing had symbolized this better than my huge map of the United States, stuck full of pins, heavy with the destination voodoo of the post-Kerouac generation.

And, like the Hungry Ghosts, I could never be satisfied—even after a trip that had taken me the better part of a year and carried me to the soil of twenty-three countries.

It was time to let that greed go. Never again would I organize a banquet as vast or as varied as the one I had devoured during my seven months abroad. If my hunger was yet unfulfilled perhaps it was time—as Nick Gregory, Carroll Dunham and even Sally had suggested—to seek nourishment elsewhere.

But if the hungry ghost inside me still wanted the world, he could have it. I swung off my daypack, unzipped the map pocket and pulled out the 1:30,000,000 scale Peters projection that had accompanied me through my entire journey.

The man who had stopped me by the trash bin had worked fast, but I was able to recall his movements. I folded my world map into a huge gold ingot and made my way through the crowd to the smoke-shrouded offering table.

Mail Call

Four days before the *Infinity* was scheduled to sail for Manila my friend returned from London and reclaimed his Clear Water Bay flat. I moved my gear into a lavish suite at the Mandarin Oriental Hotel and threw myself into a *Wired* profile on Jimmy Lai: a rag-trade tycoon-turned-media giant whose muckraking *Next* Magazine had Beijing climbing the Wall.

On the twenty-third of August—one day prior to my departure date—I received a fax at the Foreign Correspondents' Club. It consisted of a single sentence:

> *Hapag-Lloyd is agreeable to provide free passage to Mr. Jeff Greenwald from Hong Kong to Oakland aboard the Bremen Express, departing Hong Kong 4 September.*

I phoned Albert Lau, an operations manager employed by the shipping agency that handled Hapag-Lloyd. The *Bremen Express* was a container turbine ship, he explained, nearly a thousand feet long. It would make the trans-Pacific crossing in just over two weeks, stopping at ports in Taiwan and Japan.

This was it. This was the way to go. But the thought of waiting in Hong Kong another twelve days was intolerable. Not only that—I'd been totally seduced by the prospect of a week in the Philippines, cultivating melanomas on a sun-basted beach while assessing, with a long drink in my hand, the lessons of the past months.

I telephoned Fleet Trans and, receiving their assurance that there were frequent ships commuting between Hong Kong and Manila, made my decision.

Life was too short to spend twenty-five days reading Stephen King novellas. I would have my cake and eat it, too.

• 45 •

To: **Allen Noren, O'Reilly & Associates**
From: **Jeff Greenwald, Hong Kong Island**
Subject: **Big World/The Bardo of Beepers**

This morning, as I was working on a *Wired* story, my hard disk crashed—leaving me in the position of a cartoon character who, having inadvertently stepped off a cliff, has just enough time to cast the audience a look of droll regard before plummeting to the ground. After spending an hour tearing the Hong Kong directory to shreds looking for a service center (good luck on Sunday; this place shuts down like the Vatican), I booted up again and got about five paragraphs in before the dreaded bomb icon reappeared.

It can happen again, any minute. I'm writing on borrowed time. Somewhere in the bowels of this finicky 80-megabyte beast is a disaster waiting to happen, a silicon Sword of Damocles poised above the neck of this *Big World.*

How long have we got? Who knows—but we better eat fast. Here, then, is a platter of snacks, hastily prepared and easily swallowed. May as well call it . . .

Hong Kong Dim Sum

Plate 1: Sweet and Sour Soap Leaves

So here I am in a room at the Mandarin Oriental, a five-star hotel overlooking the neon-dappled waters of Victoria Harbor. Beyond the harbor lie the hills of Kowloon, and beyond them the whole world that I've crossed, from Kathmandu to Canton, since May. My horizon ends, as per Saul Steinberg's famous cartoon, with Nepal; the preceding ten thousand miles are a foreshortened procession of place names, lost over the curve of the Earth. That the world is round I'm almost certain, though I won't know for sure until North America heaves into view. On that day I will face the crucible of all the hopes and regrets I have alloyed into this trip. More and more, though, the very fact of having "done it" (assuming I do) seems enough, and I am coming to the understanding that, when it's all over, everything on Earth that rolled out from under my feet will roll back beneath them again. . . .

"But what," you shrilly interrupt, "are you doing in a $514-a-night suite in the Mandarin Oriental Hotel?"

Good question. The answer is that I am currently the honored guest of this venerable establishment. Patrons of fine journalism, the hotel management has generously agreed to put me up for three days and nights, that I might experience the polar opposite of my bus trek through the wilds of southern China. All they ask in return is that I write about them—and now I've done that, haven't I?

You can always tell how posh a hotel is by the stuff they put in your bathroom: two indigo-blue plastic boxes containing round bars of perfumed British soap, a miniature imported shaving kit with an adorable little aerosol can of shaving cream, scented talcum powder, two designer toothbrushes (for uppers and lowers?), bath salts, cotton buds, "soap leaves" (I have no idea), shower gel, body lotion (pink), two industrial-strength terrycloth bathrobes, eleven towels (one for each hand, foot and limb, a head cloth, a torso towel and a butt polisher), and of course shampoo, conditioner, bubble bath, Q-tips and shower cap. The desk drawers contain embossed stationery, phone books, a plethora of Mandarin Oriental propaganda, a Gideon's, a fire escape map, a blow-dryer, souvenir luggage stickers and something called a shoe-shine sponge, which jumped out of my hand and ran from the room the minute it saw my boots.

The bedroom is dominated by a huge stereo TV. There are ten channels but, except for CNN, nothing remotely of interest. I switch to channel 3, the on-line movie station. The Mandarin was among the first hotels in Hong Kong to install a high-tech video bank that lets one choose at will from titles listed on-screen. Of the sixty movies available, twenty are so-called "adult" films: ten American, ten Japanese.

Few gnomons of cultural dissimilarity are more obvious than the difference between Japanese and American porn titles. While the Yank channel features such flicks as *Talk Dirty to Me, Penetrating Thoughts* and *Dripping with Desire,* the ever-subtle Japs humbly offer such classics as *Ari, the Sex Beast; Chihiro, the Schoolgirl* and—my favorite—*Rie, An Imprisoned Woman Teacher.*

I tell you, this place is elegant. It's nothing like the bus. For one thing, breakfast is truly expensive. The maid (one of six dozen) slides a room service menu beneath the door. Yikes! Thirty dollars for ham 'n' eggs! Ten clams for pancakes! What's "Scottish kipper . . ."? I must confess something. My favorite breakfast in Hong Kong, no lie, is an Egg McMuffin with one of those hash brown wedges that tastes like an overcooked latke. A little ketchup, some half-and-half . . . but I digress. It's time for our next dim sum course, the irresistible:

Plate 2: Flash-Fried Octopus with Liquid Crystals

One memory that will stay with me forever is the image of scores of glassy-eyed men and women—riding the MTR, walking along Ice House

Road or driving sleek German cars—muttering into the slim fold-down jaws of cellular phones. To a Luddite like me, who thinks that even Walkmen are escapist, these phones are the harbingers of a new Age of Isolationism. The fact that these people are talking to other people is inconsequential. The reality is that they're utterly removed from their environments, walking down the avenues in electronic comas. They glide through the masses of humanity debarking at Admiralty and Tsim Tsa Tsui like pod-people, responding to voices as ethereal as those that beguiled Saint Joan.

Pocket phones are one sign of technological affluence—there are others. Woe to the child who can afford only a Walkman, or a GameBoy. Here in Hong Kong, even sixth-graders carry beepers. "Oh, it's very important," a ten-year-old assured me before flying off the MTR at Central. But *why?* No elaboration was forthcoming.

I'll venture a guess. Beepers, I believe, are symptomatic of the peculiar neurosis of our Neosilicate Epoch, the conviction that one dare not, even for an instant, disappear from sight. "At any moment," a New York Yankees billboard once chortled, "a great moment." It was a slogan calculated to bond you, with the Krazy Glue of perpetual anticipation, to your radio or TV set, and it's a sentiment that the young and restless of Hong Kong seem to share. In a world so thinly schmeared with great moments, no one wants to risk missing theirs.

But the trend has alarming consequences. What was once dignified as "personal space" is now damned as unsociability. Patience, already scant as helium, is evaporating by the hour. There was a time—I dimly remember—when, if a friend's line was busy, one tried back later. If there was no answer, it meant the party was out. One would call again or, if it wasn't critical, drop it. No longer. In the very near future, the inability to find someone within 120 seconds of dragging their name into one's id will be seen as a form of betrayal. *"Where the fuck were you? I've been calling for two minutes."*

The era of sweating it out by the phone has faded into adolescent history, along with "mad money" and goldfish gulping. The classic "I tried to phone but you were out" (or the more contemporary "I called but your answering machine wasn't working") doesn't cut it in Hong Kong—The City Where No One Misses a Call.

Plate 3: Chicken Skin in White Wine Gravy

The featured movie at the Hong Kong Space Museum—screening three times each afternoon—is called *Comet Crash!* The film details the discovery of comet Shoemaker-Levy and simulates, with wicked computer graphics, the cataclysmic collision between the fragmented space debris and planet Jupiter.

I tried to see the film this afternoon, but it was completely sold out. I wasn't surprised. One couldn't pick a better metaphor for the deepest fears lurking in the subconscious of every local citizen.

Hong Kong is on its own collision course. On July 1, 1997, Great Britain's ninety-nine-year lease on Hong Kong, Kowloon and the New Territories will expire, and the former colony will revert—with all the alacrity of an adopted child being forcibly returned to his or her abusive birth parents—to mainland-Chinese hands.

Did I mention "borrowed time"? Hong Kong wrote the book. The imminent transfer of power looms like the Twilight Zone, an ominous threshold beyond which nothing can be assumed. It is no longer even talked about. The Great Switcheroo of 1997 has become one of those huge scandals in which anticipation has worn itself threadbare, and speculation has dissolved into a deep existential weariness. The fact is that no one knows what is going to happen. The situation, for years the focus of intense debate, has reached the point where one person's guess is no better than another's; where the careful projections of a Ph.D. in economics are no more or less likely to prove true than the wildest ravings of the blind leper rattling his cup in the Jardine House overpass.

The result of this repressed anxiety is a universal schizophrenia, lurking beneath the surface of every enterprise and encounter. On the one hand there's denial—the conviction that nothing will really change. That nothing, in fact, is going to happen at all. But the flip side of this delusion is an air of obsessive apprehension, a collective nail biting about the future belied by the huge skyscrapers and vast land-reclamation projects under construction just outside my balcony. Two pubs, around the corner from each other, sum up the two points of view. One is called *The Time Is Always Now;* the other, *1997.* Young British bankers wearing Philippe Charriol tie bars and *GQ* smiles stagger between them, eyeing lithe Chinese beauties who bark absently into cellular phones.

The comet is on its way and the dinosaurs are very, very nervous. But whether the future will be warm- or cold-blooded is anyone's guess.

Plate 4: Prawn Wonton with Fresh Fruit and Diesel Fuel

I've just returned from a visit to the Mandarin Health Club—hot tubs, cold tubs, and more marble than the Parthenon. Luxury can be very surreal. There's nothing like sitting in a pine sauna and watching CNN coverage of the bombings in South Lebanon to remind me that this is a very big world, and to make me very glad I'm on the other side of it.

But my time in Asia is winding, at long last, to a close. Ten days from today I will carry my pack onto the eighth and final vessel of this pilgrimage: Hapag-Lloyd's *Bremen Express,* bound for Taiwan, Japan—and Oakland.

In the meantime, I'm treating myself to a desperately needed detour. Early tomorrow I'll board the *Infinity,* a one-hundred-meter cargo ship carrying oranges, apples and frozen prawns to the Philippines. Arriving in Manila, I'll make my way south, to the island of Mindoro. After five days of scuba diving I'll return to Hong Kong, spend one night repacking and begin the long voyage home.

For the Mandarin spa, lavish as it was, did not provide the cleansing I seek. I need to get myself submerged, far enough down so that the only sounds are the bubbling of released nitrogen, the swirl of currents and the scraping of parrotfish beaks on live coral. Before facing up to the Pacific, my body and soul require ritual immersion in the primal element of this

Note from Allen Noren: Greenwald's transmission ends here.

⚡   ⚡   ⚡

Oranges, Apples and Prawns

Approaching the *Infinity* was like coming upon an ancient, active Egyptian tomb, or the launchpad of a space shuttle. Spotlights flooded the area, and tremendous cranes danced in the sodium glare. The moan of winches filled the night with a siren's song, punctuated by the hollow roar of containers falling into place.

We were supposed to set sail at midnight, but the loading was behind schedule. I stood on the bow of the ship and watched as huge steel boxes, dangling from heavy-duty cranes, swung into our hold. Steel cables cut across the sky, slicing the moon like a hard-boiled egg. It was a noisy place to be. Steam hissed, cranks and pulleys moaned and squeaked, and every few minutes arose the timpanic boom of one steel container colliding heavily with another.

I clung to the handrail as I walked along the rain-slicked deck, roaring drunk after two drinks on an empty stomach. Above my head, mammoth cargo containers rocked in the air. The crane operators, bare-chested teenagers, couldn't see the boxes once they'd been lowered into the hull and had to rely on elaborate hand signals from stevedores squatting below. The precision of the process amazed me. Every container must slip exactly onto four anchor pins, located at each corner of the container below. The work was performed with surgical skill, despite the behemoth size of the cranes and the fact that both loading ferries—as well as the *Infinity* —were rocking crazily in the windy harbor.

It was a scene from Conrad, timeless and raw, played out against the pulsing neon skyline of modern Hong Kong.

· 46 ·

To Manila

gale warning—tropical storm 9418 upgraded from tropical depression 998 hpa at 18.6n 115.7e south china sea moving westnorthwest 12 knots x expected max winds 45 knots near center for next 24 hours x radius of over 30 knot winds 120 miles x

o   o   o

We struck into it the second night, sometime past eleven. The *Infinity* rolled and growled as I rewound *The Fugitive* and pulled myself up the narrow stairwell to my claustrophobic bunk in the ship's infirmary. I stripped naked and climbed into bed, hoping to reach the end of William Boyd's *Brazzaville Beach*, but reading was impossible. It didn't matter if I lay on my front, back or side. The ship was lurching wildly, and every new pitch rolled me between the retaining walls of my bed like a loose beer bottle in a Greyhound bus.

I didn't "spit." An antinausea patch, stuck behind my left ear, effectively "neutralized the part of the brain stem that controls the reflex to vomit." It also made me blurry-eyed, distracted and sort of woozy—a small price to pay to avoid seasickness. I'd forgotten how miserable it could be; how that dizzy sloshing motion kills the desire to eat, shower or even think. One night was all it took to convince me that two weeks on the Pacific would be sufficient.

Our second day at sea the tropical depression fell behind us. We cut slowly through steady vertical rain, the sky pearlescent white, the unbroken arc of the horizon sketched with chalk.

The *Infinity* was a friendly ship. The fifteen-man crew was entirely Filipino. Spark, the radio officer, made a special effort to be hospitable, inviting me into his room to look through his bin of old *Newsweeks*. A good man, that Spark. I was touched by his posters: a doe-eyed, bikini-clad Phoebe Cates, directly opposite a morose Mother Mary.

There were pinups of women all over the ship. Most featured bare arms, naked shoulders and some cleavage, but there was nothing even softly pornographic about them. The models smiled in a comely girl-next-door fashion, their procreative charms taking a back seat to the larger feminine archetype. It made sense. *Infinity* was, after all, a short-haul vessel, immune to the gnawing sexual pangs endemic on transoceanic freighters. It struck me, finally, that the universal presence of female images in all-male work environments is more than a matter of titillation. It's a deeply necessary balancing act, the soul's effort to keep the anima alive. The longer the period of isolation, the more graphic the reminders become. On the *Ursus Delmas* it was all tits and ass—but on the *Infinity*, rarely away from her home port for more than a week, even the virginal Phoebe Cates would suffice.

Our final night at sea was overcast and black; it was impossible to tell where the *Infinity* ended and the South China Sea began. I climbed the stairs to the bridge and opened the door. Red and amber instrument lights glowed like lizard eyes in the blackness, eclipsed by the pacing second mate. I stood on the starboard pilot's deck and lit a cigarette, staring outward but looking within.

o   o   o

By morning the weather was hot and fine. Soft islands appeared in the near distance; news and warnings crunched from the radio. We passed Corregidor Island, heading directly for Manila's hazy skyline. Lokanin Point appeared to portside, bristling with ships. Short-lived rainbows scattered through our wake like broken cookies, and a dark, energetic band of current swept off to port.

It was a sweet summer day in the Philippines, and I was not sorry to be there.

Jeepneys Named Yahweh

There is a special innocence about the Philippines, manifested most visibly in the Filipinos themselves: a pleasant, generous and above all numerous people who seem to have just emerged from Sunday school. Nearly every vehicle, from the wildly decorated and chrome-plated "jeepneys" with their ultraviolet headlights to the gleaming motorcycle sidecars painted with fluorescent Stealth bombers, is plastered with bumper stickers testifying to the Glory of God, love of the Lord Jesus Christ and the absolute importance of praying the rosary.

It was my impression that the whole place is an enormous extended family. There's no other way to explain how the Filipinos behave in traffic. People sit in each other's laps on the public buses. Not a single driver ever loses his temper, and rare is the motorist who will turn a blind eye to a fellow trying to edge in from the side. Faith can move mountains, but the Filipinos are the only people I've seen who trust in God to keep traffic flowing.

And Manila, a city of nine million people, had the worst traffic I'd ever encountered. Worse than Istanbul; worse than Karachi; worse, even, than Canton. It is a city living nose-to-bumper, a place where locals would no sooner lose patience in traffic than while waiting for their own piss to flow. Gridlock is a part of life in Manila, a law of the natural universe that brooks neither explanation nor argument. I spent hours in it: waiting for lights to change, for cars to creep ahead by half a length, for endless snakes of Hondas and jeepneys named "Yahweh" to nose past billboards promoting a cuisine so appalling that the national dish is a baby pig with a stick up its ass.

Imelda Marcos was right: There's nothing to do in Manila but collect shoes. I got out as quickly as possible.

o   o   o

There were sixty-two air fresheners dangling from the ceiling of the coach to Batangas, most of them shaped like trees. The alpine theme was echoed by the air-conditioning, which kept the bus just a notch cooler than Walt Disney's cryogenic tomb. I rubbed my arms and peered out the frosted window at a plethora of dubious enterprises:

Tailoring by Big Machine
Miggy's Piggies
Dabee's Sing-A-Long and Home Furnishings
Pure Luck Investment Company
Max's Restaurant: "The House That Fried Chicken Built"

And my runaway personal favorite:

Paula's Party Supply: Clowns, Jugglers, Live Chicken Eater, etc.

I disembarked in Batangas, walked toward the docks and bargained my way onto a crowded *bangka*—a narrow motorized skiff—for the ninety-minute sail to northeastern Mindoro Island. August had been uncommonly calm, and the usually tempestuous Verde Island Passage was metallic blue and coarsely mottled, like rhinoceros hide. I savored a smoke, watching the water cleave and spray under the wooden boat's bamboo outriggers.

My flight from civilization was not without its twinge of professional guilt. No doubt there were loads of insightful stories to be written about the Philippines, a splash of verdant volcanic geography that, having flourished in the spotlight of Cory Aquino's "People Power" revolution, was now wilting in the world media shadow. I could have written about the closing of the U.S. base at Subic Bay, contemplating the fate of the 120,000 newly unemployed residents thereof. I could have devised a cogent appraisal of the post-Marcos leadership, reaffirming what most educated Filipinos suspected all along (that one wealthy, privileged ruling family had been replaced by another of similar peerage). I could have thrashed my way into the bush to annoy the indigenous tribal groups as they enjoyed, I suspected, their final year or two of peace before the inevitable tourism onslaught (you've got to replace an obsolete military R&R industry with something) began in earnest.

But investigative reporting was the last thing I wanted to busy myself with the final few weeks of my round-the-world kora. In point of fact I had left Hong Kong completely exhausted with the surface of the Earth, and with an eye to escaping it—and its garrulous inhabitants—posthaste.

Reef-fringed Mindoro Island, with its geckos, garlic sellers and ant-infested bungalows, was the best place to begin.

The Size of the World

Sitting on the porch of my thatch-roofed bungalow on Small La Laguna Beach, typing away, I realized that I looked exactly like the illustration on the cover of Perry Garfinkel's *Travel Writing for Profit and Pleasure*. Well, shit; if I was becoming a cliché, it might as well be an exotic one.

A few yards away, the ocean gleamed like a turned steel blade. From the neighboring bungalow the strains of "Hotel California"—planet Earth's lowest common musical denominator—writhed toward me through the unfurling heat. The oscillating fan hummed, nearly drowning out the voices of the villagers bargaining over ropes of garlic on the beach. Geckos croaked, and tiny ants paraded into my floppy disk drive.

o   o   o

Scuba diving instructors are a breed apart. I'd be hard-pressed to explain this precisely, but a specific set of quirks seems to accompany the

vocation. Many of the professional divers I've met appear vaguely uncomfortable on land, as if hyperconscious of their mammalian bodies
and the obnoxious demands of gravity. Like dogs forced to "dance" on
their hind legs, they act edgy, awkward and generally put out.

More than posture, though, there's personality. One of the most obvious things about being underwater is that it forbids speech. Conversation consists exclusively of body language, and the rare percussive rap
of a knife hilt against an aluminum tank. When one makes one's living
in an environment where vocal contact is impossible, one's appetite for
small talk diminishes. It's not that diving teachers are hard to converse
with. They're not. But you get the feeling they engage society with a certain reticence—as if they're reluctant to admit, to themselves and the
world, that they're not really fish.

The description fit Allan Nash to a T-valve. A big, bullshit-proof
Aussie with a Friar Tuck hairline, San Miguel spare tire and spirit-level
eyes, Nash relocated to the Philippines in 1985. Previously he'd been in
Hong Kong, working as a construction supervisor and making a for-
tune as a co-owner of Rick's Café, a popular watering hole in the Tsim
Tsa Tsui district.

But it was seawater, not Stoly, that ran in his veins. Certified to dive
at twelve, he toyed with the passion for nearly twenty years before deciding to make a living at it. It's a tough racket, but Nash is one of
those quiet, straight-shooting guys who have a sixth sense about business. His career change steered him toward Mindoro Island, where he
became the course director of Asia Divers: a family of state-of-the-art
dive shops anchored on Small La Laguna Beach.

If the Philippines are world-famous for great diving, the reefs
around Mindoro are a big part of the reason. There are twenty-five individual dive sites within a few hours' motoring of Small La Laguna—
places with names like Shark Cave, Canyons, Fish Bowl and Pink
Wall—and each has its devoted apostles. I wouldn't have time to visit
them all, but I at least hoped to join Allan for a descent to his personal
favorite. When I asked if he could arrange it, he shrugged agreeably.

"Sure," he said.

I hinted that we could go anywhere—as long as it was the best place
he knew. Again the shrug, but this time with a devious grin.

"Ah, we'll go someplace close," he said. "Maybe Canyons. It doesn't
really matter. But, if it's all right with you, I'd like to make it a dawn
dive."

"A 'dawn dive'?" I'd done plenty of night dives—pestering parrotfish,
mingling with morays and blundering into the arms of exasperated octopi—but I'd never even heard of a dawn dive.

"Yep." Nash was a man of few words. "Meet me at the dive shop to-morrow morning."

"Super. What time?"

"Let's see . . . How's four thirty?"

o   o   o

The sky was a grape Popsicle as we loaded our gear into the dive shop's slim bangka and hauled ourselves in. The crescent moon hung directly overhead, and a few planets threw bright sparks onto the sea. I wasn't at all tired—the drinks I'd had with dinner had knocked me out by ten—but I felt sorry for the hapless vacationers who would wake to the roar of our motor.

Allan kept his eyes on his watch as the boatman drove us around the eastern flank of the island. When we arrived at his "spot"—a seemingly anonymous patch of water that long experience (and excellent eyesight) enabled him to pinpoint with deadly accuracy—he slipped into his tank and fins with the effortless élan of Cindy Crawford wriggling into her birthday suit.

"Come on . . . let's go . . ." He untangled my air hose from around my neck, checked my weight belt and switched on my light. "Let's do it."

Before I could nod he'd rolled backward, falling silently into the black water. A minute later I was bobbing beside him, listening to my breath hiss through my regulator and purging the air from my buoyancy vest.

We dropped steadily, two web-footed figures speared by dancing beams of yellow light. Eighty feet down the trunklike shapes of the reef appeared below us, and we angled ourselves parallel to the ocean floor.

A coral reef before dawn is not unlike midtown Manhattan at the same hour. The structures are still there, poised yet oddly silent, and the streets are nearly empty. A few early risers—sluggish but deter-mined—navigate the familiar avenues, enjoying the brief solitude and easy commute.

One of the main differences, of course, is that on a coral reef the buildings themselves are alive. Brilliant yellow polyps bloomed on the pink cup corals, coaxing microscopic nourishment out of the current. By day the polyps would retract into their calciferous abodes: ancient, infinitely branching communities built on the skeletons of their fore-bears. The caves and crannies of the living reef sheltered a few of the neighborhood's other residents. Pulsing octopi peered out from tiny hollows, their huge eyes constricting in our torch beams; snoozing par-rotfish hung comatose beneath rocky overhangs; trumpetfish drifted over fuchsia feather worms like javelins in slow motion, their tail fins fluttering as rapidly as hummingbird wings. A white-tipped reef shark twisted by, off to an early breakfast in deeper waters.

In fifteen minutes the water was suffused with a turquoise glow. The shapes of the reef, if not its colors, were now distinct.

Throughout childhood I dreamed of becoming an astronaut. I longed to visit the moon and planets and to drift, free of gravity, above strange and amazing landscapes. While waiting for that particular fantasy to materialize, I've been able to satisfy my craving—partially, at least—by diving. Weightless as a spacewalker, breathing compressed air, I could easily imagine myself footloose in some unearthly realm, hovering within an alien environment populated by weird creatures. As I floated above that dark, busy reef in the Philippines, the terrestrial world seemed impossibly distant.

I breathed slowly, conserving air, relishing the knowledge that I'd succeeded. I had escaped the planet's surface. The fact that my victory would be short-lived made no difference. Thirty minutes in this underwater realm, surrounded by creatures who knew nothing of either O. J. or Bart Simpson, was all I needed to recharge my batteries. The tough part was reminding myself that this parallel universe was anything but alien; that most of the Earth's population lives not in Beijing or the Brazilian rain forest, but beneath the undulating surface of the sexy, secretive sea.

Twenty-five minutes into our dive, there was enough light to see by. Nash snapped off his torch. We looked like Jurassic fleas, preserved in an immensity of pale blue sap. Around us, the less curious denizens of the reef conducted their business imperturbed. Puffer fish drifted between branches of bubble coral and purple sea fans; a sinister-looking moray emerged from its lair between plates of sheet coral, showing fanglike teeth as it stretched its jaws to breathe. Above the mechanical sigh of my own breathing I heard an erratic scraping as wakening parrotfish, grazing for algae, worried the corals with their hard beaks.

The divemaster rapped on his tank and, eyebrows raised, showed me the thumbs-up. It was time to ascend.

The key to ascending safely is ascending slowly. To allow residual nitrogen to leave the bloodstream, one should never rise faster than one's tiniest air bubbles. We rotated into standing position, squeezed a breath of air into our buoyancy vests and began the slow drift up.

With every meter the sea became brighter, a more luminous aquamarine. Looking up, I could see its vast surface: a rippling mercurial plain, stretching in all directions. It was tinted with pink and orange highlights; and as we continued to rise, patiently, slowly, the pink exploded with yellow flames. . . .

I've waited for the sun to come up in a hundred places, and watched its atomic disk torch the horizon over jungle, desert and sea. But this was the first time I'd ever seen a sunrise from *below the Earth's surface.* Allan looked at me through his mask, eyes alive. I nodded back, amazed. Any divemaster can show you a good wreck or a tame moray eel; not many of them will show you a miracle.

As we hung suspended, decompressing at three meters, I experienced a feeling I'd had seven months before, watching moonrise from the deck of the *Ursus Delmas.* I could actually *feel* the motion of the Earth, and sense in my bones the silent cosmic roll of our planet on its axis. Once in a while, you get it: the size of the world.

We broke the surface, buoyant as corks, and slipped off our masks. Allan grinned, broadly, and floated on his back.

"Well?" he asked.

The sun balanced on the horizon, a freshly poured doubloon.

"Thanks," I said.

• 47 •

Permission to Come Aboard

Albert Lau's white Mercedes—the Jebsen and Company car—darted through the Hong Kong streets. A thinning rainbow hung over Kowloon. It was 7:00 A.M.

Lau drove through the Cross Harbor Tunnel and out past Jordan, entering the parklike wilderness of the outer port area. He turned through the gate of berth 8 and parked near a generic white building. A small truck with a flashing blue light pulled up, and we hopped in.

The *Bremen Express* rested along the dock, as weathered and broad as a captured whale. Her slightly convex hull, jet-black, disappeared into the fog. Monstrous red gantry cranes rolled on tracks alongside the ship, swinging loaded steel containers onto her deck like toys. I watched in awe. There was an industrial majesty to the scene that one rarely sees in these days of nanotechnology, and it was deeply satisfying to watch these gigantic machines at work. A microprocessor is miraculous, but it's more or less invisible. For sheer visceral thrill, few sights can compete with the colossal choreography of a modern containerport.

The *Bremen Express* was as impenetrable as a moated castle. We gained access via a slippery aluminum gangway that angled steeply up to the poop deck as the black, oily sea gargled below.

o　　　o　　　o

Upon entering the staging room, my impression was that I'd boarded a gigantic yacht. Cushioned chairs and couches were set against the walls, facing a console TV. The floor was carpeted. The portside corner was completely occupied by a wet bar, and heavy glass steins sat in a stainless steel sink beneath a polished beer tap. Compact discs were stacked below the port windows—I spied Piaf and Belafonte—and the walls were covered with commemorative plaques and garden-variety lithos of nineteenth-century schooners.

Lau and I sat down at a low oval table. Beyond the thick, forward-facing windows, the continual loading of containers was audible as distant thunder.

Captain Netz walked in, dressed in a summer shirt, epaulets and shorts. A scarf was tied around his neck, giving him a rakish, sport sailor's air. A healthy, energetic man with an appropriately commanding manner—and a good head of hair graying only at the sideburns—he looked forty-eight. I was off, Lau whispered, by ten years.

We shook hands. Netz picked up my paperwork and glanced at the top sheet in a perfunctory way.

"So! You will be accompanying us to Oakland?"

"With your permission, sir."

"Yes, yes! You're welcome"—he directed his gaze pointedly at the bar—"so long as you pay for your beer. And soft drinks, too. I'll tell Officer Gleick to give you the meal schedule."

"In case I don't see him, what time is breakfast?"

"Breakfast? Eight to nine. Lunch, noon to one. Dinner, five-thirty to six-thirty. There! That does it! Now you don't need Gleick!"

o   o   o

My room was bright and spare, ideal for two weeks of work and reflection. There were a sofa and dining table, a desk with locking drawers, two ugly, modern chairs, a small fridge and a spacious bathroom and shower. I found myself amused, as ever, by the special touches found only on ships: a brace on the bookshelf, nylon webbing in the refrigerator, grab handles in the shower and a folding hook to keep the toilet seat from slamming down. The bed was wide, with a firm mattress and thick down comforter. I was relieved to see that the bunk—unlike the ones aboard the *Ursus* and *Infinity*—had no crib bar to keep me from rolling onto the floor during late-night storms. A good idea in theory, but the things gave me claustrophobia.

o   o   o

The *Bremen Express* would make four stops en route to Oakland. The first, less than twenty hours after our early morning departure from Hong Kong, would be Taiwan's Kaohsiung Port. Two days later we'd reach Japan, spending three consecutive days at Kobe, Nagoya and Yokohama. From there it was a straight sail—ten days—to the Golden Gate.

I showed up for breakfast at eight thirty-five the first morning, only to find the table being cleared. I found my place—at the foot of the table—and waited until Eric, the officers' steward, came back into the dining room. He was a compact, doe-eyed Filipino, unflappable. I imagined him to be a teenager and was stunned to learn that he was thirty, with a wife and two children in Manila. He brought me strawberry yogurt, a kaiser roll and coffee.

"I can do this today only," he said. "The captain told me not to serve you if you're late. He said, 'On a German ship you show up on time, or not at all.' Sorry. . . ."

I said nothing. Afterward, as I was descending the two flights to my room, I ran into the captain. He wagged his finger at me.

"Even one minute late," he said with an amused expression, "and you wait for lunch."

A charming and personable man, but I had a feeling I wanted to stay on his good side. "Sorry, sir. It won't happen again." I made a mental note to check the lunch and dinner schedule with Gleick.

The Shipping News

We spent the night loading up in Kaohsiung Port. The next morning I ate an early breakfast and strolled leisurely to the fo'c'sle. Low clouds the color of crocodile wallets occluded the sun. An unimpressive city lay in the hazy distance.

A single line, the Atlas rope, was all that held us back. At a signal from Chief Officer Rainier Krueger the stevedore loosened the noose from its bollard and tossed it into the sea. It squeegeed up through the ship's fairleads, leaving an avenue of seawater across the deck. The engines engaged, followed by the screw: a six-bladed, seventy-ton propeller balanced more precisely than the blades of a Cuisinart. Our bow thrusters engaged, and we yawed slowly to port.

A narrow passageway leads out of Kaohsiung Harbor, flanked by long jetties. Krueger leaned on the fo'c'sle rail as we approached, a walkie-talkie clutched in his hand. Ever since I'd come aboard he had reminded me of someone from my past, and I finally realized who. It was Captain Kangaroo.

The wind flew down the bow, whistling under the visor of his hard hat. "Up until, oh, ten years ago," Krueger shouted, "Taiwan had heavy artillery set up all along this entranceway. Between those two points"—he indicated stations about halfway down each jetty—"were two ends of a long chain, with netting attached to it. During the light hours it lay on the bottom of the channel, but at sundown they would raise it up, completely blocking the harbor."

"What for?"

"As a defense against mainland-Chinese submarines and divers. Back then there was a lot of tension between Taiwan and the PRC, much more than now. In those days you had better arrive here during the day. If you arrived at night they made you wait at anchorage until morning."

Rainier excused himself, leaving me alone on the fo'c'sle. A small raised platform—the "monkey bridge"—was affixed to the bow of the ship, and I climbed onto it. The wind was steady and fresh. Out to port and starboard, at the ends of two jetties marked with beacons, fishermen in peaked straw hats cast their lines into the sea.

We passed the beacons. That instant, without warning, came the loudest sound I'd ever heard, a stunning timpanic blast that loosened my teeth, juggled my eyes and scrambled my balls like duck eggs. I gripped the railing with all my might, fully expecting the acoustic wave to knock me off the deck. But the signal—coming from a horn on the foremast, some fifty feet behind me—stopped as abruptly as it had begun. I looked to the sides. None of the fishermen had even flinched.

We picked up speed. There was nothing ahead of me but sea, and the planet's razor edge.

o   o   o

Between 1955 and 1972, there were 120 vessels in the Hapag-Lloyd fleet. Six of these were container turbine ships: fast, superquiet ships expressly designed for the (then) nascent science of modularized cargo loading.

A "Third Generation," turbine-powered container vessel, the *Bremen Express* was built—for comfort and speed—in 1972. She is 944 feet long and 105 feet wide (the limit for the Panama Canal), with two engines capable of generating 40,000 horsepower. "Third Generation" means that she was designed to hold exactly 3,000 metal containers, each one twenty feet long. The newer, nonturbine containerships—Hapag-Lloyd's *Stuttgart Express*, for example—can carry 4,400.

Both the *Bremen Express* and her sister, the *Tokio Express*, were built with two propellers and maximum speeds of 28 knots. Shortly after the fuel crisis a hard look was taken at the turbine ships, and it was decided that their fuel consumption went far beyond the pale. In 1982, the aft portion of the *Bremen* was refitted. Her two props were replaced with a single screw, reducing both her top speed and overall fuel consumption. There was a plan to scrap her turbine engines as well—even with one propeller they use twice as much fuel as conventional engines—but the expense of retrofitting did not justify the savings, and the idea was shelved.

"If the ship is so expensive to operate, why is she still running?" I asked Captain Netz during the afternoon coffee break.

"Well, there is nothing to replace her with. They need to keep her in service."

"Surely, then, the ship must still be profitable."

Netz threw a rogue look at Chief Officer Krueger, slapped his thigh and laughed explosively.

"I won't say no!" he declared loudly. "I don't want to say no!"

Of the six ships composing Hapag-Lloyd's original turbine fleet, only the *Bremen* and *Tokio* remained in service. The others have been sold, refitted or dismantled. In 1996, the *Bremen Express* would face a shipwide inspection to determine her fate. Peter Hübner, the cargo officer, was not optimistic.

"They will look at the hatches, and hull," he said. "And I think, after twenty-four years at sea, the steel must look like this." He showed his thumb and index finger, holding them a hair's breath apart.

o   o   o

Chief Engineer Horst Zwingmann gave me a tour of the engine room, a mammoth labyrinth of catwalks and corridors winding beneath the flaming eyes and snorting nostrils of Grimm Brothers machinery. Anything not hissing, dripping, steaming, snorting, dripping, roaring, sweating, humming, boiling or thrumming was probably broken. There was something terrifying about navigating through those roaring rooms, where superheated steam blasts through giant riveted pipes and boilers rise three stories over your head. We climbed a metal stairway back to the control room, both of us sweating terrifically. The metal rails were too hot to touch.

"Have a look." Horst, a big-bellied man with thinning red hair and a cherubic smile, bellowed loudly enough for me to hear him through my padded headset. He pointed to a thick thermometer displaying room temperature. I noted the figure down and, when we reentered the air-conditioned oasis of the control room, made the conversion to Fahrenheit on a pad.

"Holy shit! It's a hundred and sixty-five degrees in there!"

"Zat is right." The chief engineer nodded reverently, wiping the sweat from his pate. "And vee vork in zis, day for day. Now you know vy vee are drinking so much beer in zee evenings."

The Bardo of Bratwurst

We sluiced through the East China Sea, Kobe-bound. Netz, First Mate Krueger and the other eight officers enjoyed the identical breakfast: three softball-size meatballs of raw ground round, with a heaping helping of raw white onion.

I had learned to dread mealtime. Stationed at the foot of the table, I chewed molecular servings of fat-marbled meat while lively but incomprehensible conversation, strictly in German, surged around me. The menu, equally German, filled me with despair. Lunch was *Rindsroulade* with rice and boiled beets; dinner, brown bread, ham and tongue. Breakfast: beef chips scrambled with eggs and onion. Lunch: beefsteak with boiled cauliflower. Wiener schnitzel, *Ochsenschwanzsuppe*, boiled carrots, *Thüringer Mett*, bratwurst, *Knödel*, boiled cabbage, headcheese, boiled potatoes, tongue, tongue, tongue. . . . My body howled for raw carrots, green vegetables, seafood and fruit. I would have gladly trawled from the stern, or fished a half-rotten tomato out of a Dumpster.

o   o   o

During our third day at sea, I visited the bridge for the first time. The captain was on watch alone.

Netz was the only officer on board who genuinely *looked* like a captain. His long, wolfish face and hypotenusal nose—set beneath an improbable bowl haircut—reminded me of *Star Trek*'s Mr. Spock; and, like Spock's, his voice, a booming contralto, was well suited to command. But Netz's resemblance to the impassive Vulcan ended there. I'd seen him standing the Filipino crew for beer, roaring with laughter at the lunch table, and wristing away a tear (so discreetly!) during the final aria of Verdi's *Masked Ball*. My most indelible impression, though, would be that first sight of him on his bridge—bending with great concentration over the maps of the Sea of Japan, carefully penciling in the positions of tropical storms as he read them off the Satcom's daily telex.

After completing his duties Netz showed me around the command center, fiddling with the radar and demonstrating the various satellite navigation aids. All the controls had a seductively futuristic look, designed in that big-knobbed, brightly lit transition period between Pop Art and Techno-modernism. I asked if his father had been a captain.

He laughed gustily. "No, no. There were no seafarers in my family. It's not so often," he added wistfully, "that the children of a seaman go to sea."

Netz himself had three sons, twenty-seven, twenty-nine and thirty-one. None had the slightest desire to captain a ship.

"It's not the right thing, for having a family," he said. "That's one reason you see so few women officers. On Hapag-Lloyd it's better; we get one tour on, one tour off. Normally a tour is eighty-four days. But in many companies there is no such break."

Netz himself first went to sea in 1955. Germany was suffering from widespread unemployment, and his carpentry skills were in scant demand. "I was twenty," he recalled. "I traveled by train from Hamburg to Rotterdam, and signed on to a very small tanker. She was exactly twenty-point-five meters long, and five-point-eight meters wide. We were altogether five: the captain, an engineer, and three men on deck. We had the trade between Frankfurt and Felixstowe. We went up the river Rhine, up and down, then we crossed the North Sea to England. It can be very dangerous, the North Sea. . . ."

Netz looked at me narrowly, as if I'd forgotten my homework. "Is there a survival suit in your closet?"

I'd seen a large yellow sack so labeled, and nodded that there was.

"Has Officer Gleick demonstrated how to put it on?"

"No. . . . He came in yesterday and showed me how to use the life jacket and hard hat."

"He didn't show you the survival suit? Well, he should have! I'll have to speak with him." Netz turned sharply, like a setter spotting its prey. "Wait . . . I think there's one here."

The captain strode across his bridge and stopped at a low wooden cabinet. "The survival suit is very important. With it you don't need a life jacket, or even a raft. You can float exposed in the open sea, even in zero-degree water, with no problem. But speed is everything. If anything happens, you must be able to. . . ." He squatted down and yanked the cabinet door. It didn't budge. He pulled the other side; it was also locked. He patted his pockets, and burst out laughing.

"I'll try to find the key."

Netz located the key, opened the cabinet and pulled out a big duffel bag. Inside was a thick neoprene suit, Day-Glo orange. He unrolled it onto the bridge floor. It looked exactly like a huge gingerbread man coated with Halloween frosting.

"You see here, only the face—nose, eyes, mouth—is exposed. This belt loop is for helicopter rescue . . . in this pocket you have the buddy line . . . here is the light . . . watertight zipper . . . whistle. . . ."

"Does it have a secret Cap'n Crunch decoder?"

"*Vas?*"

I rephrased the question. "Has there ever been a situation where anyone on a Hapag-Lloyd ship has had to use one of these?"

"No." He frowned, pulling the industrial-size zipper that ran down the suit's chest, splitting it like a cocoon. I slid my legs inside—the booties were a tight fit—and struggled into the sleeves with their attached mitts. The thick neoprene hood encased my head like a catcher's mitt.

"So Hapag-Lloyd has never lost a ship?"

Netz pulled up the zipper, sealing me inside. I lay on the floor, the freakish spawn of Anita Bryant and the Michelin Man. "There was one time. This was about fifteen years ago, in December of 1979. The *Hamburg Express*. There was one distress call, then nothing. Even now, no one knows exactly what happened. She was an old-style ship, with a very large crane aboard. She hit very bad weather. Some people think the crane broke, and fell through the deck into the engine room. Some think a big wave hit the ship and destroyed the bridge. No one knows. The ship was never found."

"No survivors?" I could barely hear my own voice through the rubber padding.

"All hands were lost." He wandered out onto the pilot's deck.

I struggled to my feet and waddled after him. "What do you think happened?"

Netz raised his shoulders in a histrionic shrug. "When they build these ships, you know, they test them in a big tank—there they can simulate the strong wind, the biggest swells, anything. Normally the ship can withstand all these things—even a hundred-year wave."

"What's that?"

"Oh, they say one time every hundred years there may be an unusual ocean wave. Very big, very rare, and completely unexpected. Anyway, it's no problem. The designers tell us the ship can survive that. We can survive a hundred-year wave.

"But whatever hit the *Hamburg Express* must have been a *thousand*-year wave—and no one can prepare against that."

I'd had enough time in the survival suit—I was starting to look (and smell) like a bratwurst myself—and Netz unzipped me. He held on to the boots as I lay on the floor and squirmed out of the rubber. "You know," he said, "I remember something one of my captains once said. He was a very old captain, maybe sixty-five, from what we call the Spice Islands—the ones in the North Sea. I was his second officer for nearly one year.

"'Knowledge is just fifty percent of being a captain,' he told me. 'The other fifty percent, you need good luck. You can know your job inside out . . . but if you have only forty-nine percent luck, something will go wrong.'"

o   o   o

That afternoon, brushing my teeth before the mirror in my cabin, I saw a sight that made my blood run cold. My tongue was black again.

This was intolerable. I could not go home with a black tongue. But I'd long ago finished the medicine I'd bought in Xining, and there was no doctor on the ship. What to do? Darting down to the officers' staging room, I found Chief Engineer Zwingmann installed at the bar. Officer Gleick, he informed me, was the ship's all-around medic. Though trained primarily in first aid, he had several medical texts—in German, of course—that might shed light on my malaise.

I could already predict the cunning diagnosis: *schwarze Zunge*.

Gleick was on the bridge, preparing the courtesy flags for our entrance into Japanese waters. I sat next to him on a stool. He greeted me warmly—Netz, plainly, hadn't yet chewed him out about the survival suit—and asked what the problem was. Eschewing a lengthy explanation, I simply opened my mouth and stuck out my tongue. Gleick took my chin and moved my head from side to side, peering into my oral cavity. Then he chuckled, leaned away and stuck *his* tongue out at *me*.

It was black as a fudge-dipped biscotti.

I nearly fell off my seat. "But how . . . why . . .?"

"Okay," Gleick said. "I make one guess. This German food, big problem for your stomach, *jah*?"

"Yes. . . ."

"So every night, you are taking some drink. This"—he bit his lip—"*pink* drink. *Jah*?"

He was right; I'd been guzzling Pepto-Bismol since my second night on the *Bremen Express*.

"Yes, that must be it. Some people, if they make like this, it has a funny reaction in the digestion. They sleep and next morning, *bumps*, the tongue is coated black."

I laughed incredulously. "Are you telling me that this whole problem is caused by drinking Pepto-Bismol?"

"Jah, jah. Of course. But it's no problem. You stop the drink, your tongue goes red once more. It is perfectly normal. As for me, I also take such a drink—it's good for settling the stomach—and, two or three days before Rotterdam, I stop. On the ship it's all right, I can have like this;

but I don't care for my wife to see. She thinks, maybe, it's some strange tropical disease. . . ."

Live from the Spiral Arm

The night before our arrival in Kobe I left my cabin and, forgoing the ritual nightly viewing of *Ace Ventura, Pet Detective*, wandered out onto the deck.

Warm air played across my face, its motion as constant a force as the starlight. I stared down the enormous beam of the *Bremen Express* and tried to imagine what it would feel like if she were completely computerized, crossing the ocean on auto pilot—like the interplanetary spaceship *Discovery* in *2001: A Space Odyssey*. It was an unsettling fantasy. The sense of desolation was palpable, and I began whistling the *Gayne Ballet Suite*.

I walked the two hundred yards to the fo'c'sle and sat on a flat black bollard, looking straight upward. The sky was bright as a planetarium, and the Milky Way trailed across the azimuth like the smoke from a ghost ship.

We think we're sitting still, but we aren't. The Earth is spinning at 1,037 miles an hour, and we're orbiting the sun at more than sixty times that speed. Every day, every creature on this planet travels more than a million and a half miles—not counting the motion of our solar system or the spiral arm of the galaxy in which it spins.

We sit in our cafés, squat in front of our fires, and we're all pilgrims, every one of us. The immense kora of expansion and contraction, the great contra-dance of space-time, swings us through its continuum like unwitting partners, looping forward and back toward a completion that is the end and beginning of all things. . . .

Shore Leave: Three Situations in Search of a Story

It was strangely disorienting to leave the self-contained universe of the ship and, for three days running, spend my afternoons on dry land.

I loved shopping in Kobe. I loved browsing through endless shelves of Kewpie Doll stationery, Godzilla ashtrays and battery-powered lollipop spinners. I loved the way everything, from cantaloupes to condoms, was beautifully packaged. I loved the fact that there was nothing of shoddy quality. Everything seemed to carry a tangible aura of pride, of human cunning behind the finished product.

Most of all, I loved having a secret. It gave me a rush to mingle with the population at large—mothers with their infants, teens in Fred Mac-Murray T-shirts, businessmen who looked away the instant I caught them looking at me—and know that, a few hours hence, I'd climb the long aluminum gangway back into the belly of the *Bremen Express*, roll the ladder up behind me and feel the wind in my hair as we set sail again. There was a sense of being a shade, of passing through the moment without really inhabiting it. The illusion of invisibility was almost erotic. I felt like a time traveler, the hero of one of those old science fiction stories where a being from the future beams back in time to visit a city or civilization just hours, or minutes, before its cataclysmic destruction.

Ah, Kobe! How could we have known?

o   o   o

We reached Nagoya the next day. The highlight of my visit was a cup of tea, served in the Ninomaru Teahouse in the Ninomaru Garden of Nagoya Castle.

I opened the little tourist booklet—"Visitors may strengthen their leases on life five years by taking a bowl of Japanese tea at the house"—and, satisfied with the potential return on my investment, ponied up 500 yen.

An elderly, kimono-clad hostess set six objects on my table. Each of them was perfect. Of course there was the tea, a foamy green broth that looked exactly like Sally's freshly squeezed wheatgrass juice and tasted like a morning jog through a spring meadow with Keiko, your faithful hound, leaping spiritedly beside you as Mount Fuji glitters on the horizon. It was served in the sort of antique ceramic bowl that one holds with both hands, in mortal terror of dropping it. Accompanying the drink was an exquisite square plate, upon which lay a square of handmade rice paper marked with a single *kanji*. Sitting on the paper was a formidable little cake, a pillow of rice-flour dough enclosing a delicious sweet bean paste and a tiny yellow yolk. Like everything of quality in Japan, the cake was signed. I picked it up with my fingers—it was surprisingly dense, with a soft, fleshy texture—and bit into it luxuriously. It was the closest thing I'd had in eight months to oral sex.

Beside the cake was a single toothpick, a tapered spike whittled from sapling maple. It had that unbearable, almost tongue-in-cheek elegance one often sees in Japan. Someone had either picked it out of a woodpile or labored over it for a day and a half. I was irked by its arrogance; it would probably outlast my teeth.

o   o   o

Sometimes it seems the Japanese want us to believe that there was nothing before this moment; that everything predating their ability to build mega-malls and sexy suspension bridges was somehow an embarrassment. They gloss the past and buff the present to a seamless shine, punctuating their new theme parks–cum-cities with Laura Ashleys, Mikimotos and McDonald's.

The port of Yokohama was a vacuum. Its venerable history as the gateway between Japan and the west had been shrink-wrapped, and anything with the slightest air of antiquity was protected by a fence. The whole port region had about as much soul as the Singapore Airport duty-free shop. Even the new Museum of Art was an empty showpiece, a perfect architectural toy box that exhibited nothing so much as the Japanese genius for wrapping things. The self-consciously fascinating building was, in essence, a mausoleum: a place where art goes to die. There was bald incomprehension in the faces of the half-dozen visitors, seen wandering in earnest confusion amid a mixed salad of Expressionist and Contemporary work. My sense that they were searching in vain for something to buy was requited upon my departure, in the museum's gift shop. It was packed with patrons sorting among green globular earrings, shuffling Helmut Newton postcards and sizing up YOMA-emblazoned T-shirts bearing neck tags that answered, without ambiguity, the most pressing aesthetic question of the moment: "Will it shrink?"

I left the city, bored witless. There were no taxis, and it was an hour's walk back to the ship in dastardly heat. By the time I reached the ship I looked like I'd been rained on, shadowed by a cartoon cloud that had dogged my every move.

Such are the wages of minor discomfort: I failed to notice the moment my foot left Asian soil.

Buildings, Bridges, Bay

Back in my cabin I cooled off and napped. When I awoke, at 16:15, the ship was in motion. I made it to the monkey bridge in time to watch the Yokohama Bay Bridge sail by, its open-ended white towers ringing against the clouds like enormous tuning forks. Navigation Officer Zivkovic, supervising the ship's departure from the fo'c'sle, yelled something at me, jabbing a finger the breadth of a bratwurst at the foremast. I saw, but didn't hear him; my ears were already plugged with wax. A pilot boat cleaved the water ahead of us, and we navigated under half power toward the entrance of the bay.

I turned around to watch the oddly familiar visual orchestration of bay, bridges and buildings recede. A moment later I realized, with a shock, exactly *why* it was so familiar: When I saw that combination again, I'd be home.

• 48 •

To: **Allen Noren, O'Reilly & Associates**
From: **Jeff Greenwald, the Pacific Ocean**
Subject: **Big World/Fast Forward**

Our cargo ship, vast and modern as it is, has no fax machine, so I'm communicating via telex. The station aboard this vessel, at least, uses a monitor; on the *Ursus Delmas* I was up to my ears in punched paper ribbon, breathing an atmosphere suffused with the confetti of pre-Cambrian telecommunications.

Greetings, then, from Hapag-Lloyd's *CTS* (Container Turbine Ship) *Bremen Express:* Twelve days out of Hong Kong, three days past Japan, and very close to the edge of this Big World.

Here, then (with apologies to my second-favorite magazine), is everything you need to know about my current digs. I can only call it:

Hapag's Index
Length of the Bremen Express, in feet: 942.7
Age, in years: 22
Unloaded weight, in metric tons: 23,818
Maximum speed: 23 knots
Average speed across the North Pacific: 20 knots

Miles, by straight line, from Yokohama to Oakland: 4,757
By the Great Circle Route: 4,560

Number of eggs carried on each 84-day tour aboard the
Bremen Express: 4,200
Kilograms of meat: 700
Containers of Berkeley Farms yogurt: 450
Number of potatoes our chief cook can peel by hand,
in one hour: 100
Number of potatoes peeled in five minutes by the
Hobart Electric Potato Peeler: 60

Number of 0.4 lt. steins in a keg of Holsten beer: 75
Kegs consumed in Officers' Staging Room, per 84-day tour: 37
Avg. steins of beer consumed per officer per tour: 277

Number of feature films in the crew's video library: 45
Average body count, per film: 38

Approximate distance traveled by Captain Jürgen Netz
during his 35-year career at sea, in miles: 2,000,000
By moonwalker Alan Shepard: 750,000
By Magellan: 30,000

o   o   o

The *Bremen Express* lunges through the water, its vintage turbines pro-
pelling us silently northward. Clouds hang low over the ocean, their
chaotic hydrologic topology making an Abstract Impressionist statement
above the uncritical sea.

Eight months ago it seemed this moment would never come; or that,
when and if it ever did, it would arrive as a tremendous release, a final reward for all my aims and efforts. Well, here I am, less than a week from
Oakland, and I'm swimming in the dizzy unreality of it all. I literally cannot
believe that I'm here, already, with so much behind me and so much still
undone. As if all my weird nightmares of arriving home before I'd finished
the trip were coming true. Welcome, then, to the

Earth at Eye Level

Twenty-one years ago, during my second year at Nassau Community
College, my astronomy professor tacked a seemingly innocuous question
onto our final exam.

How long does a day last on planet Earth?

You could hear the jaws drop. Several students, poised for a relay of
gordian-knotty calculations (we'd already been asked to calculate the ro-
tational speed of Saturn from the red shift of its rings), hung over their
notebooks like wax figures depicting collegiate bewilderment.

Hands flew up. The queries were desperate and predictable:

"One day? You mean, a 24-hour day?"

"Is this at the north pole, or the equator?"

"Is it 'day' only when the sun's out?"

"Is this some kind of trick?"

The professor smiled, an evil glint in his eye, and simply repeated the
question. "It's for 'bonus' points," he added shrewdly. "Getting it wrong
won't count against you."

The following week the test results were in. "I'm ashamed to an-
nounce," he concluded at last, "that not a single one of you got the bonus
question right."

We waited in silence for the answer.

"One day on the planet Earth," he archly declared, "lasts 48 hours."

There was an uproar.

"C'mon kids. . . . Look." He drew a circle representing the globe, as
seen from above the North Pole. "Okay. Let's take today, May 28, 1973.
How long does any given moment of 'today'—let's say, dawn—take to
reach every part of the world's surface?" We watched the chalk tick
around the circle. "Twenty-four hours. Right?"

We nodded. This was demonstrably true.

"Good. Now, how long does it take this same day, May 28th, to *end?*"

Once again, he tapped off the hours with his chalk. The answer, impossible as it had seemed, was suddenly obvious. If a single day, which begins one hour later every time zone to the west, takes 24 hours to arrive at each time zone on Earth, then—and this was what we had failed to grasp—*it takes another 24 hours to leave.*

There was a collective gasp, followed by the thunderclap of 35 foreheads being slapped simultaneously.

"So you see," he said, juggling the chalk as we slumped in our chairs, "one day on the planet Earth actually takes *two* days: 24 hours to reel itself out—and another 24 to rewind."

I've never forgotten that odd lesson in lateral thinking, though I never expected to experience the phenomenon first hand. Few people indeed get to savor the full luxury of a long, honest Earth day. Flying west to east across the Pacific, you seem to gain a day—but you've already squandered a good 10 hours of it leaping across time zones.

It is only on a ship, gliding along at the easy speed of 20 knots, that one gets to both bite off and chew these enormously ripe dates. And for the 33 persons aboard the *Bremen Express*—10 German officers, two of their wives, 20 Filipino crewmen and me—the harvest approaches. In a few days we will break the ribbon of the International Date Line—and get an entire Wednesday to live all over again.

Just my luck, it happens to be Yom Kippur . . .

o   o   o

Played liars' dice til midnight last night with Chief Engineer Zwingmann and Radio Officer Hans 'Sparky' Boekelman. I won the game—beginner's luck—and excused myself to wander around the deck. Boekelman, the Jewish mother of the crew, was scandalized.

"What do we do if you fall overboard?," Hans asked in all seriousness as I left the room of drunken sailors.

"Come back for me in the morning."

"No, no, you shouldn't make a joke of it!"

"What can I say, Hans? If I fall off the boat I'll die."

"Exactly. That's why nobody wanders around the ship at this hour."

I took the stairs down to the main deck two at a time and stepped through the double doors onto the slick causeway. My plan was to make the full circuit, fo'c'sle and back, but it was pitch black outside and I'd forgotten my flashlight.

A thirty-knot wind blew my hair back like foam. The September stars were muted, small eyes watching my every move in the whistling darkness.

I was sauced. Sauced and philosophical. There's something addictive about being on a ship in the middle of the open sea for weeks on end. It's meditative and terrifying, unnerving and blissful. How many, I wondered, have written about this paradox? Though restricted and confined, one's horizon appears infinite. Though limited in range, one is moving continuously forward. Being on a ship, I perceived, is a perfect allegory for being on a planet.

And this planet, as Buckminster Fuller made clear, *is* a ship. Every nation I've visited on my odyssey (along with the 400 odd others I didn't) lays cabined together on this sapphire sphere, rolling silently through space. For a few score years—a wink in cosmic time—we get to share the stewardship of this vast-yet-tiny ark with the other 1.4 million species: stinkbugs and elms, elephants and fungi, salamanders and Sioux. From the Siberian phlox to the homeless guy hawking the *Street Sheet* on Market and Fifth, we're passengers one and all—animated by a spark we cannot duplicate, have never found elsewhere and struggle helplessly to define.

It's the only planet worth shit, I realized, *and I'm so in love with it I could scream.* And scream I did, a hoarse drunken howl carried by the wind and bounced between the whitecaps until I wondered, with a vague and ridiculous guilt, if I'd woken something up.

Call it an occupational hazard—but the problem with traveling around the world is that you end up caring about everyone in the world.

• 49 •

Ballad of the Soft Rock Café

Later she remembered all the hours of the afternoon as happy—one of those uneventful times that seem at the moment only a link between past and future pleasure but turn out to have been the pleasure itself.
                                        —from *Tender is the Night*

38°07' N x 146°14' E

Dolphins leap into the air along our starboard side—always an exhilarating sight. Even a bird, spotted so far from land, seems miraculous.

But the dolphins are a reminder that, empty as the horizon appears from deck, we are blazing across the stratosphere of someone else's sky.

Slicing my schnitzel as the crew sings in German, I digest a plain fact. These hours on the ship are my last chance to savor my own company, away from the distractions of Life at Large. The thought is rich with irony. How I dreaded the prospect of traveling alone eight months ago! How I paddled and floundered to evade my own company! But now the situation has reversed and I can perceive, with 20/20 hindsight, that it was the relentless momentum demanded by this voyage—more than any psychological issue—that bedeviled me most. From the day that Sally and I set off on our pilgrimage until the moment I stepped onto this ship, there was seldom a time when I didn't have to consider where I was going next, how I'd get there, and what I'd have to deal with once I arrived.

Now, at last, there ain't nowhere more to go. The ship is a village, a terrarium, a stage. The distance once around the deck is exactly one third of a mile. I walk it before breakfast, twice. Mornings are spent in my cabin, reviewing the 800 pages of notes I've made during my trip. After lunch I sit on the starboard deck, facing south, and read Fitzgerald. Stationary bicycle and yoga from 3:30 to 4:30, followed by a shave and shower. An hour playing Klondike on my computer. Dinner. Sunset from the aft deck. A couple of beers in the Staging Room. From 8 o'clock on I'm in the crew's rec room, shooting darts and watching the kinds of videos I'd never rent at home.

> "I want to be with you. I want to meet your parents, and pet your dog."
> "My parents are dead, Dexter. My dog ate them."
>   —Hot Shots: Part Deux

42°12' N x 156°00' E

Out on the tilting deck the air smells faintly of deisel. Waves beat deliberately against the hull. Sea birds, albatrosses maybe, swoop between the white crests of the sea. Through binoculars the horizon appears rough-edged and raw, like the terminator on the Moon. One hand stays on the railing—it's hard to keep a footing in an eight degree roll. The wind whips the moorings and moans through the fairleads, a mallet rings out against steel, but I hang on.

Sometimes it's like being inside a painting: the kind you see in panelled Montauk living rooms, where a billowing schooner leans into a storybook green sea. You can stand on the fo'c'sle and look forward, imagining the masted ship at your back, the breakbulk cargo lashed to the deck, the cattle and cannons below. As for the ocean, it looks just the same; the high sea, stretched like sharkskin beneath the open sky, hasn't changed a bit.

46° N x 177° E

Went up to the bridge around noon. The fog was so thick you couldn't see to the foremast. It was Cargo Officer Peter Hübner's watch. I found him sitting, with a Filipino crewman, behind a drawn curtain. Both men sat on stools, staring into radar screens. The luminous green dials made them look like sibling Frankensteins.

"This is how we do it in the fog," Hübner explained. He is a quiet, direct man with thick glasses and a philosopher's face. The radar screen was all but blank. "Twenty-four hours a day, if necessary. One time, crossing the Atlantic from Rotterdam, we had such weather as this for a week. For one full week we were behind the curtain, watching the screens. You just make a big pot of coffee and sit."

The pale fog reminded me of winter, reawakening a nostalgia I hadn't felt since the train ride up through Virginia in January.

"In Oakland," Hübner asked, "do you have the change of seasons?"

"Sort of. Suddenly, around the middle of October, you realize you're wearing a sweater."

"Where I grew up, in Germany, we have very strong seasons. Meters of snow in the wintertime. I loved it."

I nodded. "Same for me. I grew up in New York and Massachusetts. One of my earliest memories is of sledding face first into a tree."

"That's what I miss the most about this life." He sighed quietly. "There are no such seasons at sea."

It was a strange feeling to be sailing by instruments. We may just as well have been on a plane, it being impossible to see either ahead, above or below. I studied the radar screen intently, looking for blips. We had passed a considerable number of fishing boats the previous day. My romantic notion that they were welcome company on the lonesome sea vanished immediately when Hübner told me a bit about them.

"They are Japanese pirate vessels. Illegal. They fish with gigantic nets: five kilometers across, and nearly 1,000 meters down. They catch everything, until there are no more fish in the sea. Empty."

The information chilled me, and I wondered about the fate of the dolphins I saw yesterday morning.

46° N x 170° W

Cold outside, the coldest I've felt since Tibet. Cold and blustery. The *Bremen Express* sails due east, following the 46th parallel exactly. We departed from the Great Circle Route two days ago, when a severe depression around the Aleutian Islands made continuing northward inadvisable.

45°12' N x 159° 40' W

It is Yom Kippur, the Day of Atonement, when all good Jews must fast and do penance for the sins of the preceding year. By cruel coincidence, our ship has chosen just this day to break the tape of the International Dateline. If I were Orthodox I'd probably feel compelled to observe the ritual twice (having crossed the 180th meridian we have set back the clock one day). Instead, I forced myself — half-hearted Hebrew that I am — to choose one day or the other.

Yesterday won (or lost, depending on your point of view). I began fasting after last night's early dinner and continued through today. Half an hour before sunset I stood on the stern and released a paper prayer-flag into the wind. It gyrated and danced in the warm draft of the enormous ship before settling, invisibly, onto the sea.

45° N x 156° W

The clouds this afternoon were the loveliest I'd ever seen: Michelangelo angel wings descending from the sky, Renaissance perfect, as if they'd been painted with a feather. And now the sea is calm as a sleeping puppy, the circular snore of the engines oscillating through my open cabin window, stars twinkling through the spectrum like tilted CDs.

After eight months of eastward travel, I'm back on Pacific time.

I watch the hours go by—*will* them to go by—but know that, when the final hour comes, I'll want to cling like a barnacle to this lonely raft of heightened consciousness.

o   o   o

Heavenly bodies visible, at sunset, from the deck of the *Bremen Express*:
One star.
Two planets.
One moon.
No guru. No method. No teacher. Just the pale spray in the fading final

daylight, and the glossy black bollard holding my scotch and soda as the enormous moon, all but full, rises above an easterly fog bank.

There's no way to describe—or justify—how extraordinarily ambivalent I feel. There were so many times during this voyage when I felt I'd been away forever, when it seemed I would never return. How can it be, how can it possibly be, that at this moment it feels as though I've just taken a long weekend?

Gone, the anticipation and joy of meeting Paul Bowles. Finished, the ferry ride from Brendisi, the Grecian sunrise bending over Mt. Olympus and into my tired eyes. Behind me lie Istanbul, the Sirens of Ankara, the Saudi Desert. My copy of *Vineland* has long ago dissolved in the Persian Gulf. I've walked barefoot in an electrical storm at the Golden Temple, lit butter lamps for the Buddha in Kathmandu and nursed a snow leopard in Lhasa. I've spent 38 weeks traveling, a total of 40 days at sea. And it feels as if I left home four days ago.

How can it be?

It was as real as this.

42° 14' N x 135° 30' W

Twelve days ago I stood on the prow and saw it: My homecoming moon. It was the slimmest crescent, an albino eyelash floating on the cornea of dusk. From here to Oakland, I thought to myself, I will not spend a single night without it.

And I feel with this moon, with this perfect September moon, an inexpressible sense of companionship; as if it were nothing less than my personal guide and guardian, my own angel moon, a goblet of diamond wine slowly poured until the evening I arrive.

Night by night, the moon grows full. Otherwise, Time—which has alternately slept, crawled, jogged and sprinted by during my 37 weeks of overland travel—rests in a state of suspended animation. The ship's clock registers our progress far more credibly that any visual reading, as the scene outside my cabin window has hardly changed for days.

But this snowy hibernation of space-time bothers me not at all. I am waiting, for the first time in months, for nothing.

Time, though we frantically doctor it to match our speed, remains an inscrutable rhythm. The past is nothing but an agreement, with ourselves, to remember; the future consists exclusively of our memories, cast upward and outward like lures. When, then, does everything happen? Even Einstein, it seems, was discombobulated by the persistent notion that there is no Time at all. No time, that is, but Now.

One week from 'Now' I'll be home. Back to my memories of answering machines and parking meters, insurance bills and car registration, tennis and bagels and the Sunday *New York Times*. Back to a present that already anticipates future journeys, book deadlines, hot dates and slow burns. I seem to remember that I'll have a hell of a lot to do: income taxes to file, a refrigerator to fill, friends to visit, the final episode of *Star Trek: The Next Generation* on videotape.

I remember so much about my future. What, I wonder, will I remember about this past?

But those onrushing weeks of remembering—that 'present' yet to come—still seems an eternity away. For the moment I am content to spend my evenings standing silently on the monkey bridge, looking at the moon through binoculars, watching Venus and Jupiter shimmer on the sea as an ever-broadening V, broadcast by our hull, radiates toward Hawaii (starboard) and the Aleutian Islands (port).

On September 19th, the *Bremen Express* will pass beneath the shadow of the Golden Gate Bridge. I'll have orbited the world—traveled from Oakland, California to Oakland, California—by land, sand and sea. My overwhelming sense, incontestably true, is that I've barely scratched the surface. A tart realization. But how dare I feel anything but grateful? How many times, mired in Bay Bridge traffic, will I recall Oaxaca by night, or the mustard fields of Tibet?

How often, suspended in the purgatory of call-waiting, will I long for the unbroken connection of this single present moment? Out on the ocean, far from fear or choice, where the sky is free even of birds; where the moon blooms like a rose, the clouds experiment like lovers, and the evening news doesn't happen.

o   o   o

Nothing's finished. The moment never ends. Wherever you stand, it's a Big World.

N 39°30' x W 127°20'

One hundred fifty miles from the California coast. A dense, warm fog showers the bridge wings with fine droplets.

For the first time in many days I can smell land. It smells faintly of pretzels.

π

The West Oakland BART station overflows with American creatures, pulsing through the turnstiles toward the broad stone stairs. Rush-hour commuters give me the once-over, unsure if I'm an outgoing camper or incoming vagabond, and flee toward their trains.

A lifetime ago, I dropped my house key into the bottom of my red Gap toiletry bag. I shrug off my backpack, open the top compartment and fish the bag out. That's when I hear the music: A few short notes, clear and unmistakable, echoing beneath the rush of an outgoing train.

An elderly black man sits on a folding stool against the tiled wall, adjusting the reed on his Selmer clarinet. He is wearing a pressed lumberjack's shirt and a yellow bow tie.

I stand in front of him until he looks up, tilting his glasses to peer at my enormous pack.

"That's quite a load. . . . You comin', or goin'?"

I run my hand back through my hair, wondering how much I've aged. "Do you remember me?"

He chuckles and squints, tightening a screw. "Can't say I do. Am I s'poze to?"

"No . . ." I laugh. "I guess not." I unzip my belt pouch and pull out a twenty. It flutters like a leaf into his case. "Play me something?"

He looks at the bill, then back at me. His eyes flicker.

"Of course." He draws a breath, and mouths the reed.

I take the steps carefully, one at a time. *Summertime* follows me onto the crowded platform, lonesome and simple and sweet, its familiar melody swirling like cream in the vortex of the Richmond-bound train.

The doors open, and I step inside.

My journey begins at this instant.